Translated Texts for Historians

300–800 AD is the time of late antiquity and the early middle ages: the transformation of the classical world, the beginnings of Europe and of Islam, and the evolution of Byzantium. TTH makes available sources translated from Greek, Latin, Syriac, Coptic, Arabic, Georgian, Gothic and Armenian. Each volume provides an expert scholarly translation, with an introduction setting texts and authors in context, and with notes on content, interpretation and debates.

Editorial Committee
Sebastian Brock, Oriental Institute, University of Oxford
Averil Cameron, Keble College, Oxford
Marios Costambeys, University of Liverpool
Mary Cunningham, University of Nottingham
Carlotta Dionisotti, King's College, London
Peter Heather, King's College, London
Robert Hoyland, University of St Andrews
William E. Klingshirn, The Catholic University of America
Michael Lapidge, Clare College, Cambridge
John Matthews, Yale University
Neil McLynn, Corpus Christi College, Oxford
Richard Price, Heythrop College, University of London
Claudia Rapp, University of California, Los Angeles
Raymond Van Dam, University of Michigan
Michael Whitby, University of Warwick
Ian Wood, University of Leeds

General Editors
Gillian Clark, University of Bristol
Mark Humphries, Swansea University
Mary Whitby, University of Oxford

A full list of published titles in the Translated Texts for Historians series is available on request. The most recently published are shown below.

Lactantius: Divine Institutes
Translated with introduction and notes by ANTHONY BOWEN and PETER GARNSEY
Volume 40: 488pp., 2003, ISBN 0-85323-988-6

Selected Letters of Libanius from the Age of Constantius and Julian
Translated with introduction and notes by SCOT BRADBURY
Volume 41: 308pp., 2004, ISBN 0-85323-509-0

Cassiodorus: Institutions of Divine and Secular Learning and On the Soul
Translated and notes by JAMES W. HALPORN; Introduction by MARK VESSEY
Volume 42: 316 pp., 2004, ISBN 0-85323-998-3

Ambrose of Milan: Political Letters and Speeches
Translated with an introduction and notes by J. H. W. G. LIEBESCHUETZ and CAROLE HILL
Volume 43: 432pp., 2005, ISBN 0-85323-829-4

The Chronicle of Ireland
Translated with an introduction and notes by T. M. CHARLES-EDWARDS
Volume 44: 2 vols., 349pp. + 186pp., 2006, ISBN 0-85323-959-2

The Acts of the Council of Chalcedon
Translated with an introduction and notes by RICHARD PRICE and MICHAEL GADDIS
Volume 45: 3 vols., 365pp. + 312pp. + 312pp., 2005, ISBN 0-85323-039-0

Bede: On Ezra and Nehemiah
Translated with an introduction and notes by SCOTT DEGREGORIO
Volume 47: 304pp, 2006, ISBN 978-1-84631-001-0

Bede: On Genesis
Translated with introduction and notes by CALVIN B. KENDALL
Volume 48: 371pp., 2008, ISBN 978-1-84631-088-1

Nemesius: On the Nature of Man
Translated with introduction and notes by R. W. SHARPLES and P. J. VAN DER EIJK
Volume 49: 283pp., 2008, ISBN 978-1-84631-132-1

For full details of Translated Texts for Historians, including prices and ordering information, please write to the following:
All countries, except the USA and Canada: Liverpool University Press, 4 Cambridge Street, Liverpool, L69 7ZU, UK (*Tel* +44-[0]151-794 2233, *Fax* +44-[0]151-794 2235, Email J.M. Smith@liv.ac.uk, http://www.liverpool-unipress.co.uk). **USA and Canada:** University of Chicago Press, 1427 E. 60th Street, Chicago, IL, 60637, US (*Tel* 773-702-7700, *Fax* 773-702-9756, www.press.uchicago.edu)

Translated Texts for Historians
Volume 46

The Formularies of Angers and Marculf
Two Merovingian Legal Handbooks

Translated with an introduction and notes by
ALICE RIO

Liverpool
University
Press

First published 2008
Liverpool University Press
4 Cambridge Street
Liverpool, L69 7ZU

Copyright © 2008 Alice Rio

The right of Alice Rio to be identified as the author
of this work has been asserted by her in accordance
with the Copyright, Designs and Patents Act, 1988

All rights reserved. No part of this book may be reproduced
stored in a retrieval system, or transmitted, in any form or
by any means, electronic, mechanical, photocopying, recording,
or otherwise, without the prior written permission of the publisher.

British Library Cataloguing-in-Publication Data
A British Library CIP Record is available.

ISBN 978-1-84631-159-8 limp

Set in Times by
Koinonia, Manchester
Printed in the European Union by
Bell and Bain Ltd, Glasgow

CONTENTS

Acknowledgements	vii
Abbreviations	viii
Introduction	1
The scope of this book	1
The scope of formulae	4
The problem with formulae	6
Authorship and audience: what the manuscript evidence can tell us	8
The language of formulae	17
Formulae and the written word	22
Formulae and surviving documents	25
Dating formulae: original collections vs. manuscript tradition	28
Local context and diffusion	33
To conclude	34
A note on this translation	36
Part One: The Formulary of Angers	37
Introduction	38
Translation	47
Part Two: The Formulary of Marculf	103
Introduction	104
The scope of the collection	105
Date and place of origin	107
Marculf and Landeric	107
Dating the collection	110
Marculf and St Denis	113
A note on the printed editions	117
Translation	124
Book One	127

CONTENTS

Book Two	177
Supplement	230
Additamenta: additional texts from the manuscripts of Marculf	235
a, b, c: three more texts from the manuscripts of Marculf	240
Appendix 1: The original date of the Angers collection: the state of the question	248
Appendix 2: The *gesta municipalia*	255
Appendix 3: The Marculf collection: manuscripts and editions	259
The manuscript tradition	259
Editions of Marculf and the hierarchy of manuscripts	265
Map	280
Glossary	281
Bibliography	288
Index	304

ACKNOWLEDGEMENTS

I started this translation while working on my PhD thesis on Frankish legal formularies at King's College London; I hope this translation will convey some of the sense of excitement I felt at coming in contact with this unpublicised but deeply rewarding type of source. Many people have helped me a great deal during that time and since: first and foremost, I would like to thank Jinty Nelson, my supervisor, for her endless patience, encouragement and generosity, and for greeting my many successive drafts with grace and good humour, suppressing any sense of rightful indignation at being thus bombarded with attachments during her summer holidays. I am also deeply thankful to Paul Fouracre, for taking the time to read and comment on the whole book; his intervention saved me from many an embarrassing mistake. Mary Whitby was a wonderful editor, and was extremely patient with me; her help was invaluable in supplying the kind of distance necessary for this book to become accessible to students and the general reader, in contrast with the obsessively specialist nature of PhD work (I blush at the thought of the first samples of the introduction I originally sent her, which a year later even I could no longer understand – I am grateful, as well as not a little surprised, that she did not dismiss the project there and then). I also thank Marios Costambeys and Ian Wood for their comments and criticisms on the text and translation; David Ganz, for his kindness and guidance regarding manuscript work in particular; and Wendy Davies and Chris Wickham, who examined my thesis, for their insights and general helpfulness. Any mistakes not weeded out from this volume, of course, remain entirely mine. Most of the book as it now stands was written during a very happy time spent as Junior Research Fellow at New College, Oxford; I am very grateful to the Fellows of that college for electing me to that post, as well as for making my time there so pleasant and enjoyable. And, last but not least: thanks to my parents, who surveyed the experiment from afar, and to Shamus Maxwell, who now knows more about formularies than he would probably ever have wished to.

ABBREVIATIONS

Capitularia	*Capitularia regum Francorum*, ed. A. Boretius, MGH *Leges* II (Hanover, 1883)
ChLA	*Chartae latinae antiquiores*
Concilia aevi Karolini	*Concilia aevi Karolini (742–842)*, ed. A. Werminghoff, MGH *Concilia* II (Hanover, 1906)
Kölzer DM.	*Die Urkunden der Merovinger*, ed. T. Kölzer, MGH *Diplomata regum Francorum e stirpe merovingica* (Hanover, 2001)
MGH	*Monumenta Germaniae Historica*
MGH SS rer. Merov.	MGH *Scriptores rerum Merovingicarum*
Pactus Legis Salicae	*Pactus Legis Salicae*, ed. K.A. Eckhardt, MGH *Leges* I.4.1 (Hanover, 1962)
Pardessus, *Diplomata*	J.-M. Pardessus, ed., *Diplomata, chartae, epistolae, leges: aliaque instrumenta ad res Gallo-Francicas spectantia* (Paris, 1843–1849)
Zeumer, *Formulae*	*Formulae Merowingici et Karolini Aevi*, ed. K. Zeumer, MGH *Leges* V (Hanover, 1886)

INTRODUCTION

THE SCOPE OF THIS BOOK

Most of what we know of the early middle ages concerns only a very small portion of society: the political and ecclesiastical elite in whom the sources written during this period (whether histories, annals, saints' lives, laws or surviving archival documents) were almost exclusively interested. Beyond this, it is much harder to get an impression of what life would have been like for the vast majority of the population who were not so lucky as to elicit such interest from contemporary authors. As a result, our view of early medieval society can seem curiously disembodied: we may find out in great detail about the political alliances and strategies or the intellectual achievements of particular individuals, but we tend not to be told much, if anything, about how ordinary people coped with the situations that cropped up in everyday life at a more basic level: what, for instance, people did when their marriages turned sour, or when they found an abandoned baby; what preparations they made when setting out on a journey; how they might have taken out a loan and how they could arrange to repay it; what made some sell their freedom to become slaves; what happened when an unfree man married a free woman; what sort of provision parents made for their children; or how conflicts in cases of theft, rape, kidnapping, assault or murder were resolved in practice.

One kind of source tells us all of these things and more: the legal formularies (collections of model legal documents; these models are referred to individually as formulae),[1] composed and copied from the sixth to the tenth centuries in the Frankish kingdoms, that is, roughly the area now covered by France and Germany under the Merovingian (c.450–751) and Carolingian (751–987) kings. Although they contain much colourful as well as unique

---

1 The word 'formula' (plural 'formulae') can be used by modern scholars with two quite distinct meanings: either to refer to particular standard turns of phrase within an actual legal document, or to refer to the full text of a model document of the kind presented in this book. I will use the word only with this second meaning here.

information, formulae are not, by and large, a very well-known source for the early medieval world. Little work has been done on them since the first half of the twentieth century, so that in terms of modern historical scholarship and methodology they remain relatively unexplored territory.[2] They are rarely referred to outside footnotes, and general textbooks on the period seldom discuss them, so that students or non-specialist readers are rarely made aware of them. This long period of neglect may soon come to an end: formulae have undergone the beginnings of a revival in recent research, and their potential as a source is beginning to be better recognised.[3] A fuller impact, however, remains hindered by inaccessibility. There is no full translation in English for any of these texts, and precious little in any other language. The difficulty of the original Latin is a significant obstacle, and,

---

2 The main edition of formulae was made by Karl Zeumer, *Formulae Merowingici et Karolini Aevi*, MGH *Leges* V (Hanover, 1886) (now available on the web at http://www.dmgh. de/); it quickly superseded Eugène de Rozière's earlier edition, *Recueil général des formules* (Paris, 1859–71). General discussions include H. Brunner, *Deutsche Rechtsgeschichte*, 2nd edn. (Leipzig, 1906), vol. 1, pp. 575–88; H. Bresslau, *Handbuch der Urkundenlehre für Deutschland und Italien*, 2nd edn. by H.-W. Klewitz (Berlin/Leipzig, 1931), vol. 2, pp. 225–41; T. Sickel, *Acta regum et imperatorum Karolinorum digesta et enarrata. Die Urkunden der Karolinger*, vol. 1: *Urkundenlehre* (Vienna, 1867), pp. 112–25; R. Buchner, *Deutschlands Geschichtsquellen im Mittelalter: Vorzeit und Karolinger. Beiheft: Die Rechtsquellen* (Weimar, 1953), pp. 49–55.

3 Recent work includes C. Lauranson-Rosaz and A. Jeannin, 'La résolution des litiges en justice durant le haut Moyen-Age: l'exemple de l'*apennis* à travers les formules, notamment celles d'Auvergne et d'Angers', in *Le règlement des conflits au Moyen-Age, XXXIe Congrès de la SHMES (Angers, juin 2000)* (Paris, 2001), pp. 21–33; D. Liebs, 'Sklaverei aus Not im germanisch-römischen Recht', *Zeitschrift der Savigny-Stiftung für Rechtsgeschichte. Romanistische Abteilung* 118 (2001), pp. 286–311; W. Brown, 'When documents are destroyed or lost: lay people and archives in the early Middle Ages', *Early Medieval Europe* 11 (2002), pp. 337–66; W. Brown, 'Conflicts, letters, and personal relationships in the Carolingian formula collections', *Law and History Review* 25 (2007), pp. 323–44; P. Depreux, 'La tradition manuscrite des "Formules de Tours" et la diffusion des modèles d'actes aux VIIIe et IXe siècles', in P. Depreux and B. Judic, eds., *Alcuin de York à Tours: Ecriture, pouvoir et réseaux dans l'Europe du Haut Moyen Age* (Rennes/Tours, 2004), pp. 55–70; A. Rio, 'Freedom and unfreedom in early medieval Francia: the evidence of the legal formulae', *Past & Present* 193 (2006), pp. 7–40; A. Rio, 'Les formulaires mérovingiens et carolingiens: tradition manuscrite et réception', *Francia* (forthcoming). Ian Wood and Paul Fouracre had made significant earlier contributions: see I.N. Wood, 'Disputes in late fifth- and sixth-century Gaul: some problems', in W. Davies and P. Fouracre, eds., *The Settlement of Disputes in Early Medieval Europe* (Cambridge, 1986), pp. 7–22; I.N. Wood, 'Administration, law and culture in Merovingian Gaul', in R. McKitterick, ed., *The Uses of Literacy in Early Medieval Europe* (Cambridge, 1990), pp. 63–81; P. Fouracre, '"Placita" and the settlement of disputes in later Merovingian Francia', in Davies and Fouracre, *The Settlement of Disputes in Early Medieval Europe*, pp. 23–43.

when it does not make reading impossible (as it would for most students), it at least involves an investment of time and energy such as few non-specialists would be willing to spend on what remains a relatively obscure source. For English speakers, the fact that most of the literature devoted to formulae was written in German constitutes a further obstacle. The purpose of this book is to make some of the most interesting and (relatively speaking) most often discussed among these texts more accessible, as well as to offer some ideas as to how they might best be put to use as a source.

For separate reasons, the formularies of Marculf and Angers have received rather more attention from historians than other collections, though references even to them generally nest in footnotes. The formulary of Angers, as the earliest surviving example of such texts, has been privileged by legal historians keen to trace links with the late antique tradition;[4] however, the formulary of Marculf, which was the first such collection ever to elicit scholarly interest, as early as the beginning of the seventeenth century, has unquestionably attracted the greatest level of attention.[5] Discussions have focused essentially on Book I of Marculf, because it contains royal documents, which have remained a long-standing object of interest to historians and diplomatists (specialists in the study of documents) since the heyday of German legal historiography in the nineteenth century. Despite being far from typical, Marculf has come, for better or for worse, to embody our perception of what a formulary is, and its influence on historians' conceptualisation of the genre has been greater than that of any other collection.

Besides making these already relatively well-known texts accessible to a wider audience, presenting these two collections in a single volume offers other advantages: Marculf and Angers give two rather different perspectives on the Frankish world, and the contrasts that can be drawn between them may help to delineate the scope of each collection more precisely. They were aimed at different audiences: Marculf deals with relations between powerful nobles, and even in the documents unrelated to the royal court rarely goes

---

4 See W. Bergmann, 'Die Formulae Andecavenses, eine Formelsammlung auf der Grenze zwischen Antike und Mittelalter', *Archiv für Diplomatik* 24 (1978), pp. 1–53; Bergmann, 'Verlorene Urkunden nach den *Formulae Andecavenses*', *Francia* 9 (1981), pp. 3–5.

5 The first two editions of Marculf were produced at the same time by Jérôme Bignon, *Marculfi monachi formularum libri duo* (Paris, 1613) and Friedrich Lindenbruch, *Codex legum antiquarum* (Frankfurt, 1613). Marculf was also later much discussed by Jean Mabillon, in his *Vetera analecta*, vol. 4 (Paris, 1685); *Annales ordinis S. Benedicti, occidentalium monachorum patriarchae, in quibus non modo res monasticae, sed etiam ecclesiasticae historiae non minima pars continetur*, vol. 1 (Paris, 1703); and *Libri de re diplomatica supplementum* (Paris, 1704). The latter also included an edition of the Angers collection.

much below the level of rather grand persons, though it presents them in a different light to most other sources. Angers, on the other hand, gives us a much more local focus: the documents included in it tend to deal with much smaller transactions, which never involved either the king or his court. The collection documents the business of people who did not have access to royal justice, operating at a lower social level than that documented in most other kinds of evidence. Both collections, in different ways, constitute rich sources of information on the ways in which early medieval people of various statuses made their arrangements and went on with their lives, and give an idea of the depth and potential of formulae as a type of historical material. To facilitate their use by students in particular, I have given each text a short introduction.

THE SCOPE OF FORMULAE

There are a number of reasons why formularies should give us so much more by way of practical detail on everyday life than any other source. Formulae were compiled by scribes involved in recording legal transactions in documents. They were usually based on earlier documents that were then turned into models to serve as a reference and teaching tool in the future. Scribes brought these models together into collections, with varying degrees of completeness and organisation; Marculf is the most meticulously organised and the most thorough in its coverage, which may account for its popularity among historians. These collections could therefore include virtually anything that scribes thought might prove useful in the course of their own professional career or in teaching their pupils. A formulary will therefore contain a large variety of documents, relating to a wide range of legal matters, and dealing with people in very different walks of life: from standard day-to-day transactions, such as sales, loans, gifts, or wills, marriages or divorces, to situations which we would nowadays associate more with criminal law, such as judgments and settlements of disputes when crimes such as theft or murder had been committed.

This range of subjects is far greater than that of surviving actual legal documents, or charters, for this period. Although formulae and charters tend to look very much alike, as one would expect, profound differences in their mode of transmission and in the rationale for their survival have meant that they do not provide evidence for quite the same things. Charters survive almost exclusively as part of ecclesiastical archives, since only churches and monasteries had the level of institutional continuity required for the

INTRODUCTION

preservation of such documents over the long term. As a result, lay people are seriously under-represented in the surviving archival material, and this has led some historians to argue that written forms of agreement had very little currency in this period outside the realm of the church.[6] Besides being profoundly church-centred, surviving documents also deal almost exclusively with land: documents describing land transactions were virtually the only documents worth preserving in the long run, since they alone retained their value as proof of ownership. Establishing titles of land ownership was the main preoccupation of the eleventh-century compilers of the cartularies (collections of copies of charters) in which most of our documents survive. By contrast, legal actions of a more transitory nature tended to lose their significance after a relatively short time, probably soon after the persons involved in them had died: most records of settlements of disputes, unless they related to land, would thus have lost their value within a generation or so of their being produced.[7] Formulae did not undergo the same process of selection, for, unlike charters, they were not preserved because their intrinsic content was advantageous in the long run; they were selected instead according to their immediate usefulness in providing a framework for recording day-to-day legal business.

As a result, formulae can offer insights into a variety of local situations, and the stories embedded in them present some very striking vignettes. Here are a few examples to be found among the texts translated in this book. A man sold himself to another man and his wife, but a while later was able to recover his freedom through the courts when the couple could not find their deed of ownership for him. Royal ambassadors on their way to another kingdom were equipped with a list of all the food and supplies they were entitled to demand from the locals in the districts they passed through. Couples who were finding life together unbearable obtained divorces by mutual consent. Poor people belonging to a church found an abandoned newborn child, 'still covered in blood', and subsequently sold the baby to someone. Unfree men married free women without any adverse consequences. Pilgrims going to Rome got letters of recommendation to show people they met en route. A couple gave some property to their son, to thank

---

6 See M. Richter, '"*Quisquis scit scribere, nullum potat abere labore*". Zur Laienschriftlichkeit im 8. Jahrhundert', in J. Jarnut, U. Nonn and M. Richter, eds., *Karl Martell in seiner Zeit* (Sigmaringen, 1994), pp. 393–404; M. Richter, *The Formation of the Medieval West: Studies in the Oral Culture of the Barbarians* (Dublin, 1994).

7 P.J. Geary, 'Land, language and memory in Europe, 700–1100', *Transactions of the Royal Historical Society*, 6th series, vol. 9 (1999), pp. 169–84, at p. 170.

him for going to war in his father's place. Couples who had lost all their personal papers in a fire got them all replaced by the relevant local authorities. A king made a gift of property he had recently confiscated from a rebel. A man who had no one to care for him in his old age adopted another man on condition that the latter should provide him with food, clothing 'and shoes in sufficient quantity'. A father decided to make his daughter his heir on a par with her brothers, in spite of legislation against the inheritance of women. Someone sent a powerful friend the early medieval equivalent of a Christmas card.[8]

In all these cases, formulae seem to operate on a more local, even humdrum, level than most other sources. They therefore offer a unique perspective on the economic and social history of early medieval Francia. Important parts of society that are otherwise rather poorly documented, such as women or slaves, who characteristically tend to feature in the narrative sources only as passing stereotypes, are here represented in real-life situations and circumstances. Formulae bear witness to things which often fell beneath the notice of other sources, but which actually relate to priorities commonly shared by people in this as in any period: namely, the security of their property and their persons, the maintenance or bettering of their legal and social situation, and their duties in relation to others around them. By recording the interactions of people of varied status and occupation as they got on with their own concerns and strove to secure their rights and positions, formulae offer an unparalleled sense of the fabric of everyday life.

THE PROBLEM WITH FORMULAE

Why, given all these apparent advantages, have formulae not generally been rated among the major sources for Frankish history? Any source from this period is inherently valuable, given the overall scarcity of the evidence, but formularies have proved very much less attractive to historians than the main narrative and legal texts, such as Gregory of Tours's *Histories* or Salic law. This neglect is not the result of oversight: formulae have been known about for a long time and are often referred to in footnotes as additional evidence to back up arguments based on other sources. In fact, there are serious methodological problems associated with exploiting this material.

Indeed, as soon as it comes to putting their evidence in context in a

---

[8] Angers no. 17; Marculf I, 11; Angers no. 57 and Marculf II, 30; Angers no. 49; Angers no. 59 and Marculf II, 29; Marculf II, 49; Angers no. 37; Angers nos. 31–33 and Marculf I, 33–34; Marculf I, 32; Marculf II, 13; Marculf II, 12; Marculf II, 44 and 45.

INTRODUCTION

methodologically rigorous manner, it must be admitted that formulae, when first encountered, have features that make them seem a very frustrating source to deal with. Much of what historians usually like to learn from a source is simply missing from them, since scribes, in a bid to generalise the value of their texts, were often extremely thorough in their efforts to remove any specific details from a document when they transformed it into a formula. Formulae are therefore overwhelmingly anonymous texts about anonymous people, and more often than not their dates and places of origin are also unknown. This non-specificity can make formulae seem infuriatingly opaque to modern readers.

This was already seen as a problem in the nineteenth and early twentieth centuries, especially in Germany. Scholars of the German *Rechtsschule* ('school of legal history') saw their first task as dating the collections, and then attributing authors to them, rather than addressing their content as such.[9] At the same time, these scholars took it for granted that the 'factual' information in formulae could be trusted, if it could only be firmly pinned down to date and place. Their efforts met with mixed success and their results were fiercely debated; yet their faith that formulae fundamentally reflected reality remained undimmed.

Modern scholarship, however, is generally far more demanding of sources than this earlier historiographical tradition. Historians nowadays are more sensitive to the difficult relationship between text and reality, and are keenly aware that even the most outwardly utilitarian sources could be subject to distortions which may impede, or severely restrict, our ability to interpret them appropriately. The need to establish the context of a source is now seen as paramount in order to understand why and how it was produced; information obtained without such a context is generally seen as too vague to be useful.[10] This no doubt explains the fall from grace of formulae as a source, since their context is very often simply irrecoverable, because early medieval scribes systematically removed virtually all internal evidence of

---

9 For discussions of this sort regarding Marculf and Angers, see below, pp. 107–13 and Appendix 1. Fustel de Coulanges relied heavily on formulae as a source in his *Monarchie franque*, and his work can be said to represent the only serious attempt to use them comprehensively in a general history on the same level as, for instance, the law-codes or narrative histories (N.D. Fustel de Coulanges, *La monarchie franque*, Histoire des institutions politiques de l'ancienne France, vol. 3 [Paris, 1888], *passim*, but especially pp. 23–24; see also, for instance, *ibid*. pp. 29, 190, 214, 406, 409, 415–16, 420 and 499).

10 On this subject, see A. Rio, 'Charters, law-codes and formulae: the Franks between theory and practice', in Paul Fouracre and David Ganz, eds., *Frankland: The Franks and the World of Early Medieval Europe* (Manchester, 2008), pp. 7–27.

particulars (names, dates, places) in order to create a generalisable product. If the modern historian can no longer opt for blind trust that formulae reflect their creators' world in a straightforward manner, what more appropriate way might there be of exploiting these texts? The modern neglect of formulae reflects genuine problems in getting a handle on them, problems which cannot be evaded, if the value of formulae as sources is to be clarified and vindicated (and hence if this book is to justify its own existence). This introduction will attempt to deal with some of these fundamental questions of methodology, in order to put the translations included in this book in perspective.

These, then, are the main questions: how did these texts come into being, and what sort of user were they intended for? What relationship did they have with what was really going on in social and legal practice? Were they really used in the production of actual documents? And the problem of contextualisation: can they be mapped in time and space? I shall examine each of these questions in turn.

AUTHORSHIP AND AUDIENCE: WHAT THE MANUSCRIPT EVIDENCE CAN TELL US

Judging from their wide range of subjects, and because they were not templates that could be applied directly, but had to be adapted to new situations in such a way as to require a high level of skill,[11] we can be certain that formulae were both produced and used by professional scribes; but it is less clear what kind of professional scribe would have used them, for what purpose, and in whose employment. To answer these questions, it is necessary to consider not only who originally wrote them, insofar as this may be gathered from the content of our formularies, but also who copied them, who owned them, and who used them, all of which can only be inferred from the manuscripts in which they survive.

Formulae collections do not, as a rule, seem to have been compiled under the influence of the Frankish royal or imperial courts. The only certain example of a collection produced in connection with such a court is that of the group of formulae referred to as the *Formulae Imperiales*, collected during the reign of Louis the Pious, probably in the 820s, by a notary of the imperial chancery at the monastery of St Martin of Tours; but even they are far from amounting in any sense to an 'official' collection. This formulary was in

---

11 See below, p. 27.

fact copied with an exceptional degree of informality, even in comparison with other formulae collections: the manuscript in which it is found, despite containing material relating to the business of the imperial court, seems to have been intended by this notary as a notebook for his personal use. The manuscript's very idiosyncratic choice of texts and odd format, the latter suggesting that the pages were made out of scraps of parchment, complete the impression of an individualised handbook. There is no evidence that this collection was intended to be widely shared or diffused, and hardly any of the formulae contained in it were copied in later manuscripts. The collection can therefore no more be described as 'official' than the many collections similarly compiled by local scribes for their own use.[12]

There is, therefore, nothing to support the notion that formulae and formulae collections were ever produced as a result of royal initiative. Even those formularies that include documents involving the king should not automatically be associated with court notaries: there is thus no real evidence that Book I of Marculf, which contains mostly royal documents, was in fact produced in connection with a royal court.[13] Collections did not present users with a standard imposed by a higher authority, but rather with a miscellany of texts which compilers had found useful enough to copy, either for their personal use or for that of their pupils or colleagues, according to their expectation of the kind of material they would need to keep at hand. We should, therefore, think of formulae as texts shaped first and foremost by the needs of individual scribes. The overwhelming majority of our collections are concerned with issues that their compilers expected would arise in their local communities, rather than on the scale of the kingdom. Formulae collections thus fundamentally reflect the activity of local scribes,

---

12 The formulae are edited in Zeumer, *Formulae*, pp. 285–328. On this manuscript (Paris, Bibliothèque nationale de France, ms. latin 2718), see H. Mordek, *Bibliotheca capitularium regum francorum manuscripta: Überlieferung und Traditionszusammenhang der fränkischen Herrschererlasse*, MGH Hilfsmittel 15 (Munich, 1995), pp. 422–30; M. Mersiowsky, 'Saint-Martin de Tours et les chancelleries carolingiennes', in Depreux and Judic, *Alcuin de York à Tours*, pp. 73–90, esp. pp. 81–84; R.-H. Bautier, 'La chancellerie et les actes royaux dans les royaumes carolingiens', *Bibliothèque de l'Ecole des Chartes* 142 (1984), pp. 5–80, at p. 44; P. Johanek, 'Herrscherdiplom und Empfängerkreis. Die Kanzlei Ludwigs des Frommen in der Schriftlichkeit der Karolingerzeit', in R. Schieffer, ed., *Schriftkultur und Reichsverwaltung unter den Karolingern*, Abhandlungen der Nordrhein-Westfälischen Akademie der Wissenschaften 97 (1996), pp. 167–88, at p. 186; D. Ganz, 'Paris BN Latin 2718: theological texts in the chapel and the chancery of Louis the Pious', in O. Münsch and T. Zotz, eds., *Scientia veritatis: Festschrift für Hubert Mordek zum 65. Geburtstag* (Ostfildern, 2004), pp. 137–52.
13 On this issue, see below, pp. 113–17.

who found, selected and copied models as best they could, in light of their knowledge and expectations of the legal matters in which the people who sought their services would be involved.

It is difficult to determine more precisely what sort of career and environment these scribes may have had. Our only named author, Marculf, tells us he was a monk; other formularies, on the other hand, give us very little indication of what sort of person they were used by and intended for. The contents of collections are usually rather mixed, and the subjects included in a formulary very rarely relate exclusively to either an ecclesiastical or a lay sphere. Collections containing models on how to make gifts to a church, which would make sense in an ecclesiastical environment, thus also often contain documents involving civic archives,[14] or transactions involving only lay people. What sort of scribe would have needed both? Should we imagine independent lay scribes occasionally jobbing for churches or monasteries, or church scribes also writing for lay people?

Since all of our manuscripts survive in ecclesiastical archives, the short answer is that formulae, *in the state in which we find them*, that is, as they appear in the surviving manuscripts, were without doubt essentially the result of the work of ecclesiastical scribes, not lay notaries. It is impossible to show definitively that any of the surviving manuscripts containing formulae was produced in a lay context. However, this does not mean that all of these texts had *originally* been composed in an ecclesiastical context, or that their use was ever entirely confined to religious houses. Lay notaries are generally very poorly documented for this period, due to the loss of virtually all archives beyond those kept by ecclesiastical institutions, but there are indications that they existed, and they may well, for all we know, have used formularies themselves, or been trained in religious houses using the same textbooks as their monastic colleagues.[15] Indeed, it could be argued that ecclesiastical archives only document the final, and most formal, stages of the career of formulae as a genre.

It is important in this respect to consider why and under what conditions the manuscripts containing these texts survived. Virtually all of them can be dated to the Carolingian period, that is, from the mid-eighth to the tenth centuries. This is in itself a little surprising, since we can be certain, on grounds of internal evidence, that several formulae collections were produced long before that, during the Merovingian period: the two collections translated in

---

14 The *gesta municipalia* mentioned in Angers and Marculf; see Appendix 2.

15 See in particular R. McKitterick, *The Carolingians and the Written Word* (Cambridge, 1989), pp. 77–134.

this book, Angers and Marculf, thus seem to date from the late sixth and the late seventh centuries respectively, but only survive in manuscripts copied in the Carolingian era, from the late eighth century onwards.[16] The entire corpus of the manuscript evidence for formulae surviving from the Merovingian period amounts only to three manuscript folia, written in an early eighth-century cursive script, which only survive because they were later inserted in a manuscript otherwise containing texts copied in Carolingian script.[17] Why, then, is there so little contemporary manuscript evidence for Merovingian formulae collections? What particular set of factors allowed formularies to leave a manuscript trace of their existence under the Carolingians, but not under their predecessors?

The uneven state of our manuscript record may well be due to accidents of survival, since far fewer books survive overall for the Merovingian period than for the Carolingian period in any case. Certain factors, however, could have contributed to making the survival of such texts more likely for the Carolingian period than previously, possibly through changes in the physical shape given to formulae collections and in the institutional framework in which they were produced. It may be that the reason why so little material evidence for formulae survives from the period before the mid-eighth century is that these texts only began to be copied out formally into properly bound manuscripts from the beginning of the Carolingian period onwards. Up to that point, they may have been kept in a more casual form, as scraps or bundles of parchment, which would have had virtually no chance of surviving. This may have been the case with our three surviving folia containing formulae copied in Merovingian script: the texts were numbered, and thus clearly formed part of a collection, but most of it was lost, perhaps because the sheets were originally kept loose rather than bound. Keeping formulae in this less durable form would have been perfectly adequate and sufficient if they were only intended to serve the needs of individual scribes compiling models exclusively for their own use. This would have been the situation for all lay notaries in the late antique tradition, who would have worked independently: the absence of formulae from our surviving manuscript record before the Carolingian period may have been due to the lack of any institutional continuity for independent notaries working outside religious houses, which meant that the use of their models would rarely have outlived them or, at most, their apprentices.

16 For the dating of these collections, see below, pp. 41–42 and Appendix 1, and pp. 107–13.
17 Paris, Bibliothèque nationale de France, ms. latin 10756, at fols. 62–64.

Their collections were therefore at a high risk of being lost or discarded within the space of only a few generations. The higher risk of loss associated with collections belonging to independent notaries may also explain why no Roman versions of these texts survive, even though the survival of traces of similar documentary models in other post-Roman kingdoms besides Francia, such as Visigothic Spain and Ostrogothic Italy,[18] and the existence of formal continuities between surviving private documents from the Roman period and early medieval documents and formulae indicate that they derived from the documentary tradition of the late empire.[19]

The situation was very different under the Carolingians, and there would have been a number of reasons why a more formal approach should have become favoured then. Perhaps the most important of these would have been the growing need of ecclesiastical communities to train new scribes in order to produce and issue documents. Religious houses experienced a very significant growth throughout this period, in wealth and size as well as in their importance as centres for the production of documents. By the ninth century, and for some time before that, churches had become major providers of documentary records, both for their own sake, to record their transactions and administer complex networks of grants and tenures, and also to record the transactions and disputes arising among the lay people living under their lordship or in their neighbourhood. That last point accounts for the presence of models involving only lay people in formulae collections compiled in churches or monasteries.[20] The development of a more formal approach to these texts would have been a likely response to this increased teaching need: it meant that collections were no longer intended only for a single user, but to train present and future pupils. The Marculf collection, compiled in the late seventh century, and explicitly intended for teaching, as indicated by its preface, may constitute an early example of this process of formalisation: it is in many respects unusual for its time.[21]

18 See below, n. 26.
19 On continuities between late Roman and early medieval documentary practices, see the classic article by P. Classen, 'Fortleben und Wandel spätrömischen Urkundenwesens im frühen Mittelalter', in P. Classen, ed., *Recht und Schrift im Mittelalter*, Vorträge und Forschungen 23 (Sigmaringen, 1977), pp. 13–54.
20 The St Gall archive, though it also reflects the activity of independent local scribes, shows that the monastery played an important part in providing scribal services to the lay communities under its lordship; see McKitterick, *The Carolingians and the Written Word*, pp. 77–134.
21 On teaching, see Marculf's preface, below, p. 126; on Marculf's exceptional character, see below, p. 104. The later St Gall collection, with its sporadic commentary and advice, was clearly intended for teaching from the very start.

INTRODUCTION

Preserving collections in more formal, durable and clearly laid-out books only became necessary when the use of a collection expanded beyond the individual scribe, and became intended for a community rather than a single user. A large number of surviving manuscripts containing formulae were clearly designed for teaching.[22] Formulae are often found in manuscripts alongside a bewildering array of miscellaneous texts, all broadly concerned with setting out ways of getting things right: from genealogies of Frankish kings to chronologies detailing the passage of time from creation to the present day; calendars; treatises on grammar and spelling; basic catechistic texts, often in question-and-answer form; sermons by standard authors, often by or attributed to Augustine; hymns and prayers; extracts from Isidore of Seville's *Etymologies*, a compendium of general knowledge widely copied in ecclesiastical *scriptoria* during this period; explanations on the different degrees of family relationships; or even lists of useful medical supplies. Some of the manuscripts containing formulae may also have been used as reference books by more advanced legal scribes: many of them also contain law-codes, usually Salic law or the Breviary of Alaric, a Visigothic abbreviation of the Theodosian Code, which were perhaps included as an initial point of reference to solve disputes, though this point remains much debated.[23] All of these manuscripts were still very much tailored according to scribes' personal preferences and their understanding of what constituted useful material, but by the Carolingian period they were also intended to cater for the needs of a wider audience. All this gave formulae a level of continuity, and allowed them to be preserved in the long run, which would not have been likely to happen if they had remained the preserve of independent scribes.

Besides the growth of ecclesiastical communities and the demand for scribes, this formalisation of the genre may also have been linked, more indirectly, to the new concern for standards of correctness in written forms

---

22 Brown, 'When documents are destroyed or lost', pp. 356–57. This category includes, for instance, Paris BnF lat. 2123, 2400, 4410, 4627, 4629, 4841, 11379, Leiden Voss lat. O. 86, and Vatican reg. lat. 612.

23 Some of these manuscripts have been linked to a hypothetical '*leges*-scriptorium' dedicated to the production of official lawbooks, though it remains uncertain whether these books would have belonged to lay royal officials or to religious houses keen to uphold their legal rights (see B. Bischoff, 'Die Hofbibliothek unter Ludwig dem Frommen', in J.J.C. Alexander and M.T. Gibson, eds., *Medieval Learning and Literature: Essays presented to Richard William Hunt* [Oxford, 1976], pp. 3–22, reprinted in B. Bischoff, *Mittelalterliche Studien* vol. 3 [Stuttgart, 1981], pp. 171–86; McKitterick, *The Carolingians and the Written Word*, pp. 57–60; Mordek, *Bibliotheca capitularium*, pp. 422–24).

characteristic of the rule of the early Carolingian kings.[24] There was a clear increase under the reigns of Charlemagne (768–814) and Louis the Pious (814–840) in the production of both new formulae collections and new manuscripts of older collections: the vast majority of our manuscript evidence was produced during the late eighth and ninth centuries. Although formulae collections were not produced at the initiative of the royal court, it seems likely that their extraordinarily successful diffusion in this period was a response to a more document-minded style of rule, and to a new emphasis on recording transactions in appropriately written and carefully composed documents. It is striking that these collections, when their place of origin can be determined,[25] seem to have originated mostly in Northern Francia: they are nearly all distributed along or to the north of a rough latitudinal line running along the middle of the Frankish kingdoms through Angers, Tours, Bourges and Salzburg. The only exceptions are a very small fragment from Clermont, and the only non-Frankish collection of this kind, the *Formulae Visigothicae* or Visigothic Formulae, thought to have been produced in Cordoba.[26] This is not what one would expect, given the stronger documentary tradition generally attributed by historians to Mediterranean regions in this period; but there could be good reasons why formularies should have had a harder time surviving in the South than they did in the North. Not only were the churches and monasteries situated in the royal heartlands of Northern Francia some of the largest and most powerful religious houses, and thus perhaps those most in need of an organised system for the training of scribes, they were also those most closely linked to the activities of kings, and those most likely to be affected by them: they were closer to royal centres, were placed on the routes on which kings travelled most regularly, and may thus have had a greater ability, or at least more opportunities, to appeal to the king in cases of disputes. Northern bishops and abbots also tended to have stronger personal

---

24 See J.L. Nelson, 'Literacy in Carolingian government', in R. McKitterick, ed., *The Uses of Literacy in Early Medieval Europe* (Cambridge, 1990), pp. 258–96; McKitterick, *The Carolingians and the Written Word*.

25 Which is not often: see below, pp. 33–34.

26 The most recent edition is by J. Gil, '*Formulae Wisigothicae*', in *Miscellanea Wisigothica* (Seville, 1972), pp. 70–112. Books VI and VII of the *Variae* of Cassiodorus, from Ostrogothic Italy, also contain some examples of documentary models analogous to those found for Francia (see in particular T. Mommsen, ed., *Cassiodori Senatoris Variae*, MGH *Scriptores Auctores Antiquissimi* XII [Berlin, 1898], VII, 33–47). A translation of a small sample of formulae from these two books is included in S.J.B. Barnish, *Cassiodorus: Selected Variae* (Liverpool, 1992), pp. 94–100. A hitherto unknown formulary from tenth-century Catalonia, found in Archivo de la Corona de Aragon ms. Ripoll 74, has also been edited by M. Zimmermann, 'Un formulaire du Xème siècle conservé à Ripoll', *Faventia* 4 (1982), pp. 25–86.

or family connections with members of the royal or imperial court, which would again have improved their ability to appeal to the king. All this would have led to a certain pressure for these institutions to keep an appropriate record of transactions and disputes according to external norms of correctness, which in turn would have led to the more systematic development of formularies as a response.

Perhaps the initially less deeply implanted Roman style of documentary practice in the North may itself have contributed to the success of formal textbooks of this kind: with a less strongly rooted local tradition to draw on, scribes may have been in greater need of such reference tools. The production of formulae collections seems to have moved more or less progressively eastwards with the passage of time, with our earliest collection being compiled in Angers in the late sixth century, and our latest ones in the great monasteries of Eastern Francia. This fits in rather neatly with a spread of documentary norms through the influence of Carolingian government into the more recently acquired Eastern lands. Exchanges and regular contacts between different ecclesiastical communities, which formed a very close-knit network across Carolingian North Francia, led to a greater number of manuscripts being produced for these texts, which would again have increased their chance of survival. Such exchanges are evident in the manuscript tradition: individual texts or groups of texts often became integrated into several different collections, while undergoing a continuous process of selection and adaptation according to the needs of different scribes.[27] Scribes or their ecclesiastical superiors seem to have sent each other these texts, with each institution borrowing and copying them to add to its own resources. Marculf sent his collection to a bishop with precisely this need in mind: his formulary, an unprecedented success story in terms of diffusion, is our earliest example of a collection moving away from its initial place of composition to serve as a reference and teaching tool elsewhere, thus foreshadowing the wide-ranging influence of such collections during the Carolingian period. Our forty or so surviving manuscripts, it seems, were only the tip of an iceberg: formularies found in multiple manuscripts, such as those of Marculf, Tours and St Gall, invariably have a very complex tradition, and rarely look the same in any two manuscripts, so that one needs to presuppose the existence of many non-surviving intermediary manuscripts to make any sense of them at all.[28] This may give us an idea of what we are missing of the history of the vast majority of collections which are only known from a

---

[27] See below, pp. 30, 118–23.
[28] For Marculf, see below, Appendix 3.

single witness, as is the case with the Angers collection. The impression is one of a wide pool of available material transmitted according to a complex pattern of diffusion, in which collections mattered less than individual texts: connections and intersections in the manuscript tradition show a very fertile and changing ensemble, of which the surviving manuscripts can offer us only glimpses.

The formalisation of our corpus of formulae, and its survival, therefore depended on a combination of factors specific to Northern Francia under the Carolingians: the need for growing ecclesiastical communities to train new scribes; the existence of a tight, grid-like network of religious houses through which these texts could be diffused and exchanged; and a level of external pressure for documents to be written according to particular standards of correctness, which created a demand for such textbooks, though it should again be stressed that they were never the object of any centrally driven imperial programme. This brief window of visibility under the Carolingians came to a close after the end of their rule in the tenth century, when these texts, whether or not they were still being used, disappear again from the surviving manuscript evidence. Perhaps the reason why formulae were no longer produced or copied in the same way after the tenth century comes from the disappearance of some of the pressures which had led to their success under the Carolingians: in a situation in which the influence of the royal centre was lessened, it is possible that monasteries could have become less concerned with adhering to external norms of validity, and have started simply using documents from their own archives as models. The disappearance of formulae from our record coincides with a profound rethinking of archival practice, with the appearance of the first cartularies compiling the documents belonging to particular religious houses,[29] as well as substantial changes in documentary practice, with charters becoming replaced by longer, more narrative and less standardised *notitiae*, less suited to being derived from a model.[30] The disappearance of formulae may also have been due to the emergence of a different style of teaching, relying primarily on memory rather than on written models; perhaps such a difference in teaching styles may also account for the near-absence of formularies in the South throughout our period.

---

29 See especially P.J. Geary, *Phantoms of Remembrance: Memory and Oblivion at the End of the First Millenium* (Princeton, 1994), pp. 81–114. See also R.F. Berkhofer, *Day of Reckoning: Power and Accountability in Medieval France* (Philadelphia, 2004).

30 See in particular D. Barthélemy, *La société dans le comté de Vendôme de l'an mil au XIVe siècle* (Paris, 1993), pp. 19–127.

INTRODUCTION

The decline of formulae may not in fact require much explanation at all: these texts only managed to leave a trace in our surviving evidence for a brief period of time, thanks to a very specific set of circumstances, and their disappearance from the record once these circumstances no longer applied in a way merely amounts to a return to normal. As a rule, documentary models of this kind tend not to survive, even when they were manifestly being used, as shown by their near-absence from the manuscript record in Francia during the Merovingian period, when collections such as Marculf and Angers are nevertheless known to have existed, and from Italy and Spain, where the overall standardisation of documents as well as occasional surviving examples suggest such models would also have been in use.[31] What should cause wonder is that any formularies survived at all: their drastically improved chances of survival in the eighth to tenth centuries allow us a rare glimpse into a type of text lost to other times and regions.

Formulae, although they no doubt originated in the late antique documentary tradition of local lay scribes, thus only had the chance of leaving a trace in the manuscript tradition when they moved beyond this local level and into ecclesiastical archives. As we find them in the manuscripts, formularies thus show us the end-product of the incorporation into church archives of a long and rich documentary tradition. This need not mean that there were not still a number of lay notaries working independently during this period; but if there were, we do not have their collections.

THE LANGUAGE OF FORMULAE

The transmission of formularies in manuscripts compiled by ecclesiastical scribes makes it difficult to tell how representative these documents would have been of legal practice as commonly experienced by the lay majority of the population. How far the written word would have been relevant to lay transactions has been much debated, and some historians have dismissed documentary evidence altogether as unrepresentative of all but a very narrow clerical section of society.[32] Do formulae, then, essentially reflect a church

---

31 Besides the Visigothic formulae in Spain and the few examples preserved in the *Variae* for Italy (see above, n. 26), another exception is the papal *Liber diurnus*, compiled in response to a strong demand for standardised documents associated with the highly developed bureaucratic apparatus of the papacy.

32 See Richter, "'*Quisquis scit scribere, nullum potat abere labore*'" and *The Formation of the Medieval West*. In the opposite corner, see McKitterick, *The Carolingians and the Written Word*, and McKitterick, ed., *The Uses of Literacy in Early Medieval Europe*.

view imposed on the laity, or were they the object of a more active demand? Any assessment of the impact of these texts on the lay population at large must consider the question of their accessibility: if the documents produced using formularies had no chance of being understood by lay people, this would bring into question their ability to reflect lay concerns accurately. The use of Latin and of written forms would have constituted two major potential obstacles. In this context, it is worth looking in more detail at the language of formulae, before moving on to consider what they can tell us about the use of the written word in this period.

The Latin used in formulae is often strikingly unorthodox, and nowhere more so than in Merovingian collections such as Angers and Marculf.[33] This non-classical style of expression has been interpreted in two opposite ways: according to one, the written Latin of formulae reflected changes in the spoken language, in which case its idiosyncrasies would have made it more accessible to users; according to the other, the Latin of formulae still reflected an exclusively learned language, but one distorted and jumbled beyond recognition by scribes' poor command of classical Latin,[34] in which case it would have helped no one's comprehension, since it would no longer have corresponded to any coherent system of language, whether spoken or classical. Ultimately, the question is whether the language of early medieval documents was a language of communication (if it was designed to be accessible to a wide variety of people) or a language of exclusion (if it was designed to function as the exclusive domain of a specialised elite).

The influence of the school of thought that considered the distortions of Merovingian Latin to be a reflection of spoken forms was relatively short-lived,[35] and, from the 1950s onwards, the consensus among philologists

---

[33] For an excellent introduction to Merovingian Latin, see P. Fouracre and R.A. Gerberding, *Late Merovingian France: History and Hagiography, 640–720* (Manchester, 1996), at pp. 58–78. On the Latin of formulae in particular, see J. Pirson, 'Le latin des formules mérovingiennes et carolingiennes', *Romanische Forschungen* 26 (1909), pp. 837–944; L. Beszard, *La langue des formules de Sens* (Paris, 1910); L.F. Sas, *The Noun Declension System in the Merovingian Period* (Paris, 1937). For Merovingian legal documents, see also J. Vielliard, *Le latin des diplômes royaux et des chartes privées de l'époque mérovingienne* (Paris, 1927); R. Falkowski, 'Studien zur Sprache der Merowingerdiplome', *Archiv für Diplomatik* 17 (1971), pp. 1–125.

[34] See, for instance, P. Riché, *Education et culture dans l'Occident barbare, VIe-VIIe siècles* (Paris, 1962), pp. 284–85.

[35] This school essentially involved Muller and his students, who allowed formulae pride of place as an important measure of linguistic change in the context of the shift from Latin to Romance languages: see H. F. Muller, 'When did Latin cease to be a spoken language in France?', *The Romanic Review* 12 (1921), pp. 318–34; H. F. Muller, *L'Epoque mérovingienne:*

increasingly came to be that the language of formularies instead pointed to the gradually loosening grip of their users on written forms. The great linguist Dag Norberg, who discussed formularies extensively and was very influential in this respect, argued that by *ca.* 700 Latin was no longer a coherent system, and that it was no longer capable of being used as an adequate tool for communication, because it had become too chaotic to be much use to anyone.[36] Norberg denied that written documents of the Merovingian period provided an accurate testimony of the evolution of spoken, 'popular' Latin, and insisted on their conservative character and rigid norms. The use of formularies in particular, he argued, was conducive to the fixation of archaic expressions, and its effect was inevitably to isolate written forms from the changes occurring in the spoken language.[37] Norberg found it quite unbelievable that a Gallic peasant should have been able to read and understand what a royal chancellor had written, and insisted on the fundamental linguistic conservatism of legal documents.[38]

The Angers formulary was used as an example by both sides in this debate.[39] Its Latin is undeniably very far from classical norms. This was understood either to show the existence of a linguistic barrier hindering comprehension of the text, even for the scribe who was copying it, or to reflect changes in the language of the documents paralleling those of the spoken language, which would on the contrary have helped comprehension for all those involved. Norberg argued that the collection showed a general lack of understanding of Latin case endings, since cases used in set phrases were often left unchanged even when these phrases were taken out

---

Essai de synthèse de philologie et d'histoire (New York, 1945); Sas, *Noun Declension System*; M.A. Pei, *The Language of the Eighth-century Texts in Northern France: a Study of the Original Documents in the Collection of Tardif and other Sources* (New York, 1932).

36 D. Norberg, *Manuel pratique de latin médiéval* (Paris, 1968), p. 31.

37 D. Norberg, *Syntaktische Forschungen auf dem Gebiete des Spätlateins und des frühen Mittellateins* (Uppsala, 1943), p. 17.

38 Norberg, *Syntaktische Forschungen*, p. 17: 'Ein gallischer Bauer hätte also nach Pei auf dieselbe Weise reden sollen, wie die Schreiber des Königs bei der Ausfertigung von königlichen Erlassen und Diplomen schrieben! Das ist ja schon an sich ganz unglaublich.'

39 Norberg, *Manuel pratique de latin médiéval*, pp. 29–31; G. Calboli, 'Aspects du Latin mérovingien', in J. Herman, ed., *Latin vulgaire – Latin tardif, Actes du premier colloque international sur le latin vulgaire et tardif* (Pécs, 2–5 septembre 1985) (Tübingen, 1987), pp. 19–35; J. Herman, 'Sur quelques aspects du latin mérovingien: langue écrite et langue parlée', in M. Iliescu and W. Marxgut, eds., *Latin vulgaire – Latin tardif III, Actes du Troisième Colloque International sur le latin vulgaire et tardif (Innsbruck, 2–5 septembre 1991)* (Tübingen, 1992), pp. 173–86.

of context.⁴⁰ This, however, would not have made these sentences incomprehensible; indeed, leaving these standard phrases unchanged could only have helped to make them more recognisable. More recent philological work has focused less on such formal 'incorrectness' and more on the issue of comprehension.⁴¹ The reduction of the case system to the basic opposition between subject and object, for instance, since it is likely to have been close to the spoken language of the time,⁴² would almost certainly not have hindered these texts' accessibility, though it might make them somewhat confusing for a modern reader trained in classical Latin; in terms of ease of comprehension, the increased use of prepositions to indicate grammatical function would in any case largely have made up for this vagueness in the use of cases.

On the other hand, some phrases in the Angers formulae do seem not to have been clearly understood even by the notary himself. These are the cases Norberg pointed to as evidence that the language had become fossilised.⁴³ Virtually all of these, however, are found not in the main body of the models, but only in those few cases in which formulae contained formal standard introductions: a degree of confusion as to the exact meaning of these introductions would not therefore have had any serious consequences in terms of grasping the general intent of the formula. A certain vague and ponderous form of legal-speak seems to have been *de rigueur* in such introductions, and it probably would not have mattered very much whether anyone understood those particular passages: these isolated expressions would have been

---

40 The phrase 'cum aquis aquarumve decursibus' was thus often transferred in the Angers collection to 'cido tibi... pascuas, aquas aquarumvae decursibus', with 'decursibus' being kept in the ablative despite having moved to the position of direct object.

41 G. Calboli, 'Il latino merovingico, fra latino volgare e latino medioevale', in E. Vineis, ed., *Latino volgare, latino medioevale, lingua romanze, Atti del Convegno della S.I.G., Perugia 28–29 marzo 1982* (Pisa, 1984), pp. 63–81; Calboli, 'Bemerkungen zu einigen Besonderheiten des merowingisch-karolingischen Latein', in Iliescu and Marxgut, *Latin vulgaire - Latin tardif III*, pp. 41–61. Norberg himself later nuanced his view, particularly in the case of the Angers formulae, which he thought was representative of the spoken language by the time he wrote his *Manuel pratique de latin médiéval* (pp. 29–31): he thus accepted that the spelling of the Angers formulae reflected contemporary pronunciation.

42 Calboli, 'Aspects du Latin mérovingien', pp. 16–17; Herman, 'Sur quelques aspects du latin mérovingien', p. 181.

43 See, for instance, Herman's comparison of two passages from nos. 54 and 58 of the Angers collection: although the same expression was being used in both, no. 58 gives the wording 'consuetudo pacem' ('the tradition [of] peace') where no. 54 has 'consuetudo pagi' ('the tradition of this district'). 'Consuetudo pacem' obviously makes no sense here (Herman, 'Sur quelques aspects du latin mérovingien', p. 177).

used chiefly for the purpose of conferring upon the text, and by extension the transaction, the sense of dignity associated with the written tradition.[44] The essential content of documents based on such formulae, such as the names of the persons involved, the nature of the settlement, or the object of the transaction and its value would still have been easy to extract from the rest of the text.

The idea that different levels of language were used within a single text may in fact be the key to accounting for the mixture of archaism and innovation that is typical of the Latin of formulae: a distinction should be made between standard formal documentary traits and the essence of the text, between what needed to be understood and what did not. In contrast with the more convoluted opening statements, which were intended to impress more than to communicate meaning, the bulk of the text of both Angers and Marculf shows a degree of effort to make content clear. One example of this is in the increased, Romance-like use of prepositions to replace the classical case system, in order to clarify grammatical function.[45] This type of construction is very frequent in the Angers collection. It is comparatively less frequent in Marculf, but, significantly, Marculf used far more prepositions in Book II than he did in Book I:[46] he thus seems to have used 'vulgar' forms more often in documents recording local transactions, but to have avoided them in the more formal models for royal documents included in Book I. This suggests that Marculf was adapting his language according to the type of audience and context involved in his documents: for local transactions, his language was closer to spoken forms, which must have been intended to make content clearer, whereas in royal documents his language was more high-flown. Judging from this evidence, the use of non-classical forms was not simply a matter of having lost the ability to write classically, or the result of an unconscious and uncontrolled linguistic shift: the deliberately differentiated use of such forms by Marculf indicates that grammatical usage would have been a question of register as much as of linguistic competence.

44 Herman, 'Sur quelques aspects du latin mérovingien', p. 177.
45 The genitive case was for instance often replaced by *de* + nominative, accusative or ablative (as in Marculf II, 21, 'Vinditio de campo').
46 There are thus only three examples in Book I of *de* + –a being used instead of a first declension genitive, but the same construction appears in Book II no less than 28 times. The analytic form *ad* + –a or –am instead of a first declension dative similarly appears only seven times in Book I, but 44 times in Book II. This discrepancy was not noted by Sas in his comparison between the language of the Angers formulary and that of Marculf (in his *Noun declension in the Merovingian Period*).

This does not amount to saying that formulae could by any means be described as 'popular' texts.[47] Although their Latin has been judged 'bad', they were still specialised texts designed for the use of trained professionals. On the other hand, the presence of occasional fossilised or complicated literary expressions should not make us think that these texts were necessarily unrepresentative of the lives of the people who employed these professionals to record their transactions. Marculf's more frequent use of Romance-like forms in local documents indicates an effort to make these texts more accessible and communicable. The language of formulae can thus neither be considered an accurate witness of changes in the spoken language, nor as too archaic to be useful, but rather as somewhere in-between: a learned and specialised language modified in some key ways to make these texts accessible to their intended audience. This fits in rather well with more general trends in recent scholarship emphasising the possibility that Merovingian Latin was not perceived as conceptually separate from Romance, and focusing instead on more nuanced ways of understanding the social context of linguistic change, by distinguishing between the different levels of language used according to what was being communicated to whom.[48]

FORMULAE AND THE WRITTEN WORD

If some of the language used in formulae could be understood by non-clerical people (at least in Western Romance-speaking regions, where both Angers and Marculf appear to have been compiled, though the possibility of fairly widespread, utilitarian bilingualism in Germanic-speaking regions should not be underestimated), their written form brings up a different set of problems, linked with the debate over the extent of literacy in this period.[49] It has been argued that the very use of formulae denoted a slump in literate forms, implying that notaries were no longer able to write documents on

---

47 As Pirson noted (Pirson, 'Le latin des formules mérovingiennes et carolingiennes', p. 838).

48 R. Wright, *Late Latin and Early Romance in Spain and Carolingian France* (Liverpool, 1982); see also the articles collected in R. Wright, *A Sociophilological Study of Late Latin* (Turnhout, 2002). See also M. Banniard, *Viva voce: communication écrite et communication orale du IVe au IXe siècle en Occident latin* (Paris, 1992).

49 This is now thought to have been rather wider than had previously been assumed: see McKitterick, *The Carolingians and the Written Word* and *The Uses of Literacy*; M. Garrison, '"Send more socks": on mentality and the preservation context of medieval letters', in M. Mostert, ed., *New Approaches to Medieval Communication* (Turnhout, 1999), pp. 69–99.

their own.⁵⁰ But the existence of stereotyped or standardised forms, on the contrary, can be considered as a sign of a widespread and routine use of the written word: modern solicitors, after all, still use standard contracts, and this practice is not generally attributed to a poor command of written English.⁵¹ The sixth-century Italian scholar Cassiodorus, who included some formulae for private business in his *Variae*, can certainly not be said to have had difficulties in writing Latin.⁵² These texts were used by professionals, who were clearly trained and literate. Indeed, the use of formulae for common transactions and practical, day-to-day business constitutes one of the most convincing signs that the written word was still being used on an easy and *ad hoc* basis during the early middle ages. Formularies preserve a large proportion of the rare surviving examples in which the written word was being used for relatively mundane purposes, as with messages arranging food and shelter for the king's ambassadors,⁵³ or sending Christmas greetings.⁵⁴ It is a formulary which preserves our only surviving example of an early medieval lay love-letter.⁵⁵ This is precisely the kind of text seldom found in collections of actual letters: formulae offer a view of relatively widespread lay literacy in the early middle ages that other sources do not.

Formularies may similarly constitute a decisive piece of evidence for the ability of written forms to reflect lay concerns. Despite their ecclesiastical context, formularies give significant room to transactions involving only lay people, and thus show that at least some among the laity, like their clerical

---

50 I.N. Wood, 'Administration, law and culture in Merovingian Gaul', p. 64; P. Heather, 'Literacy and power in the migration period', in A. Bowman and G. Woolf, eds., *Literacy and Power in the Ancient World* (Cambridge, 1994), pp. 177–97, at pp. 192–93: 'The beginnings of decline [of literate administration] can perhaps already be seen in the sixth century. The appearance of books of formulae may in itself suggest a loss of vitality, if we take their existence to mean that official letter-writers now needed models to follow.' This statement is qualified further on, however, with a note that one cannot assume these collections had no Roman precedents.
51 See M. Clanchy, *From Memory to Written Record: England 1066-1307*, 2nd edn. (Oxford, 1993), p. 31, for Anglo-Saxon England; see also H. Pirenne, *Mahomet et Charlemagne* (Paris, 1937), pp. 170–71, on formularies as evidence for a wide use of the written word, rather than for any discomfort in using written documents; see also W. Davies and P. Fouracre, 'Conclusion', in Davies and Fouracre, *The Settlement of Disputes in Early Medieval Europe*, pp. 207–40, at p. 212.
52 See above, n. 26.
53 Marculf I, 11; *Formulae Imperiales* no. 7.
54 Marculf II, 44 and 45.
55 *Formulae Salicae Merkelianae* no. 47 (Zeumer, *Formulae*, p. 258); Garrison, '"Send more socks"', pp. 98–99.

counterparts, were prepared to take advantage of the written word in order to vindicate their rights or property. This impression is confirmed by charter collections when these survive outside cartularies, as Rosamond McKitterick has shown with the St Gall documents,[56] as well as by references within charters showing lay people coming forward to support their legal cases using earlier documents in their possession.[57] Orality and literacy are not best understood as contradictory opposites, but rather as two complementary modes used in variable balance.[58] One cannot ascribe the choice between one or the other form of communication simply to the parties' ability or inability to read and write; nor can one necessarily assume that it would have been based only on social status. The opposition between literate forms of agreement and oral ones, such as oath-taking, allegedly more relevant to the lay world, is therefore a false opposition, particularly since oaths seem often to have been recorded in written contracts as well.[59] Conversely, documents would also have been read out to the participants, which in effect would have removed much of the barrier between those who could read and those who could not.[60]

Formulae thus ought not to be construed as evidence for declining literacy or for a lessened relevance of the written word, but in fact indicate the very reverse: a widespread use of literate forms in early medieval Francia. Although lay persons may not have been able to follow the more flowery stylistic efforts of scribes, they may well have been able to follow the essential points of the text when it was read out to them. As Jinty Nelson has suggested, there may also have been a more widespread, specialised and 'pragmatic' type of literacy current among propertied lay people, allowing them to scan documents for information without necessarily taking in their

---

56 See McKitterick, *The Carolingians and the Written Word*, pp. 77–134. See also K. Bullimore, 'Folcwin of Rankweil: the world of a Carolingian local official', *Early Medieval Europe* 13 (2005), pp. 43–77; on this part of the St-Gall archive, see McKitterick, *The Carolingians and the Written Word*, pp. 110–11.

57 See especially J.L. Nelson, 'Dispute settlement in Carolingian West Francia', in Davies and Fouracre, *The Settlement of Disputes in Early Medieval Europe*, pp. 45–64, at pp. 53–59.

58 See Nelson, 'Literacy in Carolingian government', pp. 266–67; M. Innes, 'Memory, orality and literacy in an early medieval society', *Past & Present* 158 (1998), pp. 3–36.

59 Nelson, 'Literacy in Carolingian government', pp. 267–68. There is a large number of examples of this in the formularies: see, for instance, Angers nos. 10b, 11b, 50b.

60 At least in Romance-speaking Western Francia; for Germanic-speaking Eastern regions, the situation would have been more complicated, though propertied people may have learned as much Latin as they needed to in order to understand their documents, and the text of documents could also have been translated orally (Geary, 'Land, language and memory', pp. 175–84).

standard introductions.[61] Formulae are hardly evidence of mass literacy, but they do again and again show lay people with a strong vested interest in keeping documents, and replacing them when they were lost.[62] Whether lay people accessed these documents through reading or by hearing them read out, they clearly cared strongly about them, and formulae are thus one of the most important pieces of evidence to suggest the existence of a commonly shared literate mentality in this period. These texts, in short, reflect a wider world than that of the ecclesiastical communities which preserved them: although our collections survive essentially through the work of ecclesiastical scribes, they give us insights into the lives of the lay people whose needs were served by these texts' production.

FORMULAE AND SURVIVING DOCUMENTS

If formulae are taken to be representative of legal practice in early medieval Francia, one would expect this to be confirmed by a comparison between them and the archival documents surviving from this period. Secure textual links between formulae and actual documents are, however, extremely difficult to establish in all but a very few cases. It could be argued that this casts doubt on whether formularies really were used to draw up actual documents at all, and further that, if they were not, the whole case for counting them as evidence for actual legal practice collapses. It is therefore necessary to look more closely at the reasons why such textual connections are rare. I will argue that this rarity need not necessarily undermine the hypothesis that formularies were used to produce new documents during this period.

It is important to be clear about how much is at stake here. Apart from internal evidence, which very seldom gives us much by way of contextual information, the main method of dating formulae used by editors, diplomatists and historians in the late nineteenth and early twentieth centuries was to identify the original datable documents on which they would have been based, in the hope that this could at least provide a *terminus post quem*. Textual links between formulae and documents therefore played an important role in the classic discussions of these collections.[63] Since the

---

61 On 'pragmatic literacy', see Nelson, 'Literacy in Carolingian government', pp. 269–70; Clanchy, *From Memory to Written Record*, pp. 236 and 247.

62 For instance with the *appennis* procedure in Angers nos. 31–33, Marculf I, 33–34; *Formulae Arvernenses* no. 1ab; *Formulae Turonenses* nos. 27–28; *Cartae Senonicae* nos. 38–46; see Brown, 'When documents are destroyed or lost'.

63 See, for instance, K. Zeumer, 'Über die älteren fränkischen Formelsammlungen', *Neues*

mid-twentieth century, however, most of this dating work has had to be abandoned, because the most convincing of these textual links relied on documents which have been shown to be later forgeries, and are therefore of no use for the dating of formulae or formularies.[64]

Furthermore, textual links between formulae and authentic documents are rarely as convincing as those that were made with these forgeries.[65] Identifications often rely on common traits which may be due more to the standardised wording of legal documents in general during this period than to the use of a particular known formula. Commonplace observations on the need for Christian charity and the eternal rewards of giving to the Church in the opening statements of documents (what diplomatists call the *arenga*), unless they correspond word-for-word, cannot be held as the basis for a secure link; the same can be said of the use of the same biblical quotes, since scribes tended to rely on a standard stock of useful citations. Even descriptions of the property involved in particular transactions can look very much alike without necessarily being textually related, since these descriptions were intended to cover anything that a piece of land *might* contain rather than to provide an accurate inventory. Often the resemblance between two texts is only due to their dealing with the same type of legal action, for instance if both recorded a gift of land to the church. Similarity of purpose

---

Archiv 6 (1881), pp. 9–115; K. Zeumer, 'Über die alamannischen Formelsammlungen', *Neues Archiv* 8 (1883), pp. 473–553; B. Krusch, 'Ursprung und Text von Marculfs Formelsammlung', in *Nachrichten von der Königlichen Gesellschaft der Wissenschaften zu Göttingen, Phil. hist. Klasse* (Berlin, 1916), pp. 234–74. For links between formulae and documents in general, see H. Zatschek, 'Die Benutzung der *Formulae Marculfi* und anderer Formularsammlungen in den Privaturkunden des 8. bis 10. Jahrhunderts', *Mitteilungen des Instituts für Österreichische Geschichtsforschung* 42 (1927), pp. 165–267; W. John, 'Formale Beziehungen der privaten Schenkungsurkunden Italiens und des Frankenreiches und die Wirksamkeit der Formulare', *Archiv für Urkundenforschung* 14 (1936), pp. 1–104; I. Heidrich, 'Titulatur und Urkunden der arnulfingischen Hausmeier', *Archiv für Diplomatik* 11 and 12 (1965–66), pp. 71–279; U. Nonn, 'Merowingische Testamente: Studien zum Fortleben einer römischen Urkundenform im Frankreich', *Archiv für Diplomatik* 18 (1972), pp. 1–129.

64 A famous example is the link made by Zeumer and Krusch between Marculf I, 1 and 2 and, respectively, Bishop Burgundofaro's document for Rebais and Dagobert I's immunity for the same monastery (Pardessus, *Diplomata*, vol. 2, p. 40; Kölzer DM. †49, vol. 1, pp. 126–27). See below, n. 312.

65 One exception to this is the indisputable link between *Collectio Flaviniacensis* nos. 8 and 43 and the two testaments of Widerad (*Cartulary of Flavigny*, ed. C. Bouchard [Cambridge, MA, 1991], nos. 1 and 2); see J. Marilier, 'Notes sur la tradition textuelle des testaments de Flavigny', *Mémoires de la Société pour l'histoire du droit et des institutions des anciens pays bourguignons, comtois et romands* 23 (1962), pp. 185–99; Nonn, 'Merowingische Testamente', pp. 33–34, and pp. 110–21 in particular in connection with *Collectio Flaviniacensis* no. 8.

between a formula and a document has thus often been mistaken for an actual textual correspondence. Penalty-clauses were equally standard, and the same expressions occur in many unrelated formularies.

Similarities which would be perfectly adequate to establish a textual connection between two literary texts are therefore often not sufficient to identify a secure link in the case of formulae and documents. The case for a very widespread use among existing documents of Marculf in particular, as distinct from other formularies, may have been overstated: the fact that more links have been hypothesised between Marculf and actual documents may simply reflect the exceptionally high degree of attention given to this collection in modern scholarship. The formal similarities between texts of this kind are usually enough to ensure that, if one sets out to look for links between a formulary collection and documents from a particular archive, one will indeed tend to find them. Finding clear evidence of actual use of a particular formula in a particular document is thus made difficult, rather paradoxically, precisely because of the strong resemblances between these texts in general: the problem is not that there are too few connections, but that there are too many. But this, if anything, should make us rather optimistic as to the ability of formulae to reflect legal practice accurately. What these similarities show us, above all, is that formulae participated in the same commonly shared legal culture as our surviving documents, and that they were anchored in the same tradition.[66]

Another factor affecting our ability to recognise the use of a formula in any given piece of archival evidence is that the wording of these models would have been modified in the process of copying out a new document, in order to suit the different circumstances under which they were being produced. Even if a formula was used as the basis for a known document, such a use would be masked by these contextual differences. It is hardly surprising that exact textual matches should have been found mostly in forgeries: forged documents relied far more extensively on their models precisely in order to supply a plausible pre-existing contextual background.

The difficulty of establishing secure textual links between formulae and documents does not, therefore, constitute grounds to suppose that formulae were not used in just the way that they purported to be. The scarcity of these links is also due, more fundamentally, to the *kind* of document contained in formulae. Surviving actual documents were selected and preserved in such a way as to privilege documents dealing with land transactions or immunities,

---

66 Classen, 'Fortleben und Wandel', pp. 32–33.

virtually to the exclusion of any other subject. It is no accident, therefore, that most of the links found between the Marculf collection and surviving archival documents should involve only the first four formulae of Book II, which deal with gifts of property to the church. Since formulae, as we have seen, cover a much wider range of subjects than surviving documents, the difficulty of finding links with actual documents for the majority of these texts does not indicate that formulae were not used, but simply reflects the fact that there is limited scope to compare them, because the documents which would have been based on them were not worth preserving in the long run. Indeed, it is this ability to fill the gaps in our knowledge of the range of documentary practice which makes formulae invaluable. After all, formulae that can be linked to existing documents, such as gifts to the church, tell us little that is new; what we should be paying attention to are those transactions for which they constitute our sole evidence.

DATING FORMULAE: ORIGINAL COLLECTIONS VS. MANUSCRIPT TRADITION

Although it does not fundamentally affect the reliability of formulae as a source, the lack of firm textual correspondences with datable actual documents does leave formulae hard to date. This brings us to the most significant methodological problem associated with these texts: that of finding a context for them. One of the issues that have consistently hindered the use of formulae by historians is the question of exactly what period they constitute evidence for. This question has two parts: one, the date of the original compilation of any given formulary, and the other, the time-span over which any particular formula would have remained relevant after this date; that is, what I will call its shelf-life. As we have seen, there is virtually no surviving manuscript evidence for these collections from the Merovingian period, since most manuscripts date from the Carolingian period, and these often present vastly different renderings of the same original collection.[67] The lack of contemporary material evidence makes the earlier phase of production of formularies difficult to identify, while the presence of these texts in later manuscripts may raise doubts about whether these older texts might still have been relevant by the time the Carolingian copies were being made.

---

67 See above, p. 15. For the manuscripts of Marculf and the different ways in which they presented this collection, see below, pp. 118–23.

Beyond these problems lies a further one: the date of composition of a given individual formula could be earlier than that of the earliest recognisable state of the collection in which it was included. We cannot automatically assume that all of the formulae presented in a single collection were originally composed at the same date: formularies often included texts borrowed from earlier collections, and even 'new' formulae could be based on much older documents, according to what material had been available to the compiler. Editors long ignored this problem by identifying the date of the earliest state of a collection with that of the composition of its constituent texts. This had important repercussions not only on the dating of individual collections, but also, in a more fundamental way, on editors' ideas about what could be said to constitute a collection in the first place. Karl Zeumer, whose 1886 edition, in its own way a monumental scholarly achievement, continues to provide the standard printed version of these texts, was mostly concerned, in accordance with the traditional editorial methods of his day, with reconstituting the earliest form of each collection, in order to obtain the result he thought would have been closest to the intentions of the original compiler.[68] Zeumer attempted to achieve this by subdividing the material he found in manuscripts into distinct smaller groups, ascribing similar dates to all the texts included in each group on the basis of internal evidence or of identifications with surviving documents, and analysing groups separately, even when the texts comprising them were presented as part of a single collection in the manuscript. Zeumer supposed that the collections before his eyes were only the result of a gathering of these 'original' groups of formulae at a later stage, and he therefore dismissed the manuscript evidence as unrepresentative of the work of the original authors.

The idea that the original core for each collection would only have included models based on relatively recent documents was a largely self-fulfilling prophecy, since Zeumer simply excluded all texts that did not fit in by placing them in different groups. As a result, very few of his printed collections actually correspond to anything that can be found in existing manuscripts. His edition may be seen as unrepresentative, particularly in the case of formularies surviving in more than one manuscript witness.[69] For by breaking up existing collections to fit in with his idea of what a formulary should be like, rather than engaging with the texts as they actually

---

68 See Zeumer, *Formulae*, and 'Über die älteren fränkischen Formelsammlungen'. For a fuller analysis of Zeumer's work methods, see Rio, 'Les formulaires mérovingiens et carolingiens'.

69 For a similar point, see Brown, 'When documents are destroyed or lost', p. 354.

appear in the manuscript evidence, Zeumer gave his 'core' collections an artificial appearance of homogeneity. It is no accident, therefore, that his reconstructed clusters should have ended up looking both tidy and chronologically limited. This approach largely dismissed any issues of time scale, with each group of formulae simply being taken as evidence for a single moment in time, that of the putative 'original' date of composition, rather than taking into account the long-term processes which led to the particular shape in which these texts appear in the manuscripts.

By forcing formularies into imaginary subdivisions and reconstructions, Zeumer's edition therefore masks the mixture of old and new that is the hallmark of these collections. It also masks the significant diversity of the manuscripts. Scribes copied formulae collections not with the intention of reproducing the original text, but of reworking it to suit the needs of new users: rather than copying their model word for word, they selected, adapted and added to their material according to their understanding of their own needs and those of their user-community. Such reworkings and additions can sometimes be observed in the physical evidence of the manuscripts themselves: new users sometimes jotted down more formulae alongside those included in the main text, in the margins or on the front or back pages of books which had already been bound.[70] Formulae and formularies thus clearly remained work in progress for as long as they continued to be copied, that is, until the tenth century. As a result, no two manuscripts containing formulae ever look exactly alike: in this sense, one could say that there are almost as many collections as there are manuscripts. Privileging the original compiler of a collection of formulae as one would the author of a literary work means taking an inappropriately narrow view of these texts: a compiler was only one link in a long chain of scribes working on the same material, beginning with the authors of the documents on which the individual formulae of the collection were based, and ending with the last scribe to reuse these texts in his own manuscript. Although this complex reality makes the editor's job considerably more difficult, it is a blessing to historians: scribes' willingness to modify their texts offers us the opportunity to observe the ways in which formulae were put to use with more nuance and detail. Zeumer's reconstructions, whether or not they would have been close to the original, will always be less valuable than collections for which we have actual material evidence. It is only from the manuscripts that we can get a sense of what real users wanted. Exploiting the complexity

---

70 There are clear examples of this in Paris BnF lat. 2718, 4627 and 11379.

of the manuscript evidence is therefore more fruitful than battling with it against the odds.

This approach may also allay anxieties over these texts' continued relevance during the Carolingian period. The sheer diversity of the manuscript evidence and the freedom with which scribes continued to modify and adapt these texts show that formulae were not simply being copied mechanically, as prestigious vestiges of a venerable but defunct written tradition. Since scribes clearly had no qualms when it came to interfering with or even discarding the texts they found in their models when they did not consider them useful, the evidence of the texts they *did* choose to include emerges as more secure. The inclusion in a new manuscript of formulae extracted from sources composed over a long period of time implies that even the older among these texts were still seen as relevant. One possible exception to this is Book I of Marculf, which tended to be copied as a whole, with few or no changes, in manuscripts of the Carolingian period. By this time much of its contents would have been obsolete, since Book I contains mostly royal documents, the style of which was affected by dynastic change far more extensively than that of private documents, and which were therefore no longer written under the Carolingians in the same way that they had been under the Merovingians. Even these texts, however, could have been partly reused in new documents, and they can be found in an updated version in two Carolingian manuscripts, in which Merovingian features, such as references to the mayor of the palace, were eliminated, and phrases typical of Carolingian titulature added, as with the title of *rex Dei gratia* ('king by the grace of God').[71] In general, therefore, the continued copying and inclusion of particular formulae in new manuscripts may be seen as a good indication that these same texts were still being used to produce new documents.

Attempts to reconstruct a particular context for formulae at the earlier end of their chronological span have, as we have seen, been largely unsuccessful, not least because of the scarcity of internal evidence and lack of secure links with surviving documents. Yet we should resist any temptation to over-react by abandoning formularies altogether as evidence for the Merovingian period, in order to embrace their various avatars found in Carolingian manuscripts as the only secure and reassuringly tangible evidence for their use. A context may yet be found for these texts at the opposite end of the time-scale, through the manuscripts. Warren Brown, in an important recent article, has attempted to recreate precisely such a context for manuscripts

---

71 Munich lat. 4650 and Leiden Voss. lat. O. 86; see below, Appendix 3, p. 265.

containing formulae relating to the replacement of lost documents, with interesting results.[72] But this approach, were it to be relied on exclusively, would also have its limits. Although palaeographical studies can get us very far in terms of reconstructing geographical and chronological context, this context could never be precise enough for the type of micro-study for which charters have proved so fruitful.[73] Furthermore, although the inclusion of particular formulae in a manuscript does document the *expectation* of the scribe that these models would be needed in the future, it does not amount to evidence that new documents were necessarily being produced on the basis of these formulae close to the time at which the manuscript was copied: these texts were, after all, meant to be used as long-term teaching and reference tools. The date of a single manuscript, like the date of a single collection, therefore documents only one stage in the life of these texts. Tying down formulae to the context of the surviving manuscripts, much like earlier attempts to reduce them to the context of their 'original' textual state, would therefore still only give us a partial view, albeit in a more convincing way than Zeumer's reconstructions did.

Although it may remain as tempting as it was for Zeumer to try to pin down these texts to a particular place and time, whether at their putative point of origin or through the manuscripts, this approach proves in the end to be not only very difficult, but also fundamentally reductive: the quest for contextualisation, at either end of our time scale, still amounts to a doomed attempt to make up for the perceived failure of formulae to give us information comparable to that obtainable from charters, by seeking to undo scribes' efforts to make these texts generally applicable, instead of exploring formulae for what it is that makes them unique as a source. Unlike charters, formulae cannot tell us that a particular action took place at a particular time and place, however much we might wish they could; what they can tell us, however, is that what had happened once was thought likely to happen again, whereas charters will only ever give us isolated instances. Formulae can offer us a unique insight into scribes' expectations, articulated through different arrangements of a fertile and fluctuating range of texts borrowed from a variety of different sources, coalescing into collections only to be divided up again, before being assembled into new groups further down the line. Formulae are therefore useful as evidence for scribes' understanding

---

72 Brown, 'When documents are destroyed or lost'.

73 An exemplary treatment of this kind is Wendy Davies's study of the region of Redon, in Brittany, through its surviving charters: W. Davies, *Small Worlds: The Village Community in Early Medieval Brittany* (London, 1988).

INTRODUCTION

of legal practice over the long term, not for identifying particular events or circumstances. For historians, such evidence for continuity, rather than being lamented as a weakness, ought to be valued distinctively.

LOCAL CONTEXT AND DIFFUSION

Establishing a geographical context for these texts presents us with similar problems. Formulae sometimes preserve the name of the city or monastery where the documents on which they were based were produced, but this is only the case for a few formularies: the collections associated with Angers, Clermont, Tours, Bourges, Sens, Laon, Murbach, Salzburg, St Gall and Reichenau.[74] In some of these cases, the place-name is mentioned only in a few of the texts, so that we cannot assume that the whole collection originated there. For most other formularies, there is simply no way of knowing even vaguely where a collection was originally produced. Zeumer's reliance on textual links with surviving documents, as with dating, did not yield very satisfactory results in this respect.[75] Many formulae therefore cannot be placed geographically with any degree of precision: a broad affiliation to a North Frankish context, in many cases, seems to be as close as we can get, as in the case of Marculf or the three collections of so-called 'Salic' formulae.[76]

Here as with dating, rather more information may be gleaned from the manuscripts, but it is rarely very precise. There have been relatively few detailed palaeographical studies of manuscripts containing formulae, partly because so much of the research concerning them has focused on the quest for the *Urtext*, the hypothetical original version for each collection, rather

---

74 *Formulae Andecavenses, Formulae Arvernenses, Formulae Turonenses, Formulae Bituricenses, Formulae Senonenses recentiores, Formulae codicis Laudunensis, Formulae Morbacenses, Formulae Salzburgenses, Formulae Sangallenses* and *Formulae Augienses Coll. C*, all edited in Zeumer, *Formulae*. The *Formulae Collectionis S. Dionysii*, although they do not preserve place-names, are associated with St Denis because they contain several letters written by and to abbots of that monastery; the *Collectio Flaviniacensis* is associated with Flavigny because of the use in the collection of the two testaments of Widerad (see above, n. 65). All of these collections are included in Zeumer, *Formulae*.

75 On the link made between Marculf and the monastery of Rebais, see below, p. 108.

76 The *Formulae Salicae Lindenbrogianae, Merkelianae* and *Bignonianae*, after the names of their earlier editors; all are printed in Zeumer, *Formulae*, pp. 227–84. These collections were called 'Salic' because it was thought that they had been written in an area dominated by Salic (rather than Roman) law, though the idea that these two legal sources worked as mutually exclusive systems has been rejected in more recent scholarship (for an introduction to these questions, see Wormald, *The Making of English Law*, pp. 29–92).

than seeing what can be done with later versions.[77] Zeumer often assumed that the surviving manuscripts had been copied in the same places as those mentioned in the formulary texts (the manuscript for the Angers collection in Angers,[78] the manuscripts for the Bourges collection in Bourges,[79] and so on), but this is a problematic assumption, since these texts could have been copied in areas other than that in which they had originated. This can be seen plainly from the evidence of those collections which survive in several manuscripts: no one would suggest that all of the manuscripts containing Marculf were copied in the place where Marculf himself originally wrote, wherever that may have been.[80] The manuscripts for the Tours collection were similarly not all copied in Tours, and many texts from that corpus were reused in collections which we know to have been assembled elsewhere, as in the case of the Flavigny collection, which includes texts from both Tours and Marculf. The frequent reintegration of parts of old collections into new ones shows that individual texts, at least, were exchanged and diffused widely; this is what allowed them, as I argued earlier, to develop a significant manuscript tradition, as scribes searched for suitable models from whatever resources fell within their reach.[81] The idea that the content of legal documents was profoundly embedded in particular local conditions and cannot be interpreted correctly when such conditions are not known, although it is certainly true of charters, is therefore not necessarily true of formulae: these texts could clearly still be used to produce new documents even once they had been uprooted from their original context. The ability of formulae to function beyond the particular set of circumstances that had led to their creation, far from being limiting for the purposes of historical analysis, thus gives them a more general value than charters.

TO CONCLUDE

As we have seen, formulae do not lend themselves easily to being tied down to a particular time and place. This has been seen as their essential weakness

---

77 Though those manuscripts which also contain capitulary texts are described in admirable detail in Mordek, *Biblioteca capitularium*. For a handlist of manuscripts see A. Rio, *Legal Practice and the Written Word in the Early Middle Ages: Frankish formulae, c.500–1000* (Cambridge, forthcoming), Appendix.

78 Fulda D1.

79 Leiden BPL 114, Paris BnF lat. 4629 and the fragment in Paris BnF lat. 10756, fols. 62–64.

80 On this problem, see below, pp. 108–17.

81 See above, pp. 15–16.

INTRODUCTION

as a source, and, in a modern historiographical context which rightly emphasises the local diversity of the medieval world and the importance of context for the correct interpretation of sources, it is no surprise that formulae should have been somewhat underused. However, this non-specificity should not be seen as wholly negative. The problems that have plagued formulae as a historical source are due more to what historians have traditionally looked for in them than to any inherent lack of value. Given the lack of success of this traditional approach, it is time to start asking different questions. Although for a historian the absence of a known context would make a legal document useless if it took the form of a charter, this is not the case for formulae: the evidence they give us is strengthened by a large and complex manuscript tradition, which shows us that scribes consistently found them fit for purpose. In order to grasp more fully what it is that formulae can tell us about the early medieval world, we need to stop focusing on the problem of context, which is in most cases irrecoverable, and instead take advantage of their possibilities as normative texts: in other words, their capacity to transcend local context, and to draw the general out of the specific.

Formulae, although they do not allow us to reconstruct particular cases with any degree of precision, document commonly shared ways of thinking about social relationships, and this in itself makes them an important and valuable addition to our view of legal practice in the early medieval period. Formulae were at an intersection between norm and practice: they encompassed practical solutions arrived at in real cases, while at the same time extending the value of these solutions in order to cope with new situations. The evidence they offer therefore escapes some of the fundamental problems usually associated with normative texts. Unlike the law codes, formulae document legal practice from the perspective of demand, not imposition: their scope was defined by what it was that people actually wanted to do with law, rather than by the more abstract understanding of how society should function characteristic of the law-codes.[82] Like charters, they document legal practice; but they can also give us more than just one isolated case. They include documents produced in a larger sample of different situations, and show that the written word was used in a wide range of contexts, even for transactions that were rather modest, or that involved only lay people.

---

82 On the relationship between formulae and law-codes, see A. Rio, 'Charters, law-codes and formulae'; 'Formulae, written law and the settlement of disputes in the Frankish kingdoms', in P. Andersen, ed., *Law Before Gratian: III. Carlsberg Academy Conference on Medieval Legal History* (Copenhagen 2007), 21–34; and, with respect to the question of slavery more specifically, 'Freedom and unfreedom in early medieval Francia'.

As handbooks intended for teaching and future reference, they show us the methods scribes thought they should follow in order to express a variety of legal, social and economic relationships in the most useful and appropriate way. In this sense, the evidence they give us is unparalleled by any other source. Although much of the social history of early medieval Francia has been written without resorting to the evidence of formulae, this has meant neglecting a large amount of varied and wide-ranging material, and ignoring important ways in which it can help to refine and deepen our understanding of legal practice in the early middle ages.

A NOTE ON THIS TRANSLATION

I have tried to keep as close to the Latin text as possible, insofar as this did not hinder comprehension. As already mentioned, a certain vagueness with respect to cases is one of the characteristics of the Latin of formulae, with the result that it is sometimes difficult to tell exactly who is doing what to whom.[83] The removal of the names of all participants compounds this difficulty, since all persons tend to be referred to indiscriminately through pronouns such as *ille* or *illa* ('this man' or 'this woman'). This can make these texts difficult to interpret, particularly in the Angers collection, which often switches between third-person and first-person narrative in the course of a single formula, and between different participants within the first-person narrative. To make the meaning clearer, I have used letters of the alphabet to translate *ille*. Naturally, in some cases the meaning of the text could be reconstructed in different ways; I have chosen the readings which seemed to me most likely to correspond to scribal intentions. Where interpretation is uncertain, I have indicated it in the notes.

83 See above, pp. 19–20.

PART ONE

THE FORMULARY OF ANGERS

INTRODUCTION

Unlike Marculf, the Angers formulary (*Formulae Andecavenses*) is set firmly at the local level, and mostly includes fairly small-scale transactions, too limited ever to involve either the king or his court. It thus only contains transactions involving parts of a *villa*, never the whole of one. The records of disputes included in it give the same small-scale impression: nos. 11 and 13 show the negotiations and different methods of resolution available even for so comparatively small a matter as the theft of a mare, while no. 24 shows us one man accusing another in court of having scattered his cattle, resulting in the death of some of his animals. Others show us people selling their freedom; people selling land and other people; people manumitting their servants; people making gifts to their spouses, their children or the church; people renting or exchanging property; people making and receiving loans of land or money, and performing work for the lender for a certain number of days a week in return; people making claims and receiving compensation for crimes such as theft, murder, witchcraft, assault, kidnapping or rape; people clearing themselves by oath against the same accusations; people involved in boundary disputes; people petitioning to have their documents replaced after they were lost in a fire; people marrying or divorcing; people dealing with claims made on their freedom by others; free people taking unfree spouses, and the consequences of these marriages; people finding abandoned babies and selling them on to be raised as servants; and people not turning up for their trials. All this was clearly thought worth putting in writing, though it was not worth preserving for so long as to give us any chance of finding it in our record of surviving actual documents: this formulary therefore constitutes important evidence for the use of the written word to record and validate everyday transactions, and shows a relatively high demand for written documents during this period, even from lay people, and at a comparatively low level.[84]

---

[84] See O. Guillot, 'La justice dans le royaume franc à l'époque mérovingienne', in *La giustizia nell' alto medioevo (secoli V–VIII)*, Settimane di studio del centro italiano di studi

This formulary was given its name because the documents used as the basis for its composition, in spite of their anonymised state, regularly retain mentions of the city of Angers as the location in which they were originally written. Since no other place-name is mentioned in any of these texts, this does indeed seem the most likely conclusion to draw from such references.[85]

This collection is generally accepted as the earliest surviving example of a legal formulary, perhaps dating from as early as the sixth century, or at the latest the seventh.[86] If this dating is indeed correct, it could constitute an important missing link in the available evidence for the use of written documents from late antiquity to the early middle ages, since virtually no actual documents survive from this very early period. Because the sixth century is generally so poorly documented in terms of archival evidence, the Angers formulary has been of particular interest to historians hoping to trace continuities and breaks in legal and documentary practice in the period immediately following the end of the Roman Empire in the West. Just how much remained of Roman institutions at the local level of the city by the time the Angers formulary was put together is an important and much-disputed point. Since the late antique heritage is generally supposed to have survived longer in the Loire Valley, where Angers is situated, than anywhere else in the Frankish kingdoms (though this may be a trick of the light, due to the exceptionally rich source of evidence provided for this region by the works of Gregory of Tours), we would expect to see traces of such Roman institutions in this formulary; and indeed, we are not disappointed, as the very first of the texts included in it describes for us in great detail the full procedure involved in entering a legal document in the city's

---

sull' alto medioevo XLII (Spoleto, 1995), vol. 2, pp. 653–731, at pp. 690–702; Rio, 'Formulae, legal practice and the settlement of disputes in the Frankish kingdoms'.

85 The possibility of a link with the Spanish Visigothic formulae, brought forward by Karl Lehmann, was convincingly discarded by Schwerin, who argued that the resemblance was only superficial, and due to the similar nature of the actions taken rather than to any real textual link: K. Lehmann, 'Monumenta Germaniae Historica. Legum Sectio V: Formulae Merowingici et Karolini aevi, edidit Karolus Zeumer', *Kritische Vierteljahrschrift für Gesetzburg und Rechtswissenschaft* 29 (1887), pp. 331–46, at p. 336; J.G.O. Biedenweg, *Commentatio ad formulas Visigothicas novissime repertas* (Berlin, 1856), p. 5; J. Beneyto Pérez, *Fuentes de Derecho histórico español* (Barcelona, 1931), p. 107; R. Schröder, *Lehrbuch der deutschen Rechtsgeschichte*, 6th edn. revised by E.V. Künssberg (Berlin, 1922), p. 294; against the link, see C. von Schwerin, 'Sobre las relaciones entre las Fórmulas visigóticas y las andecavenses', *Annuario de Historia del derecho Español* 9 (1932), pp. 177–89.

86 For a full discussion of the various arguments for the dating of this collection, see Appendix 1.

municipal archives (*gesta municipalia*), which are generally thought to have disappeared in Francia at the very latest by the end of the seventh century.[87] The existence of such tantalising evidence has meant that more attention has been given to the formulae in this collection which relate most obviously to late antique institutions than to the great majority of texts included in it which do not refer to them, and which would often look perfectly at home among formulae produced much later.[88] Since the early date of this formulary has been seen as its most distinctive and interesting feature, most of the work devoted to it has focused on its earliest stage of existence, that is, the date of its original composition.[89]

One may wonder, however, how far it is really possible to access this earliest state of the collection. The formulary of Angers only survives in a single late eighth-century manuscript, possibly originating from the Loire valley, though it is now in the municipal library at Fulda (Landesbibliothek D1, fols. 136–184). This manuscript was thus copied much later than any of the various dates of composition proposed for the collection, at a point when the Roman institutions described in some of its texts are unlikely to have still been extant in the same form. This makes the evidence found in this formulary for such Roman features as the *gesta municipalia* difficult to interpret, particularly in view of the fact that few references are made to them outside the first formula, which is not representative of the kind of text included in the rest.[90]

---

87 On the question of the possible survival of these public archives, see Appendix 2.

88 Apart from the evidence relating to the *gesta municipalia*, another 'Roman' practice has been identified in the formulae relating to the replacement of lost documents (*appennis*); see Angers nos. 31–33. This procedure has been much discussed; see K. Zeumer, 'Über den Ersatz verlorener Urkunden im fränkischen Reiche', *Zeitschrift der Savigny-Stiftung für Rechtsgeschichte, Germanistische Abteilung* 1 (1880), pp. 89–123; L. Gobin, 'Notes et documents concernant l'histoire d'Auvergne. Sur un point particulier de la procédure mérovingienne applicable à l'Auvergne: "l'institution d'*apennis*"', *Bulletin historique et scientifique de l'Auvergne* (1894), pp. 145–53; and, most recently, Lauranson-Rosaz and Jeannin, 'La résolution des litiges en justice durant le haut Moyen-Age', and, for a different approach, Brown, 'When documents are destroyed or lost'.

89 Zeumer, 'Über die älteren fränkischen Formelsammlungen', pp. 91–95; W. Felgenträger, 'Zu den Formulae Andecavenses', in M. Kaser, H. Kreller and W. Künkel, eds., *Festschrift P. Koschaker zum 60. Geburtstag überreicht von seinen Fachgenossen*, vol. 3 (Weimar, 1939), pp. 366–75; Bergmann, 'Die Formulae Andecavenses, eine Formelsammlung auf der Grenze zwischen Antike und Mittelalter'; Bergmann, 'Verlorene Urkunden nach den *Formulae Andecavenses*'; for an outline of the arguments relating to the dating of this collection, see Appendix 1.

90 See Appendix 2.

Attempts to deconstruct the collection as it is found in the manuscript in order to piece together its earliest form have not been altogether successful. The arguments involved in the dating of the Angers formulary are very complex, and I have set them out fully in Appendix 1; suffice it to say at this point that Karl Zeumer, whose edition was the most influential, divided it into three distinct groups, to which he attributed different dates. The whole collection contains 60 formulae. Zeumer identified formulae nos. 1 to 36 as the earliest group, which he dated to the early sixth century; nos. 37 to 57 as slightly later, from the late sixth century; and nos. 57 to 60 as the latest group, from the late seventh century. He inferred these dates on the basis of a few fragments of information left from the text of the original documents used as sources in these formulae: two formulae, nos. 1 and 34, are dated to the fourth year of King Childebert, and Zeumer therefore put them in a first group, along with all the formulae found near them in the manuscript; he started his second group at no. 37, because that text mentions a war against the Bretons and Gascons, which Zeumer took as a reference to Chilperic's campaign against the Breton ruler Waroch in *c*. 574–578; and his third group brought together the last three formulae, nos. 57–60, which are separated from the rest of the collection in the manuscript by a short chronological text which mentioned a King Theuderic as the current ruler. None of these, it has to be said, are very helpful markers, since several Merovingian kings were named Childebert and Theuderic, and there is no way of knowing which ones were meant here. Similarly, the war with the Bretons and Gascons hardly offers us a secure indication of date, since we cannot assume, given the scarcity of our sources, that we will know of every expedition launched against them by the Franks. But even if these indications were to be accepted as reliable, there would still be no reason to see them as mutually contradictory, or to suppose that the fact that different texts offer different indications of date necessarily implies that each belonged to different stages of composition of this formulary. A simpler and far more likely explanation would be that the compiler of a formulary could base his models on documents of varying age, from the very recent to the very old, according to what material was available to him as he was writing. Zeumer supposed that formularies would only have been compiled on the basis of fairly recent documents. This assumption, although there is no real evidence to support it,[91] led him to extend to whole groups, defined largely arbitrarily, tiny fragments of infor-

---

91 See above, pp. 29–30. The same assumption was made in Bergmann's study of the lost documents on which the Angers formulae were based (Bergmann, 'Verlorene Urkunden nach den *Formulae Andecavenses*').

mation that only relate to very few among these texts, and which are in any case difficult to interpret. Such artificial regroupings are due to a fundamental confusion between formulae *per se* and the documents used as their sources: since all of these indications of date were left over from the text of the documents on which our formulae had been based, they could only be used to date the sources used in making these models, and not the formulae themselves. This means that the best that we can hope to get from them is not a secure date, but only a *terminus post quem*.

Zeumer's delineation of groups of different dates within this collection also relied on a very reductive view of the input of later scribes, namely, the idea that texts would have been added gradually, following a regular process of accretion, and with their order remaining unchanged, resulting in a neat progression from the earliest texts placed at the beginning of the manuscript to the latest at the end. This view, however, is unsustainable: it is enough to look at those formulae collections which survive in several manuscripts, as in the case of Marculf, to see that scribes tended to be very free with their models, and did not shy away from modifying and reordering their texts to suit their own purposes. The idea that later scribes would merely have added to existing collections, without wishing to interfere with them any further, pervades most of Zeumer's work, and obscures the more active role these scribes can often be shown to have taken.

Not everyone agreed with Zeumer's dating; the most recent counter-argument was made by Werner Bergmann, who thought that the entire formulary should be dated to the late sixth century, essentially through ascribing the regnal dates found in our texts to a different Childebert and a different Theuderic. This has the virtue of restoring overall coherence to this collection, which is remarkably consistent in its language and style; but disregard of the possible input of later scribes blocks any serious attempt to reconstitute the earliest state of the collection, no matter when one places the original date of its composition. Even if Bergmann's interpretation of the internal evidence were correct, it would be a mistake to see this formulary as a straightforward 'snapshot' of late sixth-century Angers. Although the origins of the whole collection may well be dated to the late sixth century, in the sense that its sources are likely to have been written around that time, it is difficult to establish a precise date for the creation of these models, because they were not composed definitively at any one time: the original compiler of these formulae worked on the basis of pre-existing documents, of which he was not necessarily the author, and later scribes may well have revised his work substantially.

All this does not mean that this collection cannot in any way be used as evidence for Merovingian Angers, but it does suggest that these late antique texts, by the time we find manuscript evidence for them, had been transferred into a quite different context. This has adverse effects in terms of our ability to reconstruct the earliest state of the collection, but this change in perspective is also worth examining in itself. Taking into account the whole range of time between the date at which these documents first came into existence, probably in the late sixth century, and the date of the particular form in which we find them, that of our single surviving late eighth-century manuscript, has important repercussions for our reading of the evidence they provide. Since scribes found these models useful enough to keep through this two-hundred-year period, their presence in the manuscript constitutes a good indication of continuity in practice; but it also signals a displacement in terms of context.

The manuscript was very clearly the work of several scribes, trained in very different styles of handwriting. Most of the text was copied by a single scribe, who seems to have had a special fondness for stylised bird-shaped initials. This main scribe wrote in a rather clumsy early Caroline minuscule, a handwriting style which became current from the end of the eighth century onwards, but he often fell back to a script closer to the earlier style of Merovingian documentary cursive, which by then was no longer the preferred style, and disappeared altogether after the eighth century. Aside from this main copyist, another scribe wrote exclusively in Merovingian documentary cursive, while yet another wrote in a style closer to uncial, a more formal type of script which remained in use throughout the Merovingian and Carolingian periods. Despite these differences, the layout of the text remained regular and coherent: the text runs smoothly from one leaf to the next; all pages contain a similar amount of text, between 19 and 20 lines, with similar margins and unified spacing between the lines; the chapter-headings are also regular, with red colouring in rustic capitals (another formal type of script), and each new chapter beginning with a larger initial.[92] The result was therefore clearly a collective work, involving several scribes of different ages (since some of these scribes used antiquated scripts while others used more current ones, the likelihood is that they had been trained at different times), but working together closely, in the same institutional context. All

---

92 Bergmann, 'Verlorene Urkunden nach den *Formulae Andecavenses*', pp. 4–5. Zeumer's edition includes a plate on which the alternation between early Caroline minuscule and Merovingian cursive is very visible (Zeumer, *Formulae*, plate 2, immediately preceding the printed text of the collection).

this strongly suggests that all these scribes belonged to a single ecclesiastical *scriptorium*. Although, therefore, the collection may well have had its roots in the work of an independent lay scribe in the late antique tradition, the manuscript evidence shows that by the late eighth century it had been transferred into the use of a church. Indeed, as I have argued in the general introduction to this book, such a transfer would have been one of the conditions necessary for its survival.[93] This collection could therefore bridge a gap in our understanding of the evolution of documentary practice, by showing the transfer of the responsibility for the provision of legal documents from Roman institutions to churches, while at the same time giving evidence for a strong level of continuity between these two providers in terms of the nature, style and content of the documents they produced.

This puts the references to Roman institutions contained in this formulary in a somewhat different perspective, though we should not assume that models dealing with them had turned into useless relics of an earlier age, wholly without practical application, by the time the manuscript was copied. One constant problem involved in working with medieval sources is that old Latin words and expressions continued to be used in the same way for centuries, even when they referred to things which, in concrete terms, had changed so much as to have become virtually unrecognisable. Although the eighth-century scribes who copied our manuscript probably did not have actual surviving Roman institutions in mind when they copied such phrases as *forum publicum* or *curia publica* (municipal council) in some of the Angers formulae (nos. 1, 32, 48), such references were not meaningless either: these expressions could refer to many different kinds of 'public' space, and changed meaning over the time span during which these texts were used.[94] With respect to the *gesta municipalia*, it is also possible, for instance, that the church or monastery in which our scribes worked had assumed, by the late eighth century, many of the functions previously held by these municipal archives, which would explain why these scribes would still have needed to keep model documents relating to them.[95]

Lay people during this period seem to have increasingly relied on

---

93 See above, pp. 11–17.

94 For a case-study of evolutions in the language of 'public' space, see M. Innes, *State and Society in the Early Middle Ages: The Middle Rhine Valley, 400–1000* (Cambridge, 2000), pp. 94–140.

95 For this hypothesis, see in particular Davies and Fouracre, *The Settlement of Disputes in Early Medieval Europe*, p. 209.

ecclesiastical scribes to have their transactions recorded in writing.[96] Although our manuscript was copied in a religious house, the great majority of the formulae included in the Angers collection thus deal with the private business of lay persons. The lands mentioned in this formulary, however, are often said to be located on the territory of an unnamed saint ('supra territorium Sancti illius'), which seems to imply that they were under the lordship of a church or monastery.[97] This does not necessarily mean that these lands were owned outright by this religious house, but it does suggest that they somehow fell under its jurisdiction. The formulae relating to settlements of disputes indicate that the religious house in this case is likely to have been a monastery, since many of the disputes included in this collection seem to have been settled before an abbot. Many were also settled through mediation or the intervention of *boni homines*, that is, prominent locals authorised to intervene in judicial proceedings, who seem to have often negotiated compromises. A count is also occasionally mentioned, though only in the more important cases, involving murders or the replacement of lost documents (nos. 12, 32 and 50; the documents produced in these cases could nevertheless still all have been issued by the same religious house which kept this collection). There is no trace, however, of the late antique judicial structures featuring so heavily in Angers no. 1 in documents relating to disputes. This shows that the use of the vocabulary of Roman institutions was selective, and apparently confined to the expression of some aspects of documentary practice (as in the case of the *gesta municipalia*). Since such references were not echoed in descriptions of the practicalities of dispute settlements, the presence of these isolated expressions does not necessarily imply an actual survival of these institutions.

The collection as it appears in the manuscript thus seems to have been produced by and kept for the scribes of a monastery, in order to help them to record both the business of their own institution and the transactions and disputes of the lay population living in its neighbourhood or on its estates. The collection shows some signs of deliberate organisation, though that is far from being consistent. The presence of some clusters of texts with similar functions could indicate that compilers or later scribes tried

---

96 See above, p. 12.
97 See H. Brunner, 'Die Erbpacht der Formelsammlungen von Angers und Tours und die spätrömische Verpachtung der Gemeindegüter', *Zeitschrift der Savigny-Stiftung für Rechtsgeschichte, Germanistische Abteilung* 5 (1884), pp. 69–83; P.W.A. Immink, 'Propriété ou seigneurie? A propos des « baux perpétuels » des formules d'Angers et de Tours', *Tijdschrift voor rechtsgeschiedenis* 29 (1961), pp. 416–31.

to make these texts easier to consult: for instance, documents of *solsadia*, noting the failure of one of the parties involved in a lawsuit to turn up to the hearing, are brought together in nos. 12, 13, 14 and 16, and connected to deeds of annulment (nos. 17 and 18); nos. 34–37 (cutting across the dating division hypothesised by Zeumer) relate to gifts to relatives, and nos. 42–45 to records of agreement after a dispute; but documents relating to all of these questions are also found in other parts of the formulary, and there seems to have been no effort to impose an overall organisation according to documentary types. The formulae are also fairly evenly spread in terms of subject, length and level of formality. An altogether different and irrecoverable system of organisation may have been at work; it is impossible to tell, and perhaps scribes were expected to know their way around the text well enough to be able to consult the book without the need for any systematic organisation.

TRANSLATION

In Christ's name the documents begin.

No. 1

This first formula stands out in comparison with the rest of the Angers formulary, both in terms of length and in its emphasis on Roman institutions. The procedure described here relates to the entry into a public archive of the obligatory gift made by a husband to his wife after their marriage (*dos*).[98] The record is made in three phases: no. 1a is a record describing the ritual dialogue leading up to the opening of the archive; it is followed in no. 1b by the reading out of the mandate given by the wife to her husband, allowing him to act as her legal representative in order to have the gift recorded on her behalf (since technically women were not supposed to represent themselves before a court).[99] These initial steps were needed in order to give official sanction to the third document, recording the marriage-gift itself, which was the real point of the procedure. This form seems to have been fairly standard: these proceedings are very similar to those described in Marculf II, 37–38, which is again presented in three phases, with a dialogue and mandate preceding the terms of a donation (though in Marculf the text of the donation itself is not given). On the question of the possible survival of the *gesta municipalia*, see Appendix 2.

---

98 On *dos*, see the recent volume edited by F. Bougard, L. Feller and R. Le Jan, *Dots et douaires dans le Haut Moyen Age*, Collection de l'Ecole Française de Rome 295 (Rome, 2002). Compare Angers nos. 34, 35, 40 and 54; Marculf II, 15.

99 For another mandate apparently entered in the municipal archives, see Angers no. 52; for mandates in different contexts, compare Angers nos. 48 and 51 below, and Marculf II, 31. See also Marculf I, 21 and 36.

48 THE FORMULARIES OF ANGERS AND MARCULF

(a) Here is an archival document.[100]

In the fourth year of the reign of our lord King Childebert,[101] in month x, on day y,[102] as, according to custom, the municipal council of the city of Angers there was assembled in the public square, the magnificent A, *prosecutor*, said: 'I ask you, praiseworthy *defensor* B, *curator* C, master of soldiers D, and the rest of the municipal council, to order that the public books should be opened, because I have something which I must enter among [their] deeds.' The *defensor*, together with the chief magistrate and the entire municipal council, said: 'Let the public books be opened for you; enter whatever you choose.' 'This document orders me by its mandate to act as *prosecutor*,[103] in order to enter into the municipal archive "this mandate, which I made for my dearest husband A in order that he should represent me in all of my legal affairs, in the *pagus* as well as in the palace[104] and in any place, and appear in court, make claims and litigate against my relatives or any other man regarding these properties of mine which came to me, will come to me or are most justly owed to me from the inheritance of my relatives according to the laws; I checked this mandate, which I made for my dearest spouse A".'[105] The council then said: 'Let the venerable E, deacon and notary, be given the mandate which you say you have.' The *prosecutor* A said: 'I ask all my lords of the council that, when you see that this mandate was made according to the laws, you should order this document for a marriage-gift, which I hold

---

100 Literally 'here is a *gesta*' ('hic est iesta').

101 It is unclear which king named Childebert this refers to; see Appendix 1, pp. 249–51.

102 The Angers formulary uses two different methods for giving dates, either according to the day of the month (as in this case, and in nos. 14, 15 and 53) or according to the older Roman system of kalends (as in nos. 12, 50 and 60). Formulae using the kalend system may have been based on older documents, but it is impossible to be sure of this, since this method of dating remained in use for a long time.

103 Literally 'that there should be a *prosecutor*' ('ut prosecutor exsistere deberit'). Zeumer thought this should be translated as 'with a *prosecutor* being present', though since the speaker is the *prosecutor* himself this does not make much sense; Zeumer thought that either *prosecutor* A or the notary did not understand the words of the mandate very well and confused the role with that of the *defensor* (Zeumer, *Formulae*, p. 4 n. 4). The translation given here, however, seems equally likely, since the Angers formulary often switches from first- to third-person narrative.

104 This is a standard phrase, emphasising the validity of a document or the legitimacy of legal representation 'in local as well as royal courts'.

105 This sentence is somewhat confusing, because it partly reproduces the text of the mandate in no. 1b and mixes up the grammar of the two texts, so that, as often in this collection, this passage switches several times between subjects: both husband and wife are thus alternately referred to in either the first, the second or the third person.

in my hands, to be read aloud in your presence in the public square.' And the council said: 'Let E, deacon and notary of the city of Angers, be given the document for a marriage-gift, which you say you hold in your hands, so that it may be read in our presence.' Once this had been given, [E] said:

(b) The mandate begins.

'To my lord and husband A. I ask and beg your sweetest grace that you should represent me in all our legal affairs, in the *pagus* as well as in the palace[106] and in any place, and appear in court, make claims and litigate against my relatives and any other man regarding these properties of mine which came to me, will come to me or are most justly owed to me from the inheritance of my relatives according to the laws; and whatever you do, perform or accomplish on my behalf regarding this, know that I will accept it. Mandate sworn in the city of Angers, at the municipal council.'

(c) The gift begins.

'I, A, to my dearest wife, loved with full affection, daughter of F, named G. Since, by God's favour, I married you according to custom and with the consent of your parents, I therefore give to you out of what little I possess,[107] as a wedding gift as well as a present to you, a house with its enclosure, with moveable and non-moveable goods, vineyards, woods, fields, pastures, water and water courses, appurtenances and adjacencies; and by this gift document I assign and transfer to you all the things mentioned above, my sweetest wife, on the most happy day of our marriage, so that you may receive it into your ownership. I give to you a bracelet worth *n. solidi*, *n.* tunics, a bed cover worth *n. solidi*, gold earrings worth *n. solidi*, a ring worth *n. solidi*. I give to you a horse with a saddle and a complete harness, *n.* oxen, *n.* cows with their calves, *n.* sheep, *n.* pigs. You are to receive all of the property written above into your ownership and authority, and leave it to your children, if any are born to us, without prejudice to the rights of Saint H, whose territory this is known to be.[108] And if at any time someone, whether myself or one of my heirs or relatives, or any man or any deceitful outsider, wants to oppose or dares to act or make a claim against this gift

---

106 See above, n. 104.
107 Literally 'out of the property of my poverty' ('de rem paupertatis meae'); such claims of poverty were standard statements of humility rather than relating to actual financial situation.
108 This implies that the property described here fell in some sense under the jurisdiction or ownership of a church or monastery, perhaps involving the payment of specific dues, though the saint's rights over the property could also have remained largely symbolic. See above, p. 45.

document, which I asked with good will to be written for you, let him, when he brings his case to court, pay you twice the value of what is contained in this gift document, together with any of its added value at that time, and let his claim have no effect, and let this gift document and my decision remain firm for all time.'[109]

After this, the council said: 'If you have anything else to do regarding this claim, say it now.' The *prosecutor* said: 'I thank your greatness for having the written marriage-gift which I presented entered into the municipal archive, as your kindness permitted, and having it recorded according to custom.'

No. 2: This is an act of sale, for one who is selling himself.

> This is the first of four documents of self-sale found in this collection (compare Angers nos. 3, 19 and 25; Marculf II, 28).[110] In this case, a man (C) puts himself into the service of a couple as a result of a dispute in which he lost his case, and was unable to return the money and pay his fine: the theft mentioned here could refer either to actual stealing or to an unpaid debt. C nevertheless managed to negotiate an additional payment for his free status as well as cancelling the debt.

To my lord A and his wife B, I, C. Because all my errors[111] conspired to make me steal your property, and because I am unable to settle this in any other way than to give my entire [free] status over to your service, it is therefore established that I put my entire [free] status into your service on account of this error, not constrained by any power, but out of my own free will, because I have been shown to be guilty of this. I am to receive from you the price which pleased me, namely *n. solidi*, so that from this day you may have the power, with God's favour, to do whatever you want with me in every way,[112] as with the other unfree servants[113] in your service. And if anyone, whether myself or one of my relatives or any other person, tries to act against this act of sale, which I asked to be made with good will, let him pay *n. solidi*

---

109 This is known as a penalty or comminatory clause, and is typical of documents and formulae from this period.

110 See Liebs, 'Sklaverei aus Not'; Rio, 'Freedom and unfreedom in early medieval Francia', pp. 27–32.

111 Literally 'carelessnesses' or 'negligences' (*necligencias*).

112 This phrase is typical of formulae relating to transfers of property; compare Angers nos. 4, 8, 21, 27.

113 The word is *mancipia*, often used to refer to unfree servants or tenants.

THE FORMULARY OF ANGERS 51

[to be divided] between you and the fisc,[114] and let him be unable to assert his claim, and let this act of sale and my decision remain firm.

No. 3: This is an act of sale for a man [sold] in compensation [for a crime].[115]

> The situation here is significantly more grim than that described in the preceding formula. B is also convicted of theft (or perhaps of failing to repay a debt) and is unable to return the money and pay his fine, but, unlike C in no. 2, he is tortured, and does not enter into the service of the person from whom he stole, but into that of a different person, A, who is said to have paid his debt on his behalf. Given the use of torture and the threat of capital punishment, it could be argued, to explain the difference between the solution envisaged here and that found in no. 2, that B had been unfree before this theft, in which case the document could correspond to a provision in Salic law regarding thefts committed by slaves ('and if [the slave] does not confess [after 120 lashes], let the person who is torturing him [i.e. the claimant], if he wants to go on torturing him against the wish of the master, give a pledge to the slave's master; and if the slave is submitted after this to greater torture and confesses, let him not be released to the master, but let him be in the ownership of the person who has tortured him, and let the master of the slave, having already received the pledge, receive payment for his slave...');[116] but this does not seem to fit the situation, since B here seems to be giving up what he describes as a fully free status, and no previous master is said to be involved. This text is more likely to indicate that free persons could also be tortured: the discrepancy in the treatment of the accused in these two formulae is more likely to have been due to differences in social status or in the specific circumstances of the dispute than to differences in legal status.

To my own lord A, I, B. Because my crimes and my great errors[117] became combined with respect to the theft which I committed, as a result of which I was tortured and convicted[118] and could have been put to death, had your

---

114 The royal treasury (*fiscus*) in principle received a share of all fines, and is therefore often mentioned in penalty-clauses.

115 The meaning of the phrase 'in esceno posito' is unclear: Zeumer suggested that *esceno* should be read as *scamno*, from *scamnum*, a torture rack, judging from the reference to torture in the text (Zeumer, *Formulae*, p. 6, n. 1), and comparing the situation to *Pactus Legis Salicae* 40, 1 (p. 145): 'If a slave is accused of a theft, for which a free man would have to pay 600 *denarii*, equivalent to 15 *solidi*, let the slave be tied to a rack ('super scamnum tensus') and receive 120 lashes'. It seems more plausible that the word instead relates to *excambium*, meaning 'exchange' or 'compensation', which could be spelled in a great variety of manners.

116 *Pactus Legis Salicae* 40, 4 (pp. 146–47).

117 See above, n. 111.

118 For *eologias* read *elogia*.

piety not given *n. solidi* out of your property, I therefore took care to have this act of sale issued to you for my entire [free] status along with all that I possess, so that from this day you may have the power to do whatever you want with me in every way,[119] with God's favour, as with the other unfree servants[120] born into your service. And if I myself or any of my relatives or any other person tries to act against this act of sale, which I asked to be made with good will, let him pay *n. solidi* [to be divided] between you and the fisc;[121] let him give you compensation, and let him be unable to assert his claim, and let this act of sale remain firm for all time.

No. 4: This is an act of sale for a leased piece of land.

> This is a straightforward act of sale. The title suggests the land was leased (it is described as 'terra conducta'), though this is not mentioned in the text itself; this probably only implies that the land was being farmed by tenants.

I, A. It is established that I sold to the venerable brother[122] [B], as indeed I did sell it, this small vineyard, [measuring] more or less *n. juchi*, and which lies on the territory of Saint C,[123] on the land of this villa, and that I received from you the price which pleased me, that is, *n. solidi*, so that from this day you, the said buyer, may have the free power in every way to do whatever you want with this vineyard. And if someone, which I do not believe will happen, whether I myself or any of my heirs or any opposing person, dares to go against or oppose this act of sale, which I asked to be made with good will, let him pay twice the value of what is contained in this act of sale, and let him be unable to assert his claim, and let this act of sale remain firm for all time. Made in Angers.

No. 5: Here begins a deed of security.

> This deed of security (*securitas*) was apparently made as a result of a dispute in which the accuser proved unable to back up his claim. Such documents were issued regardless of the outcome of the dispute, whether or not the accused had been made to pay compensation, in an effort to ensure that neither party could engage in any further litigation regarding the same matter. Compare Angers nos. 6, 26, 39, 42, 43 and 44; no. 43 is virtually identical to this formula.

119 See above, n. 112.
120 See above, n. 113.
121 See above, n. 114.
122 This should be understood in the Christian sense rather than as a real family link.
123 See above, p. 45

As it is not unknown that a certain man named A brought to court a certain man named B regarding his property, when this B had done him no wrong regarding this, therefore this A agreed before good men[124] that he should make this document [stating] that he would never [again] presume to act against B [regarding this matter]. And if either he or any person on his behalf dares to oppose this, let him pay *n. solidi* [to be divided] between you and the fisc,[125] and let him be unable to assert his claim, and let this deed of security remain firm.

No. 6: Here begins another deed of security; this is about an assault.

It is difficult to work out exactly what is happening here, because the text switches from third- to first-person narrative, and because it not always clear which party the phrase 'ipsus homo' ('this man') referred to. It seems relatively clear, however, that the dispute was here resolved in favour of the claimant, who then had to give this deed of security to his attacker, stating that he would not seek any further compensation. An actual deed of security would probably have included the specific details of the compensation payed by the attacker, though this model leaves out such information.

As it is not unknown that *n.* days ago a certain man named A had a quarrel with B on a public road and dealt him some blows, this man thus agreed before the good men[126] mediating [in this matter] that this man should make this deed of security regarding these blows and this quarrel which he had with me; and this he did. And if, as I do not think will happen, either myself or one of my heirs or any opposing person dares to oppose this deed of security, let him pay him *n. solidi*, and let him be unable to assert his claim, and let this deed of security remain firm for all time.

No. 7: Here begins a deed of security.

Although this document is also described as a deed of security (*securitas*), it does not relate to a dispute, but to the lease of some land belonging to a monastery. C does not seem to have belonged to this religious community, and the reference to 'our congregation' probably only implies that he lived on the territory owned by this monastery. This document is effectively a *precaria*, an arrangement whereby

---

124 These are the *boni homines* often involved in the settlement of disputes in this formulary, both in and out of court.
125 See above, n. 114.
126 See above, n. 124.

lands were granted as a favour (*beneficium*) for the recipient's lifetime.[127] Such rights (often described as rights of usufruct, limited to the land's revenue, as opposed to outright ownership) could be granted in exchange for specific duties or, as in this case, for a yearly payment (*census*), though *precariae* seem to have been issued most often as a result of a gift of land to a monastery, in order to allow the giver to retain its revenues.[128] The document takes pains to protect the rights of the monastery, since there was a high risk, given the long-term nature of the arrangement, that it might fail to recover its property after the death of the beneficiary, if the land was claimed by his heirs.

To the venerable lord and father in Christ Abbot A and all of our congregation and Lord B's, I, C. In response to my request, your piety gave me the benefit of your property and that of Lord B, that is, the small place named [D] in the *pagus* of E, so that I[129] should hold and possess [it] together with its houses, fields, lands, unfree servants,[130] tenants, meadows, pastures, water and water-courses, [without] any prejudice to you or to Lord B. And I promise to you an annual payment of *n. solidi*; and after my death, let whatever is found in this place, together with any value added [to it], be returned and received back under your authority and that of Lord B, without any contradiction or claim from my relatives, with God's favour. As is the custom, I have asked this to be confirmed by great men.[131]

No. 8: Here begins an exchange.

Exchanging tracts of land seems to have been fairly common practice in this period, both for practical purposes and in order to forge or strengthen links between the persons involved; compare Marculf I, 30 and II, 23 and 24. The fields exchanged here seem to have both been situated within the territory of the same church or monastery, which accounts for the clause 'without prejudice to Saint D, whose land this is known to be', though the precise nature of the rights of the monastery over these lands is left unclear.

127 Compare Marculf II, 5 and 40; for lands not belonging to a church, see also Marculf II, 9 and 41.

128 On *precariae*, see I.N. Wood, 'Teutsind, Witlaic and the history of Merovingian *precaria*', in W. Davies and P. Fouracre, eds., *Property and Power in the Early Middle Ages* (Cambridge, 1995), pp. 31–52; B. Rosenwein, 'Property transfers and the Church, eighth to eleventh centuries: an overview', *Mélanges de l'Ecole Française de Rome: Moyen âge* 3:2 (1999), pp. 563–75; H. Hummer, *Politics and Power in Early Medieval Europe: Alsace and the Frankish Realm, 600–1000* (Cambridge, 2005), pp. 19–22, and, on the payment of a *census*, pp. 84–104.

129 The text has the third person here.

130 See above, n. 113.

131 It is unclear who these 'great' witnesses may have been; they were probably members of the local elite.

In God's name. It pleased A and B and was agreed between them that they should exchange their small field[s]; which they did. A gave for his part the field of C, yielding *n. modii*, and which is on the territory of Saint D, and adjoins on one side the field of E. In a similar way B gave for his part the little field of F; yielding *n. modii*, in another place on this territory, and adjoining on one side the field of G, so that A[132] should have the free power in every way to do whatever he wants with it, without prejudice to Saint D, whose land this is known to be. If either of them dares to act against or oppose the other, let him give up the portion which he received to the other, and furthermore let him incur the fine prescribed by the law, and let the identical copies[133] of this document which we asked to be made for each other remain firm.

No. 9: Here begins an act of sale, which one makes when selling oneself.

> The title does not fit the content of this formula, which is a straightforward act of sale for a slave (compare Marculf II, 22). In all likelihood such sales involved mostly domestic slaves, as opposed to unfree rural tenants (who only tended to be sold along with the land on which they lived, which would no doubt have been less disruptive to their lives than relocation). Domestic slavery is also suggested here by the use of the more specialised term *vernaculus* instead of the more common *mancipia*.[134]

To the lord brother[135] A and his wife B, I, C, living in the *pagus* of D. It is established that I sold to you my slave named E, and for this I received a price of *n.* ounces of silver, so that from this day you may have the free power to do whatever you want with this slave, and to have, hold, give, sell or exchange him, as with the other unfree servants in your service. And if anyone, whether myself or any of my heirs or any other person, tries to act against this act of sale, which I asked to be made with good will, let him pay *n. solidi* [to be divided] between you and the fisc,[136] and let him be unable to assert his claim, and let this act of sale and my decision remain firm for all time.

---

132 The text addresses A in the second person here.
133 'Documents containing the same text' ('epistola uni tenorum conscriptas'); see below, pp. 172–73. Compare Angers no. 45, Marculf I, 38.
134 See Rio, 'Freedom and unfreedom in early medieval Francia', pp. 32–33.
135 See above, n. 122.
136 See above, n. 114.

No. 10

This is one of the few cases of disputes over labour in our surviving record to have been resolved in favour of the accused, who succeeds here in clearing himself of the charge by swearing an oath on the altar of a church (which presumably contained relics, as suggested in Angers no. 50, though the need for all altars to contain relics did not become a requirement until the reign of Charlemagne).[137] The fact that an abbot was in charge of the court may suggest that A (the claimant) and C (the defendant) both lived on the lands of a monastery, or simply that this monastery acted as a trusted arbitrator and accepted source of authority for the people living in this area. Before demanding the swearing of an oath, the abbot seems to have first tried to ascertain whether C had any relatives in A's service: the Latin here is rather confusing, and a number of words seem to be missing, but it seems likely that the phrase 'de sua agnatione alius homines' does refer to a consideration of family precedent, which was often used to reach a verdict in such cases.[138] The unfree status of relatives could have grave consequences for other members of the same family: a capitulary (dated to 803) thus ruled that anyone whose free status was being questioned should be punished by death if he murdered an unfree relative whose status might harm his case.[139] Since in this case C claimed not to have any relatives in A's service, he was made to swear an oath relating to his own status over the past thirty years.[140] Although oath-swearing could technically be seen as a form of ordeal, since it relied in principle on the idea that the presence of relics guaranteed that a false oath could not be given,[141] an important part of this way of reaching a verdict was the party's ability to present oath-helpers to boost his case and swear the oath with him:

---

137 Compare the Catalonian case discussed in Wormald, *The Making of English Law*, p. 80. For Charlemagne's legislation on altars and relics, see *Capitularia* no. 77, vol. 1, p. 170; *Concilia aevi Karolini* no. 36, vol. 1, at p. 270 (P.J. Geary, *Furta Sacra: Thefts of Relics in the Central Middle Ages*, 2nd edn. [Princeton, 1990], p. 37).

138 Compare, for instance, *Formulae Senonenses recentiores* nos. 2 and 5 (Zeumer, *Formulae*, pp. 212–14).

139 *Capitularia* no. 39, cap. 5, vol. 1, p. 113.

140 This number of years seems to have been standard: another example of the 'thirty-year rule' for labour disputes can be found in a document from Cormery dated to 828, discussed in Nelson, 'Dispute settlement in Carolingian West Francia', pp. 49–51.

141 Some relics were thought to be especially good at this: see Gregory of Tours's *Histories*, VIII, 16, for relics of Saint Martin (*Gregorii Turonensis Opera* Teil 1: *Libri historiarum X*, ed. B. Krusch, MGH SS rer. Merov. I, 1 [Hanover, 1937]; for an English translation, see Gregory of Tours, *The History of the Franks*, trans. L. Thorpe [Penguin, 1974]). On ordeals and judgments of God, see Wood, 'Disputes in late fifth- and sixth-century Gaul', pp. 14–18 (for oaths) and pp. 18–19 (for ordeals); R. Bartlett, *Trial by Fire and Water: the Medieval Judicial Ordeal* (Oxford, 1986); for an overview of ordeals, see Brunner, *Deutsche Rechtsgeschichte*, vol. 2, pp. 537–60. On modes of proof in the Angers formulary, see Guillot, 'La justice dans le royaume franc', pp. 697–702.

these were typically twelve in number and of equivalent status to the oath-giver (since C was claiming free status, he had to bring 'free men' to swear the oath with him). Although oath-helpers were not witnesses in the modern sense, the need to procure them in order to assert one's claim points to the importance of local consensus in resolving disputes (compare Angers nos. 11, 15, 24, 28, 29, 30 and 50; in practice, the other party could refuse to accept the oath as valid, as in Angers no. 16).

(a) Here begins a judgment.

The man named A, having come before the venerable Abbot B and other venerable and magnificent men, whose named are entered below, accused the man named C of owing him service; and C was also present, and denied strenuously that he ever owed him service. This C was asked whether [A] had other persons from his family in his service or not; and he said that he did not, and that he himself did not owe him service, whether from birth or as a result of a sale. When it was put to them that this [A] did not receive [service] from other persons from [C's] family, it was decided by the abbot and those who were with him that this man [C] should swear, together with twelve men, thirteen including himself, in the church of Lord D, after a delay of *n*. nights, that he had never owed him service in thirty years or more. If he managed to do this, this A should give compensation regarding this claim against C; but if did not manage it, [C] should strive to give compensation to [A].

(b) Here begins the record for the above judgment.

Record of an oath, [stating] in what manner and in whose presence C came, along with *n*. free men, to the altar of Saint D, in the city of Angers, because the man named A had accused him of [owing him] service on behalf of his father and mother.[142] Having sworn, he said, according to what had been said in the judgment regarding this: 'By this sacred place and all the divine things which take place here, I have lived under a free status for thirty years or more; and I have not given, nor will I give service to this man mentioned above; [I say this] with reverence for this place.' These are the persons in whose presence...

---

142 It is not entirely clear whether this refers to the parents of A (in which case A would have been representing his family's interests) or C (in which case C would have been accused of having to perform service on behalf of his own parents); the construction suggests that A is more likely.

No. 11

Like the preceding formula, this text shows a dispute solved through the swearing of an oath. This time the dispute related to the theft of a mare, and did not merely involve the accuser and the accused, but also a wider family group, as suggested by the presence of C's father, who was here made responsible for swearing the oath (which was nevertheless worded as if it was being sworn by his son). The case is continued in Angers no. 13. The oath record in this case is very similar to that given in Angers no. 15, which also relates to the theft of a horse. This formula shows that even very small-scale disputes such as this one could come to trial and be resolved in much the same way as the disputes over property that feature more prominently in our record, and that they could be the object of equally detailed written records, which suggests a use of the written word and of the legal system on a common, everyday basis. There is no equivalent for this type of dispute in our surviving charters, since records for such matters would not have been worth preserving in the long run.

(a) Here begins a judgment.

The man named A, having come to the city of Angers before the representative[143] B and others who were with him, accused a certain man named C of being in possession of his mare as a result of theft; and this C was there with his father, and denied strenuously that he had ever had this mare in his possession. The representative B [and] those who were with him thus decided that his father, D, should clear this C of [this charge] on behalf of his son C, because he was his father, together with *n.* men, in the church of Lord E, after a delay of *n.* nights. If he managed to do this, this A should make peace with this C; if he could not, C should compensate him.

(b) Here begins the record for the above [judgment].

Record of an oath, [stating] in what manner and in whose presence D entered the church of Lord E, according to the judgment of the representative B. Having sworn, he said: 'By this holy place and all the divine things which take place here, and which are here offered plentifully to God: with respect to the charge that A has brought against me, namely, that I have his mare in my possession as a result of theft, and that he lost this mare through my contrivance, I never had this mare, nor has he lost his mare through my contrivance; and I will not give you anything regarding this claim save for this unchallengeable oath.'

---

[143] Whose representative (*agens*) is left unclear, though elsewhere in this formulary this word is linked more specifically with representatives of a church or monastery as opposed to state officials (Angers nos. 21 and 58).

THE FORMULARY OF ANGERS

No. 12: [Here begins a notice of default.][144]

This type of text is called a *solsadia*, a document recording one party's failure to appear in court to defend his case at the time appointed to settle a dispute (compare Angers nos. 13, 14, 16 and 53, and Marculf I, 37).[145] A period of three days was normally allowed to elapse before a party was declared to have defaulted on their obligation to attend the hearing, but 'A' is here unusually said to have waited only 'from morning to evening'. In this case, the party who failed to turn up was a woman accused of murdering someone by witchcraft (*per maleficio*: this probably refers to poisoning, which was strongly assimilated with witchcraft in this period).[146] As in no. 11, this formula shows the involvement of a wider kin group in defending the interests of their family member: the woman is accused along with her two sons and their uncle, even though only she is supposed to have committed the crime, and it is likely that A was making his accusation because G had been his relative. It is not entirely clear what was meant to happen as a result of such failures to attend: although it seems that technically the absent party would automatically have lost their case (as they explicitly did in Marculf I, 37), it is possible that other means of settlement could then be explored. The involvement of the count, as opposed to the abbot more frequently involved in this formulary, is no doubt due to the seriousness of the crime; the woman's family's apparent refusal to participate in the *placitum* arranged by the count could suggest that they wished to appeal to a different authority.

Record of default, [stating] in what manner and in whose presence the man A attended his *placitum* in the city of Angers, on the kalends of x,[147] according to the judgment of the illustrious Count B and his assessors,[148] against these men named C and D and their mother named E along with their uncle F, because he had said that this woman named E, their mother, had killed [the man] named G through witchcraft. And the aforementioned A was seen to remain at his *placitum* from morning to evening according to the laws.[149] And this woman did not come to the *placitum*, nor did she send

---

144 The space for the title of this formula was left blank in the manuscript; this title was supplied by Mabillon in his edition (*Libri de re diplomatica supplementum*).

145 On the vocabulary of *solsadiae* (and the related verb *solsadire*), see P. Fouracre, 'The nature of Frankish political institutions in the seventh century', in I.N. Wood, ed., *Franks and Alamanni in the Merovingian Period: An Ethnographic Perspective*, Studies in Historical Archaeoethnology 3 (Woodbridge, 1998), pp. 285–316, at pp. 287–88.

146 Compare the 'herbae maleficiae' in *Cartae Senonicae* no. 22 (Zeumer, *Formulae*, pp. 194–95); see also *Pactus Legis Salicae* 19.

147 See above, n. 102.

148 The word is *auditor*, an assessor at the count's tribunal.

149 This sentence still seems to refer to A, despite referring to its subject in the plural.

any representative on her behalf to announce the reason for her absence.[150] Therefore it was necessary for the persons mentioned above to issue this record signed by the hands of good men;[151] which they were seen to do.

No. 13: Here begins another notice of default.

> Like the previous formula, this is a *solsadia*. This text apparently documents further developments in the case of the theft of a mare already featured in no. 11. Which party failed to turn up to this *placitum* is left unclear, since A could refer either to the original plaintiff from no. 11 or to the accused. This formula could imply that the oath given in no. 11b was not accepted by the claimant (Angers no. 16 makes it clear that refusing to accept an oath also counted as a *solsadia*), but it is also possible that this text was intended to function as an alternative to no. 11b, in case the father of the accused did not turn up to swear his oath.

Record of default, [stating] in what manner and in whose presence the man named A attended his *placitum* in the city of Angers, in the church of Lord B, against a man named C, with whom he had been in dispute before the representative[152] D regarding his mare. And this A went to his *placitum* and remained there for three days according to the laws, and established the default of his opponent. For C did not come to the *placitum*, nor did he send anyone on his behalf to attend this *placitum* and announce the reason for his absence.[153] In the presence of these men [A] attended his *placitum* and established the default of his opponent, and they signed this record below by their hands.

No. 14: Another notice of default.

> This is a third example of *solsadia*. Although here the defaulting party was not the one who was supposed to swear the oath, their presence was nevertheless apparently needed in order to allow the others to proceed.[154]

Record of default, [stating] in what manner and in whose presence A, having come to the church of Saint B in the city of Angers, attended his *placitum* against a man named C, with whom he had been in dispute before the

---

150 The word used to designate a legitimate reason not to turn up at a court hearing was *sonia*; see Fouracre, 'The nature of Frankish political institutions', p. 287.
151 See above, n. 124.
152 See above, n. 143.
153 See above, n. 150.
154 On oaths, see above, pp. 56–57.

representative[155] D about some silver, regarding which [A] was to swear an oath together with his men on this day, that is, day x of the month of y.[156] And A went to the *placitum* together with his oath-helpers, and remained there for three days according to the laws, and established the default of his opponent. And C did not come to the *placitum*, nor did he send anyone on his behalf to attend this *placitum* and announce the reason for his absence.[157] [A] attended his *placitum* and established the default of his opponent in the presence of these men, and they signed this record below by their hands.

No. 15: Here begins an oath document.

This text, again dealing with the theft of a horse, is very similar to no. 11b.[158]

Record of an oath, [stating] in what manner and in whose presence the man named A came to the city of Angers on this day, that is, day x of the month of y,[159] in the church of Lord B. Having sworn, he said: 'By this holy place and all the divine things which take place here, and which are here offered plentifully to God: with respect to the charge that the man named C has brought against me, namely, that I stole his horse and kept it as a result of theft,[160] I swear this, that I never stole his horse regarding which he has accused me, nor was I ever complicit in this theft, nor have I ever kept this horse as a result of theft; and I will not give you anything regarding this save for this unchallengeable oath, which I was made to give by judgment and completed according to the laws.' These are the persons who heard this oath; they signed below by their hands.

No. 16: Here begins a record of judgment.

This document strongly resembles a *solsadia*, but was made in different circumstances to those given in nos. 12, 13 and 14: here both parties do turn up to their *placitum*, but the claimant (E, a woman, who was apparently making her claim directly, without being represented by a man) refuses to accept the oath made by the accused, thus effectively refusing to abide by the ruling made by

---

155 See above, n. 143.
156 See above, n. 102.
157 See above, n. 150.
158 On oaths, see above, pp. 56–57.
159 See above, n. 102.
160 The word 'taxatum' in the manuscript should here be read as 'texaca', 'theft', a word of Germanic origin.

the *praepositus*.[161] Like not turning up to the *placitum* at all, this amounted to refusing to play the game, which explains why this is effectively presented as defaulting: A and B are said to have 'established the default of their opponent' (*solsadire*), as in nos. 12, 13 and 14.[162] E clearly intended to appeal to a different authority.[163] The word *praepositus* simply means 'man in charge', and could be applied to both lay and ecclesiastical contexts, so that it is impossible to tell whether it here referred to a count or other state official, or to the abbot frequently involved in settling disputes in this formulary.

Record [stating] in what manner and in whose presence A and B attended their *placitum* in the city of Angers, in the church of Lord C, according to the judgment of the *praepositus* D, because a woman named E had accused [A] regarding the property F. And A and his brother B came to this *placitum* and presented their men there, so as to clear him of the charge by an oath. But this woman E came to this *placitum* and refused to accept this oath. And A and his brother B remained at their *placitum* according to the laws and established the default of their opponent. Therefore it was necessary that they should receive a [written] record regarding this; and we made it in this manner.

No. 17: Here begins a deed of annulment.

This surprising text shows us an unfree man regaining his freedom from the couple to whom he had previously sold himself, because they could not find the contract of self-sale he had given them. This outcome is all the more surprising as the basis for ownership itself is not contested, since A admits having sold himself to the couple:[164] it was the loss of the document itself which was apparently seen as determinant (even though lost documents could apparently by replaced as long as the rights they recorded were recognised, as in the *appennis* procedure described in Angers nos. 31–33).[165] Since A sold himself entirely, rather than for a specific period of time, as in no. 18, there would have been no natural point at which the couple would have had to present their deed of ownership publicly, which implies that this document was issued as a result of a dispute, in all likelihood initiated by A. If so, this would constitute important evidence that unfree

---

161 Compare Gregory of Tours's *Histories*, VII, 23, and the rather extreme case described in V, 32, in which an argument arising as a result of the accusers' refusal to accept the oath of the accused resulted in a sword fight and killings in front of the altar in the church of St Denis in Paris.
162 On this word, see above, n. 145.
163 On oaths, see above, pp. 56–57.
164 For documents of self-sale, see Angers nos. 3, 19 and 25 and Marculf II, 28.
165 See Rio, 'Freedom and unfreedom in early medieval Francia', pp. 29–30.

people could bring a claim to justice in much the same way as the free; the details are sadly lacking, since this would probably only have been the final document among several produced as a result of the dispute.[166]

As it is known that the man named A gave an act of sale for his entire [free] status to the man named B and his wife C, and they could not find this act of sale at all, therefore I[167] took care to issue [this deed of annulment] to you signed by our own hand: if at any point this act of sale is found, let it remain void and useless, and let this act of annulment remain firm.

No. 18: Here begins another deed of annulment.

This formula is similar to no. 17, in that the loss of a document leads to a man being freed from the service of another, but there are also some important differences between these two texts. Rather than an act of sale (*vinditio*), the lost document in this case was a deed of security for a loan (*cautio*, to be distinguished from *securitas*, which refers to a deed of security intended to put an end to a dispute): A seems to have agreed to give up his free status on a temporary basis in exchange for the loan.[168] The phrase 'as if you had given me back my property' ('dum tu ris meas rededisti') implies that the money was to be repaid after a certain number of years, at which point A was to recover his freedom, with the service he had rendered in the meantime counting as interest on the loan. It is likely that this document was made at the appointed time when A was meant to return the money and recover his deed of security: since B could not find the document, A was freed without having to repay the debt.[169] Compare Angers no. 38 and Marculf II, 27 for other examples of loan securities of this kind; on the need to return deeds of security when a loan was repaid, see also Angers nos. 22 and 60; for another deed of annulment, see Marculf II, 35.

As it is known that this man named A had a deed of security for a loan issued to this man named B concerning his [free] status, whereby [B] gave [A] *x* ounces of silver in order that [A] should perform whatever service [B] demanded of him for *y* number of years, and this man [B] could not find this deed of security at all, therefore I[170] gave you this deed of annulment

---

166 On documents of *evacuatio* (or *vacuaturia*, which is the word used for 'annulment' in this case) in Visigothic and Catalonian documents, see Wormald, *The Making of English Law*, pp. 80–81.

167 This almost certainly refers to B, with a switch from third- to first-person narrative often observed in this formulary.

168 See Rio, 'Freedom and unfreedom in early medieval Francia', p. 30.

169 Compare *Cartae Senonicae* no. 24 for a more detailed account of a similar case (Zeumer, *Formulae*, p. 195).

170 See above, n. 167.

[signed] by my hand and those of good men,[171] as if you had given me back my property: and if at any point this deed of security is found, let it remain void and useless, and let this deed of annulment remain firm.

No. 19: Here begins an act of sale.

> Like Angers nos. 2 and 3, this is a self-sale, but this time it seems to have been made voluntarily rather than as a result of B being convicted of a crime in court. Although formulae of self-sale, with their frequent references to 'hunger and poverty', as in this text, have been counted as evidence that the poor had little choice but to sell themselves to more powerful persons during this period, such self-sales were not always the result of a truly desperate financial situation (compare Angers no. 25).[172]

To A, forever my lord, B. Both because of the necessity of these times and of life,[173] and also because I am oppressed by the combined weight of hunger and poverty, I am unable to act in any other way than to transfer my entire [free] status into your service. It is therefore established that I, compelled by no one, but with my fullest will (...),[174] and I received from you in exchange for my aforementioned [free] status the price which pleased me, worth *n. solidi* in gold, so that from this day you may have the power in every way, with God's favour, to do whatever you want with me,[175] as with the other unfree servants[176] in your service. And if anyone, whether myself or any of my relatives or any other person, attempts to act against this act of sale, which I have asked to be made with good will, let him be compelled to pay *n. solidi* [to be divided] between you and the fisc,[177] and let him be unable to assert his claim, and let this act of sale and my decision remain firm for all time.

---

171 See above, n. 124.

172 See Liebs, 'Sklaverei aus Not'; Rio, 'Freedom and unfreedom in early medieval Francia', pp. 27–32.

173 For 'vidi' read 'vitae' (Zeumer, *Formulae*, p. 10).

174 Part of this sentence is missing, probably as a result of a copy error in the manuscript.

175 See above, n. 112.

176 See above, n. 113.

177 See above, n. 114.

THE FORMULARY OF ANGERS

No. 20: Here begins an act of manumission [taking effect] from the present day.

This formula gives a model for a manumission (the freeing of a slave by his master) taking effect from the time the document was made, as opposed to manumissions which only took effect after the death of the master (as in Angers no. 23; compare Marculf I, 22 and II, 32–34). B was being manumitted 'as if [he] had been born of free parents', and therefore in principle would not owe any further service as a freedman to either A or his heirs; but he appears to have still remained linked in some sense to the church of Saint C, since he was to live under its protection or tutelage (*defensio*, sometimes also referred to by the Germanic term *mundeburdium*): the right to choose his own protector and place of residence, sometimes found in formulae of this kind, is not given in this case. What duties freedmen would have had to perform in exchange for such protection varied, and could include the payment of annual gifts in money or in kind. Transferring freedmen into the authority of a church by naming that church as their future protector seems to have become an increasingly common feature of manumissions in later formularies.[178] This may have been intended to combine the spiritual benefits of freeing slaves with those of giving to the church, since both were considered to be good Christian acts, likely to contribute to the giver's salvation (which is why documents recording either of these actions often, as in this case, threaten possible future opponents with excommunication as well as a fine; compare Angers nos. 23 and 46).

A, in God's name, to our dearest B. Know that, out of respect for God and for the redemption of my soul and eternal rewards, we order that you should be free from this present day, as if you had been born of free parents; and know that you will not owe any duty or service to any of my direct or indirect heirs, but instead may live in full freedom, under the protection of Saint C. And if one of my heirs or any other person dares to go against or resist this deed of manumission, which I have asked to be made with good will, first let him incur the judgment of God and be excluded from holy places,[179] and furthermore let him be liable by law to a fine of one pound of gold, *n*.

---

178 Compare *Formulae Salicae Bignonianae* no. 2 (Zeumer, *Formulae*, pp. 228–29); *Formulae Salicae Merkelianae* no. 14 (p. 246); *Formulae Salicae Lindenbrogianae* nos. 9 and 11 (pp. 273–74); *Formulae Argentinenses* no. 2 (p. 337); *Formulae Augienses coll. B* nos. 21 and 34 (pp. 356 and 360); *Formulae Extravagantes* I, 19–20 (pp. 545–46). For a later example assimilating manumission with the transfer of an unfree person to the church, in the eleventh-century *Book of Serfs* of the monastery of Marmoutier, see D. Barthélemy, 'Qu'est-ce que le servage, en France, au XIe siècle ?', *Revue historique* 287(2) (1992), pp. 233–84, at pp. 255–57.

179 This refers to excommunication.

pounds of silver, and let him be unable to assert his claim, and let this deed of manumission remain firm for all time.

No. 21: Here begins an act of sale.

> Like the vineyard sold in Angers no. 4, the field involved in this transaction was part of the territory of a church, which accounts for the clause according to which the buyer could do anything he liked with the property, provided this was done 'without prejudice to Saint C'. In this case, remarkably, the penalty-clause stipulates that the cut of the fine normally collected by the royal treasury was to be given to the representative (*agens*) of the church. This suggests that the responsibility for enforcing the agreement made in this document was also being assigned to church rather than state officials. This may have been the result of an immunity in favour of that church, preventing any interference from royal officials, though one cannot exclude the possibility that this church had simply appropriated that role on its own initiative.[180]

I, A. It is established that I sold to B, as indeed I did, a little field yielding *n. modii*, which is on the territory of Saint C, in the villa of D, and adjoins on one side the field of E, in exchange for the price which pleased me, worth *n. solidi*, so that from this day you may have the free power in every way to do whatever you want with this field, without prejudice to Saint C, whose land this is known to be. And if either I myself or any of my heirs or any other person attempts to act against this act of sale, which I have asked to be made with good will, let him pay twice [its value], [to be divided] between you and the representative of Saint C; let him be unable to assert his claim, and let this act of sale and my decision remain firm for all time.

No. 22: Here begins a deed of security regarding a vineyard.

> This is a *cautio*, a deed of security for a loan. In this case the loan was given in exchange for the right of usufruct over a vineyard, rather than in exchange for labour, as in nos. 18 and 38. The phrase according to which A is to recover his deed of security 'either from yourself or from whomsoever you will have given this deed of security to enforce' ('aut tibi aut cui caucione ista dederis ad exagendum') probably refers to B's legal representative, or to his heirs, in the event of his death before the time appointed for the repayment of the loan; it could also mean that B could transfer this deed of security to someone else as payment in the course of another transaction (compare Angers nos. 38 and 60).

---

180 On immunities, see below, p. 132.

I, A. It is established by this deed of security that I received a loan, as indeed I did, from this man named B, for the amount that pleased me, that is, n. *solidi* in silver. And for this I entrust to you as a pledge for this favour a vineyard measuring half[181] a *juchus*, which is on the territory of Saint C, in the villa of D, and adjoins on one side the vineyard of E, for a duration of n. years, so that, while I have your property in my possession, you will keep for yourself the produce[182] which God will grant in that place. And after these n. years have elapsed, as is customary, I am to return your property, and I will recover my deed of security, either from yourself or from whomsoever you will have given this deed of security to enforce.

No. 23: Here begins a deed of manumission.

This is a manumission taking effect only after the master's death, unlike the situation described in Angers no. 20. This is the only significant difference between these two texts: here again, the servant is free from service to his master's heirs, but remains under the protection of a particular church, in exchange for a (presumably lighter) type of service. As in no. 20, the penalty-clause again includes the threat of excommunication, though in this case it does not prescribe a fine.

To our dearest A, I, B. Know that, out of respect for God and for the redemption of my soul and eternal rewards, we are freeing you from the yoke of servitude, so that, for as long as I[183] live, you will not leave my service, but after my death you may lead your life as a free man, with all the possessions which you have now or that you may obtain through your work [in the future], as if you had been born of free parents, and know that you will not be required to pay any duty or service to my direct or indirect heirs, except for the service that you will give under the protection of the holy church of Lord C. If someone, which I do not believe will happen, either one of my heirs or any opposing person, tries to act against this deed of manumission, which I asked to be made with good will, first let him incur the judgment of God[184] and be excommunicated from churches, basilicas and all places of

---

181 'Vinia medio iucto tantum': Zeumer thought this meant 'half a vineyard measuring n. *juchi*' (which would imply that B would get half the revenue of this vineyard), but 'a vineyard measuring half a *juchus*', though small, seems equally likely. The compiler may have forgotten to remove the word for 'half' ('medio') when he added the *tantum* ('n. amount') at the end of this phrase in an attempt to generalise the content of the document.

182 The word *blada* refers here to the produce of the vineyard, though the word was normally used in reference to grain.

183 The text has 'for as long as you live' ('quamdiu advixeris') here, but the rest of the text suggests this actually refers to B.

184 This seems to refer to divine punishment in general rather than an ordeal.

worship; let him incur the same curse as that incurred by Judas Iscariot, and let my decision find favour before Christ. Let him never be able to have his way regarding what he claimed, and let this deed of manumission and my decision remain firm for all time.

No. 24: Here begins a [record of] judgment.

> C is here accused not of stealing A's livestock, but specifically of rousing and scattering his animals, apparently purposefully, in order to obtain the skins of the animals that died as a result (though this may seem like an odd strategy).[185] This unusual case again shows that even fairly low-level disputes could be settled through a court and in writing, just as in cases involving land, which are more commonly found in our surviving evidence for this period.

Having come to the city of Angers before the *praepositus* B and other men who were with him, A accused a certain man named C of having driven his animals[186] astray by rousing them, and that some of these animals died as a result of his having roused them, and that C had skinned these beasts after they had died. This C was asked to answer this accusation. And this C said that he had never roused [A]'s animals, and that he had never driven these animals astray as a result of having roused them, and that they had never been skinned by his hand. Therefore it was decided by this *praepositus* and those who were with him that, after a delay of *n.* nights, this C should clear himself of the charge in the church of Lord D, together with *n.* men. If he managed to do this, this A should let the matter rest; but if he could not, let him pay in compensation whatever the law prescribes regarding such cases.

No. 25: Here begins an act of sale [for someone] who is selling himself.

> This formula shows that self-sale was not necessarily a decision adopted only in cases of penury:[187] the couple selling themselves here seemed to own a relatively substantial amount of land, at least in comparison with the other land transactions included in this formulary. The reason for the sale in this case may have been a desire for protection or association with a more powerful lord. The fine amounts to twice the value of both C and D and their property, which could imply that

---

185 On the fines prescribed for the killing and skinning of horses in particular, see *Pactus Legis Salicae* 65.

186 This word (*animalia*) seems to have referred to either cattle or sheep.

187 As suggested in Liebs, 'Sklaverei aus Not'; see Rio, 'Freedom and unfreedom in early medieval Francia', pp. 27–32.

their property, although it had technically become the property of A and B, still remained tied to them in some sense. It is possible that C and D would have continued living on their lands as tenants, or through a *precaria*, perhaps giving A and B a share of their revenue along with performing particular duties.

To the magnificent lord brother[188] A and his wife B, we, C and his wife D. It is established that we sold to you, as indeed we did, our [free] status along with all the possessions that we may own or rent, *mansus* and land and vineyards, however much we are known to possess at this present day on the land of the villa of E, on the territory of the church of Angers, together with everything that we are known to have anywhere. For this we received from you the price that pleased us, worth *n. solidi* in gold, so that from this day the said buyers may have the free[189] power to do whatever they want with us and our heirs.[190] And if someone, whether ourselves or any other person, wants to go against this act of sale, which we asked to be made with good will, let him pay twice the value of our [free] status and of our property, along with any value added to it at that time, and let him be unable to assert his claim, and let this act of sale remain firm.

No. 26: Here begins a deed of security.

This deed of security (*securitas*) apparently deals with the settlement of a dispute over the rape of a woman by the dependant of a church ('homo sancti illius'). The Latin text is somewhat confusing, and the details of the situation (such as the nature of the compensation) are left unclear in any case, since this document was intended to prevent further litigation rather than to act as a record of the dispute. Whose ruling this was is not specified, and the intervention of the *boni homines*, often referred to as mediators in other similar documents from this formulary (nos. 5, 6, 39, 43 and 44), is not mentioned here; the reason for this may perhaps be that the dispute had been settled entirely out of court (compare Angers no. 42).

It is not unknown that this woman named A brought a charge against the man of Saint B named C regarding the rape[191] of which she was the victim, and

188 See above, n. 122.
189 The manuscript had 'licentiam abeant potestatem' ('let them have the right [and] the power'), but this should probably be read as 'liberam habeant potestatem' ('let them have the free power'), a more common reading in this standard phrase.
190 See above, n. 112.
191 The Latin word is *raptus*, which can mean either 'rape' or 'abduction', or even 'elopement' (when it was done with the woman's consent, as was clearly not the case here). The first meaning seems more plausible in this case, since the other two tended to be done with the

the decision [was taken] that he[192] should make reparations to this woman in order that peace be restored; which he[193] did. And it was decided that the man should receive [a document] signed by her hand regarding this, which he did, to the effect that, if this woman wants to litigate against the man after this day, she should pay *n. solidi*. Deed of security made...

No. 27: Here begins an act of sale concerning land.

> This is a fairly straightforward act of sale, showing an abbot buying a piece of land (*proprietas*) from a couple on behalf of his monastery.

To the venerable lord and father in Christ Abbot A, I, B, and my wife C. It is established that we sold to you, as indeed we did, our land in the place called D, and for this I received from you the price which pleased us, that is, *n. solidi* in silver, so that you may have the free power in every way to do whatever you want with this land of ours, which we sold to you with good will. And if one of us or one of our relatives or any other person attempts to act against this act of sale, let him pay *n. solidi* in compensation, [to be divided] between you and the fisc,[194] and let him be unable to assert his claim, and let this act of sale remain firm for all time. With confirmation given below.[195] This was done.

No. 28: Here begins a [record of] judgment.

> It is highly likely that this document related to a boundary dispute, and that the digging of the ditch ('fossado') had been intended to function as a boundary between two pieces of land belonging to different people:[196] if so, D would have been accused not of being a ditch-digging enthusiast, but of having appropriated a part of his neighbour's land in the process of defining this boundary. The speci-

---

intention of resulting in marriage.
192 The text has the plural here.
193 See above, n. 192.
194 See above, n. 114.
195 This is the standard phrase 'stipulatione subnixa', often found in Frankish formulae and documents. The *stipulatio* in late Roman documents referred to a solemn promise to abide by the terms of the contract, usually in short question-and-answer form ('Do you promise this? I do'). In Frankish documents, however, the meaning of this expression seems to have changed, and it was sometimes apparently used to refer to the signatures of witnesses included at the end of the document.
196 On this practice in Brittany, see Davies, *Small Worlds*, pp. 33–34. On the word *fossatum* in the region of Angers, see E. Zadora-Rio, 'De la haie au bocage: quelques remarques sur l'Anjou', in L. Feller, P. Mane and F. Piponnier, eds., *Le Village médiéval et son environnement: Etudes offertes à Jean-Marie Pesez* (Paris, 1998), pp. 671–82, at p. 673.

fication that the three oath-helpers (as opposed to the twelve normally required for oaths in cases of theft and murder) whom D needed to find in order to clear himself of the charge had to be neighbours was clearly intended to ensure that they were acquainted with the layout of A and D's properties: this shows that the outcome was meant to be decided according to a generally accepted idea of what belonged to whom, and points again to the decisiveness of local consensus in cases settled by the swearing of an oath.[197]

A, having come to the city of Angers before the representative[198] B, C, and others who were with him, accused a certain man named D of having dug a ditch on his land in the place called [E], which belongs to the villa of [F]. And this man gave this answer, that he had a dug a ditch on his [own] land, but that he had never dug [one] on the land of the man A. It was decided by these magnificent [men] that, after a delay of *n.* nights, D should clear himself of ever having wrongfully dug a ditch on A's land, together with *n.* men, neighbours living close to this *condita*, himself counting as a fourth, in the main church of Lord G. If he managed to do this, he should be left in peace and security; but if he could not, he should give this man compensation.

No. 29: Here begins a [record of] judgment.

In this case, the accusation brought against E seems to be that, having been entrusted some property by someone, he failed to return it to its owner's heirs after that person had died. Here as in the previous formula, pains are taken to ensure that A must find his oath-helpers only among those qualified to determine the truth of his claim: 'neighbours living nearby, who had been alive at that time and knew that the said late C had entrusted these valuables to this E' ('vicinis circa manentis qui de presente fuissent et vidissent...'). The oath-helpers were therefore here meant to act as witnesses, rather than merely giving their support without knowing the particulars of the case.

The man named A, together with the woman named B, who had been the wife of his late brother C, having come before the venerable Abbot D, accused the man named E regarding the valuables[199] which had belonged to this late C and had been entrusted to E, namely this thing. This E was present, and strongly denied all of this. They asked this A if there were men alive at

---

197 See above, pp. 56–57.
198 See above, n. 143.
199 The text has the word *servicium*, here apparently not in its standard meaning of 'service' or 'duty', but as a synonym for the word *rauba*, 'valuables', used further down in the text.

present who would have seen when this C had entrusted these valuables to E. Thus it was decided by this abbot and those who were with him that, after a delay of *n.* nights, [A] should produce *n.* men of good faith, neighbours living nearby, who had been alive at that time and knew that the said late C had entrusted these valuables to this E, so that [A] could swear to this in the church of Lord F. [If he managed to do this,] this E should compensate him according to the law; but if he could not, this E would be able to remain for all time free from litigation, in peace and security regarding this claim.

No. 30: Here begins another [record of] judgment.

> The scarcity of the details given about the case, combined with the habit of referring to all persons through indefinite pronouns, makes it difficult to work out exactly what is happening in this text; I have given what seemed to me the most likely interpretation. What is certain is that the point of the dispute was to establish who had what rights over the vineyards in question: whether C held them by virtue of a lease, or whether he owned them outright. Since this text is placed just after a dispute in which heirs tried to recover the property of their dead relative, it seems likely that this was a similar situation, this time concerning not valuables, but vineyards that had been leased to C by their original owner in exchange for a share of the crop ('ad parciaricias'); if the accusation against him was founded, C might have tried to retain the land without paying the dues prescribed by the lease.

A, having come before the Abbot B and others who were with him, accused a certain man named C, claiming that his vineyards, which had belonged to D, had been leased to him by the late D in exchange for a share of the crop, so that, for as long as it pleased this [D], he was to have the lease for these vineyards in exchange for a share of the crop. This C was asked whether or not these vineyards were his. He said that he had never made this agreement that this A spoke of. Abbot B decided that, since he denied that he had ever made this agreement, this C should clear himself of this charge together with *n.* men in the church of Lord E, [by swearing] that they had never had this agreement between them. If he managed to do this, [A] was to give him in compensation the amount that he would have received from this C; but if he could not, [C] should compensate [A].

THE FORMULARY OF ANGERS

No. 31: Here begins a document of *appennis*.

This model, like the two immediately following it, relates to a procedure known as *appennis*, which one needed to follow in order to re-establish the various rights recorded in documents that had been lost or destroyed, in this case as a result of what seems to have constituted burglary on a grand scale. The full procedure is not given here, but only the initial steps, consisting in ascertaining the loss of the documents. This text shows a clear concern to ensure the presence of appropriate witnesses in order to support the claim that was later to be made in court. Judging from the description of their house (with both a gate and front doors) and of their property, this couple seems to have been of fairly high status. The list of documents counted as lost in this formula is not very specific: like the lists of property found in descriptions of estates, it was no doubt intended to cover every eventuality and every possible type of document rather than to offer a detailed account of what the couple's archive actually contained (and it is very similar as a result to the lists given in nos. 32 and 33). Nevertheless, this formula, together with the two that follow it, constitutes strong evidence for the existence of lay archives, by showing that lay people could keep a variety of documents in their homes, and that they thought them important enough to take immediate steps to replace them when they were lost. This is understandable, given that they were clearly at risk of losing some rights altogether if they did not undertake to have these lost documents replaced, as suggested by formulae of annulment (Angers nos. 17 and 18). Compare Marculf I, 33 and 34.[200]

It is not unknown that this man named A and his wife B both[201] experienced a terrible disaster during the night in the place [called] C, and as a result lost their money and moveable property as well as many documents containing sales, marriage-gifts, dispute settlements, gifts, contracts, exchanges, agreements, deeds of security, annulments, judgments and records of judgments. Therefore it was necessary for him to summon state officials and neighbours living nearby and the whole of that community,[202] and there they found his

---

200 Formulae of *appennis* are also found in other collections: see *Formulae Arvernenses* no. 1, *Formulae Turonenses* nos. 27, 28 and *Add.* no. 7, and *Cartae Senonicae* nos. 38 and 46 (Zeumer, *Formulae*, p. 28; pp. 150–51 and 162; pp. 202 and 205–06). These formulae have generated an unusually high level of interest: see above, n. 88.

201 The manuscript has *inter eorum in loco illo* here; Mabillon suggested this could also be read as *in terra eorum in loco illo*, 'on their land', but this is not a common phrase in this formulary (Mabillon, *Libri de re diplomatica supplementum*; Zeumer, *Formulae*, p. 14).

202 The word *parochia* is used here, but this word did not take on the modern meaning of 'parish' until a later period, between the tenth and the twelfth centuries (see E. Zadora-Rio, 'The making of churchyards and parish territories in the early medieval landscape of France and England in the 7th–12th centuries: a reconsideration', *Medieval Archaeology* 47 [2003], pp. 1–19).

front doors broken through and the gate destroyed, and the place itself greatly devastated. Therefore he put a request to these good men,[203] whose names are listed below, and who went to the scene and ascertained what the situation was, asking them to confirm the record that had been made ready; which they did, so that it might be better authenticated in the city of Angers.

No. 32: Here begins another *appennis*.

> This is effectively the next step in the procedure for the replacement of lost documents described in no. 31: the victim had to present the signed account before a court in order to recover the rights and property that had been recorded in the documents he had lost. The joint involvement of the count and bishop, sitting in judgment to deal with the 'more important lawsuits' ('principale negotio'), shows that such a procedure required the sanction of a higher authority than most of the other cases recorded in this formulary. The pains taken to ensure the validity of C's claims, by comparing his own account with the separate testimony of the neighbours who signed it (who were relied upon because they lived nearby 'and knew about this very well'), shows that people were conscious that the procedure could be open to abuse, for instance if people pretended to lose their documents in order to claim greater rights or a larger property than the original documents had given them. This may be why, although no discrepancy was detected between the account presented by the claimant and that given by his neighbours, the ruling placed restrictions on what the claimant could recover from his property: it seems he could recover the main bulk of it, but not what had been included in transactions completed before a certain cut-off date, presumably in order to ensure that these transactions would be remembered by witnesses, since the replacement of documents seems to have relied entirely on the memory of local inhabitants.

Whoever in this province has suffered violence and wrong at the hands of brigands, criminals, conspirators or arsonists must make this known before all and make a public denunciation before city officials or members of the municipal councils of the province in which this is said to have been perpetrated. Therefore, as, in order to deal with the affairs of the church and the more important lawsuits, the apostolic man the lord Bishop A and the illustrious Count B sat in judgment in the city of Angers, together with other venerable and magnificent men of the state, the man named C came there and publicly stated that evil men had come in the darkness of the night to his house in the place called D, and broken down his doors and stolen his possessions, gold, silver, valuables, clothes, his jewellery, bronze

203 See above, n. 124.

THE FORMULARY OF ANGERS

utensils and many other things, including documents of sale, loan securities, transfers of property, donations, marriage-gifts, dispute settlements, gifts, contracts, exchanges, agreements, deeds of security, annulments, judgments and records of judgment, contracts of obligation, and many other things, which there is not enough room [to list] one by one,[204] and he said that many pieces of land had been sold to him through these documents. And after the arrival in that place the following day of good and industrious[205] persons, neighbours living nearby, they confirmed this in this place [by signing a document] by their own hands. And they gave this informed account to be read out before the lords mentioned above, so that these lords could learn how this crime was done and perpetrated. Since they were seen to investigate with such diligence, it was asked of these good and industrious[206] persons, neighbours living nearby, who knew about this very well, that they should give a true account of what they knew regarding this. And the testimony given by these men was such that, when it was compared with the letter presented by C, it corresponded truly to his claim. And since the matter was thus clarified in all its particulars, the prelate mentioned above and this count and those who were with him advised this C that he could keep as his own whatever he had possessed by right and according to the law through the space of years from *n*. time ago up to this day, [and], for the time before that, his principal possessions, verified according to the due course of the law; and that his heirs would [be able to] hold and possess these things. And it was decided that, for time present and future, he should receive and confirm this document, which is called *appennis*, authenticated by the lords mentioned above and the other citizens by their own hands; and this was done, so that he might receive two identical copies of the confirmed deed of *appennis*, one for him to keep, the other to be displayed in the public square. *Appennis* made...

No. 33: Here begins a record to confirm the *appennis*.

As in Angers no. 31, this formula only gives a model for the preliminary document drawn up before the court hearing and used to establish the facts of the matter. The detailed description of the evidence seen by the neighbours proving that an

---

204 The manuscript has the obscure phrase 'quod locum est per singula minustre'.
205 The phrase is 'bonas et straneas personas'. The word *straneas* should probably be read as *strenuas* ('industrious') rather than *extraneas* ('foreigners', 'outsiders'), which would be in contradiction with the statement made in the same sentence that these people were neighbours.
206 See above, n. 205.

attack had taken place was probably needed in order to ensure that A had indeed lost his documents, and was not merely looking to make larger claims than his documents had originally given him (compare no. 32).

Since through blind greed the Old Enemy[207] is forever stirring up conflicts in urban areas, and it has become common for intolerable wrongs to be endured at the hand of perfidious and evil men, great injuries are set in motion and instigated in this age by both enemies and brigands, through robbery and theft, by despoilers and robbers.[208] Indeed, it is not unknown that a certain man named A suffered a great loss, as his house in the villa of B was broken into at night and all his moveable property, gold, silver, bronze, clothes, tools, money and many documents of sale, loan securities, transfers of property, donations, marriage-gifts, dispute settlements, contracts, exchanges, agreements, deeds of security, annulments, judgments and records of judgment, and every written deed by virtue of which he had held his possessions for a long time up to that day, were taken away as a result of this theft. Therefore it was necessary for the aforementioned A to summon neighbours who lived close to this place to the public assembly on the following morning. And having come to that place they found that this had been done, that his enclosure had been cut down, his gates broken down, his walls pierced, torn apart, and that everything that we mentioned above had been taken away by this theft. Since this was shown to be true, in order that he should be better able to request a deed of *appennis* regarding this and to have it validated in the city of that region, he asked [his] neighbour C and the state official, who were both involved in this claim, to confirm this report in view of this by signing it by their own hands; which they did.

No. 34: Here begins a marriage-gift.

This model only presents the bare bones of a *dos* document: no description for the property is given, and the penalty-clause is shortened (compare Angers nos. 1c, 35, 40 and 54, and Marculf II, 15). Greater detail would no doubt have been added in the process of drawing up an actual document on the basis of this model.

In the fourth year of the reign of our lord King Childebert,[209] I, in God's name A, decided that this deed for a marriage-gift to my sweetest wife

207 Namely, the devil.
208 This is a very flowery opening statement, no doubt intended to convey a sense of solemnity to the document; understanding it would not have been essential to the overall comprehension of the text. See above, pp. 20–21.
209 This is the same date as that given in no. 1a; see above, n. 101.

named B should be written for me; which was done. Out of love for your sweetness, I give to you, in this document for a marriage-gift, a house; and let the said girl, my wife B, have, hold and possess it, and do what she wants [with it]. And if someone, whether myself or any opposing person, dares to act against this decision of mine and against what is written in this marriage-gift, let him be made to pay *n. solidi*; and let [his claim] not have any effect.

No. 35: Here begins a document.

> As with no. 34, this model seems less thorough than most of those included in this formulary, and looks more like a draft than a fully fledged *dos* document. The word 'service' (*servitium*) could be used to refer to a variety of different types of duty, and did not necessarily imply the status of a servant; it is here used to refer to the duty of a wife to her husband (compare no. 56, where it is used to refer to the duty of a servant to his lord, and nos. 37 and 58, for the duty of a son to his father).

I, A, have decided that I should have this document made for my wife B, which I did. Because of my love for your sweetness and of the service which you devote to me, I give you and transfer to you [by this] document[210] a house, together with the estate on which this house is situated, so that from this day you may have, hold and possess the aforesaid property, and do what you want [with it] from this day. And if someone, whether myself or any opposing person, dares to go against or resist this document, let him pay *n. solidi*, and let him be unable to assert his claim in any way, and let this document [remain firm for all time].[211]

No. 36: Here begins another deed of transfer.

> The wording of this text is almost identical to that of no. 35, which shows that the formulation of marriage-gifts did not differ significantly to that of gifts made to other family members.

I, A, have decided that I should have this document made for my sweetest

---

210 The manuscript has *capsade* here, which should probably be emended to *cartole* (Zeumer, *Formulae*, p. 16).

211 There is an error in the manuscript, which repeats 'vindicare non valeat' from the previous clause instead of the standard 'perenni tempore firma permaneat'; this latter expression appears at the end of no. 36, the wording of which is very similar to that found in this formula.

78   THE FORMULARIES OF ANGERS AND MARCULF

nephew[212] named B, which I did. I give to him, out of love for his sweetness, a house, so that from this day you may have, hold and possess this property written [in this document], and do what you want [with it] from this day. And if someone, whether myself or any opposing person, dares to go against or resist the decision I made, let him pay *n. solidi*, and let him be unable to assert his claim, and let this act of sale[213] remain firm for all time.

No. 37: Here begins a document which a father and mother make for their son.

> In this case, a son is given a piece of land by his parents as a reward for undertaking military service on behalf of his father 'in the service of [our] lords' ('in utilitate domnorum'). The plural in this expression probably means that he was fighting for the king under his own lord; if so, perhaps the latter would have been the 'illustrious man' on whose lands the estate is said to be situated.[214] The estate was clearly being given outright, rather than constituting an advance on C's inheritance, since the document indicates that he was to share the rest of his parents' property equally with his brothers.

The law prescribes, and a long tradition supports it, that it is permissible for every person to do what they want with the property which they are seen to have in this life, whether to give it to holy places or to their relatives. Therefore I, in God's name A, and my sweetest wife B, to our son C, loved by us with full affection. Since you have been seen to serve us faithfully in all things and in every way, and have endured on our account many hardships and injuries in various places, and went in my place to fight the Bretons and Gascons[215] in the service of [our] lords, we therefore decided to give you something from our property; which we did. Therefore we give to you in writing our small *mansus* of D, on the territory of the illustrious man E, together with houses, buildings, unfree servants, vineyards, woods, fields, pastures, water and water[-courses], adjacencies and appurtenances, along with everything that we are seen to possess there, and we transfer it from the present day and for all time into your ownership, for you to have, hold

---

212 The word *nepos* could also sometimes be used to mean 'grandson' (as in Marculf II, 10).

213 This is in contradiction with the real purpose of the document, which is a gift; the word should have been *cessio*, not *vindicio*.

214 On military service in this period, see G. Halsall, *Warfare and Society in the Barbarian West, 450–900* (London, 2003), pp. 46–48.

215 This expedition was identified as the campaign led by Chilperic against Waroch in ca. 574–578, though it is impossible to be sure (see above, p. 41).

or exchange it, and to leave to your children or to whomsoever you decide. And when anything else from our [property] which is not entered[216] in [this] charter is left to our children,[217] you should share it with them equally.[218] And we decided to specify in this document that if ourselves or our heirs or our relatives or any other opposing[219] persons [bring up] a challenge or a dispute or [offer] any resistance regarding this document and against our wishes, let them pay *n. solidi* [to be divided] between you and the fisc,[220] and let them be unable to assert their claim; and this our decision, signed by our hands, must remain unperturbed for all time, according to the Aquilian law.[221]

No. 38: Here begins a loan security, regarding a man.

This curious text shows us someone handing over 'half' his free status ('statum meum medietatem') to another. In many respects this formula is similar to the situation described in Angers no. 18, or in Marculf II, 27, in which the beneficiary of the loan gave up his free status for a few days each week for a certain number of years, but this text adds some significant restrictions: A could order B to carry out only 'appropriate' work ('operem legitema'), and, unlike the beneficiary in Marculf II, 27, did not seem to have the right to inflict corporal punishment on him. These formulae, and this one in particular, show that the boundaries between

216 'Oblegatum' should here be read as 'adlegatum'.

217 It seems more sensible to read *remutare* as *remittere* here (as opposed to the meaning given in J.F. Niermayer, *Mediae Latinitatis Lexicon Minus*, 2nd edn. [Leiden, 2004], 'remutare' 1).

218 The phrase here is 'tu cum ipsis equalis lanciae devidere facias'. For a similar expression ('equo lance') in other cases of inheritance, see Marculf II, 12 and 14.

219 Zeumer read *militans* as referring to a soldier or servant (Zeumer, *Formulae*, p. 17), but it is also used in no. 45, which has no military background of any kind, and it seems more likely that it is here used in a less specialised sense, as a synonym to the more common *opposita persona*.

220 See above, n. 114.

221 This precise reference to the Aquilian law is unusual, in that formulae normally refer to written law only as a general source of authority rather than in such specific terms (as in the first sentence of this formula, or in Angers nos. 46 and 58, in which 'Roman law' is presented as guaranteeing the validity of property rights in general, alongside royal and scriptural authority). Even this apparently specific reference, however, remains rather vague, since it does not refer to the content of the Aquilian law (which related to compensation for damage to property), but instead seems to use it only as a general source of validation for property transactions. The Aquilian law is the only law ever referred to specifically by name in formulae; it may have been mentioned in formulae and documents of this kind only as a matter of routine (compare *Formulae Bituricenses* no. 2, *Formulae Turonenses* no. 17, and *Formulae Visigothicae* nos. 1, 6, 7, 20; Zeumer, *Formulae*, pp. 169, 144–45, 575–79 and 583–85). See Rio, 'Formulae, legal practice and the settlement of disputes in the Frankish kingdoms: the formulary of Angers', pp. 27–30.

free and unfree were not all that strictly defined in practice (though it clearly mattered a great deal to B that he was not handing over his entire free status to A), and that each arrangement was negotiated on a case-by-case basis, depending on what each party wanted from the other: freedom, like unfreedom, was not a monolithic status, but could be fragmented and bargained over at will.[222]

To the magnificent lord brother[223] A, I, B. It is established by this deed of security that I received from you, as I did indeed receive, a loan of *n*. ounces of silver. I give to you as a pledge half my [free] status, so that I will have to do whatever appropriate work you order me to do for *n*. days out of every seven. After *n*. years have elapsed, I will have to return your property, and I will recover my deed of security. And if I am slow or negligent regarding this work or [in returning] this property at the appointed *placitum*, or if I do not act according to your wish in this matter, I am to pay you back twice the amount of the loan you gave me, either to you or to whomsoever you will have given this deed of security to enforce.[224]

No. 39: Here begins a deed of security.

This case shows us a dispute, which was going to be settled formally, being in the end settled out of court: this seems to have happened after an initial court hearing, since it had already been decided that B should swear an oath to clear himself of the charge, but a different solution was apparently reached before the appointed time of his *placitum*. Given the absence of any specific details regarding the negotiations, it is difficult to understand the nature of the agreement brokered by the *boni homines*: the solution arrived at is not exactly a compromise, since A appears to drop all charges, even though there would have been little incentive for him to do this, since he had initiated the dispute. It is possible that he agreed to this as a result of intimidation or in exchange for a counter-favour, or that he had received some compensation behind the scenes.

I, A. As is not unknown, *n*. days ago a certain man named A accused [B], as he said, of having broken into his house and stolen his possessions from it, and this B was to swear an oath regarding this in the church of Saint C together with *n*. men. But they were led to an agreement through the mediation[225] of good men.[226] And I understood that B was in no way guilty of this,

---

222 See Rio, 'Freedom and unfreedom in early medieval Francia', p. 31.
223 See above, n. 122.
224 Compare Angers nos. 22 and 60; see above, p. 66.
225 *Metuantes* should here be read as *mediantes*.
226 See above, n. 124.

and I agreed to have [a document] made [and signed by my] hand regarding this matter, which I did, to the effect that I should never make any accusation or claim against B [regarding this], but, as I said, you will remain secure and in peace.[227] And if someone, whether myself or anyone else, wants to make a claim against this, let him pay *n. solidi*, and let this document signed by my hand remain firm.

No. 40: Here begins a transfer of property.

> This *dos* document differs from the others included in this formulary (Angers nos. 1c, 34, 35 and 54) in that the wife's property rights are intended to last only for the length of her own lifetime, after which the land was to return to her husband or his heirs, rather than allowing her to leave it to her own heirs or family: she therefore only enjoyed a right of usufruct, that is, use of the land and its revenue, as opposed to full ownership.[228] Unusually for formulae and documents from this period, the list of property seems to have been intended as an accurate description of the property rather than allowing for every eventuality: this may be because the gift did not involve a whole estate, but only specific parts of it, so that this particular combination of lands would not already have been described in previous documents relating to that estate.[229] The reference to marriage 'according to Roman law' seems to be essentially decorative, and did not refer to a different institution.

I, A, son of B, to my sweetest wife named C, loved with full affection. Since it is not unknown, but is known by many, that I married you according to Roman law, the thought has filled my mind that I should give you something out of what little I possess;[230] which I did. That is, I give to you the out-building of a house, with its moveable and non-moveable goods, on the land of the villa of D, on the territory of Saint E, with its estate and all that is in its enclosure next to the house of F: bedding; *n.* pieces of clothing; jewellery worth *n. solidi*; *n.* unfree servants[231] named G and H; *n.* oxen; *n.* cows with *n.* calves; *n.* sheep; *n.* pigs; a field and woods yielding *n. modii*, adjoining on one side the field of I; a vineyard measuring *n. juchi*, adjoining on one side the vineyard of J; and a meadow measuring *n. juchi*. You may have all the things listed above from the very happy day of our marriage, that

---

227 This sentence again switches continually from first- to third-person narrative, and between different persons as subjects of the first-person narrative.
228 On *dos* and women's property rights, see below, n. 233.
229 See below, p. 207.
230 The phrase is 'aliquid de rem paupertaticola mea'; see above, n. 107.
231 See above, n. 113.

is, from the present day, for as long as you live, and enjoy a permanent right of usufruct over them, without prejudice [to the saint] whose land this is known to be. And if, as I do not think will happen, either one of my relatives or any other person dares at any point to act against or breach or resist this gift, let him pay twice [the value of] what he claimed, and let him be unable [to assert his claim]; and let this gift and our decision remain firm.

No. 41: Here begins [a document awarding] the right of children.[232]

This is an example of a testament made by a couple in each other's favour, in the absence of children as direct heirs (compare Marculf I, 12 and II, 7 and 8). Formulae of this kind show that the property owned respectively by the couple remained separate in principle, since both found it necessary to guard against claims to their inheritance from their relatives: if the couple had remained intestate, the implication is that the property of each, or at least a significantly larger share of it, would have automatically reverted to their respective relatives rather than the surviving spouse.[233] Unlike Marculf II, 7 and 8, this formula does not give merely a right of usufruct over this property for the lifetime of the surviving spouse: the clause in the document made by the wife according to which her husband could then bequeath his share of her property to whomsoever he liked clearly implies that it was not to revert to her own family. This clause is remarkable in that the result would have proved highly disruptive to patterns of property-holding within the wife's family, which would have been an unusual solution in a context in which rights over land tended to be held not so much by individuals as by entire families, within which the property broadly tended to remain despite being held by different members. This clause is not present in

---

232 *Jus liberorum*, that is, when a childless couple made wills in each other's favour, a document granting the legal rights normally reserved for a son or daughter to the surviving spouse. Compare *Formulae Visigothicae* no. 24 (Zeumer, *Formulae*, p. 587); see also Isidore of Seville, *Etymologiae* V, 24, ed. W.M. Lindsay (Oxford, 1911); *Lex Romana Visigothorum Novellae Valentinianae* III, 4, Interpretatio, ed. Gustav Hänel (Berlin, 1849); *Codex Theodosianus* VIII, 17, 2–3, ed. T. Mommsen and P.M. Meyer (Berlin, 1905).

233 On the property rights of women in general and widows in particular, see J.L. Nelson, 'The wary widow', in Davies and Fouracre, eds., *Property and Power in Early Medieval Europe*, pp. 82–113. For an essentially statistical study, see also D. Herlihy, 'Land, Family and Women in Continental Europe (701-1200)', *Traditio* 18 (1962), pp. 89–120. For property exchanges between spouses (in Bavaria and for a later period), see G. Bührer-Thierry, 'Femmes donatrices, femmes bénéficiaires: les échanges entre époux en Bavière du VIIIe au Xe siècle', in Bougard, Feller and Le Jan, eds., *Dots et douaires*, pp. 329–51, at p. 332. On family strategies in the transmission of landed property, see also R. Le Jan, F. Bougard and C. La Rocca, eds., *Les transferts patrimoniaux en Europe occidentale, VIIIe–Xe siècle*, in *Mélanges de l'École française de Rome, Moyen Âge*, 111–12 (Rome, 1999). On testaments, see Nonn, 'Merowingische Testamente'.

the document issued by the husband, which may be significant, though it may have been implied in the rest of the text (in particular with the clause 'you may receive it into your possession and own it for all time, as it was owned by me, and have the free power to do whatever you decide [with it], because I prefer [to leave] this property to you rather than to my heirs', which strongly suggests full ownership, including in terms of inheritance). There are few differences between the two testaments, though it should be noted that the only lands envisaged as part of the wife's property are said to have been received from the inheritance from her relatives, as opposed to the husband's, which could also have been obtained by contract ('de qualibet contractum'). No mention is made of the property the wife would have received from her husband as part of her *dos*; whether or not this property would have counted as belonging to her or her husband would no doubt have depended on the nature of the *dos* agreement itself.[234]

To my sweetest wife[235] A, loved with full affection, I, B, in God's name, healthy of mind and body.[236] Fearing the frailty of the human body, and in order that, when we leave the light of this life and have completed the course of nature, our last day may not come to us without our having made a testament, which God forbid, and since we do not have any children between us, we have decided by our common resolve, with God's help, to have our wishes written down in this document. Therefore I, the said B, transfer to you, if you, my sweetest wife A, should survive me when I have left this light and completed the course of nature, and if we do not have any children, three [quarters] of all my property, which is in the *pagus* of C, and of that which came to me according to the laws from the inheritance of my relatives or through any contract, so that, whatever you want to do with it from then on, including houses, buildings, unfree servants,[237] vineyards, woods, meadows, fields, tenants, water and water-courses, adjacencies and appurtenances, and moveable goods in their entirety and in every particular, you may receive it into your possession and own it for all time, as it was owned by me, and have the free power to do whatever you decide [with it], because I prefer [to leave] this property to you rather than to my heirs. But the fourth part I reserve not for you, but for my relatives and legitimate heirs, so that you, my wife A, must receive and have three parts in your possession, and these heirs of mine the fourth.

---

234 On *dos*, see above, Angers no. 1.
235 The beginning of this sentence describes both A and B as feminine and masculine alternatively, so that it is difficult to tell whether this initial addressee was the husband or the wife; the rest of the document suggests that this first section was addressed to the wife.
236 This phrase was fairly common in early medieval wills.
237 See above, n. 113.

Similarly, I, A, according to the testament[238] which is contained above in this charter written for me by your wish, have also asked to have [one] written in a like manner. Therefore, if you, my sweetest husband A, should survive me when I leave this light and complete the course of nature, then three parts of my entire property, which I am seen to own in the *pagus* of E and from the inheritance of my relatives, will pass on to you [as] my heir, so that, if there are no children between us, whatever you want to do with these three parts of my property, you may possess [them], including houses, buildings, unfree servants,[239] vineyards, woods, cultivated and uncultivated fields, meadows, tenants, as they were possessed by me, and you will receive under your ownership the things which I am seen to have at present and those which are to come to me in the future, in so far as this is seen to be my property, [for you] to manage [as you like], that is, to have, hold, give and bequeath it to whomsoever you want. But the remaining fourth part I have reserved for my relatives and heirs, because I prefer to leave the property listed above, which I have assigned to you, to you rather than to my other heirs.

And although, as the law prescribes, it is not necessary to add [a penalty-clause][240] in a document such as that which we have had written between us, and [by which] we reserved one quarter [of our property for our heirs], [nevertheless,] in order to make it more secure, so that it is established more strongly between us, if [either] of us or anybody tries to initiate a dispute or put forward a challenge or make a claim against the text of this document, let him be forced to pay five pounds of gold, ten pounds of silver [to be divided] between you[241] and the fisc,[242] and let the text of this document have firm effect. Let it be entered in the municipal archive,[243] so that it may have full effect for all time. Document given.

No. 42: Here begins a deed of security.

This is a deed of security (*securitas*) made after a dispute settlement, in order to prevent further litigation on the same matter. Compare Angers nos. 5, 6, 26, 39, 43 and 44.

---

238 The manuscript has *relegionis* here, but this should no doubt be read as *relegationis* (Zeumer, *Formulae*, p. 18).

239 See above, n. 113.

240 The word *poenam* or *multam* is missing from this standard phrase; compare Marculf II, 4, *Formulae Turonenses* Add. 1 and *Formulae Bituricenses* no. 15a.

241 The manuscript has the plural *vobis* here, which could refer either to both spouses together or to the surviving spouse.

242 See above, n. 114.

243 *Gesta municipalia*; see Appendix 2.

I, A, living in the villa of Saint B [called] C. I have decided with good will to have a deed of security made for this man named D, which I did, regarding the property which he obtained by theft, on account of which I received *n*. amount of silver. Therefore I gave to you [this document] regarding this, signed by my hand and those of good men,[244] so that from this day you may remain at peace and secure regarding this matter. And if either myself or any person wants to make a claim against this deed of security, which I gave to you signed by my hand, let him pay *n. solidi* [to be divided] between you and the fisc,[245] and let him be unable to assert his claim, and let this deed of security and my decision remain firm.

No. 43: Here begins a document from a man who made a claim regarding his property.

This formula is virtually identical to Angers no. 5.

As it is known that the man named A brought a certain man named B to court regarding his property, and this B had never done him any wrong regarding this, therefore this A agreed before good men[246] to have this document made, so that he should never [again] dare to act against B [regarding this]. And if A or anyone on his behalf dares to make a claim regarding this matter, let him pay *n. solidi* [to be divided] between you [B] and the fisc,[247] and let him be unable to assert his claim, and let this document remain firm.

No. 44: Here begins a deed of security regarding an abduction.[248]

This text is fairly unclear, not least because it often switches between subjects in the first-person narrative, but it seems clear that A was issuing this deed of security (*securitas*) as a result of a dispute, to confirm that he had obtained compensation for the abduction of his female servant ('puella sua'), and that he would not pursue the matter any further. Beyond that, it is difficult to tell what exactly has happened: 'tradendi' ('to betray', 'give up' or 'hand over') in the first sentence should perhaps be read as 'traducendi' ('to carry away, transfer, remove'), as suggested in the title, with its reference to *raptus*. Both verbs can also mean 'to give in marriage' or 'to marry', which could possibly imply that

---

244 See above, n. 124.
245 See above, n. 114.
246 See above, n. 124.
247 See above, n. 114.
248 On *raptus*, see above, n. 191.

C (who may have been a free or unfree dependant of B, since B was brought to court on behalf of the two of them and must therefore have been seen as responsible for C's actions) had married the woman; the association of this text with the following formula (no. 45), which deals with the marriage of two slaves belonging to different masters, could support this interpretation, though it can only remain conjectural at best, especially in view of the absence of any settlement regarding future children. The vagueness of the word *raptus* used in the title, which could mean anything from rape to marriage without the consent of the woman's parents, contributes to this uncertainty.

I, A. It is established that I, [A], received full compensation from B on account of his having carried away[249] my[250] girl,[251] together with[252] the man named C; I [B] gave this A *n. solidi*. I [B] therefore received [a document] signed by his hand and that of good men,[253] so that from this day neither A nor any of his heirs should make any claim or accusation [regarding this], but, as I [A] said, you [B] will be left in peace regarding this matter. And if either myself or any of my relatives or anyone dares to make a claim against this deed of security, let him pay *n. solidi* [to be divided] between you and the fisc,[254] and let him be unable to assert his claim, and let this deed of security remain firm.

No. 45: Here begins a record document.

This arrangement sets out to establish exactly who and what would belong to whom after the marriage of slaves (a *servus* and *ancilla*) belonging to two different masters. The children appear to have be seen as tied more closely to the mother, since two thirds of them were to belong to her master, while the property obtained by the couple seems to have been linked more closely to her husband, since two-thirds of that was to belong to his own master. What this would have meant for the couple in practice would no doubt have depended on the type of service performed by the couple: if they were unfree rural tenants, the document

---

249 The phrase is 'pro eo quod... puella sua tradendi fuit'; 'tradendi' should probably be read as 'traducendi'.

250 As is often the case in this formulary, 'sua' should here be read as 'mea'.

251 The word *puella* could refer to a young girl or to a slave woman of any age; the latter seems more likely in this case.

252 The phrase 'aput homine nomen illo' could also mean 'before the man called C' (if C was, say, the president of the court judging the case), but since this sentence seems to be merely stating the events of the crime, it seems more likely that it here means 'with the man called C'.

253 See above, n. 124.

254 See above, n. 114.

would simply have been intended to clear up which master had rights over whose labour and property, and the family would probably not have been split up.[255]

Record [stating] in what manner A and B [reached a settlement]. It is not unknown that the slave named C and the slave-woman belonging to A, named D, got married without permission. But we both agreed to a peaceful settlement, to the effect that, out of any children who may be born to them, A will receive two thirds for his slave-woman, and B the remaining third for his slave, and out of any property which they may obtain while they are married, B will receive two thirds of this property [for] his slave and A the remaining third for his slave-woman. Accordingly, in order that there should be no dispute between us in the future, we [decided] to have two copies of the same document[256] written [and signed] by our hand regarding this; which we did. And to make this more secure, we state that if ourselves or any of our heirs or relatives or any other opposed[257] person want to go against these documents, let them be liable to pay twice the value [of what they claimed], and let this claim not have any effect, and let these contracts have unshaken and undisturbed validity.

No. 46: Here begins a document for someone who is giving some of his property to a church.

> This seems to be a gift on an altogether larger scale than most of those included in this formulary, and constitutes the only major church donation in the Angers collection. The couple is described as 'illustrious' (*illustri*), making it clear that they were of high status. They are said to be relatives of the abbot from whom they had originally bought the land; it is possible that this was the abbot of the monastery which is mentioned consistently throughout this collection, and for the use of which this formulary is likely to have been compiled, which would explain why this text, despite concerning a gift to an abbess and her convent, was included in this collection. The couple is also said to have founded the convent to which the gift was being made, so that this document may have been intended to complement a foundation charter.[258] The convent is explicitly described as 'their' monastery ('monastirio nostro'), which implies that it was still very

---

255 Charlemagne referred in a capitulary to marriages between slaves belonging to different masters, and the question of which master their children would belong to (*Capitularia* no. 58, *cap.* 1, p. 145 (*a.* 801–14).
256 See above, n. 133.
257 On *militans*, see above, n. 219.
258 Compare Marculf II, 1.

much regarded as their private property.²⁵⁹ The text puts a particular emphasis on denying any rights on this property to the heirs of the couple after their death. Since a gift to the church was meant to increase the givers' chance of salvation, the penalty-clause includes the threat of excommunication, as in the case of the two manumissions included in this collection (nos. 20 and 23).

Roman law and an ancient tradition teach that any man, if it is his wish, has the right to decide to give something out of his own property for the redemption of his soul, and that that which he has given to holy places or to a congregation of monks will never be lost, but will remain for [his] eternal grace and commemoration.²⁶⁰ Therefore I, in God's name, the illustrious man A, and my wife, the illustrious woman B, have decided by a common resolve that we should give something out of our property to our monastery, which we built together in honour of Saint C and which is built within the walls of the city of Angers, and where Abbess D is known to preside as guardian; which we were seen to do from the present day. This [gift] relates to our property in the small place called E, in the *pagus* of F, that is, in the *pagus* of G,²⁶¹ which we bought with our own money from our relative, the venerable Abbot H, and which is in our possession at present, including lands, houses, buildings, unfree servants,²⁶² tenants, vineyards, woods, meadows, pastures, water and water-courses, with moveable and non-moveable goods, with adjacencies and appurtenances belonging to it. We want this property, as we said, to be given and granted, along with what is listed above in every particular, to the said church, its congregation and its abbess, so that from this day forward the congregation of this monastery may have the free power in every way, by its own firm right, to do whatever it chooses with it for its [own] use, because we prefer [to give it to] you, the holy church built in this monastery in honour of Saint C, rather than to the rest of our heirs. And if any of our heirs decides²⁶³ to go against, oppose or make a prosecution

---

259 This is what is referred to as an *Eigenkirche* in German historiography; on this subject, see S. Wood, *The Proprietary Church in the Early Middle Ages* (Oxford, 2006), especially at pp. 111–18.

260 On gifts to the church and the idea of *memoria*, see the recent volume edited by F. Bougard, C. La Rocca and R. Le Jan, *Sauver son âme et se perpétuer: Transmission du patrimoine et mémoire au haut moyen-âge*, Collection de l'Ecole Française de Rome 351 (Rome, 2005).

261 The presence of the second reference to a *pagus* is confusing; perhaps this was a copy error, or it may have been intended to refer to a wider district which included the first one; if the latter, this would imply an unusually loose use of the terminology.

262 See above, n. 113.

263 The phrase is 'venire aut contrarius vel pulsator secterit'; the last word is probably derived from the verb *sectari*, in the sense of pursuing a course of action.

against this gift document, which we gave with good will for the remission of our sins, first let him be expelled from the community of the catholic Church and condemned to eternal damnation, and furthermore let him pay *n.* pounds of gold, ten pounds of silver to [this monastery] in association with the fisc,[264] in compensation for what he claimed, and let this document and our decision remain equally firm and stable for all time.

No. 47: Here begins a record [of judgment], in which a man defeats [his adversaries] in his lawsuit.

> This dispute relates to the appropriation of a vineyard to which A, C and D all thought they had a claim: C and D claim that the vineyard had been taken away from A and transferred to them on the authority of a *maior*. It is not exactly clear who this *maior* may have been and where his authority came from, though it seems plausible that the title here referred to the overseer of an estate, perhaps belonging to a church or monastery, who had apparently decided to reallocate some of its land, as he technically may well have had the right to do, since A does not appear to have owned this vineyard outright, but only to have been granted it as a benefice (*beneficium*), as the last sentence suggests. The authority of the *maior* to give away this property is not itself contested: rather than having to clear themselves by oath, C and D merely needed to produce him as a witness at the appointed time in order to confirm their claim. See Angers no. 53 below for the conclusion to this lawsuit; the eventual outcome is anticipated in the title given to this formula.

Record [stating] in what manner A, having come to the city of Angers before the venerable Abbot B and many other good men[265] who were with him, and whose names and signatures and marks[266] are entered below, accused certain men named C and D, and said that they had wrongly seized his vineyard in the place called E. To which C and D [gave] this answer, that they had the legitimate authority [to do this] from the *maior* named F, because he had given them this vineyard. Thus it was decided by these men that this F should appear as a witness[267] on day *x* in the city of Angers; if he did not,

---

264 See above, n. 114.
265 See above, n. 124.
266 The word *signacula* could also refer to seals, but it is unlikely that *boni homines*, even as members of the local elite, would have owned any, since seals seem to have been restricted to kings during this period.
267 The phrase is 'in autericio', which usually refers to the testimony of the person from whom a property in dispute has been bought, confirming the lawfulness of the buyer's ownership of it (see Niermayer, *Mediae Latinitatis Lexicon Minus*, 'auctoricium').

the benefice of this vineyard should be returned to this A according to the law. Done.

No. 48: Here begins a mandate.

> Unlike the formula given in no. 1b, this mandate is not made because the person issuing it could not in principle represent themselves in court; instead, B is asking someone more powerful (described as a 'dominus magnificus') to act on his behalf, effectively as a patron, in order to improve his chances of success in recovering his money. Compare Angers nos. 51 and 52, and Marculf I, 21 and 36 and II, 31.

To the magnificent lord A, B. I ask, beg, beseech and implore you by this mandate to prosecute, accuse and bring to justice on my behalf the man named C, to whom I lent n. ounces of silver, by any means by which you may recover this debt; and, whatever you may want to do, perform or accomplish on my behalf regarding this matter, know that I will accept it. Mandate [made] in the city of Angers, at the public assembly.[268]

No. 49: Here begins a document regarding a newborn child[269] found by the poor of a church.[270]

> In this case, a group of poor people officially listed among those benefiting from the material support of a church find a baby in the church, who had no doubt been left for them to find, and are allowed by a priest to sell him on to someone, apparently at a significant discount, as suggested by the reference to their being paid with a meal and 'a third' (a third of what is not entirely clear, but this may have referred to the market value of a newborn child).[271] The fact that the church

---

268 The phrase is *curia publica*, which had been used to refer to a municipal council in the late Roman empire, though it probably took on a different meaning here; see above, p. 44.

269 The child is described as 'sanguinolentus', literally 'still covered in blood', i.e. a newborn child.

270 These poor are here called *matricularii*, which referred to persons listed among the poor who received alms from a church on a regular and permanent basis. See M. Rouche, 'La matricule des pauvres: évolution d'une institution de charité du Bas-Empire jusqu'à la fin du Haut Moyen Âge', in M. Mollat, ed., *Études sur l'histoire de la pauvreté* (Paris, 1974), vol. 1, pp. 83–110; M. De Waha, 'À propos d'un article récent: quelques réflexions sur la matricule des pauvres', *Byzantion* 46 (1976), pp. 354–67; J.-P. Devroey, *Puissants et misérables: Système social et monde paysan dans l'Europe des Francs (VIe–IXe siècles)*, Classe des Lettres series 3, vol. 40 (Brussels, 2006), pp. 323–24.

271 This practice was found particularly shocking by Liebs, who counted it as evidence for the lack of social solidarity which was, in his view, characteristic of early medieval times

allowed them to keep the proceeds would no doubt have been counted as part of its duty of charity towards them, and the reference to 'custom' suggests this was a regular arrangement. This formula is similar to no. 11 of the Tours Formulae (*Formulae Turonenses*), which confirms explicitly that the child was intended to become a servant, and refers to a clause of the Theodosian code guarding the buyers of abandoned children against future claims from their parents or original masters.[272]

As we brothers,[273] in God's name [A–B], who are known to belong to the list of the poor of Saint C, and whom Almighty God is seen to feed there through the donations of Christians, found a newborn child there, who did not yet have a name, and as we were unable to find his parents among all the people, we therefore agreed unanimously, and following the wish of the priest named D, keeper of relics, that we should sell this child to the man named E; which we did. And we received for this, as is the custom among us, one third [of his value] along with a meal. And we asked for it to be written down that if we ourselves or his lord or parents want to go against this document, first let Christ the son of the living God condemn them to a terrible and fearsome eternal punishment, so that they will obtain no joy from this, but only ruin, and let them be unable to assert their claim, and let our [document] remain firm for all time.

No. 50

This is another example of a judgment in which the accused was ordered to clear himself by oath, in an effort to settle the case once and for all. In this case, the accusation related to murder, though the dispute seems to have been settled along similar principles to judgments made regarding other crimes or wrongs (compare Angers nos. 10, 11, 15, 24, 28, 29 and 30), with the difference that the judgment was here made by a count, as opposed to the abbot more often involved in settlements of disputes in this formulary. As in no. 12, which also dealt with a murder, this was no doubt due to the greater seriousness of the crime. The judgment again placed restrictions on the choice of oath-helpers to be produced by the accused, since they had to be neighbours (as in nos. 28 and 29) and of similar status to himself ('vicinus circamanentis sibi simmelus'). The phrase enlisting the 'divine

---

(Liebs, 'Sklaverei aus Not', p. 311). See also J. Boswell, *The Kindness of Strangers: The Abandonment of Children in Western Europe from Late Antiquity to the Renaissance* (New York, 1988), pp. 198–227, and especially pp. 202–04.

272 Zeumer, *Formulae*, p. 141; *Lex Romana Visigothorum Codex Theodosianus* V, 8, 1 *Interpretatio*.

273 See above, n. 122.

protection of all the saints who rest here' ('divina omnia sanctorum patrocinia qui hic requiescunt') is a direct reference to the power of relics, which were meant to act as a guarantee of the truthfulness of the oath, though in practice the oath could still be rejected by the accusers (as in Angers no. 16).[274]

(a) Here begins a judgment regarding a murder.

This man A and his brothers B–C, having come to the city of Angers before the illustrious Count D and the other *rachinburgi* who were with him, and whose names are inserted below with their signatures and marks,[275] accused a certain man named E, and said that x years before he had killed their relative F. The aforementioned E was asked what answer he would give to this accusation, and he denied it vehemently in its entirety. It was therefore decided by the judgment of these persons, with the agreement of the aforementioned brothers, that after a delay of forty [nights],[276] that is, on day y of the kalends of z,[277] he should swear together with twelve men, thirteen including himself, neighbours living close by, of similar status to himself, in the main church of this place, in this city, that he had never consented to the death of the aforementioned [F], that he had not killed him, and that he had never known or agreed that this should be done. If he is able do this, let him remain free from this charge throughout the days of his life; but if he cannot, let him pay in compensation however much the law prescribes.

(b) Here begins the record of the above judgment.

Record of an oath, [stating] in what manner and in whose presence this man named E, on day y of the kalends of March, came to the main church of this place, in the city of Angers. According to what his judgment prescribed, having sworn together with twelve men, thirteen including himself, he said: 'By this sacred place and the divine protection of all the saints who rest here, with respect to the charge that this man A and his brothers B–C have

---

274 On oaths, see above, pp. 56–57.

275 See above, n. 266.

276 The meaning of the phrase 'quatrum in suum' is unclear, though the rest of the sentence shows that it must have referred to a specific length of time. Zeumer thought it referred to a delay of forty nights, which he judged to be typical, though this is only one among several standard lengths of time prescribed by written law (forty-two nights seems to have been typical according to the late sixth-century Edict of Chilperic, *Capitularia* no. 4, cap. 8, vol. 1, at p. 9); A.C. Murray reads it as 'quadriduum', 'four days', which seems a very short time for 'E' to have found oath-helpers (Zeumer, *Formulae*, p. 22; A.C. Murray, *From Roman to Merovingian Gaul: A Reader* [Broadview, 2000], p. 578).

277 See above, n. 102.

brought against me, namely, that I killed their relative, the late F, or ordered to have him killed: I did not kill him, nor did I order that he should be killed, nor was I ever aware of or complicit in his death; and I do not owe anything in this matter save for this unchallengeable oath, which I was made to give by judgment and completed according to the laws.' These are the persons who were present and heard this oath and signed this account below by their hands. Record made...

No. 51: Here begins a mandate.

> Like no. 48, this formula deals with a man's request to a more powerful person, asking him to take up his case before the courts so as to ensure a better chance of success; in this case, the request also involves tracking down an escaped slave ('servus meus...quem mihi confugio fecit'). This escaped slave is said to be *natione gentile*, a pagan, which could indicate that he had been a war captive subsequently bought by B, who is described as *negotiens*, a merchant.

To the lord brother[278] A, I, B, a merchant. I ask, beg and implore you by this mandate to bring to justice on my behalf my slave named C, a pagan, who has fled from me, wherever you may find him, in the *pagus* or in the palace,[279] or in whatever place you may find him, by whatever [means by which you may] accuse and prosecute him on my behalf regarding this. And whatever you may do, perform or accomplish through this mandate, know that I will accept it. Mandate [made] in the city of Angers.

No. 52: Here begins another mandate.

> This is another mandate; unlike nos. 48 and 51, however, it does not relate to a specific dispute, but instead appoints A as B's legal representative for all of his transactions in a particular region; in this sense it is more similar to no. 1b, which also gave its recipient the power to act on the sender's behalf in every way for an indefinite length of time. The standard phrase 'and whatever you may do, perform or accomplish regarding this, know that I will accept it in every way' ('et quicquid exinde egeris feceris gesserisve etenim mei in omnibus habitaturis tibi essit cognuscat ratum'), which assured the legal representative that his decisions would not later be contested, but would be accepted on trust, would have taken on an even more crucial meaning when the mandate gave the recipient such wide powers.

---

278 See above, n. 122.
279 See above, n. 104.

To the magnificent lord A, I, B. I ask and implore your kindness by this mandate to pursue and bring before the courts on my behalf all of my legal affairs in the *pagus* of C, both in the *pagus* and, if need be, in the palace,[280] or in any appropriate place. And whatever you may do, perform or accomplish regarding this, know that I will agree to it in every way.

Mandate sworn and entered in the public archives;[281] and in order that it should be believed with more certainty, I have signed it below by my hand, and asked it to be signed below [by the hands of] these great men. Mandate given in the city of Angers.

No. 53: Here begins a record [of judgment].

> This is the conclusion to the lawsuit initiated in no. 47. The *maior* who had supposedly granted the vineyard to C and D failed to show up, which could suggest either that they had never had his permission in the first place, or that he had withdrawn it since then in the face of opposition from the previous occupant (A). A is therefore said to have established his opponents' default (*solsadire*), which is why the document follows the pattern of a *solsadia* (compare Angers nos. 12, 13, 14 and 16).[282] Unlike most other formulae recording the default of one of the parties, this document explicitly awarded victory to A, as had been prescribed in no. 47, though he was to get compensation only 'later' (*in postmodum*); this may imply that another hearing was necessary, as a result of which A would probably also have had to issue a deed of security to C and D in return for this compensation.

Record [stating] in what manner A, having come to the city of Angers, in [this] region, on day x of the month of y,[283] attended his *placitum* against certain men named C and D, with whom he had been in dispute z days before regarding his vineyard in the place known as E, as a result of which they had promised to produce the giver named F, [who] had granted them this vineyard. But A, having come to this *placitum*, remained at his *placitum* from morning to evening according to the laws, and established his opponents' default. For C and D were there, and they were completely unable to fulfil what they had promised. Therefore it was necessary for this A to receive this record regarding this [signed] by the hands of good men;[284] which he did, so that he should later obtain from them whatever the law prescribes.

---

280 See above, n. 104.
281 *Gesta* [*municipalia*]; see Appendix 2.
282 On these words, see above, n. 145.
283 See above, n. 102.
284 See above, n. 124.

THE FORMULARY OF ANGERS

No. 54: Here begins a transfer of property.

> This is another *dos* model, this time offering a version with more strings attached.[285] The marriage-gift to the woman is in effect to be owned by both spouses, rather than by her alone, for as long as her husband is alive; this feature is absent in the other *dos* formulae found in this formulary, which tend to emphasise, on the contrary, that the property is to be held under the wife's full ownership (nos. 1c, 34, 35 and 40). This document also controls the way in which this property is to be disposed of after the death of the couple: if they had children, the property could only be left to them, and the widow was to keep it only under what seems to be equivalent to a right of usufruct. On the other hand, if there were no children, the widow could keep the property under full ownership, and would have the right to leave it to her own heirs. Only in the latter case would the property pass fully under her family's ownership, rather than reverting to her husband's heirs (compare Angers no. 41).

What a good and joyful thing! The rights of happiness are enough to allow, and Roman law [also] prescribes, and the tradition of this place agrees, and the power of the king does not forbid, that when the most happy and desirable day of [one's] wedding arrives...[286] Therefore I, in God's name A, give in writing to my wife named B, daughter of the late C, and transfer to her in this gift document a house, together with its estate and enclosure, including moveable and non-moveable goods; bedding; a field yielding *n. modii*, adjoining on one side the field of D; a vineyard [measuring] *n. juchi*, adjoining on one side the vineyard of E; woods measuring *n. juchi*, adjoining on one side the woods of F; a meadow measuring [*n.*] *juchi*, adjoining on one side the meadow of G, [all of] which is on the territory of Saint H, on the lands of the villa of I; *n.* oxen; *n.* cows with *n.* calves; *n.* sheep; *n.* pigs; *n.* pieces of clothing; earrings worth *n. solidi*; a ring worth *n. solidi*; a bracelet worth *n. solidi*. All the things listed above, for as long as we live, we shall hold and possess jointly; [but after my death][287] you will have and possess the things listed above. And if God gives us children, they should receive it, along with any added value, in every particular; and we should confirm this, which we did, that [this property] is to revert to them after your death. And if we do not have any children, you should hold and possess all the

---

285 On this formula, see R. Le Jan-Hennebicque, 'Aux origines du douaire médiéval (VIe–Xe siècles)', in M. Parisse, ed., *Veuves et veuvage dans le haut moyen âge* (Paris, 1993), pp. 107–21, at p. 116; Nelson, 'The wary widow', p. 86.

286 Some words are missing from the manuscript here.

287 The words 'post transitum vero meum' seem to be implied here (Zeumer, *Formulae*, p. 23).

property listed above, and you may leave it to whomsoever you want. And if someone were to attempt to go or litigate against or to violate this gift document, which I asked to be made and signed with good will, with no-one compelling me, let him be forced to pay *n. solidi* [to be divided] between you and the fisc,[288] and let him be unable to assert his claim.

No. 55

This formula shows us two brothers dividing some property between them. This document almost certainly relates to a partition of inheritance made after the death of their parents. Compare Marculf II, 14 for a very similar formula (in which the property is explicitly described as an inheritance).

In God's name. The brothers A and B agreed and decided that they should divide their property between them; which they did. A received the house C, with all [that is situated within] its enclosure, and the unfree servants[289] and moveable and non-moveable goods which are seen to be contained within this house, and vineyards, woods and meadows, however much is seen to belong to this house, complete and in its entirety. And for his part his brother B received another small place [called] D, with all that belongs to it. And it was decided that they should give each other [these documents] signed by their hand, which they did, so that each should have, hold and possess what he received, and leave it to whomsoever he wants. And if one of us dares to act or make a claim against the other, let him give his share to the other, and furthermore let him pay *n. solidi*, and let him be unable to assert his claim, and let this agreement on the division [of this property] remain firm for all time.

No. 56

This is a gift made by someone to their dependant. This dependant is referred to as a *nutritus*, that is, a servant or armed retainer 'fed' in his lord's household. It is not made clear whether he was of free or unfree status;[290] retainers of either status seem to have received gifts of land in return for their service (compare Marculf

---

288 See above, n. 114.
289 See above, n. 113.
290 On the ambiguity of the terminology of freedom and unfreedom in early medieval sources, see H.-W. Goetz, 'Serfdom and the beginnings of a "seigneurial system" in the Carolingian period: a survey of the evidence', *Early Medieval Europe* 2 (1993), pp. 29–51, at p. 49.

II, 36, for a similar gift of a small piece of land to a servant).[291] The document grants him full ownership of the land, as opposed to a right of usufruct for the duration of his service.

I, A. We decided, in response to the request of our servant [B], that we should give him a certain small place named C, in the place called D, in recognition of his assiduous service and the good will which he has been seen to show us; which we did, so that from this day he may have this small place granted to him in its entirety, so that you may have the free power in every way to do whatever you want with it. And because of the attacks of evil men, we should include a penalty-clause here; which we did. And if any of my heirs or any man or other person wants to make a claim against this document, let him pay him [B] *n. solidi*, and let his claim not have any effect, and let this document remain firm for all time. With confirmation given below.[292]

No. 57

This is a formula for a divorce by mutual consent; in this case it seems to have been initiated by the woman, who is the only active party in the document. This formula and others like it (compare Marculf II, 30[293]) suggest that this kind of divorce still had currency during the early middle ages, and was generally recognised: church councils seem to have made little effort to suppress it.[294] The provision according to which a share of the fine was to be kept by the ruling judge in the event of a dispute was clearly intended as an incentive to have this agreement enforced.

To my lord husband, not the sweetest, but the most bitter and mocking A, I, B. As is not [unknown], God having divided us and turned [us] into enemies, so that we cannot be together, we therefore agreed before good men[295] that we should let each other go; which we did. If ever my husband wants to marry a woman, let him have the free power to do so; similarly, she [B]

---

291 See also *Addenda ad Formulae Senonenses recentiores*, nos. 18 and 19 (Zeumer, *Formulae*, pp. 723–4). See Rio, 'Freedom and unfreedom in early medieval Francia', pp. 25–27.
292 See above, n. 195.
293 See also *Formulae Turonenses* no. 19, *Cartae Senonicae* no. 47 and *Formulae Salicae Merkelianae* no. 18.
294 See D. d'Avray, *Medieval Marriage: Symbolism and Society* (Oxford, 2005), pp. 74–81; see also J.-A. McNamara and S.F. Wemple, 'Marriage and divorce in the Frankish kingdom', in S.M. Stuard, ed., *Women in Medieval Society* (Philadelphia, 1976), pp. 96–124.
295 See above, n. 124.

agreed that, if ever this woman named above wanted to marry, she should have the free power to do so.[296] And if after this day one of us dares to act or make a claim against this document, let him/her pay *n. solidi* to the other and to the judge mediating [in this matter], and let him/her be unable to assert his/her claim, and let this document remain firm for all time.

No. 58: Here begins a transfer of property.

> This document is not a testament, though the sharing out of claims to A's lands between his heirs makes it look like one: in this case, C gets all of his inheritance before his father's death, in exchange for his past and future service to him (compare Angers no. 37). C's duty to his father is related to the idea of service in general: the phrase 'in recognition of his assiduous service and good will' ('pro adsidua servicia sua vel benevolencia') was also used in Angers no. 56, in the case of a gift to a servant. The type of arrangement described here could also be made with someone other than a family member, in which case they were seen as amounting to an adoption (compare Marculf II, 13). All of the property given is again said to be situated on the lands of a church, and that church had the responsibility to ensure that the document was enforced, as suggested by the share of the fine earmarked for its agent in the event of a dispute. The threat of excommunication in the penalty-clause is unusual for a document concerning neither a manumission nor a gift to the church.

Roman law teaches, and the tradition of this place agrees, and royal power does not forbid, that every man should do what he wants with the property he owns at present. Thus I, in God's name A, living in the villa of B, have determined in my mind to give two [thirds] of all the property which I am seen to own in this life to my son [C] by this gift document, so that he may have it in his possession from this day, including houses, dwellings, buildings, unfree servants,[297] fields, vineyards, woods, meadows, pastures, water and water-courses, adjacencies and appurtenances, moveable and non-moveable goods. I give and transfer to him from the present day, as I said, two [thirds] of all my property, in recognition of his assiduous service and good will (but reserving the third part for my relatives and heirs), with this condition, that while I live, he should take care of me, and feed and clothe me. And let him obtain this land, and have the free power in every way to do whatever he wants with these two parts, to have, hold, give, sell or exchange

---

296 See above, n. 189; note the brief switch to the third-person narrative in the second part of this sentence.
297 See above, n. 113.

them, without prejudice to Saint D, whose land this is known to be. And if someone, as I do not believe will happen, whether myself or any of my heirs or any man or any other person, should at any time dare to go or act against this gift document, first let him incur God's judgment and be excluded from holy places, and furthermore let him pay *n*. [to be divided] between you and the representative of Saint D, and let him be unable to assert his claim by any means,[298] and let this document remain firm for all time.

No. 59

This type of document was usually referred to as *carta conculcatoria* or *de agnatione*, and was intended to allow a woman who had married an unfree man to retain her free status along with her children; there are several examples of this in formularies (compare, for instance, Marculf II, 29).[299] This solution goes against the explicit prohibition of such marriages in most of the legislation in place during this period, which condemned the woman at the very least to losing her free status as a result of her marriage to an unfree man.[300] As this formula

---

298 For *congenio* read *ingenio*.

299 Compare also *Cartae Senonicae* no. 6; *Collectio Flaviniacensis* no. 102 (= Marculf, II, 29); *Formulae Salicae Merkelianae* no. 31; *Formulae Salicae Bignonianae* no. 11; *Formulae Salicae Lindenbrogianae* no. 20; *Formulae Morbacenses* nos. 18 and 19; *Formulae Augienses Coll. B* no. 41. On marriages between free and unfree, see P. Bonnassie, 'Survie et extinction du régime esclavagiste dans l'Occident du haut moyen âge (IVe-XIe s.)', *Cahiers de civilisation médiévale* 28 (1985), pp. 307–43, at pp. 320–21; H.-W. Goetz, *Frauen im frühen Mittelalter: Frauenbild und Frauenleben im Frankenreich* (Weimar, 1995), pp. 263–67; J.L. Nelson, 'England and the Continent in the Ninth Century: III, Rights and Rituals', *Transactions of the Royal Historical Society* 14 (6th ser.) (2004), pp. 1–24, at pp. 9–10; C. Wickham, *Framing the Early Middle Ages: Europe and the Mediterranean, 400–800* (Oxford, 2005), pp. 405 and 560–61; Rio, 'Freedom and unfreedom in early medieval Francia', pp. 16–23. On the situation in the later Carolingian polyptychs, or estate-surveys, see E.R. Coleman, 'Medieval marriage characteristics: a neglected factor in the history of serfdom', *Journal of Interdisciplinary History* 2 (1971), pp. 205–19; see also J.L. Nelson, 'Family, Gender and Sexuality', in M. Bentley, ed., *Companion to Historiography* (London, 1997), pp. 153–76, p. 157.

300 *Codex Theodosianus* IV, 12; *Pactus Legis Salicae* 13, 8 and 25, 4 (pp. 61 and 94). The results of such marriages in other early medieval codes vary widely in harshness: see, for instance, *Lex Ribuaria* 61, 14–18, ed. F. Beyerle, MGH *Leges* I, 3, 2 (Hanover, 1954), pp. 112–13; *Liber Iudiciorum: sive, Lex Visigothorum* (*Leges Visigothorum*) III, 2, 3, ed. K. Zeumer, MGH *Leges* I, 1 (Hanover, 1902), pp. 134–35; *Liber Constitutionum* in *Leges Burgundionum* XXXV, ed. L.-R. von Salis, MGH *Leges* I, 2, 1 (Hanover, 1892), pp. 68–69; *Leges Alamannorum* 17, ed. K. A. Eckhardt and K. Lehmann, MGH *Leges* I, 5, 1 (Hanover, 1966), pp. 80–81. The prohibition was confirmed in subsequent legislation issued under the Carolingians (see, for example *Capitularia* no. 142, cap. 3, vol. 1, p. 292, dated to 819), though one capitulary mentions 'slaves who marry free women and whose masters then give them charters

shows, this principle was open to negotiation, and did not necessarily reflect what happened in practice. In this case, A and B added a clause, not found in any other formula of this kind, prohibiting C and her children from subsequently selling themselves to anyone but themselves or their heirs: although C and her children retained a free status, they therefore did not have the right to dispose of it outside the remit of A and B's own family. The woman's right to a third of the property acquired by the couple is a similar calculation to that made in no. 45, in which a third of the property of an unfree couple fell under the jurisdiction of the woman's master.

I, A, and my wife B. Since it is not unknown that this woman called C has married our slave called D, we decided with good will that, for as long as they are united in marriage, this woman is not to be put in our service, and her children, if she has any, must remain of free status. And, if they find it necessary to put themselves into someone's service, let them not have the right to do so, unless it is into that of ourselves and our heirs and relatives. And let this woman have a third of any property which may be acquired by them as a couple, without any claim from ourselves or our heirs. We then decided to state in this document that if we ourselves or any of our heirs or relatives or any opposing person wants to oppose the agreement given to this woman or act against this document, let him who was tempted to do this pay *n. solidi*, and let him in no way succeed in his claim, and let this document stand forever firm.

No. 60

This is a security for a loan, similar in many ways to Angers nos. 22 and 38 (see also Marculf II, 25, 26 and 27). Curiously, however, this formula does not specify what interest for the loan was involved, whether in the form of money, labour (as in no. 38) or by granting a right of usufruct over a piece of land (as in no. 22). This detail would no doubt have been included in the process of drawing up a new document on the basis of this formula.

I, A, living in the villa of B. It is established that I received, as indeed I did, a loan of *n.* ounces of silver for [my] benefit[301] from the man named B. Thus is was decided that I should hold and keep this silver from your kindness

---

to the effect that, if the couple have any children, they should remain free' (*Capitularia* no. 58, cap. 8, vol. 1, pp. 145–46, dated to 801–14), which clearly refers to the kind of document given in this formula.

301 The word is *beneficium*, though not in the more technical meaning it would later acquire in relation to grants of land.

until day [x] of the next kalends of y,[302] and that on that day I should return your silver and recover my deed of security. And I decided to have it written in this deed of security that, if I am negligent or slow in doing this, or do not act according to your wish, I should give back twice [the value of] your property, either to yourself, or to whomsoever you will have given this deed of security to enforce.

---

302 See above, n. 102.

PART TWO

THE FORMULARY OF MARCULF

INTRODUCTION

The Marculf collection has acquired the reputation of being the archetypal formulary. It has been the constant reference point in defining our idea of the genre of formulae as a whole, and largely retains its status as the most dominant collection, and the standard against which to judge all other formularies. Marculf enjoyed, and still enjoys, this special status because it is the longest collection, the best known, the most studied, and that to which the greatest number of manuscripts is relevant. On the whole it is perceived as a fixed text transmitted coherently. It is widely seen as typical, despite being in many respects exceptional: it is usually more clearly marked out in the manuscripts than most other collections, though even there the tradition is less coherent than we might expect; it is organised deliberately and rather neatly, according to a distinction between centre and locality pleasing to the modern reader; and, last but not least, it boasts a preface and a named author, when other collections offer neither. The temptation is great to give it the same treatment as a literary text, if only because such a treatment is so much more rewarding in Marculf's case than for other formularies: we have some biographical detail on the author (a monk, aged seventy or more, with bad eyesight and trembling hands); we know the collection was commissioned by a certain Bishop Landeric, probably at some point in the second half of the seventh century, and that it was intended to help to train apprentices as well as to serve as a source of inspiration for scribes. Above all, we are here dealing with actual people, and this has proved appealing in a context of otherwise almost complete anonymity. Paradoxically, it is precisely these exceptional aspects, and in particular the presence of an unusually strong authorial voice, that have proved most enduringly appealing to modern historians, and have led them to accept this collection as the ideal form to which all other formularies aspired, but which they failed to take on.

THE SCOPE OF THE COLLECTION

Far more has been written about Marculf alone than about all other formularies put together. This consistently high level of interest has been mostly due to the presence of the models for royal documents included in Book I, which were given particular prominence due to the long-standing interest of early medievalists in royal power and politics, and in the organisation of the royal court as a legal and administrative centre. Unlike private charters, a few royal documents have survived from this period, essentially through the archive of the monastery of St Denis, so that models drawn from Book I also offered better grounds for comparison between formulae and actual documents. The presence in such numbers of formulae linked with the king is indeed atypical, and no other collection presents us with a comparable array of royal documents, save for the *Formulae Imperiales*, which are exceptional in having apparently been written in connection with the chancery of Louis the Pious.[303] By contrast, there is no evidence that Marculf wrote in connection with any royal court.[304] The success of his collection, as opposed to the apparently short-range influence of the *Formulae Imperiales*, which survive in only one manuscript, shows that this formulary answered the needs of a variety of different institutions over a very long period of time, since it survives in no fewer than seven manuscripts dating from the late eighth to the tenth centuries, and many individual formulae extracted from it can be found reused in other formularies.[305] If, as I suggested, adaptations and modifications subsequently brought to these texts can be held to constitute a rough index of their continued usefulness,[306] the formulae of Book I cannot be considered to have been the most crucially useful part of this formulary, since they underwent fewer changes in their text and organisation during the process of copying than Book II. Even these, however, can be found in an updated version in two manuscripts, in which Merovingian features were replaced with Carolingian ones:[307] the whole collection therefore seems to have continued to prove useful, to a lesser or greater degree, to many ecclesiastical institutions down to the end of Carolingian rule.

As Marculf's dedication of the book to a bishop also suggests, the view of royal activity given in these formulae responded not to the needs of the

---

303 See above, pp. 8–9.
304 See below, pp. 113–17.
305 The formularies of Tours, Merkel, Reichenau and St Emmeram all use texts extracted from the Marculf corpus (Zeumer, *Formulae*, pp. 128–65, 239–63, 339–64 and 461–68).
306 See above, pp. 30–31.
307 See above, p. 31.

royal court itself, but to those of separate religious institutions. Many of the royal documents included in this collection would have been needed by these institutions in order to record the gifts and immunities bestowed on them by royal favour, and to enable them to keep up a relationship with the court at a distance, as with the model letter of greetings to members of the royal court given in II, 44. Other formulae among those included in Book I are linked with the presence of the king himself, as in the case of *placita* or records of disputes: these formulae would clearly have been needed mostly by the monasteries and episcopal cities placed on the itinerary of kings, which would have been responsible for providing records for the decisions taken there through their own *scriptoria*.

Although Marculf, instead of enjoying a particularly close connection with the royal court, is therefore in principle as much bound to the local sphere as the formulary of Angers, its scope is nevertheless different. It contains many formulae concerning the same subjects as those found in the Angers collection, particularly among the formulae included in Book II, dedicated to local matters: sales; loans; records of dispute; self-sales; a divorce; a testament made by a childless couple in each other's favour; a description of how to enter deeds into an archive according to the procedure appropriate for the *gesta municipalia*; the replacement of lost documents; an agreement to let the bride of an unfree man retain her free status along with her children. To this extent, the two collections reflect similar expectations of what situations a legal scribe would need to be prepared to encounter in the course of his career. As a rule, however, Marculf seems to relate to a wider, and far grander, world than that of Angers: the properties transferred are larger, and the people involved often of a higher status, even outside Book I. The figure of the bishop, which makes an appearance only once in the Angers formulary, in order to deal with what is described as an unsually important case (no. 32), here constitutes a major character, as could be expected given the identity of the collection's dedicatee. Marculf's disputes were settled before kings, counts and bishops; abbots and *boni homines* intervening in local disputes feature far less prominently. This was not due to a fundamental difference in the nature of these transactions: as we have seen, the matters they dealt with often had a similar purpose, so that a distinction emphasising the civic 'Romanness' of Angers, based on references to late antique institutions, and the 'Frankishness' of Marculf, based on its interest in the Frankish elite and its references to Salic law, would only be artificial. It seems more probable that the difference was linked with social status: the people involved in Marculf's formulary brought their business before

THE FORMULARY OF MARCULF 107

higher authorities, often even before the king, simply because they had the power to do so, and because this gave their transactions greater validity and prestige, whereas those involved in the Angers formulary did not enjoy such a privileged access to them, and accordingly settled their disputes and transactions only in the local courts. It is telling that documents written for such different classes of persons should display so many similiarities, since it suggests a level of continuity across the social spectrum: the people described in the Angers collection thus seem to have been equally active and shrewd in using the legal system to their advantage as the members of the higher social spheres with whom Marculf was concerned.

DATE AND PLACE OF ORIGIN

Marculf and Landeric

The identity of Marculf himself has been the object of less discussion than that of the Bishop Landeric who, according to Marculf's preface, commissioned the work. It is generally assumed that one should look for Marculf's monastery in the diocese of which Landeric was bishop: the main problem has therefore been seen as simply that of identifying this diocese. A Landeric is known to have granted a privilege to the abbey of St Denis as bishop of Paris in 658. Bignon, the first scholar to express a view on the subject in 1613, concluded that this was Marculf's Landeric, and that Marculf must have been a monk at St Denis.[308] This placed Marculf firmly in the Merovingian period, which fits in with the text's occasional references to the mayor of the palace, a Merovingian high office which disappeared after Pippin, a mayor of the palace himself, deposed the last Merovingian king in 751. However, many scholars did not consider this identification as decisive, and other hypotheses were put forward. Launoy, Du Pin and Fabricius all suggested that there was also a Landeric who was bishop of Meaux from 680: although he does not appear in any list of bishops, he is mentioned in the *Gesta* of the bishops of Cambrai.[309] Somewhat less convincingly, Adrien de Valois

308 Bignon, *Marculfi monachi formularum libri duo*. Mabillon agreed with him: Mabillon, *Annales ordinis S. Benedicti*, vol. 1, p. 418.
309 J. de Launoy, *Inquisitio in chartam immunitatis quam beatus Germanus parisiorum episcopus suburbano monasterio dedisse fertur* (Paris, 1689), p. 26; L.E. Du Pin, *Nouvelle bibliothèque des auteurs ecclésiastiques*, vol. 6 (Paris, 1692), p. 36; J.A. Fabricius, *Bibliotheca latina mediae et infimae aetatis* (Hamburg, 1735–46), vol. 25. See *Gesta episcoporum Cameracensium*, in *Chronica et gesta aevi Salici*, ed. G.H. Pertz, MGH *Scriptores* VII (Stuttgart, 1846), II, 46, p. 465.

thought that the name 'Landericus' should be read as 'Candericus', Bishop of Lyon; however, if he had any reasons to suppose this, he did not disclose them.[310] Even more improbably, Marculf was identified with a 'Marculphus' named in the *Life* of Saint Austregisel, as a later abbot of the saint's monastery in Bourges;[311] this is neither here nor there, as Marculf was apparently not a particularly uncommon name.

Bignon's opinion that Marculf must have written at St Denis at some point in the 650s has generally been accepted. Its only serious competitor was that of Zeumer, who edited the text in the early 1880s, and who, like Launoy, Du Pin and Fabricius, argued that the Landeric of the preface must have been the Bishop of Meaux, which would place Marculf towards the end of the seventh century. Zeumer supported this argument by claiming that Marculf I, 2 was based on a royal exemption given in 635 to the monastery of Rebais, which is in the diocese of Meaux. This argument no longer holds good, because the diploma which Zeumer thought had provided a model for Marculf was later convincingly shown to be a forgery.[312] The two parties, the Bignonists and the Zeumerists, pursued a lengthy dispute over whether Marculf wrote in or near Paris in the 650s (upheld by French scholars in general) or in Eastern Francia in the late seventh century (upheld by their

---

310 A. de Valois, *Disceptationis de basilicis defensio* (Paris, 1660), p. 152.

311 *Vita Austrigisili episcopi Biturigi* 7, in *Passiones vitaeque sanctorum aevi Merovingici et antiquorum aliquot (II)*, ed. B. Krusch, MGH *Scriptores* IV (Hanover, 1902), p. 196; M.A. Dominicy, *De treuga et pace in bellis privates* (Paris, 1669), p. 3; *Histoire littéraire de la France*, vol. 3 (Paris, 1735), p. 567.

312 Both of the documents thought to be the basis for Marculf I, 1 and 2, Dagobert's diploma and Burgundofaro's privilege for Rebais (Kölzer DM. †49, vol. 1, pp. 126–27; Pardessus, *Diplomata* no. 275, vol. 2, p. 40), are now thought to be forgeries. See Zeumer, 'Über die älteren fränkischen Formelsammlungen', pp. 39–40; Krusch, 'Ursprung und Text', pp. 241–44; H. Sprömberg, 'Marculf und die fränkische Reichskanzlei', *Neues Archiv* 47 (1928), pp. 77–142. The authenticity of the Rebais documents was contested by F. Beyerle, 'Das Formelbuch des westfränkischen Mönchs Marculf und Dagoberts Urkunde für Rebais a. 635', *Deutsches Archiv für Erforschung des Mittelalters* 9 (1951), pp. 43–59, and L. Levillain, 'Le formulaire de Marculf et la critique moderne', *Bibliothèque de l'Ecole des Chartes* 84 (1923), pp. 21–91. See also E. Ewig, 'Beobachtungen zu den Klosterprivilegien des 7. und frühen 8. Jahrhunderts Adel und Kirche', in Ewig, *Spätantikes und fränkischen Gallien: Gesammelte Schriften (1952-1973)*, vol. 2, ed. H. Atsma (Zurich/Munich, 1979), pp. 411–26, at p. 420; E. Ewig, 'Das Formular von Rebais', in Ewig, *Spätantikes und fränkischen Gallien*, vol. 2, pp. 456–84, at p. 463, n. 36; E. Ewig, 'Marculfs Formular "De privilegio" und die merowingischen Bischofsprivilegien', in H. Mordek, ed., *Aus Archiven und Bibliotheken. Festschrift für Raymund Kottje zum 65. Geburtstag* (Frankfurt, 1992), pp. 51–69; Heidrich, 'Titulatur und Urkunden', p. 181; B. Rosenwein, *Negotiating Space: Power, Restraint, and Privileges of Immunity in Early Medieval Europe* (Ithaca, NY, 1999), p. 67.

German counterparts).[313] The issue was complicated by the fact that in one manuscript the name given for the commissioning bishop was 'Aeglidulf' instead of 'Landeric'.[314] Some got so excited over this as to suggest that Marculf dedicated his work to several different bishops at the same time, and simply changed the name in each of the manuscripts he sent out, using his own preface as a formula.[315] But this is contradicted by Marculf's implication that his dedicatee had commissioned the work (with his reference to 'the task assigned by you' and the bishop's 'orders'), since it is highly unlikely he would have received several such requests at the same time. On the whole, Bignon's opinion has triumphed, but the argument generated a curious compromise, according to which Marculf wrote in or near Paris, probably at St Denis, around 700. This contradicts both of the hypotheses put forward: either the Landeric of the preface was bishop of Paris, in which case Marculf wrote in the 650s, or Marculf wrote *ca*. 700, in which case his Landeric most definitely cannot have been bishop of Paris, which eliminates any reason why Marculf should be placed there rather than anywhere else in the kingdom.[316]

---

313 The dating of Marculf was the object of a long-standing feud between Zeumer ('Der Maior domus in Marculf I, 25', *Neues Archiv* 10 [1885], pp. 383–88; 'Neue Erörterungen über ältere fränkische Formelsammlungen', *Neues Archiv* 11 [1886], pp. 313–358) and A. Tardif ('Etude sur la date du formulaire de Marculf', *Nouvelle revue historique de droit français et étranger* 8 [1884], pp. 557–65; 'Nouvelles observations sur la date du formulaire de Marculf', *Nouvelle revue historique de droit français et étranger* 9 [1885], pp. 368–75). The debate was continued by Krusch ('Ursprung und Text') and Levillain ('Le formulaire de Marculf et la critique moderne'); see also K. Zeumer, 'Zur Herkunft der Markulfischen Formeln. Eine Antwort an G. Caro', *Neues Archiv* 30 (1905), pp. 716–19; W. Levison, 'Zu Marculfs Formularbuch', *Neues Archiv* 50 (1935), pp. 616–19; W. Levison, 'Kleine Beiträge zu Quellen der fränkischen Geschichte', *Neues Archiv* 27 (1902), pp. 331–408, at pp. 331–56; and Beyerle, 'Das Formelbuch des westfränkischen Mönchs Marculf und Dagoberts Urkunde für Rebais a. 635'. Krusch, writing during the First World War, was particularly scathing: 'one cannot hold it against the Parisians that they should look to resist the possibility that they could be robbed of such an illustrious fellow-countryman; but perhaps their advocate Tardif did his work a little too lightly, and in any case he lacked the knowledge to be able to join in the study of the text' ('Ursprung und Text', p. 237).

314 Paris BnF lat. 2123, fol. 105v.

315 Sickel, *Acta regum et imperatorum Karolinorum*, vol. 1, p. 112, n. 1. C. Pfister, 'Note sur le formulaire de Marculf', *Revue Historique* 50 (1892), pp. 43–63, at pp. 58–59, even suggested that Marculf first dedicated his work to Landeric, but that Landeric left then for one of his monasteries in the Hainaut before Marculf got the chance to send it to him, so that Marculf then decided to dedicate his book instead to Clodulf (for Aeglidulf) in Metz, which is rather far-fetched.

316 See, for instance, I.N. Wood, *The Merovingian Kingdoms, 450–751* (London, 1994),

So was Landeric bishop of Paris? Metz? Meaux? Was he both bishop of Paris and auxiliary bishop of Meaux at the same time? Was he the Landeric who was the son of Saint Vincentius and Saint Waldetrud, who himself has had his bishopric variously attributed to Metz and Meaux? Since Landeric, judging from this sample, was clearly not an uncommon name, it is doubtful whether any of these identifications can ever be securely established as the correct one. Furthermore, despite general tacit agreement to the contrary, one cannot assume in any case that this Landeric would necessarily have been Marculf's diocesan bishop, so that even if it was possible to identify the Landeric of the preface, which seems increasingly unlikely, this would bring us no further to establishing where Marculf himself wrote and lived.[317] This conclusion might be disappointingly vague, but at least it should cause no further worry.

Dating the collection

As Zeumer pointed out, the text itself seems to support the idea that Marculf wrote *ca.* 700, since the mention of the mayor of the palace as having a major role in the royal tribunal in I, 25 fits with a similar situation in a document from 697, whereas the attendance of the mayor of the palace at the royal tribunal is not attested in earlier *placita* drawn up closer to the time of Landeric of Paris.[318] It was argued against this by both Tardif and Krusch that this document from 697 was rather atypical, in the sense that the accused was Pippin II, the mayor of the palace, and that his two sons Drogo and Grimoald were both present, the former in his capacity as defendant.[319] Both Tardif and Krusch agreed that these exceptional circumstances would have ensured a role for the mayor of the palace even if it had been normally unthinkable for him to fulfil such a function in the court tribunal. This, however, is not in itself an argument against Zeumer's view, but rather tends to confirm it, if one considers that this presence at the court tribunal can only be explained by the change in the position of the mayor of the

---

p. 241: Landeric of Paris could not have commissioned Marculf's work in the late seventh to early eighth centuries, since he died a long time before this date.

317 Hraban Maur, writing in Fulda, thus dedicated his *Expositiones in Leviticum* to Bishop Freculph of Lisieux, who was not his diocesan bishop.

318 Kölzer DM. 149 (*a.* 697), pp. 374–76; compare Kölzer DDM. 93, 95, 94 (*ca.* 658), and 88 (*ca.* 659). On the debate over the dating of the Marculf collection, see above, n. 313.

319 Tardif, 'Nouvelles observations sur la date du formulaire de Marculf'; Krusch, 'Ursprung und Text', pp. 237–38.

palace, by then all-powerful. The *maior domus* is mentioned three times in the main text of Marculf, at I, 24, I, 25 and I, 34. I, 34 also suggests an all-powerful mayor: the citizens address him and the king without apparent differentiation. I, 24 even refers to the mayor as a *princeps*, a prince, which was a title normally used by the king.[320] It should be noted, however, that the importance of the mayor of the palace in this collection is not completely decisive in terms of dating, since there were also some powerful mayors in the mid-seventh century.

Another argument against the dating of Marculf to the 650s is the reference to Saint Martin's cape in Marculf I, 38 ('the said B... should swear on Saint Martin's cape (*capella*) in our palace, where the other oaths take place').[321] Saint Martin's cape is not documented in the royal palace until the reign of Theuderic III, in 682.[322] Ewig speculated that Balthild, Theuderic's mother, had been responsible for adding this relic to the royal collection.[323] If that is true, this obviously argues against an early dating of Marculf, although the reverse case could admittedly be made, if an early dating of Marculf were used as an argument against Ewig's suggestion. In view of the uncertainty surrounding the dating of Marculf, however, such an argument would not be very sound.

Uddholm, on philological grounds, also placed Marculf in the late seventh century.[324] He placed the formulary after 688, arguing that Marculf, in his standard descriptions of landed property, places the word *accolabus* (rural tenants) before the word *mancipiis* (unfree servants or tenants).[325] Uddholm argued that, from 688–695, the royal chancery, which before had systematically used the order *mancipiis – accolabus* in the documents

---

320 The mayor also appears in Marculf Supplement no. 3, a model for a formal letter of greetings.
321 Fouracre, '"*Placita*" and the settlement of disputes in later Merovingian Francia', p. 36, n. 47.
322 Kölzer DM. 126; see also *Chartae latinae antiquiores* XIII, ed. H. Atsma and J. Vezin (Dietikon-Zurich, 1981), no. 567, p. 76: 'in oraturio nostro, super cappela domni Martine'.
323 J.L. Nelson, 'Queens as Jezebels: Brunhild and Balthild in Merovingian history', in D. Baker, ed., *Medieval Women: Essays dedicated and presented to Professor Rosalind M.T. Hill* (Oxford, 1978), pp. 31–77, reprinted in J.L. Nelson, *Politics and Ritual in Early Medieval Europe* (London, 1986), pp. 1–49, at pp. 40–41; E. Ewig, 'Das Privileg des Bischofs Berthefrid von Amiens für Corbie von 664 und die Klosterpolitik der Königin Balthild', in Ewig, *Spätantikes und Fränkisches Gallien*, vol. 2, pp. 538–83, at p. 581 and n. 98.
324 A. Uddholm, *Formulae Marculfi: Etudes sur la langue et le style* (Uppsala, 1953), p. 20.
325 Marculf I, 13, 14, 33; II, 3, 4, 11, 19 and 23.

it produced,[326] switched with equal consistency to the order *accolabus – mancipiis*, as found in Marculf.[327] He therefore concluded that Marculf wrote after this change took place. Most of these diplomas are originals, so that there can be no doubt as to their authenticity. It is of course possible to argue, on the contrary, that this change in the order of this expression in original documents actually reflects the influence of Marculf's work on chancery practice, which would mean that Marculf must in fact have written *before* the 690s, but this view would be hard to sustain: it would be strange for Marculf's work to have influenced chancery practice only in this minute way and not to have left any other traces of its influence until a later time. Although the language of the Marculf formulae is not otherwise very different from that of mid-seventh-century documents,[328] it would be unrealistic to expect it to present an entirely consistent stage of diplomatic development: the seventy-year-old Marculf, who refers to a lifetime of scribal activity, would have undergone his initial training as a scribe several decades before compiling his formulary, and many of his formulae could well have been based on older documents in any case.

The *terminus ante quem* was thought by Heidrich to be 721, since Marculf I, 16 is thought to have been used as the model for the immunity given by Theuderic IV to St Bertin, though this argument again no longer holds good, as this is now also thought to be a forgery.[329] One has to admit that using similarities with diplomas in order to date formulary collections is a risky strategy, especially given that we are most of the time not dealing with originals: later scribes often changed the style of documents in the process of copying them into cartularies, and sometimes their content too, in the hope of securing more extensive rights than had originally been envisaged, often to such an extent as to result in outright forgery.[330] On the other

---

326 Kölzer DDM. 89, †120, 124, 131; this order also appears in the formulary of Angers, no. 46, though the order of items in such lists is not systematic in that collection.

327 Kölzer DDM. 142, 153, 159, 167, 187. Kölzer gives different dates for these diplomas, but the general pattern can still be observed, so that Uddholm's point is altered only in placing the change at some time between *ca.* 690 and 694 instead. The same order is found in later formularies, as in *Formulae Turonenses* no. 1b or *Formulae Salicae Merkelianae* no. 9.

328 I. Woll, *Untersuchungen zu Überlieferung und Eigenart der merowingischen Kapitularien*, Freiburger Beiträge zur mittelalterlichen Geschichte 6 (Frankfurt, 1995), pp. 225–27.

329 Heidrich, 'Titulatur und Urkunden', pp. 182–184; Kölzer DM. †180.

330 All of the royal documents which Krusch thought had provided models for Marculf (Krusch, 'Ursprung und Text'), and which he used to support the idea of a very late date, have turned out to be either forgeries (as in the case Kölzer DDM. † 49, 102, 125, 180) or interpolated (Kölzer DDM. 128 and 134). Their similarity with Marculf is sometimes only

hand, the fact that the use of Marculf in royal and private documents can only be documented from the 730s or slightly before also tends to support a later date.[331]

Although it is difficult to narrow down the date of this collection to anything more precise than the second half of the seventh century, the consequences of this are not so great as to reduce its usefulness as a source. As suggested in the introduction to this volume, narrowing down the chronological scope of formularies is not in any case the most fruitful way of looking at these texts, since the texts included in these collections would have been based on actual documents often produced decades earlier, and the same formulae were to continue being copied and used for centuries afterwards.[332]

Marculf and St Denis

The identification of Marculf as a monk of St Denis, first suggested almost four hundred years ago by Bignon, is now generally accepted as correct, perhaps more as a result of the action of time than because the case to be made for this is particularly compelling. The arguments put forward in favour of this hypothesis are:

1) that the contents of some Merovingian diplomas in favour of St Denis show some similarities with Marculf;[333]
2) that the models on which Marculf would have based the formulae included in Book I, concerning royal charters, could only have been found in a royal archive; and

---

superficial: Kölzer DM. 126 thus does show a similar situation as Marculf I, 38, but it is unlikely that Marculf was based on it because the circumstances of the dispute are different (and Marculf is unlikely to have changed them just for the sake of it), and because the solutions are also different: in Marculf the accused is the one that has to give the oath, whereas in the document it is the accuser. The other examples given by Krusch were linked with Marculf only by virtue of a similar subject, which is not enough to suggest a direct link (Kölzer DDM. 137 for Marculf I, 37; 86 for I, 11; 166 for I, 4; 167 for I, 38). Kölzer DM. 145 for St Sergius in Angers (694–711) does have evident textual links with Marculf I, 4 and 17, but it is difficult to say whether it is based on Marculf or the other way around (and the early as well as vague date for this document does not help to support Krusch's argument in any case). On formulae and charters, see above, pp. 25–28.

331 Heidrich, 'Titulatur und Urkunden'; see also Zatschek, 'Die Benutzung der *Formulae Marculfi*'.
332 See above, pp. 28–33.
333 For instance Kölzer DM. 137.

3) that St Denis was more likely to have needed formulae linked with the royal court than other monasteries, because it was a major beneficiary of royal patronage from the seventh century onwards.[334]

Let us begin with the question of the diplomas. Although it may have been a clinching argument at one time, it can no longer be held as such now: as we have already seen, a large number of the diplomas which at one time or another have been thought to be linked with Marculf have since been shown to be forgeries.[335] As to surviving original charters, textual correspondences are never very close, and the presence of Marculf-like diplomas at St Denis could simply be due to the disproportionately high level of survival of royal diplomas in the St Denis archive, which offers far greater grounds for comparison than other archives.[336] Links made between Marculf and royal *placita* preserved by St Denis are particularly unrepresentative, since there is little else to compare them with: the majority of the surviving *placita* for the Merovingian period only survive through the St Denis archive in any case.[337] The charter evidence is therefore not enough in itself to make a convincing case for placing Marculf at St Denis, both because of the debated authenticity of many of the documents considered, and because of the comparatively very low rate of survival of such documents for other monastic archives of the Merovingian period.

As for the presence of models for royal letters in Marculf's formulary, and the idea that he would have needed access to the royal archives to write them, we are here dealing with only two formulae written from one king to another, I, 9 and 10, and their presence is hardly enough in itself to prove a link with St Denis simply because it was close to Paris. Model royal letters can also be found in other collections which were not linked to royal centres,

---

334 Uddholm, *Formulae Marculfi: Etudes sur la langue et le style*, p. 21.

335 Such as Kölzer DM. †102, a gift from Childeric II to Bishop Amandus written at St Denis (pp. 147–48 and 262–63).

336 Uddholm presented the same characteristics in the same diplomas (Kölzer DM. 142, 159, 167 and 187) once as reflecting a change in royal chancery practice over time, and a second time as reflecting the particular house-style of St Denis (Uddholm, *Formulae Marculfi: Etudes sur la langue et le style*, pp. 20–21; note that Kölzer DM. 153 is a *placitum* referring to St Germain-des-Prés and not St Denis, yet still uses the *accolabus – mancipiis* order). If this order was the result of a general change in chancery practice, then it does not reflect a link between Marculf and St Denis; on the other hand, if it simply reflects a version particular to St Denis, it can no longer be used for dating.

337 Fouracre, '"*Placita*" and the settlement of disputes in later Merovingian Francia', pp. 26–27.

as for instance in the St Gall collection.[338] It is furthermore a little difficult to assess exactly for what use the royal letters in formularies were intended. An analogy may be made with a rather curious feature of the Flavigny collection (*Collectio Flaviniacensis*), a formulary merging Marculf together with other formulae, which begins with a letter purportedly written by Helena to Constantine, followed by Constantine's reply. The following formulae contain a number of letters attributed to other fourth-century imperial and Christian figures, among them Athanasius. It is undeniable that these are indeed imperial and episcopal letters, but they were obviously impossible to reuse in the same form. The intent here seems rather to have been to provide model letters with an impressive pedigree, very little intrinsic content, and smooth beginnings and endings, which, as everyone knows, are the hardest bits to write. One does not necessarily need a royal archive at hand in order to obtain this result: despite the presence of these Byzantine letters, no one has yet thought of suggesting that the Flavigny collection was compiled in Constantinople.

One should be careful in any case in thinking about what a royal archive would have looked like in the late seventh century. Even if one insisted that Marculf would have had to be writing close to a royal centre, St Denis would still not be the only candidate, as there were other royal centres in the Frankish kingdoms which could just as easily have allowed access to royal documents, such as, for example, the Austrasian city of Metz, where the *Liber epistolarum*, containing a large number of royal letters, was compiled in the sixth century.[339] Judging by its contents, Marculf would in fact seem to make more sense in Eastern Francia, since this is where surviving documents echo Marculf most early and regularly, for instance in the documents issued by the mayors of the palace;[340] but sadly even this last hypothesis does not point to a definite geographical anchor for Marculf, since it is equally, if not more, likely that Marculf's collection came to be distributed primarily through its recipient, Landeric, rather than through the author himself, in which case this would only constitute evidence for Landeric's presence in the East, but not necessarily for Marculf's.

---

338 *Formulae Sangallenses* (Zeumer, *Formulae*, pp. 378–437).

339 E. Malaspina, *Il* Liber epistolarum *della cancelleria austrasica (sec. V-VI)* (Rome, 2001), p. 20.

340 Pfister also cites the fact that I, 40, in which an unnamed king orders oaths to be given to himself and his son, whom he has just made king, could refer to Dagobert I and Sigibert, who became king of Austrasia, as support for an East Frankish location ('Note sur le formulaire de Marculf'). On the documents of the mayors of the palace, see Heidrich, 'Titulatur und Urkunden', pp. 171–95.

Let us now consider the argument that St Denis would have needed model royal letters more than any other monastery or episcopal see because it stood in high favour with the kings of the later Merovingian period. This is by far the least convincing part of the argument in favour of placing Marculf at St Denis. A large number of copies of Marculf were made to suit the purposes of other institutions even during the Merovingian period: although St Denis no doubt did need royal formulae, other monasteries clearly also did, as did Landeric and his episcopal chancery. Since institutions other than St Denis were interested in copying these formulae very soon after Marculf put his text together, there is no reason to think that St Denis is necessarily where they would have been compiled in the first place. Indeed, one could just as easily put forward the point that a monastery which did not enjoy the same level of royal favour as St Denis, but desired and sought it actively, would also have been interested in having model documents ready and keeping themselves up to date with royal practice. Krusch even suggested that Marculf was not in fact quite up to the standard of royal chancery practice, although his devastating description of Marculf's incompetence as a notary is rather too extreme: after all, if it was good enough for a large number of early medieval scribes, who copied all or part of Marculf in their manuscripts and their own compilations, it should be good enough from the perspective of any modern historian.[341]

W. John suggested, because Marculf includes models for royal acts, that Marculf must have been at the head of a royal school destined to train notaries; Riché agreed, and thought that he may have been a royal notary who, having retired to St Denis, offered Landeric some of the models he had used to teach young notaries.[342] This way of ultimately placing Marculf

---

341 According to Krusch, Marculf comes across more as a 'bookish' type following literary conventions than as a scribe involved in 'practical' matters ('Überall tritt er uns vielmehr als reiner Buchgelehrter entgegen, der bei seiner Arbeit literarische Zwecke verfolgt, und auch die weitere Untersuchung wird noch zeigen, wie wenig er sich auf den praktischen Geschäftsverkehr verstanden hat', 'Ursprung und Text', p. 243); but this distinction does not really apply to the early medieval period, since even great writers such as Einhard also wrote charters (for a translation of these, see P.E. Dutton, *Charlemagne's Courtier: The Complete Einhard* [Broadview, 1998], pp. 41–62).

342 John, 'Formale Beziehungen'; Riché, *Education et culture dans l'Occident barbare*, p. 286. See also P. Riché, 'La formation des scribes dans le monde mérovingien et carolingien', in W. Paravicini and K.-F. Werner, eds., *Histoire comparée de l'administration (IVe-XVIIIe siècles): Actes du XIVe colloque historique franco-allemand (Tours, 27 mars-1er avril 1977)*, Beihefte der Francia 9 (Munich, 1980), pp. 75–80, at p. 76, and P. Riché, *Enseignement du droit en Gaule du VI au XIe siècle* (Milan, 1965), pp. 9–10; Bresslau, *Handbuch der Urkundenlehre*, vol. 2, p. 231. This view of Marculf has become very pervasive: in a recent textbook,

in the secular sphere is not necessarily wrong.³⁴³ The main problem with it is that it relies on explaining away the evidence rather than relying on it: Marculf was after all a monk writing for a bishop, and there is no mention in the preface of a lay context, or even of a lay person. When Marculf refers to a lifetime of writing charters, it would seem from his own statement that he was taught, presumably as a young man, in the same monastery as that in which he was living at the time of writing ('I have put together... these things which I have learned from my elders according to the custom of the place in which we live'). Nowhere is there a hint that Marculf ever worked for anybody or anything apart from his own monastery. The evidence for Marculf's 'special' connection with the royal court therefore seems tenuous to say the least. It is not impossible, as Riché thought, that he became a monk only in his old age, after spending his life as a layman drawing up documents and teaching pupils at a royal chancery, but this remains a far-fetched hypothesis. Even Marculf's putative involvement with the royal chancery, in itself highly dubious, did not imply a lay status, since that role could also be fulfilled by particular monasteries: although these included St Denis, it was only one among several. Naturally, none of this rules out St Denis as the place where Marculf compiled his formulary, but it suggests that it was by no means the only possibility.

A NOTE ON THE PRINTED EDITIONS

Unlike the formulary of Angers, Marculf survives in several manuscripts giving more or less different versions of the collection, which creates problems in reconstructing the original. It is therefore worth considering how the Latin text translated in this book was arrived at.³⁴⁴

The sheer prominence of Marculf, the fact that it was for centuries perceived as the Frankish formulary *par excellence*, had an important impact on the manner in which the corpus of formulae as a whole was assembled. The volume of the *Patrologia Latina* including '*Marculf et alii*' exhibits a distinct tendency to consider all formulae, whether isolated or even part

---

Jean Durliat thus referred to Marculf simply as 'un haut fonctionnaire en retraite', 'a retired high-ranking civil servant' (J. Durliat, *De l'Antiquité au Moyen-Age: l'Occident de 313 à 800* [Paris, 2002], p. 100).

343 Although to some extent Riché has his cake and eats it, since he goes on to cite Marculf's writing of his book for a bishop among the evidence for the exclusion of lay persons from administrative spheres (Riché, *Education et culture dans l'Occident barbare*, p. 476).

344 See Appendix 3 for a fuller discussion of the manuscripts and editorial work.

of other formularies, as appendices to Marculf, which seems to have been regarded as the original fount from which all other formulae flowed.[345] Bignon, Etienne Baluze and the eighteenth-century catalogue of the Bibliothèque Nationale all described the formulae from Sens, found together with Marculf in one manuscript,[346] as an *appendix Marculfi*, even though their relationship went no further than the fact that they were copied into the same manuscript; the Sens collection was even occasionally referred to before Zeumer as 'Marculf III'.[347] Bignon included in his edition of Marculf a group of formulae from a completely unrelated manuscript (the *Formulae Salicae Bignonianae* of Zeumer's edition).[348] Mabillon himself had referred abundantly to Marculf in his edition of the formulary of Angers, for formulae with a broadly similar subject but no obvious formal similarities, as if to point to what may be termed a spiritual rather than textual link.[349]

From this point of view, Zeumer's edition was considerably more cautious than his predecessors', and his rationalisation of the Marculf material was in many respects a remarkable achievement. His whole volume, indeed, was a *tour de force* of traditional scholarship, attesting to his colossal work power and cleverness in detecting textual links and constructing manuscript stemmata. His reconstructions are if anything rather too clever, and that is their essential flaw.

All seven manuscripts of Marculf are Carolingian, and all in this sense could be called 'Carolingian versions' of Marculf.[350] Zeumer reserved that title for only two manuscripts among them, because they alone removed all references to the mayor of the palace and introduced the phrase 'rex Dei gratia', both of which constituted obvious 'updates'.[351] But the other manuscripts also testify to the free adaptation of Marculf in its Carolingian afterlife, although they do not update the text in the same way. As was normal at the time he was working, Zeumer was not primarily interested in the Carolingian end of this story, and instead focused on reconstructing the

---

345 J.-P. Migne, *Patrologia Latina* (1844–55), vol. 87, col. 691 to 967.
346 Paris BnF lat. 4627.
347 Zeumer, 'Über die älteren fränkischen Formelsammlungen', p. 69; *Catalogus codicum manuscriptorum Bibliothecae Regiae* 3, 3 (Paris, 1744), p. 615.
348 Paris BnF lat. 13686; Bignon, *Marculfi monachi formularum libri duo.*
349 Mabillon, *Libri de re diplomatica supplementum.*
350 These manuscripts are Paris BnF lat. 4627; Paris BnF lat. 10756; Leiden BPL 114; Paris BnF lat. 2123; Copenhagen, Kongelige Bibliothek coll. Fabric. 84; Munich lat. 4650 and Leiden Voss. lat. O. 86. See Appendix 3.
351 Munich lat. 4650 and Leiden Voss. lat. 86, branch 'C' of the manuscript tradition (see Appendix 3).

Urtext, that is, the 'original' text as it was written by its author: his edition thus deliberately obscures the fluidity of the text and its many different incarnations. The fact that the Marculf matter was still being modified, abridged, lengthened, reorganised and integrated into new collections in its Carolingian copies clearly shows that it remained a work in progress down to the ninth and tenth centuries, accounting for the wide variety in the form of this text given in the different manuscripts.[352]

The formulary in its post-Zeumer state contains 92 formulae divided into two books, one of *cartas regales* (40 formulae for royal documents), one of *cartas pagenses* (52 formulae for private documents), but it is sobering to realise that it is recognisable in this form only in two manuscripts (Paris BnF lat. 4627 and 10756) out of the seven considered in recent editions.[353] The other five show no intention of preserving Marculf as a distinct unit so much as to use it as a source for what, to all intents and purposes, may be considered new collections. In one of them (Leiden BPL 114, a manuscript curiously favoured by editors as being somehow exceptionally authentic[354]) the preface and two-book structure are ignored, and the Marculf matter is mixed up with other, unrelated formulae (for a list of the contents of this manuscript, see Appendix 3, table 2). The Marculf material itself was cut down, and a number of formulae were omitted. At no point does the collection even explicitly claim to be Marculf's. Much the same situation occurs in the other four manuscripts (Paris BnF lat. 2123, although that manuscript does preserve the title and preface, and in Copenhagen Kongelige Bibliothek coll. Fabric. 84, Munich lat. 4650 and Leiden Voss. lat. O. 86). In Paris BnF lat. 2123, the new collection was still attributed to Marculf, and the substitution of the name 'Aeglidulf' for 'Landeric' as patron of the work shows the manner in which an older collection could keep its old name while being appropriated and modified to suit a new compiler's needs (or his patron's): Marculf's preface itself was being used by this new compiler as a formula. These manuscripts were evidently not compiled with the concern of preserving anything of the original form of the Marculf collection: it would therefore make more sense to consider them all as new, distinct collections. With the rather mysterious exception of Leiden BPL 114, however, all of these manuscripts simply appear in Zeumer's edition as 'bad' manuscripts of

---

352 See Appendix 3.
353 As in A. Uddholm, *Marculfi formularum libri duo* (Uppsala, 1962); see also his article 'Le texte des *Formulae Marculfi*', *Eranos* 55 (1957), pp. 38–59, for his assessment of the manuscript tradition.
354 On these issues, see Appendix 3.

Marculf, branches 'B' and 'C' of the tradition, rather than as altogether new collections. Zeumer had to resort to blaming the incompetence of scribes to explain the chaotic state of the material rather more often than a modern editor would feel comfortable with: he thus explained the changed order of Leiden BPL 114 by supposing there had been a flaw in the binding of the scribe's exemplar, despite the fact that this new order makes quite a lot of sense in the context of the new collection taken as a whole.

Some of the formulae found in the same manuscripts as Marculf, but which did not properly belong to it, were sometimes shepherded into other collections. The Paris BnF lat. 2123 collection got out of this process fairly lightly, since it gained a place both in the edition of Marculf and as a separate collection, the *Collectio Flaviniacensis* or Flavigny collection, which at least reproduced the order found in the manuscript.[355] The extras in Leiden BPL 114 were not so fortunate: they were put in a separate collection, baptised 'Formulae of Bourges' (*Formulae Bituricenses*), together with texts similarly extracted from two other manuscripts (Paris BnF lat. 10756 and 4629), despite the lack of any discernible relationship between these different parts beyond the fact that all of them mention the city of Bourges as their locality.[356] This is an extreme example, but it is revealing of Zeumer's approach. He was working in an editorial tradition that privileged the *Urtext*, and his treatment of the five unorthodox Marculf manuscripts reflects his concern with recreating original states. His priority was Marculf, but he was also doing his best, as he saw it, for the texts that had been merged with it: since some or all of these texts were likely to have been taken from earlier collections themselves, Zeumer saw it as his duty to try to recover as much as possible of their own 'original' form. In practice, however, this meant culling the new collections in such a way as to rob them of all internal coherence, sometimes only to merge them again with texts that had somewhat less of a claim to be related to them, which led to such unhelpful constructions as the Bourges formulae.

This prompts the question of just how different a version needed to be from the reconstructed 'original' to qualify as a new collection in Zeumer's eyes. After all, the manuscripts chosen by him to represent the Marculf tradition are not the only ones to contain Marculf's texts. Many formularies which Zeumer was happy to consider as self-standing new collections drew on the Marculf matter too. The *Formulae Salicae Merkelianae* ('Formulae

---

355 Zeumer, *Formulae*, pp. 469–92.

356 Zeumer, *Formulae*, pp. 166–81; the formulae from Leiden BPL 114 found intermixed with Marculf are given as nos. 8–19, while those preceding it are given in the Appendix.

of Merkel', named after their first editor) and the *Formulae Turonenses* (Formulae of Tours) thus made fairly extensive use of Marculf as a source, and the modifications in text and order introduced in the course of these borrowings were not more extreme than those observed in the five 'Marculf' manuscripts discussed above. Why, then, did Zeumer not split up the Merkel formulae, isolating the Marculf material and putting the rest in a separate collection, as he did for Leiden BPL 114? Why are they not 'branch D' of the Marculf tradition? It is likely that Zeumer's decision rested not on an evaluation of the level of creative scribal input, but on the fact that these formulae had already been edited by Merkel, so that they would already have constituted a collection in their own right in Zeumer's mind before he approached the manuscripts. This shows the influence of previous editing work on Zeumer's approach to his collections: when work had already been done by illustrious scholars on a particular group of formulae, such as Merkel for the *Formulae Salicae Merkelianae* or Sirmond for the *Formulae Turonenses*, he automatically granted it independent status, while those groups that had been virtually ignored until his edition were forced willy-nilly into the stemmata of pre-existing collections. Zeumer's reasons even when deciding what constituted a discrete manuscript tradition can therefore seem rather arbitrary.

Zeumer's desire to pin down once and for all the fluid shape of the manuscripts also led to the isolation of a small number of satellite texts, appearing in some of the manuscripts of Marculf but not in others. Some of these satellite texts were incorporated into the numerous supplements, appendices and *addenda* to Marculf in Zeumer's edition; others were simply discarded. The fate of these texts was largely governed by assumptions regarding content suitability, as can be seen in the treatment reserved by modern editors for the three formulae referred to by Zeumer as 'a', 'b' and 'c', discarded in both Zeumer's edition and in Alf Uddholm's later edition,[357] even though they are found in association with Marculf in all of its three main manuscripts (Leiden BPL 114, Paris BnF lat. 10756, and Paris BnF lat. 4627), and should therefore have as much of a claim to be included in the Marculf corpus as the formulae admitted as part of the Supplement. One would need a very good reason to discard 'a', 'b' and 'c', which are transmitted coherently in three manuscripts in association with Marculf, while keeping the *Additamenta e codicibus Marculfi*, a group of texts found together with Marculf in some of the manuscripts, and which are really just a

---

357 Uddholm, *Marculfi formularum libri duo*.

compilation of the formulae Zeumer was unsure what to do with: *Add.* 1 a–e are found only in Leiden BPL 114, and *Add.* 2 and 3 in Paris BnF lat. 2123, in which they are substituted for Marculf I, 24 and Marculf Supplement no. 1. Since both Leiden BPL 114 and Paris BnF lat. 2123 also contain many other non-Marculfian formulae, there is no reason to link the *Additamenta* automatically to Marculf.

The *Additamenta*, however, do have quite 'proper' subjects for formulae, something which Zeumer did not think was true of 'a', 'b' or 'c'. He admitted that 'a', a prologue encouraging powerful men to give property to the Church, could have been part of a formula, or perhaps the draft of a formula; but the other two he discarded completely. In 'c' a man expresses his joy at being admitted into a monastery, while 'b', the strangest of all three, expresses the indignation of a teacher at the uselessness of his pupils after their failure to complete the exercise he had set for them. Zeumer explained away the consistent presence of these texts in the Marculf manuscripts through the device of scribal error. He argued they could have been inserted into an early copy of Marculf and reproduced in subsequent copies because later scribes failed to realise that they were not dealing with 'real' formulae, probably because they were not sure of what these texts really meant. Zeumer also hypothesised that they had originally been written into this earlier Marculf manuscript in Tironian notes, a form of shorthand used in the early middle ages, and that the surviving text must have been the result of a well-meaning but garbled transcription.

And yet it is dangerous to think one could know what medieval scribes were trying to do better than they did themselves. All three texts might qualify as prologues to formulae: the headings in the manuscripts refer to 'a' and 'c' as prologues, while 'b' is more prudently defined only as *dictum* or *dictatum*. These texts do not replace names with indefinite pronouns, but this does not tell us much, since, due to their fragmentary nature, they contain no names that needed to be eliminated. These texts should therefore be reintegrated into the Marculf corpus, and I have included the Latin text and a translation in this volume.[358] Assumptions of modern scholars regarding what a formula is, what a formulary is, and how medieval scribes wanted to copy them, have had important repercussions on the way in which we approach the genre as a whole as well as the manuscripts: one cannot take for granted that the corpus of even such a well-known and extensively worked-on text as Marculf has been established on a wholly sound basis.

---

358 See below, pp. 240–44.

The lessons to be learned from this point to the limits of conventional editing work on such texts in principle, rather than calling for a new edition; in spite of these problems, I have used Uddholm's edition as the basis for this translation, both because the standard modern organisation of the Marculf corpus as it currently stands is the only form in which this collection is available to the general reader, and because it is no more or less representative than could be expected from any edition of texts of this nature. Uddholm's edition is not, on the whole, all that different from Zeumer's, and readers wishing to consult the Latin text may thus refer to either; where my readings differ, I have indicated it in the notes.

TRANSLATION

In the name of God the preface of this book begins.

This is the only preface, or statement by the author, to be found in any formulary, and is therefore uniquely informative in providing an idea of the purpose and circumstances behind the compilation of a formulary. Although Marculf seems to create an opposition between his own work and the more literary pursuits of others, this does not mean that he saw them as fundamentally different in qualitative terms: his protestations of his own ignorance and unworthiness, and the fear of being derided by more sophisticated men, were not the fruit of an inferiority complex of charter-writers in relation to writers of other genres, but part of a modesty topos characteristic of prefaces in general.[359] Marculf's choice to proclaim his ignorance through a reference to Orosius is in itself enough to show that he was not being entirely disingenuous.[360] Marculf's display of humility is in fact so extreme as to suggest an occasional whiff of sarcasm, particularly in the passage in which he assures Landeric that more elegant writers need not fear that his work will contaminate the 'flowers' of their words: despite its outward lack of pretension, his preface thus comes across as a strong vindication of his work. Marculf turns what Landeric had asked him to do, which perhaps only involved sending him models for documents and letters for his own particular use, into a more ambitious project, offering models for a much wider range of subjects. He claims to have drawn his material both from the teachings of his own masters and from the body of charters he had himself written, though he does not make clear whether he only used the charters previously drawn up in his monastery or whether his sources also included earlier formularies. The phrase in which he says that he included 'royal charters as well as private documents' ('tam preceptiones regales quam cartas pagenses') reflects the overall structure of the collection, which is divided into two books, the *cartas regales* (royal charters), and the *cartas pagenses* (private charters). Marculf's explicit statement that his formulary was designed as a textbook 'to guide the first efforts of youths' ('ad

---

359 Both points are echoed in the preface to the late seventh-century *Passio Leudegarii*, a literary text; for a translation, see Fouracre and Gerberding, *Late Merovingian France*, at p. 215.

360 See below, n. 364.

exercenda initia puerorum') is significant:[361] his collection adopts the features of a textbook more consistently than most other formularies, for instance with the offering of several alternatives in the same formula, either depending on preference or in order to fit different circumstances. The collection was apparently also intended as a reference book for more experienced scribes, as suggested by the phrase 'if it pleases someone to copy something out of it, let him do so' ('cui libet exinde aliqua exemplando, faciat enim'). Marculf's reference to the impossibility of predicting the particulars of each case is consistent with what can be observed from the use of this formulary in actual documents: with the exception of forgeries, these models tended to be used as an inspiration rather than as a ready-made template.[362]

To the sainted lord, most blessed through his merits and ever to receive apostolic honour and deserving of every praise, to the most revered lord Bishop Landeric,[363] Marculf, the last and most lowly of all monks.

Holy father, would that I had been able to obey your command as efficiently as I wished,[364] as I have tried to perform the task assigned by you, although this was already beyond the capabilities of my strength, as I have now completed seventy years of life or more, and my trembling hand is no longer good for writing, and my clouded eyes are not good enough to

---

361 Compare 'b' for what seems to be a description of a classroom situation (see below, pp. 240–43). How young these pupils would have been and how they were taught is uncertain. It has often been assumed that this preface constitutes evidence for the training of lay notaries: Pirenne mentioned Marculf's school as a type of lay school (H. Pirenne, 'De l'état de l'instruction des laïques à l'époque mérovingienne', *Revue Bénédictine* 46 (1934), pp. 165–77, at p. 174), as did Riché, adding that Marculf's formulary was not likely to have been part of every child's curriculum (P. Riché, 'L'instruction des laïcs en Gaule mérovingienne au VIIe siècle', in *Settimane di studio del Centro italiano di studi sull'alto medioevo* 5 (Spoleto, 1958), pp. 873–88, at pp. 882–83). But there is little to support the assumption that Marculf's school must have been a lay institution or that Marculf himself was a former lay notary in the service of the royal chancery (see above, pp. 116–17), and a monastery would have had an equally strong vested interest in training monks or novices to write charters. It is indeed possible that this was a specialised kind of training, though there is no reason to suppose that the writing of documents in a religious institution should have been limited only to a small team of scribes.

362 See above, p. 27.

363 Landeric is addressed as 'papa', which at this time could still be used to refer to any bishop, and was not yet restricted to the bishop of Rome (see J. Moorhead, 'Papa as "bishop of Rome"', *Journal of Ecclesiastical History* 36 [1985], pp. 337–50). Paris BnF lat. 2123 gives the name 'Aeglidulf' instead of Landeric; see above, p. 109.

364 This opening is a common *topos*. Uddholm convincingly argued that it had been drawn from the preface of Orosius's *History against the Pagans*, which has the flattering effect of putting Landeric in the role of Augustine (Uddholm, *Formulae Marculfi: Etudes sur la langue et le style*, p. 222).

see, and my dull mind is not good enough to find meaning, since, according to the words addressed to you by a most experienced man, wisdom grows in children, thrives in youths, and is diminished in old men. Therefore I could not do this elegantly, as I wanted to; however, under [your] orders, I did the best I could. I have taken care, according to the simplicity and ignorance of my nature,[365] to include in these pages not only the things which you ordered, but also many others, royal charters as well as private documents. And I know that there will be many, both yourself and other most knowledgeable men and eloquent orators, skilled at rhetoric, who, if they read these things, will rate them as absurd, and of little worth in comparison with their own wisdom, or who will certainly disdain to read them. But I wrote openly and simply, as best I could, not for such men, but to guide the first efforts of youths. If it pleases someone to copy something out of it, let him do so; if it does not please him to do so, no one will force him, so that my ignorance will not disturb the flowers of words and eloquence of scholars and orators. There will be many legal cases between people, both in the palace and in the *pagus*,[366] which cannot be written down before they have discussed them together, and only then will their words and actions be recorded, according to the accusations and answers [they may present]. But I have taken care to assemble together in one place the things which I have learned from my elders according to the custom of the place in which we live,[367] and those which I made up on my own account; and I gave them chapter headings, so that the seeker may recognise more easily what he is looking for by the writing that comes before it.[368]

---

[365] 'Rusticitas mea': a literary and prefatory commonplace by this stage. Gregory of Tours used this word to represent the simplicity of his style (*sermo rusticus*) in his *Histories* and hagiographical works (on *sermo rusticus*, see E. Auerbach, *Literatursprache und Publikum in der lateinischen Spätantike und im Mittelalter* [Bern, 1958] and H. Beumann, 'Gregor von Tours und der Sermo Rusticus', in K. Repgen and S. Skalweit, eds., *Spiegel der Geschichte. Festschrift für Max Braubach zum 10. April 1964* [Münster, 1964], pp. 69–98).

[366] 'Tam in palatio quam in pago': this is a standard phrase, emphasising the validity of a document or the legitimacy of legal representation 'in local as well as royal courts'.

[367] 'Iuxta consuetudinem loci quo degimus': this passage has been taken to mean that Landeric lived in the same place as Marculf, and therefore that Landeric was his diocesan bishop (see above, pp. 107–10). This is not necessarily true, as the plural *degimus* could easily stand for a singular, and may therefore only refer to Marculf himself; or it could refer by extension to his monastic community and the 'elders' who taught him.

[368] The chapter-headings are very consistent in the manuscript tradition, even in manuscripts in which the collection was otherwise extensively reworked, so there can be no doubt that they were indeed Marculf's own.

BOOK ONE

Here begin the chapter headings.

The parts of this work.

I – How a privilege is made.
II – Document from the king regarding this privilege.
III – Immunity from the king.
IV – Confirmation of an immunity from the king.
V – Document from the king regarding a bishopric.
VI – Letter from the king to a metropolitan bishop, in order that he should give the rites of ordination to another bishop.
VII – General agreement of the citizens regarding a bishopric.
VIII – Charter concerning the office of a duke, *patricius* or count.
IX – Letter of recommendation to another king, when an embassy is sent and presents a verbal communication.
X – Answer to the king through his ambassador.
XI – List of goods and minimal duties to be provided to the envoys, after this model.
XII – Document of mutual donation.
XIII – Document of *lesewerpus*[369] by the hand of the king.
XIV – Three prologues concerning royal grants.
XV – Grant to a holy place.
XVI – Confirmation from the king to a holy place.
XVII – Another confirmation, for laymen.
XVIII – Regarding the antrustion of a king.
XIX – Document regarding the holy orders.
XX – Regarding the sharing of a property in which an agent of the king is involved.
XXI – On taking up someone else's legal cases.
XXII – Document [of manumission by throwing a] *denarius*.
XXIII – Document for the interruption of legal cases.
XXIV – Document regarding the protection given by a king and a prince.
XXV – Prologue to the judgment of a king, when two people are in dispute over a large property.
XXVI – Letter of summons to a bishop.

---

369 See below, n. 432.

XXVII – Another letter to a bishop, so that he should discipline another man.
XXVIII – Charter relating to a [legal] hearing.
XXIX – Letter to a layman.
XXX – Exchange with the king.
XXXI – Confirmation from the king regarding a whole patrimony.
XXXII – If anyone acted against the will of the king, deed of security for the man whom he has ordered to pursue him.
XXXIII – Document for those whose documents were burned by enemies or in some other way.
XXXIV – Account by *pagenses*, addressed to the king.
XXXV – Another confirmation, to a monastery, regarding the whole of its property.
XXXVI – In order that someone should have permission to take over the legal cases of those from whom he received property.
XXXVII – Clear judgment.
XXXVIII – Charter in two identical copies.
XXXIX – In order that servants be freed for the birth of a king.
XL – In order for the people to swear their submission.

Here begin the examples of how royal and local charters are written for various circumstances, for any whom it will please to take a model from here and who is not capable of doing better himself.

I, 1: Regarding a privilege.

> This is a privilege of exemption from a bishop in favour of a monastery. The purpose of such documents was to give the monastery a level of independence from the control of the bishop of its diocese. How far this independence extended varied. Ewig distinguished between two kinds of exemption: the 'grosse Freiheit' ('big exemption') included clauses intended to protect the monastery's property against possible encroachments by the bishop or his agents; it allowed the congregation the freedom of choosing their own abbot and of asking another bishop to perform rites of blessing or ordination; it made the monastery independent from the jurisdiction of the bishop and exempt from the payment of any dues to him, and gave monks the right to deny him entrance if they wished to. The 'kleine Freiheit' ('little exemption') included most of these rights, with the difference that it did not allow the monastery to ask anyone but its own diocesan bishop to give blessings and perform ordinations.[370] According to this formula, the diocesan

---

[370] Ewig, 'Beobachtungen zu den Klosterprivilegien', p. 418; see Rosenwein, *Negotiating Space*, pp. 35–36.

bishop of the monastery retained this exclusive right to give blessings and ordinations in this monastery, which puts this text in the category of the 'little exemption'. The bishop here seems to have tried to retain as tight a control as possible over the monastery within the limits of the exemption: the right of *correctio*, that is, the right for the abbot alone to discipline the monks, which was a normal part of early exemptions, was also explicitly denied, so that the bishop retained the right to discipline the monks if the abbot proved unable to deal with them himself. This text is closely linked with the royal grant of immunity given in the following formula (I, 2), made at the request of the founder of the monastery. The identity of this founder is left unclear. I, 2 allows for different possibilities, with the founder being either the bishop himself, an abbot or a layman. If he was a layman, he was clearly a powerful one, and, having founded his monastery, was able to secure the cooperation of both king and bishop. The relationship between this formula and Bishop Burgundofaro's exemption for the monastery of Rebais has been much debated.[371] The Rebais exemption is now recognised as being at least partly the result of forgery, which rules out the possibility that Marculf based his formula on it, and suggests instead that the text was rewritten using Marculf as a model. Ewig, while accepting the argument that the text contained many later interpolations, argued that its basic content was essentially authentic; if so, it would constitute the earliest example of an episcopal exemption in the surviving record.[372] The Rebais exemption was less restricted than that put forward in this formula, and gave the abbot the right of *correctio* over his monks. Barbara Rosenwein has argued that this Marculf formula was used as a model for a stricter type of exemption in a document issued by Chrodegang of Metz in 757, with key modifications ensuring even tighter control by the bishop.[373]

To the blessed lord and venerable brother in Christ Abbot A and the entire congregation of the monastery of B, built in the *pagus* of C by D in honour of the blessed E–F, Bishop G. Affection for your kindness prompts us, through ardent divine rays, to provide for your peace such things as may contribute to our salvation, and to define them in a correct and permanent way, which, God willing, will retain eternal validity, since the future reward to be expected from God is no less for one who plans for the future than for one who gives to the poor in the present time. And let no one, accusing us, think that they are seeing a new song in this,[374] since from antiquity, according to the decree of the pontiffs, [and] under royal sanction, the monasteries of

371 See above, n. 312.
372 Rosenwein, *Negotiating Space*, pp. 67–73.
373 Gorze no. 4, = *Concilia aevi Karolini*, vol. 1, pp. 60–63. See Rosenwein, *Negotiating Space*, pp. 103–06 and 221–24.
374 The phrase is 'nova decernere carmina'. The point was that there were precedents, and that this exemption could not therefore be considered as a dangerous innovation.

the saints of Lérins, Agaune, Luxeuil[375] – or simply: innumerable [monasteries] throughout the entire kingdom of the Franks[376] – have been seen to remain under the privilege of freedom. And out of reverence for the saints and in order to fulfil the requests of all my brothers[377] – [or:] to follow their advice –, I shall make public my obedience. We believe that what you and your successors are to retain from now on, under the guidance of the Holy Ghost, and in particular [the duties which] the bishop of the holy church of H will have to perform, should be included in this document: that is, that the man from your congregation who must perform the divine offices in your monastery,[378] whom the abbot will have recommended with all the congregation, will receive the sacred rites of ordination from us and from our successors, who shall receive no reward for their office. The said bishop will bless the altar in this monastery and grant the holy chrism every year, if they so choose, out of reverence for this place, without payment; and when, according to divine providence, the abbot of this monastery makes his journey to the Lord,[379] the bishop of the said city will himself ordain as abbot, without payment, the man whom the whole congregation of monks of B will have elected unanimously from their number due to his excellent knowledge of the Rule[380] and his suitability through the merits of his life. Let neither bishops, whether ourselves or our successors, nor archdeacons, nor anyone of the other priestly orders, nor any other person from the said city, presume to exert any other authority in this monastery, whether regarding its property, ordinations, or the villas already given to it or to be given later by the gift of the king or of private persons or the rest of the property of the monastery, nor dare to expect or take away anything from this monastery by way of tribute, as we do from the parishes and the other monasteries, nor

---

375 This refers to the island-monastery of Lérins near Nice, founded in the fifth century, and the Burgundian monasteries of St Maurice of Agaune, founded in the early sixth century, and Luxeuil, founded by Saint Columbanus at the end of the sixth century. All seem to have received episcopal exemptions, though this is only a conjecture based on references to these three prestigious monasteries as precedents in later documents of exemption; see Rosenwein, *Negotiating Space*, pp. 64–68.

376 For the sake of clarity, I have used dashes to isolate the alternative wordings offered by Marculf, though it should be noted that these are not marked out in the manuscripts.

377 That is, the monks of this congregation.

378 This refers to the prior of the monastery, second in command after the abbot; the gloss *prior est* ('this means the prior') is added here in Paris BnF lat. 10756.

379 That is, at his death.

380 Which monastic rule this referred to is left open: several different rules were still current in the Merovingian period, before being superseded by the Benedictine rule in the ninth century.

presume to take away anything out of that which was transferred or offered to the altar by God-fearing men, or any sacred books or precious objects which pertain to the ornament of divine worship, [whether] those that have already been given or those that will be given later. And unless he is asked by this congregation of B or the abbot to celebrate mass, let none of us be allowed to come into the seclusion of the monastery or enter the limits of its enclosure.[381] And if this pontiff is asked by them to celebrate mass, or goes there for their need, once the divine mystery has been celebrated and ended, having received a simple and moderate meal,[382] without requiring any gift, he must go back, in order that the monks, who are called solitaries,[383] may enjoy perfect tranquillity for all time, with God's guidance, and, living under the holy Rule and following the life of the blessed fathers, may pray to the Lord more fully for the state of the Church and the salvation of the king and the land. And if some of these monks become lukewarm or dry in their religion, let their abbot discipline them according to their Rule, if he can; if not, the pontiff of this city must control them, since, no matter whatever may be given to the servants of the faith for their peaceful tranquillity, canonical authority will in no way be diminished. But if one of us, which God forbid, moved by cunning or misled by avarice, should presume to violate, with a rash spirit, the things which are given above, let him be struck down by divine vengeance and subjected to the punishment of anathema, and let him count himself excluded from the communion of all [our] brothers, and let this privilege remain intact in perpetuity. And in order that our decree may stand with a firm strength, both we and our brothers the lords bishops [I–J] decided that it should be confirmed with a signature by our hands. Made here, on day *x* of year *y*.

I, 2: Grant from the king regarding this privilege.

The first part of this formula confirms the episcopal privilege given in the previous one, and shares some of its wording; this text, however, goes slightly further in also prohibiting the bishop and his clergy from exploiting the monastery in less obvious ways: they are thus not allowed to 'diminish any [of its property] under the pretext of an exchange' ('aliquid quasi per commutaciones titulum minuari'),

---

381 The phrase is 'monasterii adire secreta aut finium ingredi septa'; on the expression *secreta septa*, see Rosenwein, *Negotiating Space*, pp. 68–69 and 71.
382 The word is *benedictio*, here apparently with reference to food.
383 The word is *solitarii*, which normally referred to hermits, though this was clearly not the case here.

which implies that a monastery's dependence on its diocesan bishop, as well as involving the collection of dues, could also entail unequal exchanges of property, effectively constituting unofficial (and in practice perhaps compulsory) gifts. The second part adds to this exemption a grant of royal immunity, giving the monastery a level of independence from royal control in much in the same way as the exemption had made it independent from the bishop's jurisdiction: right of entry into the monastery was denied to royal representatives; no dues were to be collected from its people or its property, and royal agents were explicitly forbidden from interfering with its property and legal business. Although immunities are known to have been granted in the sixth century, our first surviving examples date from the reign of Dagobert I (623–39).[384] Because they formally established the relinquishing of a level of control by the king, immunities were long thought by historians to have provided the basis for feudalism, in the sense that they seemed to limit royal power and allow the development of private jurisdictions. More recently, they have been recognised instead as forming an integral and deliberate aspect of royal policies: waiving direct jurisdiction in this manner did not necessarily entail a weakening of the state, but could on the contrary strengthen alliances with particular religious institutions.[385]

King A to the apostolic men, our fathers,[386] and also to the illustrious men Count B and all royal representatives present and future. Royal clemency must, among all requests, welcome those of priests with a kindly ear, and, when a suitable request is made for the tranquillity of the servants of God, put into effect what is requested in fear of God's name without hesitation, so that salvation may be granted. Perfect faith does not doubt that what is given specifically for the servants of the faith with a devout spirit, according to Scripture, leads to the grace of the Highest, for it is written: 'blessed are the poor in spirit, for theirs is the kingdom of heaven'.[387] Therefore, since Bishop – or: Abbot, or: the illustrious man – C is known to have built a monastery in honour of [Saint] D in the *pagus* of E – or: on his property, or: on an estate of the fisc –, where at present Abbot F and a great crowd of monks are known to have gathered, at his request it pleased our clemency to issue an order[388] by our authority for the tranquillity of these servants of

384 See Rosenwein, *Negotiating Space*, pp. 59–67.
385 For a discussion of the historiography, see Rosenwein, *Negotiating Space*, pp. 6–18; A.C. Murray, 'Immunity, Nobility, and the Edict of Paris', *Speculum* 69 (1994), pp. 18-39. On this formula, see N. D. Fustel de Coulanges, 'Etude sur l'immunité mérovingienne', *Revue Historique* 22 (1883), pp. 249–90, and 23 (1883), pp. 1–27.
386 That is, bishops.
387 Matthew 5:3.
388 The word is *praeceptio* (also found as *praeceptum*), which could refer to an edict or to a royal charter.

God. We have decided to declare in full in this document under what manner of tranquillity, with God's protection, these monks may live in perpetuity, according to the norms of religion. For canonical authority will in no way be diminished, no matter what may be given to the servants of the faith for their peaceful tranquillity.[389] And let no one, accusing us, think that they are seeing a new song in this,[390] since from antiquity, according to the decree of the pontiffs [and] under royal sanction, the monasteries of Saints G–H and others in our kingdom are seen to remain under the privilege of freedom;[391] and so let this one remain, with God's help. Therefore, if something has been given to this place, or is to be given in the future, whether villas, unfree servants[392] or anything or anybody, by a gift from either the king or the said C or anyone else, according to what we know has been granted to the said monastery by the pontiff I and the other lords bishops, and according to what is contained in their privilege, which the said C presented to us for verification, no bishop, as we said, whether the present one or those who are to be his successors, nor archdeacons nor their clergy nor any other person may take it away from this place by any means, or take on any authority for himself in this monastery beyond what is written, or diminish any [of its property] under the pretext of an exchange, or take away anything out of the ornaments of the [divine] service and the offerings presented at the altar, or presume to go into this monastery and its cells in any circumstance other than to celebrate mass, if that is the will of the abbot and his congregation, without any expense on their part, so that, according to the wishes of the delegation and this solemn document, all [of the property given] there may benefit this monastery more easily, without any interference. We add that no judges[393] nor any other men will have the right to defraud illegally the said monastery of any of its property against the will of these servants of God, or to usurp it for their own use with a rash spirit, without first incurring God's wrath and our displeasure, and being liable to pay a hefty fine to the fisc.[394] It pleased us to add, for our complete salvation, that at no point may any judiciary authority, either present or future, presume to enter any

---

389 The same sentence features in Marculf I, 1, after the section denying the abbot the right to discipline his own monks.
390 See above, n. 374.
391 A similar sentence cam be found in Marculf I, 1, with the difference that this version does not refer to the monasteries of Lérins, Agaune and Luxeuil as precedents.
392 The word is *mancipia*, often used to refer to unfree servants or tenants.
393 The word is *judex*, which could also refer more broadly to royal officials.
394 The royal treasury (*fiscus*) in principle received a share of all fines, and is therefore often mentioned in penalty-clauses.

place which has been or will be given there, either through our generosity or through the gift of C or of anybody else, in order to hear legal cases or to collect anything there. Instead, this monastery and its congregation may possess this under full immunity, all dues being conceded to themselves; and whatever our fisc could perhaps have expected from the persons, whether free or unfree, who live in their fields or anywhere [on their lands] is to benefit them in its entirety, by our grant, in order to provide for lights[395] for this holy place and for the stipends of the servants of God, both while we are alive, in God's name, and in the times of future kings, to gain [our] salvation, so that it may please these monks constantly to implore God's infinite mercy for [our] eternal salvation and the happiness of the land and the tranquillity of the king. In order that our decree may stand more firmly and be kept in perpetuity, with Christ helping in all things, we have taken care to make a signature below by our hand.

I, 3: Royal immunity.

This is a straightforward royal grant of immunity, this time in favour of a bishop's church. It is rather more detailed in its description of what royal officials could demand than the previous formula. This description makes no mention of fixed taxation, and instead lists a series of possible costs, such as the feeding and lodging of royal representatives, pledges and fines, all of which would have been incurred essentially in the context of the exercise of judicial power by royal representatives on the lands of the church.[396] This power was at least partly removed by this immunity, and royal agents were no longer allowed to enter the lands of this church in order to settle court cases; it is possible, however, that this part of the immunity only related to smaller disputes (similar to those settled by an abbot in the Angers formulary), as opposed to more important ones, such as murder, which tended to be resolved before a count.[397] The transfer to the church of the

---

395 See P. Fouracre, 'Eternal lights and earthly needs: practical aspects of the development of Frankish immunities', in Davies and Fouracre, *Property and Power in the Early Middle Ages*, pp. 53–81.

396 On immunities and links to a fiscal system in this period, see L. Levillain, 'Note sur l'immunité mérovingienne', *Revue historique du froit français et étranger* 6 (4th series) (1927), pp. 38–67; E. Magnou-Nortier, 'Etude sur le privilège d'immunité du IVe au IXe siècle', *Revue Mabillon* 60 (1981–84), pp. 465–512; W. Goffart, 'Old and new in Merovingian taxation', *Past and Present* 96 (1982), pp. 3–21; Rosenwein, *Negotiating Space*, pp. 12–14.

397 See above, p. 45. Charlemagne's capitulary of Herstal, dating from 779, explicitly stated that the beneficiaries of immunities still had to surrender *latrones* (robbers) to the count's court, no doubt because of the seriousness of their crime (*Capitularia* no. 20, *cap.* 9, vol. 1, p. 48).

right to the share of legal fines normally reserved for the royal treasury meant that the exercise of judiciary power had been put under its responsibility, by turning the settlement of disputes and the enforcing of the agreements recorded in documents to its material advantage (compare Angers no. 21). The text suggests that churches were not the only likely recipients of this kind of privilege, with the comment in the first sentence offering the alternative 'or to whomever you wish to say' ('aut cui volueris dicere'): this could constitute an important indication that lay individuals as well as churches could benefit from royal immunities (as also suggested by Marculf I, 14 and II, 1).

We believe we shall erect a great monument of our reign if we grant by a benevolent decision some benefits[398] useful to churches – : or to whomever you wish to say – and, with God's protection, we prescribe that they should remain constant. Therefore let your intelligence know this: we were seen to grant, for our eternal reward, this favour, at the request of the apostolic lord A, bishop of the city of B, to the effect that no public judge[399] may ever presume, in order to hear court cases or to collect fines from anywhere, to enter the villas of the church of Lord A, whether those which it is seen to own now by our gift or anyone else's, or those which divine piety may wish to add later to the property of this holy place; and let this pontiff and his successors, in the name of God, be able to rule under a title of full immunity. We decree, therefore, that neither you nor your subordinates nor your successors nor any public judiciary power should ever presume to enter the villas of that church anywhere in our kingdom, whether those given by the generosity of the king or of private persons or those that are to be given at a later time, in order to hear disputes or collect fines from any legal cases or to demand lodgings or supplies or legal guarantors;[400] but let whatever the fisc[401] could have expected to obtain from there, whether from fines or from anything else, whether from free men or from servants of any other status[402] who live within the fields and the boundaries or on the lands of the said church, benefit [this church] in perpetuity through its representatives,

---

398 The word is *beneficium*, here with the more general meaning of 'benefit' or 'favour', as opposed to a land benefice.

399 See above, n. 393.

400 *Fiedeijussor*: this refers to someone who offered himself as guarantor in order to vouch that someone else would fulfil their legal obligations.

401 See above, n. 394.

402 The phrase is 'servientibus ceterisque nationibus', that is, 'servants of different births'. The plural seems to imply a variety of different types of unfree status (see Rio, 'Freedom and unfreedom').

by our grant [and] for our future salvation, by [providing] lights[403] for this church. And we, in the name of the Lord and for the salvation of our soul and that of our future progeny, with complete devotion, grant that neither the royal highness nor the cruel avarice of any judges[404] should be tempted to oppose this. And so that the present document may remain inviolable both in present and in future times, God helping, we decided to confirm it below with a signature by our hand.

I, 4: Confirmation of an immunity.

> This is a confirmation of a privilege of immunity, given by a successor of the king who had first granted it. This document shows that earlier privileges needed to be confirmed at the beginning of the reign of each new king, and this particular immunity seems to have been confirmed by a string of different kings ('the said pontiff showed us... the document of the aforementioned prince and the confirmation of the kings E–F, signed by their own hands'; similar phrases appear frequently in surviving confirmations of immunities). The repetitious nature of this process, besides providing increased validity for the documents, would no doubt also have fulfilled the function of strengthening links of patronage and obligation between king and bishop. This text is very similar in its wording to the previous formula (I, 3), which also concerned the lands of a bishop's church: the two were clearly intended by Marculf to complement each other. Given the significant number of years said to separate the confirmation from the initial charter of immunity, this similarity shows that the original immunity would have been used as a direct model for drawing up the confirmation; surviving actual examples of such documents give the same impression.

It befits princely clemency to lend a kindly ear to all, [and] we must in particular consider with a devout mind what we know to have been granted to churches by preceding kings, our ancestors, for the salvation of their souls, and not deny, but confirm [these] just privileges with the strongest authority by our own declaration, so that we may deserve to share in [their divine] reward. Thus the apostolic man A, bishop of the city of B, pointed out to the clemency of our rule that King C, by his charter signed by his own hand, conceded a full immunity to the villas of his church of D, both those which it owned at the time and those which were later given to it by God-fearing men, so that no public judge[405] may enter there in order to hear

---

403 See Fouracre, 'Eternal lights'.
404 See above, n. 393.
405 See above, n. 393.

legal cases, collect fines, demand lodgings, supplies or guarantors, distrain the men of this church as a result of any legal claim, or require any payment. And the said pontiff showed us, in order that it should be read, this document of the aforementioned prince and the confirmation of the kings E–F, signed by their own hands. And he states that this privilege for this and his said church has been observed in present times as it had been granted by the said princes; but out of a desire for firm validation, he asked our highness that our document should generally confirm this again regarding this and the said church of Saint D. Know that we guaranteed and confirmed his request with our fullest will, out of reverence for this holy place, so that we may deserve to have a share of [divine] mercy. We therefore order and command, since it appears that a full immunity from entry by judges[406] was granted by the said princes to the villas of the aforementioned church of Lord D, that the documents of earlier princes, having been examined, are to be upheld in every way, with God's help, in present and future times. And neither you nor your subordinates nor your successors nor anyone with judiciary power may presume to enter the villas of the said church, whether those that are known to belong to it now anywhere in our kingdom or those which will have been given in the future by God-fearing men, or, with respect to the free men, servants or men of any status living in the said villas of this church, to exercise [judiciary power], demand fines or take guarantors, or to demand lodgings or supplies, or to distrain them as a result of any legal case, or to require payments. Instead, just as this privilege was granted by the said princes to the said church and observed until now, so let it also remain unchanged in the future, and be confirmed generally and permanently in the name of God by this our document. And let whatever our fisc could have expected from this place benefit [this church, by providing] lights for this church in perpetuity.[407] And so that this document may remain inviolable in both present and future times, with God's help, we decided to confirm it below by our own hand.

I, 5: Document regarding a bishopric.

> This is a letter from a king asking a bishop to consecrate another, newly appointed bishop. The text implies that each of the bishops who had to be present at the consecration were sent this letter (compare the next formula for a slightly different version). The appointment of bishops in the Frankish kingdoms was very much

---

406 See above, n. 393.
407 See Fouracre, 'Eternal lights'.

a royal prerogative, but this formula suggests it was also a collective decision, with the king apparently consulting lay nobles as well as bishops. The formula gives two possible alternatives for the previous status of the new bishop, with variations in the list of the candidate's supposed qualities depending on whether he had previously been a layman (*inluster*, chosen for his worthy conduct and noble rank) or an abbot (*venerabilis*, honest, kind and prudent).

King A to the apostolic Bishop B. Although the burden of royal care binds us to administering and governing the affairs of the state through most elevated occupations, nothing is so princely or so worthy of a prince than, when the crowd of the flock wanders somewhat, deprived of protection, to see that, for the salvation of their souls, the pontifical dignity in the highest places is conferred upon such a person as commands both words, so that he may be the teacher of the people, and action, so that he may resemble a disciple of Christ; one who governs the people with no less piety than severity; who knows how to polish the talents given to him through the sermons of assiduous preaching; and who is able to bring to the sheepfold of the Lord the salvation of the flock which he acquired and multiplied, unstained by any sin. And because we know that the lord C of blessed memory, bishop of the city of D, has travelled from this light at the divine call, having deliberated extensively, with fitting solicitude, over his successor, together with our pontiffs and great men, we decided, in God's name, to confer the pontifical dignity in this city to the illustrious – or: venerable – E, who is much recommended to our mind by his worthy conduct, is exalted through his noble rank, and adorned by the probity of his life – or: the honesty of his kindness and prudence –. We therefore order by the present document regarding this matter that, with the crowd of the assembled bishops to whom the pious deed of our serenity has been sent in writing in order that they should bless him, as [the rites of] ordination demand, your industry should apply itself, having opened the decree of our will, to make public [this] declaration and to make it obtain effect, with God's approval, so that, when he is seen to rule and govern diligently the church given to him by divine dispensation, this choice may grant us mercy before the eternal judge, and so that he may perpetually pray to the boundless Lord for the greatness of our sins.

I, 6: Letter of the king to a bishop, in order that he should give [the rites of] ordination to another.

This text gives a shorter and formally slightly different version of the preceding formula (I, 5).

To the holy lord, caring for [his] see with apostolic dignity, [our] father in Christ Bishop A, King B. We believe [the news] have already reached your reverence that C, of blessed memory, bishop of the city of D, has travelled from the light of this present life at the divine call. Having deliberated with complete attention over his successor with the pontiffs and great men of our people, we decided to confer [this] dignity in the said city, according to custom, to the illustrious – or: venerable – man D, with Christ's favour. And therefore, sending [our] duty of salutations with due and proper honour, we ask that, when [this] reaches you, your sanctity should not delay in blessing him, as the [rites of] ordination demand, and that, all the other [bishops] of your province being assembled with you, you should consecrate him pontiff in the aforementioned city, with Christ's favour. Let your grace therefore do this, so that you may implement the piety of our decision without delay, and so that both you and he may pray more fully, with constant watchfulness, for the stability of our reign.

I, 7: General agreement of the citizens regarding a bishopric.

> The fact that this document was placed last in the sequence of formulae relating to the appointment of a bishop by Marculf suggests it is likely to have been sent as a confirmation agreeing to the new bishop's appointment after the king's decision had already been made known, rather than as a spontaneous petition from a group of citizens. The citizens referred to as the signatories of this document could in any case only have been part of a small elite group. The reference to a 'common lord' ('seniore commune') is puzzling, since it seems to suggest that someone other than the king might have had the power to appoint a bishop; this may have referred to the mayor of the palace, though it may also have been meant simply as an alternative way of referring to the king.

For the attention of the most pious and excellent lord King – or: [our] common lord – A, from your servants, whose signatures and marks[408] have been added below. The admired clemency of your eminence knows, after considering by his judgment the government [of the state], to assent favourably to just[409] requests, particularly when one is put forward by a general

---

408 The word *signacula* could also refer to seals, but it unlikely that members of a local elite would have owned any, since seals seem to have been restricted to kings during this period (see, for instance, Marculf *Additamenta* no. 2).

409 Both Zeumer's and Uddholm's editions give the spelling *juxta petentibus* (literally 'according to those requesting'), following Leiden BPL 114, but this should probably be emended to *justa petentibus* (literally 'those requesting just things'), as in Paris BnF lat. 10756 and 4627.

request, by the common voice of all, which will steadily benefit the governance of the people by the church, and which will also favour salvation and [divine] mercy for the royal clemency. Since the apostolic man B of blessed memory, bishop of the city of C, nearing his end, travelled from this light after completing the course of nature, we humbly ask, in order that the flock of the deceased shepherd should not be abandoned (may this never happen!), that you should deign to name in his place the illustrious man D – or: the venerable D – as the successor to his see, in whom there is great foresight, a free birth, shining elegance, diligence of chastity, wealth of charity. We decided willingly to confirm this agreement irrevocably by our hands.

I, 8: Charter regarding the offices of duke, *patricius* and count.

This single formula could apparently be followed to appoint either a count, a duke or a *patricius*: each of these officials governed different territories, but they are here attributed the same basic functions. Besides the payment of a yearly tribute to the royal treasury (which may or may not refer to something akin to direct taxation,[410] and could also refer to the payment of fines owed to the fisc), these functions were essentially linked with the administration of justice and the keeping of the peace. Defending the weak, and widows and orphans in particular, was also commonly associated with the responsibilities of the king and his agents.[411] The reference to the different types of people who might be found on the territory of the official and the expectation that they should be dealt with 'according to their own law and custom' ('secundum lege et consuetudine eorum') evoke the 'personality principle' characteristic of early medieval law, according to which a different set of laws would have applied to each particular ethnic group: Salic law for the Franks; the Theodosian code or its Visigothic abbreviation, the Breviary of Alaric, for 'Romans' (a category which included religious institutions); and the *Liber constitutionum* (also known as the *Lex Gundobada*) for the Burgundians, whose kingdom had been absorbed as part of Frankish territory in 534. In practice, however, identification with any particular ethnic group was not an automatic process: historians no longer consider ethnic identity as a given or objective state, but rather as a more fluid form of self-definition, determined at least to some degree by choice.[412]

410 See Goffart, 'Old and new in Merovingian taxation', and n. 396 above.

411 See Devroey, *Puissants et misérables*, pp. 326–27; Guillot, 'La justice dans le royaume franc', pp. 658–59.

412 On ethnicity in the law-codes, see, for instance, R. Collins, 'Law and ethnic identity in the Western kingdoms in the fifth and sixth centuries', in A.P. Smyth, ed., *Medieval Europeans: Studies in ethnic identity and national perspectives in medieval Europe* (London/New York, 1998), pp. 1–23; Wormald, *The Making of English Law*, pp. 29–108; P. Wormald, '*Lex scripta*

The clemency of royal foresight is celebrated perfectly when he looks for kindness and vigilance in persons from among all the people; and it is not fitting for the judiciary dignity to be conferred easily upon any person, unless his faithfulness and diligence have first been ascertained. Therefore, since we have learned of your faithfulness and usefulness, we give to you the office of count – duke, or *patricius* – in the *pagus* of A, which your predecessor B was seen to hold until now, for you to administer and govern, in such as way that you will always keep complete fidelity to our rule, and all the people living there, Franks, Romans, Burgundians or people of any other origin, will live and be disciplined by your rule and government. And you will rule them in the right way, according to their [own] law and custom; you will count as the greatest defender of the widows and orphans; [and] the crimes of robbers and evil-doers will be punished by you most severely, so that the people, living well under your rule, may, rejoicing, remain peaceful. And whatever the fisc may expect from this office will be paid by yourself every year to our treasurers.[413]

I, 9: Letter of recommendation to another king, when an embassy is sent and presents a verbal communication.

This is a letter of introduction for ambassadors apparently sent by one Merovingian king to another, who is described as his brother. The purpose of the embassy was intended to be transmitted orally, as was common practice,[414] so that introductory letters of this kind often only contained standard pleasantries, which could

---

and *verbum regis*: legislation and Germanic kingship from Euric to Cnut', in P.H. Sawyer and I.N. Wood, eds., *Early Medieval Kingship* (Leeds, 1977), pp. 105–08, reprinted in Wormald, *Legal Culture in the Early Medieval West: Law as Text, Image and Experience* (London, 1999), pp. 1–43; P. Amory, 'The meaning and purpose of ethnic terminology in the Burgundian laws', *Early Medieval Europe* 2 (1993), pp. 1–28; P.S. Barnwell, 'Emperors, jurists and kings: law and custom in the late Roman and early medieval West', *Past and Present* 168 (2000), pp. 6–29. On ethnicity in general, see P.J. Geary, 'Ethnic identity as a situational construct in the Early Middle Ages', *Mitteilungen der anthropologischen Gesellschaft in Wien* 113 (1983), pp. 15–26; P.J. Geary, *The Myth of Nations: the medieval origins of Europe* (Princeton, 2002); H.-W. Goetz, J. Jarnut and W. Pohl, eds., *Regna and gentes: the relationship between late antique and early medieval peoples and kingdoms in the transformation of the Roman world* (Leiden, 2003); W. Pohl and H. Reimitz, eds., *Strategies of Distinction: The construction of ethnic communities, 300–800* (Leiden, 1998); S. Reynolds, 'Our forefathers? Tribes, peoples, and nations in the historiography of the age of migrations', in A.C. Murray, ed., *After Rome's Fall: Narrators and Sources of Early Medieval History* (Toronto, 1998), pp. 17–36.

413 These treasurers are referred to as *aerarii*.
414 Compare, for instance, Cassiodorus, *Variae* II, 41, 3 (trans. Barnish, p. 44).

easily be based on models of this kind. The written answer required would have been equally devoid of significant content (an example is given in the following formula), since King A's answer was again to be reported orally.

To the glorious lord and excellent brother King A, in God's name, King B. A desired event has given us a worthy opportunity to present the honour of our salutations to your serenity, since we desire, plainly moved by love, to know the prosperity of your highness, since we think of your glory as inseparable from us through brotherhood. Therefore we sent into the presence of your fraternity the present illustrious men C and D, who we ask should be received with the kindest tranquillity, as is appropriate to your glory, so that when they fulfil the object of the embassy entrusted [to them], after being given notice of your answer, they may be honoured through your sacred letter to bring back news of your health.

I, 10: Answer to the king.

This is an equally standard answer to the letter given in the previous formula. It contains only good wishes and a reassurance that the king is in good health, while the main business of the embassy was again to be transmitted orally.

To the most glorious and excellent King A, to be embraced by us in the love of Christ with the ties of greatest affection, King B. Know that we received with the greatest eagerness the letter from your highness [brought] by the magnificent and illustrious men C–D, through whom we send on to your highness, as is fitting, dues of salutation. I rejoiced in learning that things were prosperous with you, and we received those [who are] in your affection, as befits such men, with the kindest devotion. They brought the business of the embassy to our ears as you had ordered them to, and when, in God's name, they have happily returned, they are to relate for the ears of your highness all the things that we gave in answer.

I, 11: List of required goods and minimal duties [to be provided] for the envoys, according to this [model].

This is a *tractoria*, a list of goods and services that had to be provided for envoys on their journey: Marculf clearly intended this text to complement the letters relating to a royal embassy in the previous two formulae (the envoys are here described as a team consisting of a bishop and a layman).[415] Krusch joked that

---

[415] Compare *Formulae Imperiales* no. 7 (Zeumer, *Formulae*, p. 292); Cassiodorus had also included one example of this type of document in his *Variae* (VII, 33), though in a far less detailed form.

this was really quite a lot of food for two men to have every day, and thought that this list enumerated all the different possibilities rather than describing realistic everyday supplies;[416] this may well be the case, but it is also likely that these two men would have been escorted by quite a large party, as suggested by Marculf I, 23, which shows a king's envoy taking a number of his men with him. These supplies were to be delivered 'at the usual places' ('loca consuetudinaria'), which no doubt refers to set stages on this particular itinerary. This formula mentions a great quantity of Mediterranean and Eastern spices.[417] A presumed decline of the commerce of spices after the Merovingian period, along with that of papyrus, formed an important part of the Pirenne thesis. Pirenne compared this formula with another formula of *tractoria* dating from the reign of Louis the Pious:[418] the latter mentions twenty loaves of bread, one pig or lamb, two chickens, ten eggs, salt, herbs, vegetables, fish and cheese as well as wood and horses, but no spices. Pirenne concluded that spices had become unavailable in Francia by the Carolingian period, arguing that exchanges across the Mediterranean had stopped due to the Arab conquest.[419] This point has been much disputed ever since: it has been argued that the Carolingians were not so wholly bereft of spices as had been supposed, and Pirenne's exclusive concentration on the trade of luxury items, obscuring more common exchanges, has also been criticised more generally.[420] One cannot exclude, in any case, the possibility that at least some of these plants were being cultivated within the Frankish kingdoms, in which case they

416 Krusch, 'Ursprung und Text', p. 256.
417 These spices are well-represented in the treatise on foods and their medical properties written by Anthemius, a Greek doctor, for the Frankish king Theuderic I (511–533), to whom he had himself been sent on an embassy by the Ostrogothic king Theoderic (*Epistula de observatione ciborum*, ed. E. Liechtenhan, *Corpus Medicorum Latinorum* vol. 8:1 [Leipzig, 1963]; see C. Deroux, 'Anthime, un médecin gourmet du début des temps mérovingiens', *Revue belge de philologie et d'histoire* 80:4 [2002], pp. 1107–24). Many of the items included in this formula are also mentioned in a charter of Chilperic II in favour of the monastery of Corbie, dated 29 April 716 (Kölzer DM. 171). Krusch even speculated that Marculf used this document as his model, and used this as part of his argument for a very late dating of Marculf. The supplies in the Corbie document were to be provided every year rather than every day, which according to Krusch explained the large quantities of supplies involved (Krusch, 'Ursprung und Text', p. 256). The textual link, however, is far from close: the correspondences are only to be found in the list itself, and even then offer an imperfect match (the Corbie document, for instance, does not include livestock). The similarity may point simply to Corbie and the ambassadors all requiring the same type of supplies, rather than to an actual textual link, as Pirenne himself argued (Pirenne, *Mahomet et Charlemagne*, p. 62).
418 See above, n. 415.
419 Pirenne, *Mahomet et Charlemagne*, p. 61 and pp. 123–26. On the Roman commerce of spices, see J. Innes Miller, *The Spice Trade of the Roman Empire: 29 BC to AD 641* (Oxford, 1969).
420 M. McCormick, *Origins of the European Economy* (Cambridge, 2001), pp. 709–16; Wickham, *Framing the Early Middle Ages*, pp. 701–06.

would not constitute evidence for long-distance trade at all: coriander, cumin and costum, for instance, are listed as garden plants in one of Charlemagne's capitularies.[421]

King A to all agents. Since we, in God's name, sent the apostolic man B[422] as well as the illustrious man C to the region of D for the purposes of an embassy, we therefore order that you should provide them with horses[423] and supplies in the appropriate places, that is: *n.* horses for main and lesser roads,[424] *n. modii* of rich bread, *n. modii* of lower quality [bread], *n. modii* of wine, *n. modii* of beer, *n.* pounds of lard, *n.* pounds of meat, *n.* pigs, *n.* piglets, *n.* sheep, *n.* lambs, *n.* geese, *n.* pheasants, *n.* chickens, *n.* eggs, *n.* pounds of oil, *n.* pounds of *garum*,[425] *n.* [amount of] honey, *n.* [amount of] vinegar, *n.* pounds of cumin, *n.* [amount of] pepper, *n.* amount of costum,[426] *n.* [amount of] cloves, *n.* [amount of] nard,[427] *n.* [amount of] cinnamon, *n.* [amount of] granulated mastic,[428] *n.* [amount of] dates, *n.* [amount of] pistachios, *n.* [amount of] almonds, *n.* one-pound candles, *n.* pounds of cheese, *n.* [amount of] salt, oil, *n.* chariots of vegetables, *n.* [amount of] firewood, and also, to feed their horses, *n.* chariots of hay, *n. modii* of bran. Each of you will procure and accomplish all these things for them each day, both on their way there and, in God's name, on their way back to us, in the usual places, so that they shall not suffer delay or wrong, if you wish to keep our favour.

---

421 *Capitularia* no. 32, *cap.* 70, vol. 1, at p. 90; see also no. 128 § 37 at p. 256.

422 That is, a bishop.

423 The world *evectio* refers more precisely to horses requisitioned for travelling officials, as do *veredus* and *paraveredus* (horses for main roads and horses for bypaths; the distinction is a little puzzling, and the two words later became synonymous). See the relevant entries in Niermayer, *Mediae Latinitatis Lexicon Minus*.

424 See above, n. 423.

425 *Garum* was a type of fish sauce that had been extremely popular under the Roman empire (many members of the local élite of Pompeii had made their fortune manufacturing and exporting it during the first century; see for instance R.I. Curtis, 'A. Umbricius Scaurus of Pompeii', in R.I. Curtis, ed., *Studia Pompeiana & Classica in Honour of Wilhelmina F. Jashemski* [New York, 1988], vol.1, pp. 19–50).

426 Costum: a Mediterranean aromatic plant.

427 This refers to an extremely expensive type of fragrant oil, produced from the rhizomes of the nard plant. The plant grows in the Himalayas, and was imported to Mediterranean regions as a luxury good; it was used to make perfume, but also for the medicinal properties attributed to it. It was sometimes confused with lavender, so that it is uncertain which plant was being referred to here.

428 This refers to chunks of resin taken from the Mediterranean mastic tree, which were apparently chewed to help digestion.

THE FORMULARY OF MARCULF

I, 12: Charter for a mutual donation [between spouses].

This formula describes a similar transaction to that found in Angers no. 41, which also gives a model for a testament made by a childless couple in each other's favour, but there are some significant differences between these two texts: this document is not formulated as a testament, but puts all of the couple's property in common ownership until the death of one of them. Unlike the Angers document, it only confers a right of usufruct over the property to the surviving partner, rather than full ownership: this transaction did not, therefore, entail any disruption of the rights of the couple's respective families and heirs. The text thus excluded the right to alienate any of this property, with the exception of gifts to the church. Although this couple could perfectly well have had their document validated through local courts, as the Angers formula shows, they chose to have it confirmed by the king, which accounts for the presence in Book I of what to all intents and purposes would otherwise constitute a private charter: the king's intervention not only gave their document greater authority, but also stressed their privileged access to royal authority. Compare Marculf II, 7 and 8 for models very similar to this one, though sanctioned through local courts.

Since the Lord almighty, creator of heaven and earth, allowed, according to what can be read, in the beginning, male and female to be associated in the union of marriage, saying: '[Therefore] shall a man leave his father and his mother, and shall cleave unto his wife: and they shall be one flesh',[429] if they have decided out of loving affection to give each other something, our serenity will not refuse to confirm this for them. Therefore, [the man] A and [the woman] B, having come here in our palace, because they are known not to have had any children born between them, were seen to give all of their property to each other by our hand, and – if this is appropriate: – they were seen to give each other certain villas. Therefore the said man A gave by our hand to his said wife B the villas named C–D, situated in the *pagus* of E, which he is known to hold at present, either through a royal gift or from the inheritance of his relatives or from anywhere else, with lands, houses – etc. –. Similarly, in compensation for these properties, the said woman gave to her said husband A the villas named F–G, situated in the *pagus* of H, with lands – etc. –; and they were seen to give each other by our hand moveable goods from their house, gold and silver, jewels, carpets, clothes and all their household implements, so that while they both live in this life, all the things written above must be owned by both parties equally; and if for [the good of] their souls they decide to give something out of this to a holy place, they shall have the freedom to do this; and let the one out of them who survives his spouse in

---

429 Genesis 2:24.

this life own the property of both by right of usufruct for as long as (s)he lives. And after both have travelled from this light, according to what is included in their documents, they must leave at their death both the villas written above and whatever is left of their moveable goods to holy places, the persons who helped them or their relatives, as their heirs. Therefore by the present order[430] we decide and command that, since such was the decision of the persons A–B written above, and [since] they are known to have given [this] to one another by our hand, whatever is included above must stand, with God's help, consolidated and confirmed by the strongest right by this order,[431] by God's grace and ours, so that no opposition, whether from our fisc or from their close relatives or from anyone, may shake it, but it will remain unshaken for all time. And so that this document may stand more firmly and be preserved through time, we decided to confirm it below by our own hand.

I, 13: Document of *lesewerpus*[432] by the hand of the king.

Although much is made of royal intervention here, this document boils down to a straightforward gift taking effect at the giver's death, which was merely being confirmed by the king: as in the previous formula, the intervention of the king did not alter the nature of this transaction significantly, but was sought as a greater source of authority, as well as to emphasise the claims of the two main parties to royal favour. Although A was technically giving his land to the king, he retained the use of it (*usubeneficium*) until his death, at which point the king was to ensure the land passed on to the heir of his choice (E). The right of usufruct mentioned in this document limited A's rights over the land in the meantime, since it only allowed A to exploit the land and retain its revenues, but did not allow him to alienate any of it or leave it to any heir but E. This arrangement is very similar to some found in surviving documents, in which laymen gave property to churches but retained a right of usufruct over it until their death, but it is exceptional in relating exclusively to lay persons: although documents which did not concern churches had smaller chances of surviving, this formula may therefore allow us to speculate that usufruct agreements could also be made between lay people.

---

430 See above, n. 388.
431 See above, n. 388.
432 The meaning of the word 'lesewerpus' is unclear. Some scribes seem to have been unable to understand it: the scribe of Paris BnF lat. 2123 tried to make sense of it by replacing the words 'de lesewerpo' with 'de lesio verbo' (turning the meaning to 'on breaking one's word', which does not correspond to the content of the formula). The Germanic verb *werpire* means to waive or to abandon (spelled 'gurpire' in *Capitularia* no. 28 *cap.* 3, vol. 1, p. 74): *lesewerpus* thus probably involved relinquishing one's rights over something, in this case some landed property.

THE FORMULARY OF MARCULF

Whatever is done in our presence and is seen to be transferred by our hand, we want and order that it should in the future remain most firm by the strongest right. Thus, A, our faithful follower,[433] having come here in our palace in the presence of ourselves and our great men, was seen, by his spontaneous decision, to relinquish and donate to us by the rod[434] the villas named B–C, situated in the *pagus* of D, in such a manner – : if this is appropriate – that, while he lives, he may possess them under the benefit of use; and after his death, according to his request, we will be seen with full grace to concede these villas to our faithful follower E. Therefore we pronounce by the present order,[435] which we order should stand in perpetuity, that, according to the decision stated by this A, he was seen to relinquish and donate to us voluntarily these villas in the said places, and, by our generous gift, according to the decision stated by this A, we will concede [them] to the said E: that is, let [A] possess lands, houses, buildings, tenants, unfree servants,[436] vineyards, forests, fields, meadows, pastures, water and water courses, whatever belonged to this A there in its entirety, under usufruct, for as long as he lives, without diminishing [the value of] any of this property, and after his death let the said E have, hold and possess this, and leave it in the ownership of his descendants or of whomever he likes. And in order that this document may stand more firmly, we decided to confirm it below by our own hand.

---

433 *Fidelis*: it is debated whether this term referred to the fidelity owed to the king by his subjects in general (S. Reynolds, *Fiefs and Vassals: The Medieval Evidence Reinterpreted* [Oxford, 1994], pp. 88–89) or whether it specifically designated a member of the Frankish aristocracy (J.L. Nelson, 'Kingship and empire', in J.H. Burns, ed., *The Cambridge History of Medieval Political Thought c.350–c.1450* [Cambridge, 1988], pp. 211–51, at p. 223). It seems clear, at any rate, that the *fideles* mentioned in Marculf had a privileged access to the royal court.

434 *Per fistuca* (or *festuca*): this 'rod' was used as a symbol to sanction various legal procedures (on this word, see Fouracre, 'The nature of Frankish political institutions', p. 287). Although this tends to be seen as a specifically Frankish phenomenon, it can also be found in a description of Roman judicial proceedings, with a description of accompanying gestures, in the second-century *Institutes* of Gaius (IV, 16). Even in his day Gaius described it as an archaic practice: on its origins, he speculated that 'rods stood for spears, as a symbol of legitimate ownership, because it was thought that the most legitimate form of ownership was over the spoils taken from the enemy' ('festuca autem utebantur quasi hastae loco, signo quodam iusti dominii, quamdo iusto dominio ea maxime sua esse credebant quae ex hostibus cepissent'). See Barnwell, 'Emperors, jurists and kings', p. 24.

435 See above, n. 388.

436 See above, n. 392.

148   THE FORMULARIES OF ANGERS AND MARCULF

I, 14: Prefaces for royal grants.

This formula offers several alternative versions for a gift, in an attempt to cover as many different types of gift as possible through permutations within a single model. Marculf's title emphasises in particular the different possible styles of preface (*arenga*).[437] Only the third allows for the formula to be used to record a gift to a church, and this is also the only case in which a biblical quote is used (though the second preface also includes a reference to salvation, which suggests rewarding followers was also seen as a Christian act). The main text, on the other hand, only corresponds to a gift to a layman, the 'illustrious' A (the model to be used for a gift to the church is given separately in the following formula). According to the alternatives offered in this model, the land being given could have come from two possible sources: it could originally have belonged to another layman (D), or it could have been part of a royal estate, which accounts for the transfer, along with the land, of any tenants of the fisc ('qualibet genus ominum dicione fisci nostri subdetum') who might be living on it. If it had previously belonged to a layman, the situation may have been similar to that described in the previous formula (if the king was only enacting D's own decision to leave his land to A), which may explain why Marculf placed this one immediately after it. Despite being made to a layman, this gift was coupled with a privilege of immunity: this could constitute important evidence for the existence, not recorded in any other source, of lay immunities as well as ecclesiastical ones (see also Marculf I, 3 and II, 1).

Those who have served our relatives and ourselves from their youth with diligent service are deservedly supported by the gift of our generosity.

Another one: – [Being] a wise benefactor in observing the service of one's faithful followers,[438] with God's favour, counts especially towards royal salvation.

Another one, to a holy place: – 'We brought nothing into this world,' as the apostle says, 'and [it is certain] we can carry nothing out',[439] except for what we are seen to give to holy places for the salvation of [our] soul, offering [it] with devotion to the Lord.

Therefore let your greatness – or: your diligence – know this: we were seen to grant to the illustrious man A, by a willing decision, the villa named B, situated in the *pagus* of C, in its entirety, with all of its benefit and territory, as it was possessed, or is now possessed, by [the man] D – or: by our fisc –. Therefore we decide by our present document, which we order should

---

437 The classic work on the ideological content of *arengas* is H. Fichtenau's *Arenga: Spätantike und Mittelalter im Spiegel von Urkundenformeln* (Graz/Cologne, 1957).
438 See above, n. 433.
439 1 Timothy 6:7.

stand in perpetuity, that the said man A, as we said, should have granted to him in perpetuity this villa of B, in all its entirety, with lands, houses, buildings, tenants, unfree servants,[440] vineyards, forests, fields, meadows, pastures, water and water courses, corn mills, dependencies, appurtenances, and with any type of person subjected to our fisc who may live there, under full immunity, with judges[441] being forbidden from entering to collect fines in relation to any legal case; so that he may have, hold and possess it by right of ownership without waiting for any judicial assembly [to sanction] the donation, and that he may leave [it] as a possession to his descendants, with God's help, or to anybody he wants, through our generosity; and let him have the free power in every way to do whatever he wants with it, by our permission. And so that this document...

I, 15: Grant to a holy place.

> Marculf seems to have intended this model for the grant of a royal estate to a church to work in tandem with the formula that precedes it. No preface is given, which suggests that this text was meant to be headed by the third preface presented in I, 14. The main text is very similar to that given in I, 14, with some minor alterations allowing for the change in type of recipient. Marculf refers the reader to that previous formula for the full description of the estate; although he skipped the grant of immunity which immediately followed that description in I, 14, it was probably also meant to be included, since it also features in the confirmation for a grant of land similar to this one given in the following formula. This text also contains the end of the last sentence of the document, which had been omitted in I, 14.

Let your greatness – or: your usefulness – know this: we were seen to grant, in the name of God, to the basilica – or: the church – of A, over which our apostolic father – or: the venerable abbot – B is known to rule, the villa named C, situated in the *pagus* of D, which our fisc – or: E – owned until now, in all its entirety, with a most ready devotion. Therefore we decide by our present document, which we command should stand in perpetuity, that the said church of A and the said pontiff – or: Abbot A –, as we said, [should possess] this villa in all its entirety, with lands – etc.; see above –, so that he and his successors may have, hold and possess it, and may have the free power in every way to do whatever they want with it for [the benefit of] the said church – or: basilica – of A, by our permission. And so that this

---

440 See above, n. 392.
441 See above, n. 393.

document may stand more firmly and be preserved through time, we decided to confirm it below with a signature by our hand.

I, 16: Confirmation.

> This is a confirmation of a grant of land to a bishop, complementing the formula given in I, 15 (compare Marculf I, 4 for the confirmation of an immunity).

It befits one whom divine piety has elevated to the kingship to maintain the deeds of his ancestors, [and] it is especially necessary to maintain in [our] time what is known to have been granted by royal clemency for the benefit of churches or holy places, for the sake of eternal rewards. Thus the apostolic man, our father in Christ, A, bishop of the city of B, brought to the attention of the clemency of our rule that King C, by his order[442] signed by his hand, had in the name of God granted to the church of D, over which [A] is known to rule, the villa named E, situated in the *pagus* of F, in its entirety, under full immunity, with judges[443] being forbidden from entering to collect fines in relation to any legal case. And he states that he has this document[444] in his hands, and that this pontiff is known to possess the said villa under these same terms for the benefit of the church. He asked our highness to confirm this regarding this matter and the said church of Lord D by our document. Know that we, in the name of God and out of reverence for this holy place and the merits of the said pontiff, guarantee and confirm this with a glad spirit, commanding, since it appears that the said villa was granted in its entirety under full immunity by the said prince to the said church of D, and since [that church] is seen to possess it at present, having read this grant, we fully confirm by this order,[445] in God's name, that by that right both he and his successors and the said church of Lord D may hold and possess it, leave it for their successors to possess, and have the free power to do whatever they decide with it for the benefit of this holy place, by our permission. And so that this document...

I, 17: Another confirmation, for laymen.

> This text complements the formula for a grant of land to a layman given in Marculf I, 14 in much the same way that I, 16 complemented I, 15. The wording is again very similar.

---

442 See above, n. 388.
443 See above, n. 393.
444 See above, n. 388.
445 See above, n. 388.

We exercise the royal custom and encourage the spirit of our faithful followers[446] if we grant the requests of our faithful followers gladly and put them into effect in God's name. Thus the illustrious man A pointed out to the clemency of our rule that *n*. years before the late King [B], our relative, had granted to him, through his order[447] signed by his hand, out of consideration for his fidelity [and because] his merits called for it, a certain villa named thus, in the *pagus* of C, which before that had belonged to his fisc, and which A held, together with everything belonging to this villa, under full immunity, with judges[448] being forbidden from entering to collect fines in relation to any legal case. And he showed us this document from the said prince in order that it should be read, and he is known to possess the said villa at present under the same terms. He asked us that our document should fully [and] generally confirm this regarding this matter. Know that, out of consideration for his fidelity, as with every one of our faithful followers who makes a just request, we did not want to deny his request, but with a glad spirit we guaranteed and confirmed it. We therefore order that, as it appears that the said villa of D was granted to A in all its entirety by this said prince B, and he is seen to possess it at present by right of ownership, [this should be] fully confirmed, in God's name, by this order,[449] this document having been read,[450] and he and his descendants may hold and possess it, and leave it as a possession to whomever they want; and let them enjoy the freedom to do whatever they decide with it, by our permission. And so that this document may stand more firmly and be preserved through time, we decided to confirm it below by our own hand.

I, 18: Regarding the antrustion of the king.

An antrustion was a member of the king's *trustis* or band of armed retainers, and may have fulfilled a role similar to that of a bodyguard.[451] The swearing 'into the king's hand' mentioned here foreshadows the rituals later associated with entering someone's service as a vassal, which typically included swearing

---

446 See above, n. 433.
447 See above, n. 388.
448 See above, n. 393.
449 See above, n. 388.
450 See above, n. 388.
451 See Reynolds, *Fiefs and Vassals*, pp. 82–83. See also W. Kienast, *Die fränkische Vassalität* (Frankfurt, 1990), pp. 3–73; P. Depreux, *Les Sociétés occidentales du milieu du VIe à la fin du IXe siècle* (Rennes, 2002), p. 158; Devroey, *Puissants et misérables*, p. 162.

an oath and touching hands.[452] As this formula shows, entering this particular type of service to the king increased one's *wergeld* (that is, the price to be paid in compensation if someone was murdered: the sum varied according to status, age and gender).[453] The *wergeld* of 600 *solidi* mentioned here does indeed correspond to the amount given in Salic law for the murder of a member of the king's *trustis*.[454] This was the highest possible *wergeld* envisaged in Salic law, only equalled by the amount to be paid for killing a free child or a free woman of child-bearing age, and thus emphasised the high status and increased protection associated with the antrustion's role.

It is right that he who promises undying fidelity to us should be protected by our help. And because our faithful follower[455] A, with God's favour, having come here to our palace along with his weapons, was seen to swear into our hands[456] military service and fidelity to us, we therefore decide and order by the present order[457] that from now on the said A will be counted among the number of [our] antrustions. And should someone perhaps dare to kill him, let him know that he will be liable [to pay] 600 *solidi* for his wergeld.

I, 19: Document[458] regarding the holy orders.

This text is linked to the formula immediately preceding it in that it also records someone's entry into service before the king; this time, however, it is into the service of the church. The fact that A needed to ask for the king's permission suggests that he owed some form of dependence to the king. Since there is no indication that he was of particularly high status or that he had a strong

---

452 On the possible reasons for the transition from 'antrustions' to 'vassals', see P. Fouracre, *The Age of Charles Martel* (London, 2000), p. 152.

453 The compensation to be paid also depended on the circumstances of the murder: the *wergeld* was multiplied by three, bringing the price up to 1800 *solidi* in the case of an antrustion, when the victim was killed inside their own house, while serving in the army, or if the murderer tried to get rid of the body by throwing it in a river or down a well or by covering it with leaves or branches.

454 *Pactus Legis Salicae* 41, 5 (p. 156).

455 See above, n. 433.

456 'In manu nostra': this is a standard phrase connected to transfers of either property or service, which were often said to be given into the recipient's 'hand'. This expression was commonly used in the writings of earlier Roman jurists to express power over something or someone; the Frankish equivalent is the word *mund* (as in the *mundeburdium*, or royal protection, in I, 24). Touching hands and swearing an oath later both became typical features of entry into vassalage.

457 See above, n. 388.

458 See above, n. 388.

connection with the king, since he is not described as a *fidelis*,[459] it is possible he could have been a dependant of the fisc, if he lived on a royal estate. The text, however, makes it clear that he could not join the clergy if he was listed as having to pay dues from his land to the royal treasury ('in poleptico publico censitus'); perhaps there could be circumstances in which dependants did not have to pay such dues, or perhaps A was simply a different type of free dependant or servant, whose land, if he had any, did not depend from the fisc. Unfree persons were not allowed to become priests (though they could be manumitted for that purpose), which accounts for the condition that A should be of 'truly free status' ('bene ingenuus': the need to specify the word *bene* may suggest that some people could be more 'free' than others).

If we do not deny permission to those who decide to transfer to the rank of the clergy, we are confident that we will be rewarded by God for this, since it is written: 'Withhold not good from them to whom it is due, when it is in the power of thine hand to do it'.[460] Thus A, coming into our presence, asked our serenity to give him permission to cut off the hair of his head [in order to obtain] the rank of the clergy, and go into the service of the church – or: the monastery – of B. Know that we, in the name of God, guaranteed this for him with a glad spirit. Therefore we command by our order[461] that, if the said A is seen to be of truly free status, and is not counted in the public register as paying dues, he may have the permission to tonsure the hair of his head and go into the service of the church – or: the monastery – written above, and pray vigilantly for God's forgiveness on our behalf.

I, 20: Regarding the sharing of a property in which an agent[462] of the king is involved.

In this case, the division of some property as a result of an inheritance seems to have become the object of a dispute, which accounts for the request of the participants that a royal *missus* (that is, an envoy or agent of the king) be sent over to sort things out. A tenth of the property was to be confiscated as a result of royal involvement in the dispute, and although this fine should apparently have gone

---

459 See above, n. 433.

460 Proverbs 3:27. Uddholm bizarrely mistranslated this quote, though it follows the Vulgate text fairly closely (Uddholm, *Marculfi formularum libri duo*, p. 89).

461 *Praecipientes*, 'ordering', or perhaps here more specifically 'by issuing a *praeceptio*' (see above, n. 388).

462 The word is *missus* (literally 'envoy'). *Missi* tend to be associated more with Carolingian government, though this formula shows that Merovingian kings already made use of them (as did bishops: see below, Marculf I, 26, Supplement no. 1 and Add. no. 3).

to the royal treasury, the king here allows the *missus* to keep it as a reward. The text emphasises that this did not merely amount to a one-off payment of a tenth of the value of the property: the *missus* was apparently to own his tenth of the land outright, as suggested in the last sentence, which guaranteed his continued rights over the land. In practice, this probably meant that he would receive a tenth of all the revenues obtained from this land from that point onwards. No doubt the obligation to hand over a share of the property as the price for royal involvement would have encouraged participants to settle out of court whenever possible (compare Marculf II, 14 and Angers no. 55 for agreements over inheritance made without judicial intervention).

Since the sharing and equal partition of the inheritance of A – or: the field of B – between C and D – or: between its joint owners – must be proclaimed, and since they requested that an agent[463] of our palace should be involved in dividing and sharing this equally between them, therefore know this: we were seen to send our agent,[464] the illustrious man E, to divide this equally between them. Therefore we decide and order by the present document[465] that you should involve him in this matter, and each of them will be limited to the portion justly owed [to them], and a tenth [of the property is to be given] to him for the cost of the dispute.[466] And this man E will have conceded to him, by our grant, whatever is to be paid to the fisc as a result of this, including land, vineyards, unfree servants[467] and from whatever source; and let him have the free power to do whatever he wants with it.

I, 21: On taking up someone else's legal cases.

This formula shows us the king allowing one lord to represent another in court. A pleaded ignorance ('simplicitas sua') to explain his inability to pursue his own

463   See above, n. 462.
464   See above, n. 462.
465   See above, n. 388.
466   This last part of the sentence is somewhat confusing. Manuscripts offer different readings: *sunt elites* (Leiden BPL 114), *suntellitis* (Paris BnF lat. 4627), and *sunt ellitis* (Paris BnF lat. 10756). The B tradition (Paris BnF lat. 2123 and Copenhagen, Kongelige Bibliothek, coll. Fabric. 84) leaves it out altogether. Bignon read this as *sumptus litis*, Zeumer as *suntelites* (as in *syncellitis*, 'companion', which makes little sense in this context), Uddholm as *sunto lites* (as in Bignon's *sumptus litis*, but with a variant spelling). Uddholm's conclusion was probably correct, though the meaning of his translation remains as mysterious as the Latin text itself ('et tous les dix X comme frais de procédure'; Uddholm, *Marculfi formularum libri duo*, p. 91; see also Uddholm, 'Le texte des *Formulae Marculfi*', p. 56). On the manuscript tradition, see Appendix 3.
467   See above, n. 392.

claims. This would imply that some form of special competence was needed in order to bring forward a legal action, which is not very plausible, since people of varied stations seemed perfectly able to do this for themselves, as can be seen from the Angers formulary. It is more likely that A was asking for B's assistance because B would have been in a better position to bring about a satisfactory outcome in court: B is described as a *vir inluster* and thus seems to have been of higher status than A, who is only described as *fidelis*.[468] This effectively amounted to a link of patronage, giving B a level of control over A. The text certainly does not imply that A was in any sense putting himself into B's service, since both were free to go back on the agreement, but some form of reciprocation or counter-gift would no doubt have been expected from him. B assumed legal responsibility not only for A, but also for his dependants, who must themselves already have put A in charge of their own legal cases (compare I, 23 below): others would therefore also have gained protection from A's association with a more powerful lord. Compare Angers no. 52 for a mandate describing an arrangement similar in many ways, but made outside the royal court.

Our faithful follower[469] A, with God's favour, having come into our presence, put it to us that due to his ignorance he could not pursue his legal cases or enter a plea in court.[470] He asked the clemency of our rule that the illustrious man B should take up all his legal cases on his behalf, in the *pagus* as well as in our palace,[471] and pursue them and enter pleas [regarding them] in court. He was seen to delegate them to him presently by the rod.[472] Therefore we order that, since this was the will of both parties, the said man B must pursue and enter pleas regarding all of A's legal cases everywhere, and must make right every legal accusation on his behalf and on that of his men, and in a similar manner obtain justice[473] from others, for as long as this is the will of both [A and B].

I, 22: Document[474] [of manumission by throwing a] *denarius*.

This is a rare example of manumission of an unfree rural tenant (as suggested by the reference to the 'reliqui mansoarii', 'the other tenants'); domestic slaves seem to have been manumitted rather more frequently. B's master, A, is described as

468 See above, n. 433.
469 See n. 433 above.
470 That is, the *mallus*, a judicial assembly (verb form: *mallare*).
471 See above, n. 366.
472 See above, n. 434.
473 The word used here is *veritas*, in the specialised sense of establishing the 'truth' in relation to the outcome of a lawsuit.
474 See above, n. 388.

either a bishop or an 'illustrious man': his privileged access to the king probably accounts for his choice to free his servant in this particularly formal way, when the same result could perfectly well have been achieved in a local court. The symbolic action of throwing a coin seems to be the only thing differentiating this form of manumission from others, though it is difficult to tell, since the text is very short, and does not specify what, if any, duties B would still have had to perform for A as his freedman. Salic law does refer to manumission by the *denarius*, though only in a clause forbidding people from manumitting slaves who did not belong to them.[475] This type of manumission was used by Charlemagne when he freed his servant woman Sigrada.[476] Four formulae surviving as part of other collections also describe the same ceremony.[477]

Because the apostolic – or: illustrious – man A freed his slave named B by his hand – or: [by the hand] of C[478] – in our presence, by throwing a *denarius*, according to Salic law, we confirm his manumission by our present charter. And we order that from now on, in the same way as the other tenants known to have been freed from the yoke of servitude in the presence of princes by this legal title, the said B, with full confirmation in God's name by our order,[479] without anyone making claims against him, may be able to remain free and secure for all time by God's grace and ours.

I, 23: Charter regarding the interruption of legal cases.

In this text, the king sends a bishop or an 'illustrious man' on an errand, perhaps on an embassy, and frees him from any obligation to appear in court for the duration of his journey; I, 21 shows us that A could have appointed someone to represent him, but this does not happen here. As in I, 21, this lord seems to have taken responsibility for all legal cases affecting his dependants: *amici*, 'friends', or sometimes 'relatives', or perhaps here referring to people under A's patronage; *gasindi*,[480] military retainers; and all those for whom he was legally responsible ('undecumque ipse legitimo redebit mitio').[481]

475 *Pactus Legis Salicae* 26, p. 97.
476 *Die Urkunden Pippins, Karlmanns und Karls des Grossen*, ed. E. Mühlbacher, MGH *Diplomata* (Hanover, 1906), DK. 115, at pp. 161–62 (only the beginning is preserved, written in Tironian notes on the verso of the original charter containing DK. 116, dated to 7 January 777).
477 Compare *Cartae Senonicae* no. 42, *Formulae Salicae Bignonianae* no. 1, *Formulae Salicae Merkelianae* no. 40 or *Formulae Imperiales* no. 1.
478 This alternative allows for A being represented by someone else.
479 See above, n. 388.
480 On this word, see Rio, 'Freedom and unfreedom', pp. 25–27; below, pp. 216–17.
481 See Wickham, *Framing the Early Middle Ages*, p. 439.

Let your greatness – or: your usefulness – know this: since we presently ordered the apostolic man A – or: the illustrious man A – to travel to this place in our service, we therefore order that, while he is detained in these parts, all his legal cases and those of his friends and retainers, or of anyone for whom he is legitimately answerable, should remain on hold. Therefore we decide and order by the present document[482] that, until he returns from these parts, all his legal cases and those of his friends, both those who are going with him and those who are remaining in their homes, or of anyone for whom he is legitimately answerable, should remain on hold, and after [his return] he is to make right every legal accusation on their behalf, and in a similar manner obtain justice[483] from others.

I, 24: Charter regarding the protection given by a king and a prince.

'Protection' is expressed here by the word *mundeburdium*, which derives from *mund*, the Frankish word for 'hand' (Marculf also gives the Latin equivalent *defensio*). The protection was here given to a church or monastery, and extended to all of A's dependants, his men, retainers and 'friends' ('cum hominebus suis aut gasindis vel amicis'), and those under his protection ('suo mitthio'). Although the word *mundeburdium* was not used in the formula in which a layman agreed to take up another layman's legal cases (I, 21), the situation was not entirely dissimilar, since both formulae relate to legal protection through patronage. In this case, however, the king undertook to do this less directly: the practicalities of this protection were delegated to the mayor of the palace (the *princeps* of the title), who himself delegated them to his own subordinate (E). A would effectively have been able to make use of his link with the king only in the sense that he would be allowed to go before the royal tribunal if he failed to get the desired result in a local court by relying on E's help alone. This right to go to the king, however, was an important favour, since those who did not benefit from the king's *mundeburdium* did not technically have the right to speak to him, and could only submit a written petition.[484]

It is right that royal power should offer protection to those who are known to be in need of it. Therefore let your greatness – or your usefulness – know

---

482 See above, n. 388.
483 See above, n. 473.
484 One formula dealing with a woman who did not have a document of *mundeburdium* thus bears the title 'if you do not have the permission to speak with the king, these are the words you should send to him regarding your case' (*Formulae Bituricenses* no. 14 [Zeumer, *Formulae*, p. 174]). For other examples of royal *mundeburdium*, see Marculf Add. no. 2 (an adaptation of the text given here), and *Formulae Imperiales* nos. 30, 31, 48, 52 and 55 (Zeumer, *Formulae*, pp. 309–10, 323 and 325–27).

that we were seen to grant, under our protection, to the apostolic – or: the venerable – man A of the monastery of B, built in honour of Saint C, along with all his property and men and retainers[485] and friends or anyone for whom he is legitimately answerable, his just request regarding the unlawful attacks of evil men, so that the said church – or: monastery – shall remain in peace along with all its property, under the protection and defence of the illustrious man D, mayor of our palace, and the illustrious man E, under [the orders of] this man D, will take up the legal cases of this pontiff – or: abbot – and [his] church – or: monastery – and of those who are known to expect [protection] from him, and of anyone for whom he is legitimately answerable, in the *pagus* as well as in our palace.[486] Therefore by the present document[487] we decide and order that the said pontiff – or: abbot – should remain in peace under our protection and the protection of the said man; and neither you nor your subordinates and successors nor anyone else should presume to wrong and trouble him with legal claims. And if legal cases are brought forward against him and his dependants that cannot be settled in local courts without causing him a great loss, let them be brought to our presence. And so that this document may stand more firmly, we decided to sign it below by our own hand.

I, 25: Prologue to the judgment of a king, when two people are in dispute over a large property.

> Marculf sadly only gives us the preface to this *placitum*, so that the circumstances of the dispute are unknown. This text introduces the different members of the royal tribunal in decreasing order of prestige and power; the possible attendance of the mayor of the palace has been taken as one of the main arguments for a late dating of Marculf.[488] The wording of this introduction is consistent with that

---

485 On the word *gasindus*, see below, pp. 216–17.
486 See above, n. 366.
487 See above, n. 388.
488 Deciding whether Marculf I, 25 does or does not have a reference to the mayor of the palace was the object of a long controversy: Leiden BPL 114 and Paris BnF lat. 10756 do have a *maior domus* present, whereas Paris BnF lat. 4627 does not (see Zeumer, 'Der Maior domus in Marculf I, 25' and 'Neue Erörterungen über ältere fränkische Formelsammlungen'; Tardif, 'Etude sur la date du formulaire de Marculf' and 'Nouvelles observations sur la date du formulaire de Marculf'). Uddholm's discovery that Paris BnF lat. 4627 was actually the result of a contact between the Leiden tradition and the Paris BnF lat. 10756 tradition (Uddholm, 'Le texte des *Formulae Marculfi*') settled the problem: the absence of a reference to the *maior domus* from Paris BnF lat. 4627 must have been due to its removal for the purpose of updating the formula at some point after the office had died out, and therefore points to a later tradition rather than an earlier one in relation to the other manuscripts. On the manuscript tradition, see Appendix 3.

found in surviving Merovingian *placita* of the second half of the seventh century, and the list of officials involved is given in much the same order.[489] The 'large property' specified in the title may imply that the full list of officials would not have been needed if the object of the dispute had been less valuable. The accuser (Q) probably appealed to the king after other means of settlement at a more local level had been exhausted, in the hope of obtaining a better outcome; he may have benefited from a similar sort of agreement with the king as that given in the preceding formula (I, 24), since, in spite of the reference to the royal tribunal as hearing 'the lawsuits of all', it is clear that not everyone would have been able to appeal to the king.

> He to whom the Lord has granted the care of ruling [the kingdom] must investigate the lawsuits of all by a diligent examination, in order to give a sound judgment according to the allegations and answers exchanged between them, so that the sharpness of a quick mind may resolve the knot of disputes and so that [our] decision may set foot where justice shines through. Thus, while we, in God's name, were sitting here in our palace to settle the lawsuits of all by a right judgment, together with bishops, our lords and fathers, and many of our great men: the bishops A–B, the mayor of the palace C, the dukes D–E, the *patricii* F–G, the referendaries H–I, the *domestici* J–K, the *senescalces* L–M, the *cubicularii* N–O and the count of the palace P, and many other faithful followers of ours; Q, having come here, accused R, and said…

I, 26: Letter of summons to a bishop.

> This formula again relates to the activity of the royal tribunal. In this case C had appealed to the king to force a bishop to return a *villa* which he claimed had been given to him by another man (E), perhaps through an inheritance. The king ordered the bishop to come to a *placitum* to settle this dispute, or else forfeit the land. It is unclear how the bishop had come to hold E's land in the first place and on what terms he had obtained it: different types of rights over a single property could be held by different people, which often created conflicts and competing claims regarding who exactly had rights over what (it is possible, for instance, that a lease or *precaria* had been involved).[490] On Marculf I, 26–29, see Guillot, 'La justice dans le royaume franc', pp. 686–89.

---

489 Compare, for instance, Kölzer DM. no. 135, pp. 342–44 (translated in Fouracre, '"*Placita*" and the settlement of disputes in the later Merovingian period', pp. 28–29) and DM. no. 149 (pp. 374–76).

490 For *precariae*, compare Angers no. 7 and Marculf II, 5, 9, 40 and 41.

To the blessed lord, caring for the apostolic see, lord and father in Christ, Bishop A, King B. Our faithful follower[491] C, by God's favour, having come into our presence, put it to us that you are unjustly keeping in your possession a certain villa called D, which was to come to him from E, and that he had been unable to obtain justice from you regarding this. Therefore we sent the present letter to your crown of beatitude, so that you should both pray for us and, if that is what happened, return the said villa of D to the said C according to the laws. Certainly, if you do not want [to do this] and have something to oppose to this, summoned by this letter, either yourself or an agent[492] representing your person should now come into our presence to give an answer to this C regarding this.

I, 27: Another letter to a bishop, so that he should distrain another man.

> This letter of summons takes the same basic form as that given in the preceding formula, even though the object of the dispute is different, since it related to a slave rather than a *villa*. One significant difference, however, is that in this case the king did not address the accused (D) directly, but asked a bishop to deal with him. D is explicitly said to be Bishop A's dependant, and therefore under his legal responsibility (compare Marculf I, 21, 23 and 24). Judging from the alternatives offered here, this bishop would have had to see to the legal cases of many different types of persons under his direct jurisdiction: D could be either an abbot (presumably of a monastery which had not been granted a full episcopal exemption[493]), a cleric or a layman (*homo vester*, which may in this case have referred to a military dependant). This formula suggests that the legal responsibility of a lord towards his dependants also involved the duty to discipline them and force them to abide by the decision of the courts. Bishop A was also responsible for obtaining a guarantor (*fideijussor*) to stand surety for D and guarantee that he would fulfil his obligation to appear in court and make reparations if he lost the case.

To the blessed apostolic lord and father Bishop A, King B. C, having come into our presence, put it [to us] that your abbot – or: your cleric – or: your man – D had taken his slave from him by force and is unlawfully keeping [him] in his possession, and that he had been unable to obtain justice from him regarding this. Therefore we sent the present letter to your sanctity, in which we ask that you should both deign to pray for us and, if that is what happened, constrain your abbot – or: cleric – D presently, so that, if that is

---

491 See above, n. 433.
492 See above, n. 462.
493 On episcopal exemptions, see Marculf I, 1.

what happened, he should endeavour to give compensation to the said C in this matter according to the laws. Certainly, if he does not want [to do this] and has something to oppose to this, then you should endeavour to send into our presence this D, after establishing a guarantor, at such a time.

I, 28: Charter relating to a [legal] hearing.

This formula follows a similar pattern to the preceding one, with some differences: here, the letter is to a count, and concerns an inhabitant of the region under his control (*pagensis*) rather than someone involved in a personal tie of dependence to him. This could suggest that little differentiation was being made between the workings of private and public jurisdictions, since much the same vocabulary is here used to refer to the count's general responsibility for the locals under his control (indeed, the word *pagensis* took on the meaning of 'dependant' from the tenth and eleventh centuries). The phrase stipulating that D should be brought before the royal tribunal 'if this is not rightly settled before you' ('si... ante vos rectae non finitur') implies that C could still bring his case before the king if Count B failed to condemn D.

King A to the illustrious man Count B. Our faithful follower[494] C, by God's favour, having come into our presence, put it to the clemency of our rule that your *pagensis* D had taken from him by force his land in the place called E, and is unlawfully keeping it in his possession, and that he had been unable to obtain justice from him regarding this. Therefore we sent the present order to you, in which we fully order that you should constrain this D in such way that, if that is what happened, he should endeavour to compensate the said C in this matter according to the laws. Certainly, if he does not want [to do this], and this is not rightly settled before you, you should endeavour in every way to send him into our presence, after establishing guarantors for the said D, on the Kalends of *x*.

I, 29: Letter to a layman.

After the appropriations of land and slaves by force described in the previous two formulae, the last kind of crime envisaged in this series is highway robbery. Sadly, no explanation is given regarding the circumstances of the attack; the phrase specifying that it was 'without cause' ('nula manenti causa') implies that there was no direct provocation, though the attack could still have been intended as an act of retaliation in the context of an existing dispute. The anxious warning in the last sentence, unusual for formulae of this type, stipulating that the attacker

---

494 See above, n. 433.

could only oppose C by coming directly into the king's presence, and 'in no other way' ('non aliter fiat'), suggests that it was feared that further violence might ensue, and thus also points to an ongoing dispute. This incident is likely to have been linked with aristocratic in-fighting: the fact that the king's letter is addressed directly to the attacker (B) rather than to his lord or a count suggests he was of high status, like his accuser, who had the power to appeal to the king.[495] Compare Marculf I, 37 for another document which may have referred to the same case, and Angers no. 6 for another case relating to an assault.

The illustrious man King A to B. Our faithful follower[496] C, having come into our presence, put it to us that you attacked him on a road without cause, and hurt him seriously, and took from him his valuables[497] worth *n. solidi* and unlawfully kept them in your possession, and that he had been unable to obtain justice from you regarding this. Therefore we sent you the present letter, by which we fully order that, if that is what happened, you should endeavour to compensate the said C immediately in this matter according to the laws. Certainly, if you do not want [to do this] and have something to oppose to this, let it be done in no other way than by coming yourself into our presence, summoned by this letter, on the next Kalends of *x*, to give him a full and valid answer regarding this.

I, 30: Exchange with a king.

The initial terms of address make this otherwise fairly straightforward contract of exchange a little puzzling, by suggesting that the exchange was being made between two kings. If so, it would constitute our only evidence that kings were interested in exchanging small landed properties with one another. The manuscript evidence, however, makes it difficult to be certain of the meaning of this initial address, since scribes (who were apparently also puzzled by it) copied it in a variety of different versions.[498] The content of the rest of the text does not fit very well with the idea that both of the protagonists were kings: the style of address is distinctly different to that of the letters from one king to another given in I, 9 and 10; only one of the two parties is said to have a fisc, and the other

---

[495] On elite highway robbery (though only for the Carolingian period onwards), see T. Reuter, 'The insecurity of travel in the early and high middle ages: criminals, victims and their medieval and modern observers', in T. Reuter, *Medieval Polities and Modern Mentalities*, ed. J.L. Nelson (Cambridge, 2006), pp. 38–71.

[496] See above, n. 433.

[497] *Rauba* tended to refer specifically to clothes taken as booty, though the meaning of the word sometimes seems to have been extended to refer to objects of value more generally (see Angers no. 29).

[498] See below, n. 499.

is only referred to as being an 'illustrious man' ('inluster vir'), which was not normally used to refer to kings without being accompanied by the word *rex*. The use of 'illustrious', at least, suggests that the person with whom the king was making this exchange was a layman; the king's expectation that his earlier gift to B was to increase his chances of salvation does not necessarily imply that the recipient was a religious establishment, since giving to a dependant could also be construed as a Christian act (as in the second preface presented in Marculf I, 14). The description of B's land as having originally been given to him by King A, however, does emphasise the unequal nature of their relationship, making the idea that B was also a king yet more unlikely. Marculf may have been trying to leave as many options open as possible, in order to allow this formula to be used for exchanges made by the king with almost anyone (whether another king, a layman or a church), which may be why the final result ended up being somewhat confusing. Compare Angers no. 8 and Marculf II, 23 and 24 for other examples of property exchange.

King A to King B.[499] Each [man] is seen to take away nothing from his [property, when] each receives something in exchange.[500] Since it was agreed in common between us and the illustrious man B that we should exchange some places between us, we gave him the little place called C in the *pagus* of D, with the tenant holdings[501] E–F and all of their dependencies and benefits, including houses, unfree servants,[502] vineyards, forests, fields, meadows, pastures and every other benefit, whatever G – or: our fisc – is known to have held in these places; and he in exchange gave us all his property that he was seen to own on the villa of H in the *pagus* of I,

---

499 The wording of this initial address varies considerably in the manuscripts, as scribes tried to make sense of it in different ways: Leiden BPL 114, Paris BnF lat. 4627 and Paris BnF lat. 2123 all have 'ille rex illo rege' ('King A to King B'), and, since the Leiden manuscript and Paris BnF lat. 2123 correspond to different branches of the manuscript tradition, this is therefore likely to be the correct reading. Copenhagen Fabr. 84 just has 'ille' ('A'). Paris BnF lat. 10756 mixes this part up with the first sentence ('nihil sibi il rex quisque il cernitur minuendo', which would translate roughly as 'each King A is seen to take away nothing of his [property]'); both of these are probably later rationalisations. See Uddholm, *Marculfi formularum libri duo*, p. 112. On the manuscript tradition, see Appendix 3.

500 Literally, 'each [man] is seen to diminish nothing for himself, each [thing] being received in exchange as a gain'. Uddholm's interpretation ('no one is allowed to diminish what he has received on the contrary in order to increase it'), besides arbitrarily changing *in augmentum*, 'as a gain', into *ad augmentum*, 'in order to increase it', does not make much sense in the context of an exchange (Uddholm, *Marculfi formularum libri duo*, p. 113). A similar expression is used in Marculf II, 23 to introduce another exchange.

501 The word is *colonicas*, which could either apply specifically to land held by *coloni* (tenants), or more generally represent the equivalent of a *mansus*.

502 See above, n. 392.

again with houses, unfree servants[503] and every other benefit, whatever he owned there and that we gave to him there for the redemption of our soul. Therefore we decided to have this document made for this man regarding the manner of this exchange, so that from this day this B shall have, hold and possess this little place, along with everything that is written above and in its entirety, whatever, as we said, G – or: our fisc – held there, and leave it for his descendants to possess, and have the free power to do whatever he wants with it, by virtue of our contract of exchange. And each of the parties whom it has pleased to receive [this] in a good and peaceful exchange should, with God's permission, rejoice through time as a result. And so that this document...

I, 31: Confirmation of the king regarding a whole patrimony.

> This document gave a broad confirmation of the whole of A's property, held in full ownership and acquired through inheritance as well as particular transactions: in spite of the reference to 'fidelity' in the introductory sentence, it should not, therefore, be mistaken for any sort of proto-feudal arrangement according to which lands granted by kings as a reward for military service would have needed to be confirmed rather than straightforwardly inherited. A probably asked for this confirmation not out of legal necessity, but because he knew he could get it, and could use it to strengthen his own relationship with the present king as well as to establish his rights more strongly in the event of a dispute. Compare Marculf I, 35 for a similar confirmation in the case of the property of a monastery.

Royal clemency deservedly decides to confirm the gifts and property of relatives transferred to those who are known to have retained a full and intact fidelity to previous kings, our relatives, and to ourselves. Thus the illustrious man A presented to us the charters of previous kings, in order that they should be read, by which certain places had been granted to his relatives. He asked that we should generally confirm for him by our order[504] regarding this [his rights over] his whole patrimony, both what he or his relatives obtained through royal gifts and that which was justly and rightly acquired up to now under the title of sale, transfer, gift and exchange, and which he is known to possess at present. Let your greatness know that we guaranteed this with full devotion, out of regard for God – or: because his merits called for this –, ordering[505] that, whatever came to him justly out of

---

503 See above, n. 392.
504 See above, n. 388.
505 See above, n. 461.

the inheritance of his relatives or by his acquisition, whether through royal gifts or any other charters, including villas, unfree servants,[506] buildings, tenants, gold, silver, valuables, ornaments, moveable and non-moveable goods, and whatever property he is seen to be legitimately master of at the present time through charters, confirmed by this document, by God's grace and ours, he may possess it in full and leave it to his descendants, with God's help. And so that this document…

I, 32: If anyone acted against the will of the king, [this is a] security for the man whom he has ordered to pursue him.

This formula is intended to deal with the consequences of a rebellion (A is described as 'faciente revello'). All those involved seem to have belonged to the aristocratic class, as suggested by the frequent reference to their retainers (*pares*, here in the sense of dependant rather than social equal, *gasindi*[507] or *amici*). Murdering B, whoever he may have been, is counted as an act against the king, showing that action taken against other aristocrats could count as rebellion, despite affecting the king only indirectly: this suggests a lack of clear division between 'public' rebellion against the state and 'private' forms of aristocratic violence. Rebellion in the Merovingian period very rarely involved direct opposition to the king,[508] but tended to be linked instead to rivalry between aristocrats: in this context, rebellion could often simply be the result of aristocratic competition gone wrong. In this case, A apparently estimated his chances of success against his opponents as too low for comfort, and he escaped to another kingdom (no pursuit is mentioned in the text, despite what is suggested in the title). The property confiscated from him and his followers, rather than being appropriated by the fisc, was given to other lords, who may have been A's opponents and competitors, who had been more successful in securing the king's support; this document ensured the relatives of the dispossessed could not subsequently challenge their ownership of it.

Those who obey a royal command must not suffer [any] wrong from anyone afterwards. Therefore, since A, having rebelled along with his other companions who were following him, killed B – or committed any other actions against the king – and removed himself from our kingdom, which was most vexing to us, we, with the counsel of our faithful followers,[509]

506 See above, n. 392.
507 On the word *gasindus*, see below, Marculf II, 36.
508 On violence in general during the late Merovingian period, see P. Fouracre, 'Attitudes towards violence in seventh- and eighth-century Francia', in G. Halsall, ed., *Violence and Society in the Early Medieval West* (Woodbridge, 1998), pp. 60–75.
509 See above, n. 433.

ordered that all his property be confiscated by the illustrious men C–D under the entitlement of the fisc; and, had he not taken himself away, we would have ordered them to make him lose not only his property, but also [his] life, for rebelling in this way. Therefore we gave the present document,[510] to the effect that, since [it was] not out of unruliness, but by our order and with the advice of lords, our faithful followers, [that] the said men C–D and their other companions and retainers took these properties placed under our fisc and seized them as a result of this along with [the properties] of the others who were involved with him [A], as we ordered by our proclamation, we thus order that, since this was done by our order, they must never have any accusation or claim made [against them] on this account at any time, neither by the said A, nor by those who were involved with him, nor from their heirs; but let these C–D, as well as their companions, retainers and friends, remain for all time free and absolved [of any guilt] regarding any of the property which belonged to the said A and was taken away [from him], since this was done on account of his crimes and by our order, and, as we said, let the men written above, C–D, our faithful followers,[511] never be exposed to any calumny or claim or penalty regarding this. And so that this document [may stand] more firmly...

I, 33: Document[512] for those whose documents were burned by enemy troops or in another way.

> This is a document for the replacement of lost documents; compare Angers nos. 31–33, which describes a similar procedure in the context of a local court (the list of possible lost documents is much more comprehensive in Angers than in Marculf).[513] In this case, A had already had his rights confirmed through local courts under the authority of *boni homines*, but was here using his access to the king to obtain additional confirmation. A seems to have recovered all of his property, and this text does not feature any of the restrictions included in the three formulae from the Angers collection; these better terms may have been secured

---

510 See above, n. 388.
511 See above, n. 433.
512 See above, n. 388.
513 See also *Formulae Arvernenses* no. 1, *Formulae Turonenses* nos. 27, 28 and *Add*. no. 7, and *Cartae Senonicae* nos. 38 and 46 (Zeumer, *Formulae*, p. 28; pp. 150–51 and 162; pp. 202 and 205–06). On this procedure, see Zeumer, 'Über den Ersatz verlorener Urkunden im fränkischen Reiche'; Gobin, 'Notes et documents concernant l'histoire d'Auvergne. Sur un point particulier de la procédure mérovingienne applicable à l'Auvergne: "l'institution d'*apennis*"'; Lauranson-Rosaz and Jeannin, 'La résolution des litiges en justice durant le haut Moyen-Age: l'exemple de l'*apennis*' ; Brown, 'When documents are destroyed or lost'.

through royal patronage. The possibility that these depredations had been caused by this king's own troops ('exercitus noster') could suggest that A lived on a territory that had only recently been acquired through war (in which case A would only have been this king's *fidelis* for a short time).

It is necessary that those who suffered wrong and violence from enemies be comforted by royal clemency. Thus our faithful follower,[514] with God's help, A, put it to the clemency of our rule that *n*. years ago – or: the year before – our army – or: that of King B – burned down his house by fire, and that much of his property was burned there, along with documents [regarding] both what he had received through a royal gift and what he owned by documents of sale, gift, transfer, exchange, or from the inheritance of his relatives, in whatever place in our kingdom. He gave us an account to be read, confirmed by the hands of good men,[515] [stating] that it was know to them that [things were] as he had said, and that he should be seen to possess securely all of his property to which the documents that were destroyed related, without any contestation, as he had done before. But out of a desire for firm validation, the said A asked that we should confirm by our document that all his property thereafter [will be] under his right and authority, both that [which he obtained] through a royal gift and that [which he owned] by documents of sale, transfer, gift, exchange, and the rest of his patrimony, which he owns at present securely according to justice. Know that we guaranteed and confirmed his request with a glad spirit. We therefore order[516] and command that, whatever the said A is seen to have owned justly and rightly anywhere in our kingdom until now, including lands, houses, buildings, tenants, unfree servants,[517] vineyards, forests, fields, meadows, water and water-courses and every other benefit,[518] [according to] what we learned through the account of the said men, since we learned that his documents were burned, he should hold and possess it, consolidated and confirmed more fully in God's name by this document concerning him, without any contestation or accusation, and leave [it] for his descendants to possess, or for whomever he wants, in God's name. We decided to confirm this document, [which is] to be valid in perpetuity, by our own hand below.

---

514 See above, n. 433.
515 These are the *boni homines*, members of the local elite often involved in the settlement of disputes in the Angers formulary, but featured more rarely in Marculf.
516 See above, n. 461.
517 See above, n. 392.
518 The word is *beneficium*, though not in its later, more technical sense.

I, 34: Account by *pagenses*, addressed to the king.

> This is the account 'confirmed by the hands of good men' referred to in the preceding formula.[519] Although the signatories are here simply described as *pagenses* (that is, the inhabitants of a *pagus*), their description as *boni homines* in the previous formula suggests that they were not just any sort of inhabitant, but enjoyed local elite status and an authoritative function in local courts.

> To be given to the most pious and excellent lord King A and to the mayor of the palace B, from your servants the *pagenses* B–C, whose signatures and marks[520] have been entered below. The admired clemency of your preeminence knows to grant just requests favourably and kindly to help the necessity of the suffering. It is indeed obvious to everyone that our region has been devastated by the enemy and the houses of many people burned by fire and their property stolen. Among them, your servant[521] E has there suffered no small damage and the loss of his property, and all the documents which he and his relatives had, [regarding] both what he possessed as a result of the munificence of kings and what he held through documents of sale, transfer, gift and exchange, are known to have been burned by fire together with his house. As a result, he asked our humble selves to make known to your clemency by this our petition what we truly knew of this; which we, your servants, took care to do. Let your piety order that he may possess from now on, with peace and security, that which he possessed securely in your kingdom until now, by a document[522] granted by you regarding him, since he lost his documents. We, your servants, have presumed to make known what we truly know of this; it belongs to you to help the necessity of the suffering.

I, 35: Confirmation regarding the entire property of a monastery.

> This is a broad confirmation of a monastery's rights over its property and of the episcopal privilege made in its favour (for such privileges, see Marculf I, 1; for another royal confirmation, see I, 4). Although this text is addressed to royal officials rather than to ecclesiastical authorities, it does not include a royal immunity. Such confirmations do not seem to have been a legal necessity (the very same king is said to have already given a confirmation to this monastery, at least regarding its episcopal privilege) so much as an occasion to reiterate and

---

519 Compare *Cartae Senonicae* no. 46 (Zeumer, *Formulae*, pp. 205–06), which gives a similar account addressed to the king by *pagenses*.
520 See above, n. 408.
521 The word is *servus*, though here clearly not in the technical sense of unfreedom.
522 See above, n. 388.

reinforce periodically the rights of those who had access to the king. Compare I, 31 for a similar document regarding a layman.

King A to the *patricius* B and all agents. We think it right that we should bring into effect the requests of priests concerning the interest of holy places, with Christ's favour. Thus the venerable man C, abbot of the holy monastery of D, asked the glory of our rule that, since this holy monastery is known to have been built through the benefaction of our relatives, with God's help, we should confirm generally by our order[523] its entire property, both that which the preceding abbots obtained there and that which the lord Abbot C, who is known to be there, was seen to add and purchase there for the property of the monastery, and which has been owned by this holy place in modern times. Let your greatness have no doubt that we, out of respect for God and to increase our [eternal] rewards, guaranteed this. And we also decided to confirm, for [its] eternal stability, the privilege of this monastery, which it was seen to obtain through the document of the apostolic see and of the other bishops, and [which] is known to have been confirmed by the document of Lord D and the other kings who succeeded him, our ancestors, [and] according to what was also confirmed by our previous order[524] regarding them, [which] they presented [to us]. We therefore order that the entire property of this monastery, whatever [it obtained] from royal benefaction or the gift of private persons or was legally acquired or purchased there by the predecessors of the abbot or by Lord C, and what was rightly added to these properties, whatever the lordship[525] of this holy place is seen to possess rightfully anywhere in modern times, villas, houses, unfree servants,[526] vineyards, forests, meadows, pastures and any other benefit,[527] let [all this], consolidated by this document, benefit it without [meeting with] any unlawful opposition, in both present and future times, with Christ's favour. We add that, [by virtue of] the privilege, regarding both the appointment of the abbot (this congregation appointing [one] of its own after the other has died) and all the rest, which this monastery was granted by a document from pontiffs from date *x* until now, and has been retained until now, and [was] confirmed regarding this by the previous kings, they may now and thereafter remain through time in this manner, without being exposed to any wrongful contestation, by our document, with God's help.

523 See above, n. 388.
524 See above, n. 388.
525 The word here is *dominatio*.
526 See above, n. 392.
527 See above, n. 518.

And you and your successors, when it is necessary, will bring just assistance to the affairs of this monastery, so that it may please them to pray more often for our salvation, and so that you may obtain our favour as a result of this. And so that this document may survive with firm stability, we decided to confirm [it] below by [our] own hand.

I, 36: In order that someone should have permission to take over the legal cases of those from whom he received property.[528]

> This curious text shows us someone (A, who could be either a bishop, an abbot, an abbess or a layman according to the beginning of the text, though he is described further on in the text only as a bishop or abbot) asking the king for legal authority over the lands he had acquired: this seems to imply that previous owners retained a degree of legal responsibility over property even after it was alienated, and that the right to appear in court to defend one's rights of ownership was not automatically transferred along with it. It is possible that this document was made necessary because of conflicting rights over the same land, but A was clearly not competing with the heirs or relatives, since the givers and sellers are explicitly said to have died without heirs as a result of a *clades*, which here probably refers to an epidemic. This document may have been needed to help recipients to assert their rights in circumstances of exceptional confusion, with an unusually high mortality rate entailing a large amount of property changing hands through inheritance, which would have been an especially contentious affair if there were no direct heirs. The references to 'evil men' suggests that there had indeed been disputes regarding these properties, and the document was apparently intended to function as a blanket confirmation for all transactions made in favour of A. The cryptic expression 'through their documents or through years' ('per eorum instrumenta aut de annis') seems to suggest that, when no written document recording the transaction was available, rights over property could also be established by virtue of a certain number of years' uncontested ownership of the land.

It is necessary for royal justice to restrain the subterfuges of evil men. Thus the apostolic man A, bishop of the city of B, – or: the venerable Abbot A, or: the Abbess A consecrated to God, of the monastery of B, or any of the lords' faithful followers[529] – informed us by a written request – or: in person – that both himself and his predecessors had purchased much by way of lands and unfree servants[530] in our kingdom with ready money from various

---

528 The word here is *auctor*, that is, the person from whom one has bought or otherwise obtained something.
529 See above, n. 433.
530 See above, n. 392.

men, with [these men's] free assent, and that other men had given property to this church – or: monastery – by their documents for the redemption of their soul, and that [this church or monastery] is seen to own this justly at present. He asked that, for future times and to restrain the wiles of evil men, since many of their benefactors and sellers travelled from this light[531] without heirs because of the pestilence that is rampant among the people, or because they had completed the course of nature, if anyone should want to trouble him by some trick regarding these properties, he or his representative should have the permission to take over their legal affairs on behalf of those from whom he received this property.[532] Know that we granted this in the name of God and out of reverence for this holy place. We therefore order by our command that the said pontiff – or: abbot, or: abbess – and his advocate should have permission, on behalf of those from whom he received this property,[533] to take over and bring to court their legal affairs, and, should they be seen to be troubled by anyone from then on, to give an answer and appear in court with justice [to support their case] in the interest of his church – or: monastery – through their documents or through years [of ownership of] this property, and to keep it through the years against anyone['s claims].

I, 37: Clear[534] judgment.

This formula is very similar to documents of *solsadia* establishing one party's failure to show up to their hearing in court (compare Angers nos. 12–14, 16 and 53).[535] The dispute dealt with an assault, in circumstances virtually identical to those given in Marculf I, 29, which may indicate that this text related to the same case (compare Angers no. 6 for another assault). This particular document was addressed by the king to a local count (as implied by the reference to B as an inhabitant of 'your *pagus*'; the intervention of this count seems to have been

---

531 That is, died.
532 See above, n. 528.
533 See above, n. 528.
534 'Judicio evidentale': the variant in Paris BnF lat. 10756 ('judicio evindicatum', 'judgment awarding victory') cannot be the correct reading here, since Copenhagen Fabr. 84, which is derived from the same branch of the tradition, shares the reading 'evidentale' with the other manuscripts (the formula is missing in Paris BnF lat. 2123). On the manuscript tradition, see Appendix 3.
535 There are also some actual examples of this procedure surviving from the Merovingian period: see, for instance, Kölzer DM. 141, from 694 (discussed in Fouracre, '"*Placita*" and the settlement of disputes in later Merovingian Francia', pp. 28–34). On the vocabulary of *solsadiae* (and the related verb *solsadire*), see Fouracre, 'The nature of Frankish political institutions', pp. 287–88.

similar to that in Marculf I, 28), who had to ensure that B paid compensation. It is possible that the reference to 'the law of your region' ('lex loci vestri') could have referred to the personality principle of early medieval law, according to which each person would be judged according to the law corresponding to their own ethnic group,[536] but this phrase seems to refer to a geographical area rather than to the ethnic origin of the participants: it may therefore have referred instead to customary local practice.[537] If so, this formula could constitute important evidence that such customs were recognised even in the king's court.

A, having come in the presence of ourselves and our great men, said that a man called B, inhabitant of your *pagus*, attacked him on a road without cause, and hurt him seriously, and took from him his valuables[538] worth *n. solidi*, and that because of this [B] had given you such guarantors[539] [as were prescribed] by our order, so that [A and B] should stand in our presence on the Kalends of *x* to litigate over this. The said A came to this *placitum* here in our palace, and remained at his *placitum* during three days or more, as the law prescribes, and exposed and established the said B's failure to attend. He established that B did not come to the *placitum* and gave no reason for his absence.[540] Therefore it happened that we, together with our great men, decided [this]: since manifestly the said B had given such guarantors to you concerning this case and did not attend his *placitum*, and since the illustrious man C, count of our palace, testified that the said A had remained at his *placitum* according to the laws and exposed and established [B's] failure to attend, and that this B had neglected to attend his *placitum*, we order that, with yourself compelling him, the said B should not refuse to compensate and give satisfaction to A [according to] whatever the custom in your region teaches about such a case.

I, 38: Charter in two identical copies.

The title brings attention not to the object of the dispute, which related to an escaped slave (expressively described as *fugitivus pedes*, 'having escaped with his feet'), but to the two identical copies to be prepared for this document (*carta paricla*), one to be kept by each party: this may have corresponded to the practice

536 See above, Marculf I, 8.
537 For this phrase, compare Kölzer DM. 137 (p. 348); see Fouracre, '"*Placita*" and the settlement of disputes in later Merovingian Francia', pp. 27–30.
538 See above, n. 497.
539 See above, n. 400.
540 The word used to designate a legitimate reason not to turn up at a court hearing was *sonia*; see Fouracre, 'The nature of Frankish political institutions', p. 287.

observed in chirographs (of which there are surviving Merovingian examples), in which the same text was copied out twice on the same page, which was then cut in two. This was apparently only done when the document guaranteed the same rights for both parties (in this case protecting them from further litigation until the appointed time of their *placitum*; compare Angers nos. 8 and 45).[541] This formula is the only one in Marculf to show a dispute being settled by an oath: the king's magnates are said to have chosen this solution while the two parties were arguing it out, so that it may have been resorted to only as a way of cutting the dispute short when no other solution presented itself. There seems to have been a concern to limit possible abuses linked with this solution, as shown by the condition according to which B had to pick half of his oath-helpers from a pre-established list of five men, thus limiting his ability to give the oath if he was generally thought to be guilty.[542]

As a man called A accused another man called B in the presence of ourselves and our great men, and said that he had taken in his runaway slave called C along with his valuables[543] worth *n. solidi*, and was keeping him unlawfully, the said B was seen to deny all this vigorously, [saying] that he had never taken for himself either the runaway slave or his valuables. But while they were arguing with each other, it was decided by our great men, as the illustrious man D, count of our palace, testified, that the same B, together with three men, picked out of five, and another three men, with himself as a seventh, should swear at such a time in our palace, on the cape of the Lord Martin,[544] where the other oaths take place, that he had never taken for himself the said runaway slave C written above or his valuables worth *n. solidi*. If he can swear to this, let him remain free from this accusation; but if he cannot, let him endeavour to return this slave to the said A along with his valuables worth *n. solidi*, together with the compensation price [stipulated] by the law. Meanwhile, so that neither of these parties may be disturbed

---

541 Compare Kölzer DDM. 137 and 141; see Fouracre, '"*Placita*" and the settlement of disputes in later Merovingian Francia', p. 35.

542 In this sense, as Janet Nelson has put it, 'oaths operated no more, and no less, as a kind of judgment of God [in the early medieval period] than in the twentieth century: they solemnised the proceedings and reduced the risk of perjury' (Nelson, 'Dispute settlement in Carolingian West Francia', p. 60). On proof in royal documents and in Marculf Book I, see Guillot, 'La justice dans le royaume franc', pp. 702–31.

543 See above, n. 497.

544 There is no evidence for the presence of the cape of Saint Martin in the royal palace before 682, when it was first mentioned in a document, in a context similar to this one (Kölzer DM. 126, pp. 319–20; *Chartae latinae antiquiores* XIII, p. 76, no. 567). This would count as an argument against an early dating of Marculf (Fouracre, '"*Placita*" and the settlement of disputes in later Merovingian Francia', p. 36, n. 47); see above, n. 323.

[regarding this] until [the time of] this *placitum*, we ordered that identical documents be made for and received by them.

I, 39: In order that some slaves be freed on the occasion of the birth of a king.

This formula is echoed in Marculf II, 52, which gives the model for the manumission documents to be issued by the count as a result of this royal order. It is rare to find manumissions from this period being made under such impersonal terms (the king left the choice of which slaves should be freed at the count's discretion); this was clearly due to the large number of servants involved here. The text emphasises the link between the manumission of unfree persons and Christian piety: in this case the manumissions were made explicitly in order to ensure that God would grant good health to the king's son. Although manumission was certainly seen as a good deed (as indeed it had been seen before Christian times under the early Roman empire), it should be stressed that the Church never adopted any sort of stance against slavery in this period: the point of manumitting was to ensure the salvation of the master rather than resulting from a particular concern for those whom he freed.

A, King of the Franks, to the illustrious Count B.[545] Since divine piety has accorded to us the great joy of the birth of our son C, according to the prayers of our faithful followers[546] and of our great men, in order that divine mercy should deign to spare his life, we order that, throughout all our villas which are under your jurisdiction and under that of the other *domestici* in all our kingdom, you should free, through our mercy, three servants[547] of either sex in each villa through documents [issued] by you.

---

545 The variant reading replacing the count by the mayor of the palace, which is only found in Paris BnF lat. 10756, cannot be correct, because Copenhagen Fabr. 84, which derives from the same branch of the manuscript tradition, also has 'illo comite' (B. Krusch, 'Der Staatsstreich des fränkischen Hausmaiers Grimoald I', in M. Krammer, ed., *Historische Aufsätze. Karl Zeumer zum sechzigen Geburstag als Festgabe dargebracht von Freunden und Schülern* [Weimar, 1910], 411–38, at p. 414, n. 6; Krusch, 'Ursprung und Text', p. 268). On the manuscript tradition, see Appendix 3.

546 See above, n. 433.

547 The word is *servientes*. Marculf seems to have used this word to refer to unfree 'servants' specifically, as this manumission indicates (see also II, 3 and 34).

I, 40: In order for the people to swear their submission[548] to the king.

This text shows us a king demanding a general oath of loyalty to himself and to his son, whom he had just made king of a sub-kingdom (Frankish territory could be divided into three sub-kingdoms, Neustria, Austrasia and Burgundy, each of which could be ruled by a different king). The source of this formula has been associated with Dagobert I's elevation of his son Sigibert III as king of Austrasia in 632 (Sigibert suffered a defeat at the hands of Radulf eight years later, at which time Fredegar describes him as still in his *adolescentia*, which implies that he would have been a young child when he was first made king).[549] Although there is some evidence for such general oaths being demanded by kings in the late sixth century,[550] modern scholars tend to consider general oaths of fidelity to the king as an essentially Carolingian phenomenon, with an assumption that the practice had been discontinued in the late Merovingian period and was not revived until the reign of Charlemagne (who demanded an oath from all persons over the age of twelve).[551] This formula suggests, however, that this practice was still current enough by the late seventh century for Marculf to think it was worth including a model for it. The king was clearly keen to receive the oaths on his own terms, and the sending out of relics along with the king's *missus* is remarkable: the king's insistence that the oaths should be sworn only on these relics could have been due simply to the practical unavailability of relics in some of the places of assembly, but the king's own relics may also have been more prestigious, which could have given the oath an additional symbolic value (he may also have been guarding against oaths being sworn on unsatisfactory relics relating to doubtful local cults).

548 *Leudesamio* (in the phrase *leudesamio promittere*) is a rare word; several scribes seem to have been confused by it, and their efforts to make sense of it led to several different readings in the manuscripts (see Appendix 3, p. 276). The content of the formula, however, makes it clear that it related to an oath of fidelity, and the word *fidelitas* is indeed paired with it in the text.

549 Krusch, 'Ursprung und Text', pp. 240–41; Fredegar IV, 87 (B. Krusch, ed., *Fredegarii et aliorum Chronica. Vitae Sanctorum*, MGH SS rer. Merov. II (Hanover, 1888), p. 165). Childeric II is another possibility (he was also a child when he became king of Austrasia in 662), but this formula is unlikely to have related to him, since he was not made king until after his father (Clovis II) had died.

550 With, for instance, the swearing of an oath to Childebert II in Gregory of Tours's *Histories* (VII, 26).

551 *Capitulare missorum* (from 802), *Capitularia* no. 33 *cap*. 2, p. 92. See, for instance, F.L. Ganshof's classic article, 'Charlemagne's use of the oath', in his *The Carolingians and the Frankish Monarchy: Studies in Carolingian History*, translated by J. Sondheimer (London, 1971), pp. 111–24; see also J.L. Nelson, 'Peers in the early middle ages', in P. Stafford, J. L. Nelson and J. Martindale, eds., *Law, Laity and Solidarities: Essays in honour of Susan Reynolds* (Manchester, 2001), pp. 27–46, at p. 38; M. Becher, *Eid und Herrschaft. Untersuchungen zum Herrscherethos Karls des Grossen* (Sigmaringen, 1993), pp. 16–17 and 195–212. On the discontinuation of the Merovingian general oath, see for instance Devroey, *Puissants et misérables*, p. 173.

King A to Count B. Since, with the unanimous consent of our great men, we decided that our glorious son C should rule in our kingdom of D, we therefore order you to summon all your *pagenses*, Franks, Romans and those of any other origin,[552] and to have them assemble in appropriate places in cities, villages and strongholds, in order that they should promise and swear fidelity and submission to our excellent son and to ourselves, in the presence of our agent,[553] the illustrious man E, whom we have sent out from our side for this purpose, in the places of the saints and on the relics which we have sent there through the same person.

---

[552] See above, Marculf I, 8.
[553] See above, n. 462.

BOOK TWO

Here begin the chapter-headings for the local charters.

I – If someone wants to build a monastery or a religious house out of a large property.
II – Prologue for someone donating a large property to a church.
III – Another prologue for this deed, with the donation.
IV – Grant of a villa to a church from the present day.
V – *Precaria* for this villa, while [the giver] lives.
VI – Donation of a small property to a church.
VII – Charter of mutual donation between a man and his wife regarding their property.
VIII – Another one, without any diminution.
IX – Charter of concession made by a father for his children.
X – Document, when grandchildren are given the status of sons by their grandfather.
XI – Charter for someone who wants to give something to his grandson.
XII – Charter, so that a daughter may inherit her father's property together with her brothers.
XIII – If someone adopts a stranger as his son.
XIV – Agreement between relatives regarding their inheritance.
XV – Document for a wedding gift.
XVI – If someone has abducted a girl against her will.
XVII – How a person may make a testament in one volume.
XVIII – Security for a murder, if [the two parties] made peace.
XIX – Sale of a villa.
XX – Sale of an area within a city.
XXI – Sale of a field.
XXII – Sale of a male or female slave.
XXIII – Exchange of villas.
XXIV – Exchange of lands or vineyards or fields.
XXV – Loan securities made in different manners.
XXVI – Another one.
XXVII – Another one.
XXVIII – For someone who is putting himself in the service of another.
XXIX – Charter regarding the children, if an unfree man has abducted a free woman.

XXX – Deed of divorce.
XXXI – Mandate.
XXXII – Manumissions made in different ways.
XXXIII – Another manumission in another manner, after the death [of the master].
XXXIV – Another one regarding this, in another manner.
XXXV – Annulment of a deed of security for a loan, if it cannot be found.
XXXVI – If someone wants to grant something to his slave or retainer.
XXXVII – How donations and testaments are entered in the [municipal] archive, according to the manner of the Romans.
XXXVIII – Mandate for the [municipal] archive.
XXXIX – Document, if someone has the use of the property of a church and gives something from his [own] property.
XL – *Prestaria* made by a bishop for property belonging to a church.
XLI – *Precaria* for someone who wants to seize another person's property, but fails, and afterwards obtains it through a *precaria*.
XLII – Letter, when a bishop sends gifts to another on [the day of] the resurrection of the Lord.
XLIII – Answer to the bishop about his gift.
XLIV – How one should write greetings sent to a king, queen or bishop after the nativity of the Lord.
XLV – Another one for the nativity of the Lord.
XLVI – Letter of recommendation to a bishop whom one already knows.
XLVII – Another letter of recommendation, to an abbot whom one knows.
XLVIII – Supplication for someone who has left a monastery, or for someone who wants to enter a monastery.
IL – General letter to all men.
L – Letter of recommendation to illustrious laymen.
LI – Letter to powerful men of the palace whom one knows very well.
LII – How the *domesticus* of a royal villa must free slaves by a royal order on the occasion of the birth of the king's son.

Here begin the pages on the manner in which local charters are made.

II, 1: This one [is for] someone who wants to build a religious house or a monastery[554] out of a large property.

---

554 *Xenodochium*: this kind of religious establishment seems to have fulfilled more or less the function of a hospice and guest house for foreigners, pilgrims, the poor and the sick.

THE FORMULARY OF MARCULF

This first formula of Book II is an elaborate set piece, and features an unusually long introduction (*arenga*), the length and formality of which were apparently commensurate with the value of the land being given (a *magna res* or large property). No *arenga* found in surviving documents from this period is quite this long, and scribes may have been expected to make a selection of the parts they wanted to keep when using this model to draw up a new document. The *arenga* describes the benefits of giving to the church, and is interspersed with several scriptural references; these apparently fulfilled more than a merely decorative purpose, and the text engages with them in a more personal way than is usual for such documents (for instance in stating a particular fondness for the quote 'As water extinguishes fire, so do alms extinguish sin'). A concern for the remission of sins pervades the whole text, which emphasises the promise of salvation for both the founder of this monastery and all those who were to abide by his decision (just as it emphasises the threat of damnation and excommunication for those opposing it, whether directly or indirectly). This text clearly shows that documents regarding local transactions could be just as carefully and finely wrought as the royal documents found in Book I (though this document, as the foundation charter of a religious institution, would admittedly have had an exceptional degree of formality). The monastery is said to be situated within a city; manuscript readings leave some doubt as to whether the initial address was made to a man or a woman, though the abbots referred to later on were clearly men. The initial contingent of monks was to consist of twelve 'paupers', linking in with the strong insistence in the *arenga* on the special power of intercession attributed to the 'poor' in praying for their benefactors. The document also sets down the provision for the monastery's financial needs: the text makes it clear that A had already benefited from a royal grant of immunity over this land before he gave it for the support of the monastery, pointing again to the granting of immunities to individual lay people as well as churches (see Marculf I, 3 and 14). A large section of the document also deals with the nature of the monastery's future relationship with its diocesan bishop. The founder made a number of demands from this bishop: his document thus demanded much of what was usually included in a privilege of exemption, specifying that the bishop could not ask for any payment or special favours from the monastery, and leaving him only the power to give blessings, as well as the power to appoint a new abbot after the death of his predecessor (the latter right was normally given up in episcopal exemptions; compare Marculf I, 1). This bishop also seems to have been made responsible for the legal protection (*defensio*) of the monastery, if it ever became involved in a dispute; indeed, the formula allows for the possibility that litigants should be dealt with by the bishop rather than by royal judges, with a share of the fine being assigned to him rather than to the fisc.

To the truly blessed lord, and shining with manifest zeal, by the clear miracles of virtue, through Christ's reward, [and] to the oratory or cell built in honour of the blessed and eternally virgin Mary, mother of our Lord Jesus Christ – or: in that of another saint –, A, guilty through [my] faults of disgraceful crimes, tainted by wanton deeds and by extreme infamy, by rank and by deed by far the last of all good Christians. This indeed all of the holy scriptures pronounce with pious exhortation to the Christian faithful, [and] the thundering voice of the evangelists, through the counsel of the [Holy] Spirit, also celebrates it by its power, that he who wants to escape the tortures of hell should give alms to the poor. For the Lord says in the gospel: 'Go and sell all that thou hast, give to the poor, and thou shalt have treasure in heaven'.[555] Let us Christian people therefore think how great the piety and the generosity of the Redeemer are, that, in exchange for alms for the poor, we are promised the treasures of the kingdom of heaven. Let us therefore atone, as our Lord and Saviour prescribes, and let us give as alms, if not all that we have, at least all that we can. And let no one hesitate, let no one delay, because if we do what our Lord and Saviour prescribed, he will without doubt do as he promised. For scripture says: 'Shut up alms in the heart of the poor, and it shall intercede before God on your behalf'.[556] Let us therefore shut up alms in the heart of the poor, so that the prayers of the poor may grant us the remission of [our] sins. We find many other statements in the holy scriptures in favour of the giving of alms, which are too intricate to quote, among which – or: out of which – I consider this sentence to be the best, which says: 'As water extinguishes fire, so do alms extinguish sin'.[557] What, indeed, can be believed to be truer, what more trustworthy or better expressed, than: 'As water extinguishes fire, so do alms extinguish sin'? He is therefore justly extinguished [himself], he who does not hasten to extinguish the fire of [his] sins through alms according to the divine promise. Let others do as they wish, and act according to their preference, since every man is led by his own sense; but I, following this example, have chosen at present to house in the said oratory or cell, with Christ's favour, twelve paupers, after the number of the apostles, for the remission of my sins – or: for the alleviation of the burden of my sins –. By the present letter of my donation I also give in this place from the present day what may help [to provide for] the lights[558] of this oratory and the support, sustenance and provision of food and clothing for these paupers

---

555 Matthew 19:21.
556 Adapted from Ecclesiasticus (Sirach) 29:15.
557 Adapted from Ecclesiasticus (Sirach) 3:33.
558 See Fouracre, 'Eternal lights'.

and the clerics [who serve] there, with God's governance and assistance. And I want this [to be] given in perpetuity, and I attach, hand over, transmit and transfer it from my possession into their authority and power: fields, the names of which are B and C, which are situated on the territory of D, and, in the same way, whatever property of mine is situated on the territory of D, in all its entirety, with unfree servants,[559] buildings, vineyards, lands, meadows, forests, and all that they contain, together with tenant holdings with all their dependencies and appurtenances, in all their entirety, as they were known to be possessed by me or to have come to me there out of a legitimate inheritance or in any other way, in all their entirety and with full benefits, with this condition and stipulation that, the power of the pontiffs along with that of all ecclesiastical and state officials being removed, no payments or exactions, refined and excellent meals, obliging and artful little gifts, nor pasture for horses nor requisitions of mounts or chariots, nor anything that could be called a payment, may ever be required from this property, but that this little property should remain under full immunity, as it was possessed by me, under the authority of Saint Mary and of the said paupers, with God's protection and help. Except for the giving of blessings and the replacement of abbots, presbyters and deacons, for which he will not be given any money, the holy and apostolic bishop of the city of E, within the walls[560] of which this religious house is situated, will have no power to give, claim or diminish anything besides this, and he will at no time be given the occasion or the opportunity to take away anything from this through exchanges of properties, but let it remain in perpetuity in the power of the said oratory and of these paupers, with Christ's favour. This also I beg and enjoin the pontiffs, that in future times, as death comes to the abbots and clerics of other ranks, they shall deign – or: they should – replace them in this place with those who are celebrated for their wisdom and knowledge of the scriptures, and who are recommended by their holy life, good conduct and honourable demeanour. I therefore beg the most clement kings, both present and future, and all of God's bishops and all powerful and great men, and also all lords, whatever persons are to become judges,[561] by the ineffable omnipotence of God, by the inseparable Trinity of the Father and the Son and the Holy Ghost, never to allow this my decision to be shaken in any circumstance (since property is often seized due to the current godless avidity), for any pretext or at any time, but rather to order that it be maintained through the solicitude and care

---

559 See above, n. 392.
560 The phrase is 'in cuius opidum', referring to a fortified town.
561 See above, n. 393.

of the bishop, out of reverence for the boundless Trinity, in your time and by your effort and action, so that He who knows that I gave alms to these holy paupers of God out of an ardent desire, for the love of our Lord Jesus Christ, should repay you with salvation in the future. If someone contradicts or makes a claim against this my decision through fallacies or designs (since the world is daily plundered through guile and deceit), or creates trouble or delay, let him be anathema, and let both the man who did it and the man who consented to it be anathema, and, as Dathan and Abiron were swallowed in a chasm of the earth,[562] descend into hell alive, and together with Zeziae, the deceitful trader,[563] let him expiate his share of damnation in present and future ages, and let him not obtain pardon until the devil himself obtains it, who, having been cast down from the ethereal throne after betraying the Lord, is forever wakeful with the cruel design of opposing good deeds. Furthermore let him pay, the most sacred fisc – or: the blessed bishop of the church of F –, being involved in both the prosecution and the collection [of the fine], one hundred pounds of gold, three hundred pounds of silver, and let the present document, which was written by me out of fear of God and love of my fellow-man, remain no less firm, uncorrupted, unsullied and inviolate. For I commit all of the property transferred and listed above – or: the defence of the property and the authority over these paupers – to the care and solicitude of the blessed and aforementioned lord Bishop G and his successors, God being his witness, and I delivered the documents according to which this property, with God's help, is to be defended by their solicitude into the hands of the aforementioned lord Bishop G; and whatever he does there that is provident, pious, right and appropriate will be acknowledged by the Lord Christ in his judgment. For myself I reserved nothing at all out of this property title, because he who wants to be saved from the mouth of hell – or: he who desires the remission of his sins through God's reward, or: he who is always thinking that he must die whether he likes it or not – easily disdains all things. With confirmation given below.[564]

562 The story is from Numbers 16:32.

563 This refers to II Kings 5:20–27. Gehazi was not a trader, but a servant of Elijah; the word *mercator* was probably meant as a slur, referring to his attempt to trick Naaman out of some money and clothes (Elijah made him a leper as a result).

564 This is the standard phrase 'stipulatione subnixa', often found in Frankish formulae and documents. The *stipulatio* in late Roman documents referred to a solemn promise to abide by the terms of the contract, usually in short question-and-answer form ('Do you promise this? I do'). In Frankish documents, however, the meaning of this expression seems to have changed, and it was sometimes apparently used to refer to the signatures of witnesses included at the end of the document.

THE FORMULARY OF MARCULF

II, 2: Prologue for someone who is donating a large property to the church.

> As in the previous formula, the preface given here is highly elaborate, and again strongly emphasises the concern for salvation. The text of the donation itself is given in the following formula, after an alternative preface.[565]

This much human intelligence and understanding can fathom through a penetrating mind and consider through industrious inquiry, that enjoying a transient happiness in the light of this age is of no greater value than what one takes care to distribute out of one's property to venerable places as alms for the poor. Therefore, before a sudden death falls upon the weakness[566] of [our] nature, which is something that all will suffer generally, we must be vigilant regarding the salvation of the soul, so as not to find ourselves unprepared and leave this age without any refuge, but rather, while the freedom of full ownership remains, to seek to gain, in exchange for a transient wealth, eternal life in eternal dwellings,[567] so as to obtain a desirable place among the community of the just and predispose the Lord [our] judge in our favour, [and] so that we may deserve to be favoured with the boundless fruit of paradise. When we drink with perfect faith from its living source, the cup is not taken away nor the flow diminished; instead, everyone that attempts it will be bathed in the sweetness of heaven and smell the pleasing fragrance of the balm of paradise.

II, 3: Another prologue for this deed, and the donation.

> This gift was only to take effect after the death of the couple who made it, who retained a right of usufruct over their property for their lifetime: this meant that they could exploit and retain the revenues of the land, but could not sell or alienate any of it, since once the gift was made they no longer had the right to diminish its value (though in this case they did reserve the right to free some of their slaves, which was also counted as a pious deed). This text is striking in displaying an unusually high level of concern regarding the possibility of the document being tampered with or forgeries being presented to contradict it, and tries to guard against this in a variety of ways. The most interesting of these is the couple's apparent decision *not* to enter their document in the municipal archives,[568] and their scornful rejection of

---

565 This text, along with the content of the donation in the following formula, also appears as part of the Reichenau formulary, as *Formulae Augienses Coll. A* no. 12.
566 Compare the opening sentence of Marculf II, 4.
567 This phrase ('eterna tabernacula') refers to Luke 16:9.
568 See below, Appendix 2.

'insignificant decurions'. This phrase, however, is difficult to interpret; it seems to have puzzled later scribes, and the manuscripts offer several different readings for the word *curiales*, many of them highly implausible.[569] It may be no accident that scribes were not really sure about this sentence, since by the time the manuscripts were copied many of the functions of the *gesta municipalia* may have been taken over by religious houses, which would have made any opposition between public and monastic archives redundant. Zeumer thought that *vilitate* ('insignificance') should be emended to *laudabilitate* ('praiseworthiness'), although, in view of the consistency of manuscript readings for this particular word, he thought that this had been a mistake on the part of Marculf himself rather than resulting from a later corruption of the text.[570] But even if the meaning of this expression is not absolutely certain, the use of the negative is: whatever their opinion on decurions, the couple clearly did *not* want their document entered in the *gesta*, and instead probably chose to leave it in the keeping of the beneficiary (the monastery). Their stated reason for this was that they did not want anyone other than the monastery to have access to it in the future, apparently out of fear of tampering. The idea that the safest way to protect the rights granted through a document was to make this document as inaccessible as possible is at odds with the original purpose of the *gesta*, which was to provide public authentication for legal actions; it certainly suggests that public archives, at least in the city in which this couple were living, were no longer seen as providing sufficient guarantee, and marks in an unusually explicit manner the shift from public authority to recipient as the repository for legal documents.

Clear signs show and evident proofs are known to announce that the end of the world is near, as disasters become more frequent,[571] and the predictions given by the Lord in the gospels some time ago to torment the foul minds of infidels are known to be at hand. Preoccupied by the vicissitudes of future times, I undertake to ensure [my] reward by my action, and to prepare for the uncertain fate of the human condition with the understanding of a penetrating mind, so that I may deserve as a result to obtain the favourable remedies of piety for the wounds inflicted by sins. Thus I, in God's name, A, and my wife B, considering the weight of sins with which we are burdened, and remembering God's kindness, saying: 'Give alms, and all things will be clean unto you',[572] trusting in the Lord's great compassion and piety,

569 See below, Appendix 3, p. 276.
570 Zeumer, *Formulae*, pp. 75–76, n. 2. Another possibility would be that what was meant was 'the by no means insignificant decurions', but that is not what the construction implies.
571 The beginning of *Formulae Turonenses* no. 1a reproduces a slightly abridged version of this sentence ('Mundi terminum adpropinquantem, ruinis crebrentibus, iam certa signa manifestantur'; Zeumer, *Formulae*, p. 135).
572 Luke 11:41.

therefore give by this document of donation, and want it to be given in perpetuity, and transfer and convey it in writing from our ownership into the power and authority of the monastery of C, built in honour of D by E in the *pagus* of F, where the venerable Abbot G is ruling and a great crowd of monks [is] assembled, the villas named H–I, situated in the *pagus* of J, with lands, houses, buildings, tenants, unfree servants,[573] vineyards, forests, fields, meadows, pastures, water and water-courses, along with dependencies and appurtenances, cattle of either sex, moveable and non-moveable goods, as it is possessed by us at the present time. And if we are able to augment or improve anything there in the future in any way, let it benefit the said monastery, for the sustenance and support of the monks who live there, with Christ's protection; with this condition, however, that while we both live we may possess the said villas under usufruct only, without any prejudice or diminution to this monastery, unless we want to free for our common salvation one of our slaves[574] from the yoke of servitude. But when we are both dead, whenever God wills it, without waiting for a transfer by a judge[575] or from our heirs, let the said monastery and the said abbot and his successors, in God's name, receive in their possession in perpetuity, together with everything that was added to it, whatever was added or is found at present in the said villas, whether goods or persons, as if [their] ownership had been effective immediately from the present day and not [left] in our use, so that they may have the freedom of decision in every way to do whatever they decide with the said villas for the benefit of this monastery. We took care and wholly decided by no means to have the present donation entered into the public archive by contemptible decurions,[576] so that no one should be able to gain access to it at any point as a result of this. And if any document in our name regarding these villas apart from this one, which we want to be most firm, is put forward by anyone at any time, [which is] to the detriment of the said monastery, acquired in whatever way and marked from an earlier or a later [date], [and] which we neither made nor asked to be made, let it not obtain any effect, but let it appear void and empty, and let the judiciary power not suffer the author of the crime and the forger to go unpunished at that time. And if someone, which we do not believe will happen, [whether] one of our heirs or the cruel greed of judges[577] or any other person, opposes

---

573 See above, n. 392.
574 See above, n. 547.
575 See above, n. 393.
576 This phrase appears in different versions in the manuscripts; see the discussion above.
577 See above, n. 393.

or makes a claim against this our decision under any pretext, let him be held outside the community of all Christians and the boundaries of the churches, and let him enjoy the company of Judas, the betrayer of our Lord Jesus Christ; and let him furthermore pay to this monastery and to the brothers who live there, the most sacred fisc being involved both in the lawsuit and in the prosecution, *n.* pounds of gold, *n.* pounds of silver, and let him thus be unable to assert his claim, [and] let the present donation, which was written by us out of fear of God and love for the paupers of Christ, remain no less firm and inviolate for all time. With confirmation given below.[578] Made here [on day x].[579]

II, 4: Grant to a church from the present day.

> This gift is described in the title as effective 'from the present day', and the document makes no reference to any right of usufruct over the land being reserved for the givers; however, this seems to be contradicted by the following formula, a *precaria* said to relate to the same *villa*, requesting precisely such a right of usufruct. If these two formulae were indeed related, the situation might not have been so different to that given in II, 3, with the same result being achieved in two distinct stages rather than in a single document.

Since the weakness of humanity fears the end of life, one should not be found unprepared by the sudden death that is to come, or leave this age without any consideration for good deeds; instead, while one retains one's authority and power, one should prepare for oneself the way of salvation, through which one may reach eternal happiness. Thus I, in God's name A, and my wife B, for the salvation of our soul and the remission of our sins, so that we may deserve to obtain mercy in the future, concede from the present day, and want it to be conceded in perpetuity, and [transfer] from our power into the power and authority of the holy church of C, built in honour of D, the villa called E, situated in the *pagus* of F, which came under our authority out of the inheritance of our relatives – or: from any source – and which we are seen to possess at present, with all its benefit and territory, with appurtenances [and] added dependencies, with lands, houses, buildings, tenants, unfree servants,[580] vineyards, forests, fields, meadows, pastures, water and water-courses, mills, flocks with shepherds, cattle of either sex, large and

---

578 See above, n. 564.

579 The phrase 'sub die illo' only appears in Paris BnF lat. 4627 and 2123, and is therefore likely to have been a later addition (on the manuscript tradition, see Appendix 3).

580 See above, n. 392.

small, moveable and non-moveable goods, and whatever can be named or numbered and is seen to be in our possession at the present time. We want the said villa of E to be conceded to the present church, so that from this day the said church and the pontiff of the city of G or the representative of this church may enjoy the free authority in every way to have, hold [and] possess it, and to do whatever they choose with it for its benefit, so that our names may be written in the book of life[581] and presented to the pious Lord after our death in exchange for our common offering. Although it is not necessary to include a penalty-clause in donations, it pleased us, for the sake of complete firmness, to insert [this]: if at any point someone, which we do not believe will happen, whether ourselves (and may this never happen) or one of our direct or indirect heirs or any person, moved by guile and misled by greed, wants to go or do anything against our present gift document, which we decided should be made through a spontaneous decision, in the name of God and out of veneration for this holy place, or tries to circumvent [it], let him be anathema, and let him make amends to the said Lord D before the tribunal of Christ.[582] Furthermore, let him pay, according to the secular punishment, *n.* pounds of gold, *n.* pounds of silver to this church, the fisc compelling [him],[583] and let him be unable to assert his claim, but let the present grant remain immoveable for all time. With confirmation given below.[584] Made here.

II, 5: *Precaria* for this villa, while [the giver] lives.

According to the title, this *precaria* relates to the gift of a *villa* made in the preceding formula, contradicting the claim that this gift was to be effective immediately. A *precaria* was a request to be granted a right of usufruct over some property, usually by benefactors wishing to retain the revenues of the land they had given to a church. In later examples, *precariae* were usually associated with the yearly payment of a *census*, a payment in money or in kind (it is not clear whether this would have corresponded to a substantial sum or to a largely symbolic repeated admission that the land was not being held under outright ownership); but this was

---

581 The reference is to Revelation 21:27. *Libri vitae* were also registers listing the names of benefactors to be commemorated and prayed for by a church or monastery; our earliest surviving examples seem to date from the ninth century (for an overview and bibliography on *libri memoriales*, see Devroey, *Puissants et misérables*, pp. 107–13).

582 This refers to the day of Judgment; the phrase is clearly used with this meaning in Marculf I, 17.

583 See above, n. 394.

584 See above, n. 564.

manifestly not the case here.[585] The stipulation that the *precaria* was to remain valid 'as if it had been renewed every five years' suggests that there were situations in which *precariae* did need to be renewed at fairly short intervals of time, though it has to be said that this need seems to have been mentioned in documents of this kind only in order to be dismissed (compare the *precaria* in Marculf II, 39, which says that, 'according to custom', there would be no necessity to renew the document). Compare Marculf II, 9 and 41; Angers no. 7.

To the blessed lord caring for the apostolic see, our lord and father in Christ Bishop A, [I,] B and my wife C. It is known by many that, in the name of God, we were seen to concede to the church of D, [built] in honour of Saint E, our villa called F, situated in the *pagus* of G, whatever was in our possession there from any source in its entirety, by our gift document, and you received it on behalf of the said church. But afterwards we requested, and your benevolence and piety agreed to it, that, while we live, or while whichever one of us survives the other lives, you should allow us to hold and cultivate this villa as a benefit[586] under the right of usufruct, with this condition, however, that we will not have the right to take away or diminish anything from this property, but should only cultivate it without any prejudice to the said church or to you. We therefore gave you this *precaria*, to the effect that our ownership, even if God deigns to prolong the span of our life, must not entail any prejudice towards you or any diminution of this villa at any time, but we must have it, while we live, only for our use. And after the death of both of us, along with all its added value, whatever we may bring or improve there in any way, you and your successors or the representatives of the church will have it returned under your authority, to be possessed in perpetuity, without waiting for any deed of transfer from any judge[587] or our heirs, by this *precaria*, as if it had always been renewed every five years. And, as our document stipulates, you will have the free authority to do whatever you choose with it in the interest of the said church of the Lord E. *Precaria* made here.

---

585 On *precariae*, see Wood, 'Teutsind, Witlaic and the history of Merovingian *precaria*'; Rosenwein, 'Property transfers and the Church, eighth to eleventh centuries: an overview'; Hummer, *Politics and Power in Early Medieval Europe*, pp. 19–22, and, on the payment of a *census*, pp. 84–104 (especially pp. 92–94).

586 The word is *beneficium*; it is difficult to tell whether this word was already being used in the seventh century to refer to its later, more technical meaning of landed benefice, or whether it simply meant 'benefit' or 'favour'.

587 See above, n. 393.

II, 6: Donation of a small property to the church.

> Although this formula is differentiated from preceding ones in the title as concerning a 'small property' (*parva res*), that is, not a whole villa, but only a part of one, it is nevertheless written in very similar terms, and even reuses parts of Marculf II, 4 and 5 (though it includes in a single document both the gift and the clause relating to usufruct).

If we give something out of our property to the places of the saints and to provide for the poor, we believe without doubt that we will be rewarded with eternal happiness. Thus I, in God's name A, out of love for our Lord Jesus Christ and for the remission of my sins, so that I will deserve to obtain the alleviation of my sins in the future, give, and want it to be given in perpetuity, to the church of B, built in honour of Saint C, my property on the villa called D, in the *pagus* of E, whatever I am seen to own there at present either from the inheritance of my relatives or as a result of any acquisition. I want it to be given completely and in full to the said church, with this condition, however, that while I live I should cultivate it under the right of usufruct only, without any prejudice or diminution of anything from the property of the said church. And after my death, whenever God wants [me] to leave this light, straight away and without waiting for a transfer from judges[588] or my heirs, and without any contradiction, the abbot of this church and his representatives must recover it under their authority, with lands, buildings, tenants, unfree servants,[589] vineyards, forests, fields, meadows, pastures, water and water-courses, and every other benefit,[590] to possess in perpetuity; and let them have the free power in every way to have, hold and do whatever they choose with it in the interest of the said church. And if someone, which we do not believe will happen, whether ourselves (and may this never happen) or one of our heirs or any opposing person, moved by guile and misled by greed, tries to go against this our document of donation, which we decided to have made by a spontaneous decision in the name of God, or to breach it, first let him incur the wrath of the triple Majesty, and let him make amends to the said Saint C before the tribunal of Christ;[591] furthermore, let him pay to this church, the fisc compelling [him],[592] *n*. [amount of] gold, *n*. [amount of] silver, and let him

---

588 See above, n. 393.
589 See above, n. 392.
590 See above, n. 518.
591 See above, n. 582.
592 See above, n. 394.

be unable to assert his claim, but let the present document remain firm and inviolate for all time. With confirmation given below.[593]

II, 7: Charter of mutual donation of their property between a man and his wife.

> This document is similar to Angers no. 41, in which a childless couple made testaments in each other's favour, with the difference that in Marculf documents of this kind were not defined as testaments, but as gifts taking effect after the giver's death (testaments in Marculf were apparently distinguished from deferred gifts as being exceptionally formal and more particularly associated with Roman law; compare Marculf II, 17). As in Marculf I, 12, this gift in fact only involved granting a right of usufruct over the dead spouse's property for the length of the other's lifetime: once both spouses had died, the property of each was to revert to their respective heirs, whose rights over this property were protected by the clause preventing the surviving spouse from alienating any of it. Unlike the following formula, however, this particular text made an exception for gifts to the church and manumissions, since both of these actions were seen as contributing to salvation.[594]

Whatever it may please spouses to give to each other out of their own property, through constant affection, out of love, it is necessary to record it in documents, so that it may not afterwards be wrested [from them] by their heirs or by anyone. Thus I, in God's name A, to you, my sweetest wife B: since we are seen not to have had any children between us, we therefore decided that we should give to each other the entirety of our property under a right of usufruct, which we did. Thus I give you, my sweetest wife, should you survive me in this age, the entirety of my property, whatever I am seen to own anywhere, whether through inheritance or through a purchase or from any other source, and that we cultivated together as a couple, with lands, villas, houses with all [their] content, tenants, unfree servants,[595] vineyards, forests, fields, meadows, water and water-courses, gold, silver, clothes, cattle of either sex, large and small, so that, while you live, you may own and have authority [over it] by right of usufruct, except for what we gave to the places of the saints for the salvation of our soul.[596] And let our donation,

---

593 See above, n. 564.

594 This formula also appears in the Reichenau formulary, as *Formulae Augienses Coll. B* no. 26.

595 See above, n. 392.

596 This refers to lands which the husband had already given to a church and had retained under a right of usufruct; this clause meant that these lands would revert to this church after his death, rather than allowing his widow to continue to hold them.

once inspected, be upheld in every way. And whatever out of our inheritance you may want to give and donate legally after my death to the places of the saints for our common salvation, you will have the permission to do so, and let this donation, once inspected, remain undisturbed. But as for the rest of all these properties, let whatever remains without heir[597] after your death revert to our legitimate heirs.

Similarly I also, B, to my sweetest husband A. Your sweetness has moved me to give [you] compensation for your property, which you have been seen to give to me. If you survive me in this age, I give you the entirety of my property, wherever [it may be] and from whatever source, whether from the inheritance of my relatives or through a purchase, and that we cultivated together, entire and in full, with villas, houses – etc. – except for what we donated for the salvation of our soul to the places of the saints.[598] And let this document, once inspected, be upheld in every way. And whatever out of this my inheritance you may want to give to the places of the saints or to give free status to after my death for our common salvation, you will have the right [to do so]; and, let this document, once inspected, be upheld in every way. And after your death, let whatever remains without heir[599] revert to the heirs closest to us at that time.

And if someone, which we do not believe will happen, whether one of our heirs or anyone else, wants to go against or breach this mutual donation, which we confirmed between us in two documents of identical content,[600] let him in no way be able to assert his claim, but let him pay *n*. pounds of gold, *n*. of silver to you, the fisc compelling [him].[601] And the present document may in no way be discarded, but let it remain firm and unchanged. With confirmation given below.[602]

II, 8: Another one, without any diminution.[603]

This formula was clearly intended to complement the preceding one, pointing out which modifications needed to be made to it if the surviving spouse was not allowed to alienate anything from the property in any way, not even to make

597 That is, whatever had not been left to the church.
598 See above, n. 596, for this clause in the husband's document.
599 See above, n. 597.
600 See above, Marculf I, 38.
601 See above, n. 394.
602 See above, n. 564.
603 This same formula is also found in the Reichenau formulary, as *Formulae Augienses Coll. B* no. 27.

manumissions or gifts to the church. This solution thus protected the interests of heirs more strictly.

This other one is identical to the previous chapter down to: – ... while you live, you should possess it by right of usufruct. And after your death, let it revert to our legitimate heirs, and you will not have the right to alienate or diminish anything out of it.

Similarly also I, B, to my sweetest husband A. Your sweetness has moved me [to give you] compensation for your property, which you have been seen to give to me. If you survive me in this age, you should own all my property, whatever I may own and from any source, with lands – etc. – under the right of usufruct; and, beyond only a right of usufruct, you will not have the right to alienate or diminish anything out of it. And after your death, let it revert to our legitimate heirs. And if someone...

II, 9: Charter of concession made by a father for his children.

This document describes a counter-gift made in exchange for a grant of usufruct over some property. C's sons are said to have been in dispute with him over the lands included in their mother's marriage-gift (*dos*), which she had left to them as part of their inheritance. According to the text, they defeated their father by turning against him the document which he had himself given to her to record this marriage-gift (showing that written documents of this kind could be crucial in determining the outcome of such disputes). The arrangement described here must have formed part of the dispute settlement. This new document allowed C to retain these lands under a right of usufruct, but his sons, rather than 'obeying his will', clearly drove a hard bargain: he could not alienate any of the property, not even to give some of it to the church; he had to give to his sons, in exchange for this favour, the ownership of some other *villas*, though he also retained those under usufruct; and, finally and most unusually, he had to agree to give up all of these lands whenever they demanded it. Since a judgment had already been pronounced against him, C had no doubt been in a very weak position to negotiate (compare Marculf II, 41).

To my sweetest children A–B, C. It is known by all that, *n*. years ago, I was seen to give some villas called D–E, situated here, to your mother F, before I married her, by a gift document – or: a document for a wedding-gift –. But she, for my sins, left this light, and you, according to what was granted by a judgment, having litigated against me in the presence of good men[604] – or: of the king –, won your case against us regarding all the

---

604 See above, n. 515.

inheritance of your mother F by [producing] this document which we had made for her, and received all of this inheritance into your power. But since I requested it, you, as befits good children, obeying my will, allowed me to hold and cultivate under usufruct,[605] without any prejudice to you, these villas and property which had belonged to your mother, and which I had given to her. Therefore it pleased us to surrender to you by this document of concession our other villas G–H in return for your benevolence and for [giving me] the said use of your villas, so that from now on I am to cultivate, by your favour,[606] both the said villas and those which I had given to your said mother by my document. And, beyond only [this right of] use, I will not have any right to sell, alienate, exchange or diminish by any ploy any of what is written above, but let them be under your authority and power by this my document of concession, and, whenever you want and it may please you to do so, you are to recover under your authority, to own in perpetuity, all that is written above, both what belonged to you from before through your mother's inheritance and those other villas called thus, which I was seen to surrender to you in exchange for this [right of] use, without any contestation or claim from me, and you will have the free power to do whatever you want with it. Let this [document], without any other intervening *precaria*, but as if it had always been renewed every five years, obtain perpetual validity by this concession. With confirmation given below.[607] Made here.

II, 10: Document, when grandchildren[608] are given the status of sons by their grandfather.

> Despite the title, this is not an adoption, but a testament, intended to allow C's grandchildren to inherit through their mother. The text emphasises that, 'by law', these grandchildren would not in principle have been allowed to share in C's inheritance: this could refer to the clause in Salic law according to which daughters could not inherit their father's lands if they had brothers,[609] as was plainly the case here (compare Marculf II, 12); but the text also mentions the inheritance that C's daughter would have received had she survived, which implies that she would have shared in C's inheritance along with her brothers. Formulae of this kind

---

605 The phrase is *ad usum beneficii*. On *beneficium* in this context, see above, n. 586.
606 See above, n. 586.
607 See above, n. 564.
608 The word is *nepos*, which normally refers to a nephew, but Marculf consistently uses it to refer to granchildren.
609 *Pactus Legis Salicae* 59, 6 (p. 223).

could in fact deal with a man's granchildren through his son as well as through his daughter, which suggests this issue was not gender-specific.[610]

To my sweetest grandchildren A–B, C. Since, for my sins, your mother, my daughter D, left this light, against my hopes, after completing the course of her life, I, mindful of blood-ties, and since by law you may not share in my inheritance with my other children, your uncles, therefore by this document I want you, my sweetest grandchildren, to receive from all my inheritance after my death, if you survive me, the said portion, that is: lands, houses, tenants, unfree servants,[611] vineyards, forests, fields, meadows, pastures, water and water-courses, moveable and non-moveable goods, cattle of either sex, large and small, and every content of the house, and anything that can be named, whatever your said mother could have received from my inheritance if she had survived me, against your uncles, my sons. And since I gave to this daughter of mine, your mother, when I gave her away in marriage, carpets and jewels and some unfree servants,[612] worth *n. solidi*, out of my moveable property, you will receive this in your share against my sons; and if anything further is owed to you out of our property in addition [to this], you will receive the share owed to you out of it, along with my sons, your uncles; and you will have the free power in every way to do whatever you want with all the things written above. And if someone, which we do not believe will happen, whether one of my direct or indirect heirs or any other person, tries to go against this document or wants to breach it, let him pay you *n*.; and let him be wholly unable to assert his claim, but let the present document remain firm for all time. With confirmation given below.[613] Made...

II, 11: Charter for someone who wants to give something to a grandson.[614]

This document deals with a gift of land, which a grandfather was giving to his grandson above and beyond what he was to receive as part of his inheritance. The gift was apparently intended as a reward for this grandson's past and future 'service' (*servitium*), and was strongly associated with a commitment on his part to continue to look after his grandfather. This type of arrangement, in which

---

610 Compare *Formulae Salicae Merkelianae* no. 24 and *Formulae Salicae Lindenbrogianae* no. 12 (Zeumer, *Formulae*, pp. 250 and 274–75). *Formulae Turonenses* no. 22 reproduces a large part of the text of this Marculf formula (p. 147).
611 See above, n. 392.
612 See above, n. 392.
613 See above, n. 564.
614 See above, n. 608.

an older man gave land to a younger man in exchange for material support, did not necessarily only involve family members (compare Marculf II, 13; see Angers nos. 36, 37 and 58 for similar gifts to family members in exchange for support).[615]

To my sweetest grandson A, B. Since old age already weighs me down, and I am unable to provide for my necessity as much as is necessary, and you never stop giving me help in my necessity and do not cease to serve me day and night devotedly, therefore, out of kindness and consideration for your service, by which you toil for me, I give you, and want it to be given in perpetuity, and transfer from my authority into your authority and power, independently from your brothers and my sons, the place called C, whatever I was seen to have there up to now, whether from the inheritance of my relatives or from other sources, together with lands, houses, buildings, tenants, unfree servants,[616] vineyards, forests, fields, meadows, pastures, water and water-courses, and every other benefit.[617] I want it to be granted to you, as we said, from the present time, so that from this day, as we said above, you will have, hold and possess it in its entirety, and you will have the free power in every way to do whatever you want with it, independently from your brothers and my sons. And if someone, which I do not believe will happen, whether one of my direct or indirect heirs or any person, wants to go against this my gift document or breach it at any point, let him pay you, the fisc compelling [him],[618] *n.* [amount of] gold, and let him be unable to assert his claim, but let the present document remain firm. With confirmation given below.[619] Made...

II, 12: Charter, so that a daughter should succeed to her father's inheritance together with her brothers.

This extraordinary text shows us a father going explicitly against what he describes as 'an ancient but impious custom' by leaving his daughter an equal share of his inheritance:[620] this 'custom' was no doubt a reference to one of the most famous clauses of Salic law, according to which daughters could not inherit land along

---

615 Compare *Formulae Turonenses* no. 21 and *Formulae Salicae Merkelianae* no. 25 (Zeumer, *Formulae*, pp. 146–47 and 251), the latter reproducing much of the wording of this formula.
616 See above, n. 392.
617 See above, n. 518.
618 See above, n. 394.
619 See above, n. 564.
620 Compare *Cartae Senonicae* 42 and 45; *Formulae Salicae Merkelianae* 23 is largely based on this formula.

with their brothers.[621] Although formulae often present solutions diverging from the prescriptions of written law, it is rare for such contradictions to be pointed out so explicitly. This contradiction is associated in the text with a concern to emphasise that the arrangement was nevertheless to be considered valid; perhaps the direct reference to this law was meant to discard it explicitly as a possible counter-argument in future disputes. We can only speculate as to how successful this preemptive discarding of legal custom may have been, and as to whether A's daughter was really able to secure her inheritance in practice.[622] Either way, this text does indicate that law, written or otherwise, was not understood as having to be observed rigidly, but rather as one possible source of authority among several, to be appealed to if it supported one's case, or discarded if it did not (other sources of authority could for instance include Christian charity, here opposed to the 'impious' custom, or even simply the free decision of the property-holder).

To my sweetest daughter A, B. An ancient but impious custom is held among us, that sisters may not have a share of their father's land along with their brothers. But I, carefully considering this impiety, [say]: just as you were equally given to me by God as children, you should also be loved by me equally, and enjoy my property equally after my death. Therefore, by this letter, I name you, my sweetest daughter, the equal and legitimate heir of my entire inheritance, along with your brothers, my sons C–D, so that you should divide and share whatever we may leave when we die, whether from my father's inheritance or from a purchase, unfree servants[623] or moveable property, in equal parts[624] with my sons, your brothers; and in no way are you to receive a portion smaller than theirs, but you must divide and share everything equally between you in every way. And if someone – and what follows.

II, 13: If someone adopts a stranger as his son.

This formula shows us a childless and apparently elderly man handing over his property to another, in exchange for the material support he could normally have expected from his sons.[625] Although B claimed to be doing this so that A would help him in his 'poverty', this claim seems to be contradicted by the list of B's

---

621 *Pactus Legis Salicae* 59, 6 (p. 223). Judging from surviving documents, which regularly show us women disposing of land, this clause does not seem to have been much observed in any case. On the possible origins of this clause as relating in the first place only to military colonies, see T. Anderson, 'Roman military colonies in Gaul, Salian ethnogenesis and the forgotten meaning of Pactus Legis Salicae 59.5', *Early Medieval Europe* 4 (1995), pp. 129–44.
622 On women and property rights, see in particular Nelson, 'The wary widow'.
623 See above, n. 392.
624 The phrase is 'equo lance... dividere vel exequare' (compare Angers no. 37).
625 For a very similar text, compare *Formulae Turonenses* no. 23.

land and property: this was clearly not a measure taken as a result of extreme poverty, since B would have had nothing to offer A if that had been the case, but rather to ensure protection and support in old age (the word *paupertas* in any case tended to be used during this period to refer to social or political 'weakness' rather than strictly to 'poverty').

To my lord brother[626] A, B. Since, for my sins, I have long been bereft of sons, and poverty and infirmity are seen to afflict me, and, according to what was decided and agreed between us with good will, I was seen to adopt you in the place of my sons, so that, while I live, you will spare and provide for me in every way food and clothing, both for my back and for my bed, and shoes in sufficient quantity, and you are to receive in your power all my property, whatever I am known to have, including *mansus*, vineyard, meadow, cattle and every other content of my house, on the condition [that you observe] this right while I live, I therefore decided to have this document made for you, so that neither myself nor any of my heirs nor anybody may be able to change this agreement made between us, but, as mentioned above, you must provide for my necessity while I live, and all my property will remain in your power, both at present and after my death, and you will have the free power to do whatever you please with it. And if someone wants to change this at any time, let him pay you *n*.; and let him be unable to assert his claim, but let the present document remain firm for all time.

II, 14: Agreement between relatives over their inheritance.

> This is a partition of inheritance between brothers. The opening sentence stresses that there had been no dispute (unlike the situation in Marculf I, 20); this agreement is similar to Angers no. 55, though the property is here larger and described in less detail.[627]

When relatives agree between them the portion justly owed to each out of the inheritance of their relatives without being compelled by a judiciary power, but voluntarily, through constant affection, this is not to be counted as damaging to the property, but rather as being to its advantage, and therefore it is necessary that their [agreement] made between them be recorded in a written document, so that it may not be thwarted by anyone in the future. Thus it was agreed and decided with good will between A and his

---

626 This should be understood in the Christian sense rather than as referring to an actual family relationship.
627 Compare also *Formulae Turonenses* 25, *Cartae Senonicae* 29, *Formulae Salicae Bignonianae* 19, *Formulae Salicae Merkelianae* 21 (the latter is partly based on this formula).

brother B, through constant affection, that they should divide and share the inheritance of their parents between them, which they did in this manner: A received the villas called C–D, situated here, with *n.* unfree servants[628] E–F; similarly B received for his part, in compensation, some other villas called G–H, situated here, with *n.* unfree servants I–J. They were seen to divide and share equally between them the moveable goods, carpets and jewels worth *n. solidi* and all the contents of the house, whatever can be named or numbered, and each party transferred it to the other and said that everything had been shared by the rod.[629] Therefore they were seen to write the present two documents, copied with identical content,[630] [to act] as a settlement between them, so that neither should thereafter have the right to claim anything further against the other out of this inheritance of their father, beyond what he received at present. And if one of them or their heirs ever wants to change this, or wants to claim or take anything more than what he received, let him pay the other, according to this document,[631] *n.* pounds of gold, *n.* pounds of silver, and let him be unable to assert his claim, but let the present settlement remain firm for all time.

II, 15: Document for a wedding gift.

> Like Angers nos. 1, 34–35, 40 and 54, this is a *dos* document, but this case is unusual in that the gift was being made not by the husband, but by his father.[632] This may be because his son, not having yet come into his inheritance, did not own enough property himself to make such a substantial gift; whatever the reason, this document certainly emphasises parental involvement in the marriage arrangements. The gift is also explicitly made before the wedding, whereas most *dos* documents seem to have been given on the day of the wedding itself.

May this be a good, happy, joyful and prosperous [occasion]![633] It is necessary that everything that is done as a result of a betrothal, marriage or the birth of children, and also a gift, should obtain fuller validity through a written document. Thus A [gives] to the virtuous girl, his daughter-in-law

---

628 See above, n. 392.
629 See above, n. 434.
630 See above, Marculf I, 38.
631 The readings 'ista tota' (in Leiden BPL 114, Paris BnF lat. 4627, Paris BnF lat. 2123, and Copenhagen Fabr. 84) or 'ista tuta' (Paris BnF lat. 10756) should probably be emended to 'statuta', 'document'.
632 On *dos*, see the recent book edited by Bougard, Feller and Le Jan, *Dots et douaires dans le Haut Moyen Age*; Nelson, 'The wary widow'.
633 Compare Angers no. 54 for a similar opening sentence.

B, to be married to his son C, before the day of the wedding, and transfers and conveys [it] in writing in the spirit of a gift, the following, under the title of a wedding-gift: the villa called D, situated here, with a house suitable for habitation and all that can be seen there in its entirety; similarly, also as a wedding-gift, some other villas called E–F, situated here, *n*. unfree servants,[634] [the men] G–H and [the women] I–J, with gold and silver and jewels worth *n. solidi*, *n*. horses, *n*. oxen, a herd of horses, a herd of cows, a herd of pigs, a flock of sheep, so that all these things should go to the said girl, his daughter-in-law, by his hand, before the day of the wedding, and be brought under her authority, and she will have the free power to do whatever she chooses with it. And if someone tries to go against this document for a wedding-gift and to breach it, let him pay *n*. to the said B – and the rest.

II, 16: If someone abducted a girl against her will.

This is effectively a variation on a *dos* document, but this time arranged after an abduction, in order to turn it retrospectively into a marriage:[635] the marriage-gift, as an essential feature of a proper marriage (indeed, *dos* documents seem to have been the only written record produced as a result of a marriage), here served as a way of legitimising the union after the fact, though this may not have been a legal requirement so much as the result of negotiations with the wife's family.[636] The word *raptus* could be used to mean 'rape', 'abduction', or even 'elopement', and did not always imply that the woman had not consented to it: as other formulae of this kind also show us, *raptus* could therefore be consensual.[637] The main point of contention was the consent of the bride's parents rather than her own: although Marculf included two alternative prefaces (*arengas*), the first to be used if this abduction had taken place against the girl's own will, the second if it had only been against that of her parents, the procedure outlined in the document itself seems to have remained much the same regardless of this. The mention that B could have lost his life as a result of his abduction, and was only saved by the intervention of priests and *boni homines*, is unexpected: according to Salic law, only people who technically counted as unfree (*pueri regis*, servants of the king, or *liti*, another type of unfree dependant) lost their life as a result of abducting a

---

634 See above, n. 392.

635 Compare *Formulae Turonenses* no. 16 and *Formulae Salicae Merkelianae* no. 19 (the latter is largely based on this formula).

636 On *dos* as a common feature of marriages rather than a strict legal requirement, see R. M. Karras, 'The history of marriage and the myth of *Friedelehe*', *Early Medieval Europe* 14 (2006), pp. 119–51, especially at pp. 138–44.

637 For apparently consensual 'abduction' in similar documents, see *Formulae Turonenses* no. 32 and *Formulae Salicae Lindenbrogianae* no. 16.

free woman, while free men were heavily fined instead.[638] This could suggest that B was indeed in some way unfree (as in the situation described in Marculf II, 29), or, perhaps more plausibly, that local practice in the area where this particular case took place differed from the prescriptions envisaged in Salic law.

To my sweetest wife A, B. Since you were [not] betrothed to me by the will of your parents, and I married you through the crime of abduction against your will and that of your parents, – Another one: Since, in my arrogance, I married you through the crime of abduction against the will of your parents –, I could have been in danger of [losing my] life because of this; but I was granted my life through the intervention of priests and good men,[639] with the condition that I should confirm [for you] what I should have given to you as a marriage-gift[640] before the day of the wedding if you had been betrothed to me, by this document of agreement – or, if that is the case: of grant –, which I did in this manner: I therefore give you the small place called C, situated in the *pagus* of D, with houses fit for habitation and all the useful necessary things inside them, with lands, tenants, *n.* unfree servants,[641] vineyards, forests, meadows, pastures and every other benefit,[642] *n.* horses, *n.* oxen, a herd of horses, a herd of cows, a herd of pigs, a flock of sheep, with gold and silver, jewels [and] carpets worth *n. solidi.* I transferred all these things listed above from the present day into your power and authority, [for you] to possess, and you will have the free power to have, hold and do whatever you choose with it. And if someone – etc.

II, 17: How a person may make a testament in one volume.

This testament is exceptionally formal, and extremely thorough in its attempt to prevent any future confusion or conflicting claims to the property (the penalty-clause is particularly vindictive and colourful, combining, as often in Marculf, spiritual and secular punishment). The text includes provision for the couple's children, but also provides for the surviving spouse, in an arrangement similar to those found in testaments or donations made in each other's favour by childless couples (Angers no. 41, Marculf I, 12 and II, 7–8), by granting a right of usufruct

---

638 *Pactus Legis Salicae* 13, 7 (p. 61).
639 See above, n. 515.
640 This rare word is found in several different readings in the manuscripts (*tanodo, tanto dono, tandono*), which could indicate that scribes were unsure of its meaning; its association with the word *dos* in the text suggests it was also referring to a gift or marriage-gift. See Appendix 3 below, Table 5.
641 See above, n. 392.
642 See above, n. 518.

over the property to the surviving spouse. In this case, the surviving spouse was also allowed to alienate some of it for charitable works, such as gifts to the church or manumissions, or to make gifts to dependants ('bene meritis nostris', 'those who deserve well from us'). There are some differences between the will made by the husband and that made by the wife: the husband is to obtain the right of usufruct over all of his wife's property, whereas she was only allowed one third of his,[643] the rest being immediately inherited by the couple's children; the wife was also to lose all the property if she chose to remarry, whereas her husband apparently would not. The property involved here seems to have been substantial, and was distributed over several *pagi*. The document did not make an issue of the inheritance of daughters, since the couple's child named E could be either a son or a daughter and still inherit some *villas*. The text emphasises the physical aspects of drawing up a document, and, like Marculf II, 3, devotes a significant amount of space to avoiding any opposition through the presentation of conflicting documents: in this case, this was attempted through a general annulment of all documents made prior to but not acknowledged in this testament. However, whereas II, 3 had been concerned with keeping the document unchanged and inaccessible, since it was a one-off gift, the terms of which could not in principle be renegotiated, this document, by contrast, explicitly warns that corrections would be visible on the parchment, since the couple expected to modify it over time, specifying that this should not bring the authenticity of the document into doubt.

Under the eternal reign of our Lord Jesus Christ, in any given place, in year x of the reign of King A, on day y, I, B, and my wife C, of sane mind and full understanding,[644] fearing the fate of human weakness, made our testament, which we appointed the notary D to write down, so that, on the correct day after our death, the seals having been identified and the string cut, as the authority of Roman law decreed, by the illustrious men E–F, whom we name as our executors in this document of our testament, it may be validated by them at the municipal archive[645] through their request. Thus, when, by God's order, we leave the course of this life, I want you, my beloved wife C, and you, my beloved children D–E, as my heirs, to have my inheritance, everything that we are seen to own on the day before our death, whatever we may have deserved to obtain out of the property of our relatives or through our own efforts or from the munificence of pious princes, and which came under our authority, with God's help, under any title and contract of sale, grant,

---

643 This fits in with the idea that the woman had a right to a third of the property that had been acquired by a couple, also found in Angers nos. 45 and 59.

644 Compare Angers no. 41 for a similar phrase.

645 The phrase is 'gesta rei publicae municipalia'; see Appendix 2.

gift, or from any [other] source. And let my other heirs thus be disinherited, apart from what I will give and order to be given to each by this testament. I call you, omnipotent God, as a witness, so that this may be done, given, granted. Let our son D receive the villas F and G, situated in the *pagus* of H; similarly let our son E – or: daughter E – receive the villas I–J, situated in the *pagus* of K. Let the church – or: monasteries – of L receive the villas M–N, situated here. This I call you to uphold, omnipotent God, so that it may be done, given, granted. Although we reserved the use of all these things for ourselves while we live, but since my said wife could have had one third of these villas which we named above, which we bequeathed to the places of the saints and our heirs, because we acquired them together as a couple, let her therefore receive in compensation one third of the villas called F–N, situated in the *pagi* of H–K, in full, if she survives us; and let her have the permission to do whatever she decides with it for our common salvation, for the poor and those who deserve well from us; and after her death, if anything remains without heir, let our heirs receive it. Let the freedmen and freedwomen whom we have freed or will want to free in the future for the salvation of our soul, and to whom we will have given documents signed by our hand, know that they will owe service to our children, and let them take care to provide hosts and lights for our tomb, according to what is contained in these documents, both themselves and their offspring.[646] And we have taken care to enter individually in this our testament each person to whom we have given something out of our property. As for the rest, if anyone presents any documents in our name, signed by our hand, and marked from an earlier date than this testament, which we did not mention here, let them remain void, except for those regarding manumissions which we made or will want to make in the future for the salvation of our soul. And let the one between us who survives the other, and whatever person, and those who deserve well from us, to whom we will have given something as a gift out of the said property through any document, insofar as the law permits, remain with firm security; let the other documents remain void and without effect. And we agreed this between us: if you, my sweetest wife, survive me and want to go to another husband, and may God prevent you from doing so, let our heirs immediately receive all that you may have out of my property, which we granted you could possess by right of usufruct, and which we gave you from this day, to be divided between them.

I also, C, your servant, to my lord and husband B, asked by a most ready

---

[646] Compare Marculf II, 34 for a manumission of this kind.

decision to have it written in this testament, for its perpetual preservation, that if you, my lord and husband, survive me, you will have the free power to do whatever you want with all my property, however much I am seen to own out of the inheritance of my relatives, or that we obtained together in your service, and that which I received for my third, in its entirety, whatever you want to do with it, to give it for the salvation of our soul to the poor or to your dependants[647] or to those who deserve well from us, without any opposition from my heirs. And after your death, let what has not been given away revert to our legitimate heirs.

And we signed this testament document with signatures by our own hands, which we did according to custom, and took care to have it confirmed by the signatures of other persons. And so that the document for this testament may not be disputed: if some erasures, scrapings, additions or corrections have been made, [that is because] we made them or ordered them to be made, since we often checked and modified our testament. If someone tries to resist our decision or question our testament with guile for any reason, we, imploring the Lord, beg the majesty of the divine name that he should be held guilty on the day of Judgment of all our crimes, on behalf of us sinners, that he be excluded from the communion and peace of the catholic church, that he be forced to submit his case before Christ's tribunal for violating the will of the dead, and let God visit his vengeance upon him with fire, as he promised to the unjust, when he comes to judge this age, and let him receive in His sight the perpetual damnation received by Judas, the betrayer of the Lord. And we wanted to include that, if any of our direct or indirect heirs or any other person wants to go against or attack this document of testament, which we asked to be made by a full and complete decision, let him pay to the person against whom he made this claim twice the value of what is written down in this testament, and furthermore, the fisc compelling [him],[648] *n.* pounds of gold, *n.* of silver. And let him be unable to assert his claim, but may the present testament remain stable for all time.

II, 18: Security for a murder, if they made peace.

This is a dispute settlement made out of court between a murderer and the family of the victim, after the murderer paid compensation (possibly, though the text does not say it, equal to the victim's *wergeld*, though the amount actually paid could no doubt be negotiated in practice). This document was intended to prevent any future litigation about the same matter; the family of the victim took

---

647 The word is *vassus*, though here not in the technical sense of 'vassal'.
648 See above, n. 394.

responsibility for this, since they would have to pay a fine if they failed to prevent further disputes arising from this. Compare the securities for disputes in Angers, nos. 5, 6, 26, 39 and 42–44; none of these, however, deal with murder, which seemed to have been settled more formally than other disputes in that formulary (see Angers nos. 12 and 50).

> To [my] lord brother[649] A, B. Since, at the instigation of the devil, you were seen to kill our brother C, which you should not have done, you could have been in danger of [losing your] life because of this; but through the intervention of priests and great men, whose names are added below, we were seen to restore the harmony of peace in this matter, so that you were to give me *n. solidi* in compensation for this, which you were seen to deliver by your pledge,[650] and we were seen to relinquish this claim against you by the rod.[651] Therefore, according to what was agreed, it pleased us to write this document of security for you, so that you should not fear any further claim or accusation or penalty regarding this death of our brother, whether from me or from my heirs or his, or from a judiciary power, or from anybody, but you will be seen as free and absolved from this in every way. And if perhaps I myself or one of my heirs or anyone else wants to trouble you regarding this, and is not prevented by me, we will pay to you, the fisc compelling [us],[652] twice what you gave us. And let him be unable to assert his claim, but let the present document of security made by me remain firm.

II, 19: Sale of a villa.

This is a sale of a large estate. The preface (*arenga*) establishes a distinction between the act of sale itself, achieved through an oral procedure, and the charter recording it, which was intended to serve as future proof: this distinction, however, rather than creating an opposition between written and oral forms, instead stresses their complementarity.[653] As in the previous formula, the seller here took responsibility for preventing any future disputes, and agreed to pay a fine should he fail. Although this did not ensure that the new owner would not be involved in disputes linked to earlier and conflicting claims to the land (for instance if the seller was proved to have 'sold it wrongly', for instance if it had in fact belonged to someone else), it did therefore ensure a sizeable compensation.

---

649 See above, n. 626.
650 The word here is *wadium*.
651 *Per fistuco... werpisse*: for these two words, see Marculf I, 13, nn. 432 and 434.
652 See above, n. 394.
653 See McKitterick, ed., *Uses of Literacy*, at pp. 320–21.

To the lord brother[654] A, B. Although a contract of purchase and sale consists only of the calculation of the price and the transfer of the property itself, and the drawing up of charters and other documents is only included in order to provide evidence of the deed according to the law, it is thus established that I sold you, as indeed I did sell, the villa in my possession named C, situated in the *pagus* of D, which I am seen to have from the legitimate inheritance of my relatives – or in whatever way it came to him – in its entirety, with lands, houses, buildings, tenants, unfree servants,[655] vineyards, forests, fields, meadows, pastures, water and water-courses, dependencies, appurtenances, and every benefit and territory belonging there. And I received from you in payment, according to what pleased me, *n.*, and presently transferred the said villa into your possession, so that from this day you may have the free power in every way to have, hold and do whatever you choose with it. And if someone, which I do not believe will happen, whether I myself or one of my direct or indirect heirs or any other person, tries to go against this act of sale, or proves me to have sold it wrongly, and is not prevented by me or my heirs, we will then pay to you and your heirs twice the money that I received from you [combined with] the value added to this villa. And let him be unable to assert his claim, but let the present act of sale remain firm for all time. With confirmation given below.[656]

II, 20: Sale of an area within a city.

> This text is very similar to the previous formula, but the exact specification of size and boundaries for this urban plot contrasts with descriptions of villas, which tend simply to refer to the property by name and include fairly standard lists of what might be found there.[657] In this case the buyer had been a bishop, though this apparently did not in any way affect the way in which the transaction was recorded (compare Marculf II, 19 and 21, in which the buyers were laymen).

To the blessed and apostolic lord, the lord and father Bishop A, B. It is established that I, compelled by no authority nor by any fictitious claim, but by the decision of my own will, sold you, as indeed I did sell, the area in my possession within the walls of the city of C, of *n.* feet in length and *n.* feet in width, which is joined on one side with D and on the other side with E, on one front with F and on the other front with G; and I received from you as

---

654 See above, n. 626.
655 See above, n. 392.
656 See above, n. 564.
657 Compare *Formulae Turonenses* no. 42, which is similar to this formula.

payment, according to what pleased me, *n*. gold *solidi*, and presently transferred the said area into your possession; you will have the free authority[658] to have, hold and do whatever you choose with it. And if someone, which I do not believe will happen, whether I myself or one of my heirs or any person, tries to go against this act of sale or attempts to breach it, let him pay to you or your representatives twice the money and however much is added to the value of the plot at that time – etc.

II, 21: Sale of a field.

This formula is virtually identical to the previous one, and gives equally precise boundary descriptions, this time in the case of a field (compare Marculf II, 24 for an exchange document concerning either a piece of land, a field or a vineyard; see also Angers nos. 8, 21, 22, 40 and 54 for similarly precise boundary clauses). The need for a written contract to record the sale of a single field suggests a very wide use of the written word, documenting even very small-scale transactions.

To the lord brother[659] A, B. It is established that I sold you, as indeed I did sell, the field in my possession, situated on the territory of C, covering [a surface of] more or less *n*., which is joined on one side with D and on the other side with E, on one front with F and on the other front with G; and I received from you as payment, according to what pleased me, *n*. gold *solidi*, and I presently transferred this field into your possession; you will have the free power to have, hold and do whatever you want with it. But if someone – etc.

II, 22: Sale of a male or female slave.

Judging by the similarity between this formula and the three preceding ones, it would seem that little difference was made during this period between the sale of persons and the sale of landed property. On the other hand, not all unfree persons would have been the object of such sales, which seem to have been largely restricted to domestic slaves (compare Angers no. 9).[660] The health check-list given at the beginning of the document may have allowed A to seek compensation

---

658 Both Zeumer and Uddholm rejected the reading 'liberum perfruatur arbitrium', which is found in Paris BnF lat. 10756 and 4627, in favour of the more standard 'liberam habeas potestatem' ('let him have the free power'), as in the following formula; but this seems unnecessary, since the same expression is also found in Marculf II, 4 and 5 and II, 22.

659 See above, n. 626.

660 Compare also *Cartae Senonicae* no. 9, in which a slave is sold 'in mercado', 'in the market-place' (Zeumer, *Formulae*, p. 189). See Rio, 'Freedom and unfreedom', pp. 32–34.

if the slave proved unsatisfactory (that is, if his value had been exaggerated by the seller). The last sentence also allowed for the possibility, on the contrary, that the slave might gain value, perhaps through training in particular tasks.

To [my] lord brother[661] A, B. It is established that I sold you, as I did sell you, the slave in my possession – or: the female slave – named C, neither thieving nor runaway nor epileptic, but healthy of mind and of his whole body, for whom I received from you as payment, according to what pleased me, *n*. good gold *solidi* weighing [the correct amount],[662] and I presently transferred this slave into your possession, so that from this day you may have the free authority to have, hold and do whatever you decide with him. And if someone, which we do not believe will happen, whether I myself or one of my heirs or any other person, tries to go against this act of sale or wants to breach it, let him pay you, the fisc compelling [him],[663] *n*. [amount of] gold, and whatever value will have been added to the slave himself at that time, and let this act of sale remain firm for all time. With confirmation added below.[664]

II, 23: Exchange of villas.

Although the title says that this exchange related to some villas, in the text itself the property is referred to as a *locellus* (a 'small place', in this case a small estate), a word which may or may not have corresponded to the same thing. Either way, this would not have had any serious repercussions for the wording of the text, since this document (as in cases involving a villa) clearly related to a full estate as opposed to a single field or small stretch of land, and therefore only included a standard list of items rather than a fuller description of boundaries (compare Marculf II, 19–21; see also Angers no. 8 for an exchange relating to individual fields). The exchange was here apparently being made between a layman and an abbot (a 'venerable man' who had to ask for the permission of his diocesan bishop).

Those who retain undiminished affection for each other should offer appropriate favours[665] to one another, since [each one] is thought to take away nothing from his own property, when he receives [something] in exchange.[666] Thus it was decided and agreed between the venerable A, with the permission of the apostolic B, and the illustrious man C that they should exchange some

661 See above, n. 626.
662 As opposed to coins from which some gold had been shaved or clipped off.
663 See above, n. 394.
664 See above, n. 564.
665 See above, n. 398.
666 Compare the *arenga* (preface) in Marculf I, 30.

small places between them, which they did. Thus the venerable A, acting on behalf of the church of Saint D, gave this small place called E, situated here, to the said C, whatever it was seen to hold there at present from any source, with lands, houses, buildings, tenants, unfree servants,[667] vineyards, forests, fields, meadows, pastures, water and water-courses, and everything that belongs there. Similarly, in compensation for this benefit, the said C gave to the said abbot acting on behalf of the said church another small place called F, situated here, whatever he was seen to have there at present from any source, with lands, houses, buildings, tenants, unfree servants,[668] vineyards, forests, fields, meadows, pastures, water and water-courses, and everything that belongs there, so that from this day each of them will enjoy the free authority to have, hold and do whatever they choose with the said places which they received, for their profit and benefit. And they agreed to add this, that if one of them, or his heirs or successors, wants to change or contest this, let him lose the property that he received, and furthermore let he who presumed to do this pay *n.* pounds of gold, *n.* pounds of silver to the other, and let him be unable to assert his claim, but let the present exchange, of which they had two [copies] of identical content written for each other,[669] remain firm and inviolate for all time. With confirmation given below.[670] Made...

II, 24: Exchange regarding a land or a vineyard.

> This document is very similar to the previous one, but deals with a smaller property. In exchange documents as in acts of sale, particular plots of land were described much more thoroughly than villas or estates. Compare Angers no. 8, which also deals with a vineyard.

Thus it pleased and was agreed between A and B that they should exchange a piece of land – or: field, or: vineyard, or whatever – between them, which they did. Therefore A gave B a field in the place named C, covering [a surface of] *n.*, which is joined on one side with D and on the other side – or: front – with E. Similarly B gave to A in exchange another field there – or in another place –, covering [a surface of] *n.*, which is joined on its sides – or: fronts – with F, so that from this day each of them will have the free power to have, hold and do whatever he chooses with what he received. And if

---

667 See above, n. 392.
668 See above, n. 392.
669 See above, Marculf I, 38.
670 See above, n. 564.

someone, one of them or their heirs or anyone else, wants to change this, let him lose the property which he received to the other, and furthermore let him pay one ounce of gold to the other, the fisc compelling [him];[671] and let him be unable to assert his claim, but let the present exchange, of which, out of a desire for stability, they had two [copies] of identical content written for each other,[672] remain firm for all time. With confirmation given below.[673] Made here.

II, 25: Loan securities made in different manners.

> This the first of three loan securities (*cautiones*) given by Marculf, showing possible variations in the nature of such agreements. This example curiously makes no mention of the interest to be paid on the loan, and the deed of security is only concerned with establishing the date on which the money was to be returned and stating the penalty for failing to meet this requirement. This may have been because the loan was very short-term, since the text suggests it was to be repaid within less than a year ('at the next Kalends of [the month of] C'). Compare Angers no. 60, which is similarly silent on the subject of what would have been expected in exchange for the loan. In this text as in the following one, the lender is addressed as the debtor's 'own' lord ('domino mihi proprio', 'domino suo'), emphasising this as a relationship of dependence and obligation (compare Marculf II, 28).

To my own lord A, B. Since, at my request and to provide for my necessity, your kindness agreed to lend us a pound of silver out of your property for our benefit,[674] I therefore promise by this bond of security that I will return this silver to you on the next Kalends of C. If I have not done this when the appointed day of my *placitum* has passed, on the next day, you or your heirs, or whoever you will have given this security to enforce, will obtain a penalty of twice [that amount] from me or my heirs. Security made here, on day *x*, in year *y*.

II, 26: Another one.

> In this case the compensation for the loan follows a straightforwardly proportional (if very steep) rate of interest, to be paid yearly; perhaps as a result of this, the debt did not have to be repaid at any predetermined date.

---

671 See above, n. 394.
672 See above, Marculf I, 38.
673 See above, n. 564.
674 See above, n. 398.

A to his lord B. It is established that I received from you, as I did receive, and that I owe [you], as I do owe [you], *n. solidi*, in exchange for which *solidi* I promise that, for as long as I will keep them, I will give back to you a third of every *solidus* every year. And if I refuse to do this or appear negligent in this matter, I promise to give back to you twice [the value of] the loan. And when I can return your *solidi* from my property, I will recover this security from you.

II, 27: Another one.

> In this case, the interest on the loan takes the form of part-time work. The reference to corporal punishment on a par with A's 'other servants' ('ceteros servientes[675] vestros') seems to imply that B was effectively agreeing to become unfree for a certain number of days each week, which makes this situation somewhat similar to a self-sale: the link was apparently also consciously made by Marculf, since a model for a self-sale is given in the following formula.[676] Arrangements of this kind could no doubt become permanent if the loan was never repaid. Compare Angers no. 38, in which a man pledged 'half' his free status, with slightly more favourable terms, and Angers no. 18 for a deed of annulment for a loan security of the same type.[677]

To [my] lord brother[678] A, B. Since, to provide for my necessity, you lent *n.* of your *solidi* for my benefit,[679] it was therefore agreed between us, according to what pleased me, that, until I can return these *solidi* from my own [property], I must [spend] *n.* days in each week in your service, to do as yourself or your agents bid me. If I seem negligent or slow in this, you will have the right to inflict corporal punishment, as with your other servants. And when I am able to return your *solidi*, I will recover my deed of security, without the need for a deed of annulment.

---

675 Marculf seems to use the word *serviens* only to refer to unfree servants (compare Marculf I, 39, II, 3 and II, 34 for the manumission of *servientes*).
676 See Rio, 'Freedom and unfreedom', pp. 28–31.
677 Compare also *Cartae Senonicae* no. 3, which is similar to the solution envisaged in this formula (Zeumer, *Formulae*, p. 186). For an annulment similar to Angers no. 18, see also *Cartae Senonicae* no. 24 (p. 195).
678 See above, n. 626.
679 See above, n. 398.

THE FORMULARY OF MARCULF 211

II, 28: For someone who is putting himself in the service of another.

> This is the only example of self-sale in the Marculf collection (compare Angers nos. 2, 3, 19 and 25).[680] The situation is similar to Angers no. 3, in which a man also sold himself in exchange for someone paying a fine on his behalf.[681] Unusually for formulae of this kind, the penalty-clause here includes the threat of being sold again to someone else if the servant proved unfaithful to his master and tried to enter another man's service.

To my own lord A, B. Since, at the instigation of the devil, my weakness taking the upper hand, I fell in a serious legal dispute, as a result of which I could have been in mortal danger, but since your piety redeemed me with your money when I had already been sentenced to death, and gave for my crimes several items of your property, and I do not have enough to repay your favour out of my property, because of this I was therefore seen to hand over to you my free status, so that from this day I may never leave your service, but I promise to do whatever your other slaves do under your order or that of your agents. If I do not do this, or want to take myself away from your service by any means, or want to go into the power of another or receive things [from him], you will have the right to impose upon me whatever punishment you want, or sell me, or do with me what you please. This enslavement made then, on day *x*.

II, 29: Charter regarding the offspring, if a slave has abducted a free woman.

> This model offers two prefaces outlining different possible circumstances, though the outcome seems to have been the same in both: in the first, A's slave, C, is said to have abducted a free woman, B (this is *raptus*, and in this case C, since he was unfree, could have been killed as a result:[682] A probably allowed B to remain free in exchange for keeping his servant alive); in the second, B married him willingly, in which case C's life was not at risk, but B and her future children could have been enslaved as a result, according to Salic law.[683] The fact that this document is

---

680 See *Cartae Senonicae* no. 4 for a case of enslavement resulting from the failure to repay a debt (Zeumer, *Formulae*, p. 187).

681 On the subject of self-sales, see Liebs, 'Sklaverei aus Not'; Rio, 'Freedom and unfreedom', pp. 27–32.

682 *Pactus Legis Salicae* 13, 7 (p. 61); compare Marculf II, 16.

683 *Codex Theodosianus* IV, 12; *Pactus Legis Salicae* 13, 8 and 25, 4 (pp. 61 and 94). On marriages between free and unfree, see Bonnassie, 'Survie et extinction du régime esclavagiste dans l'Occident du haut moyen âge'; Goetz, *Frauen im frühen Mittelalter*, pp. 263–67; Nelson, 'England and the Continent in the Ninth Century: III, Rights and Rituals'; Wickham, *Framing*

referred to as a manumission charter (*cartola ingenuitatis*) at the end of the text suggests that C's master felt he had a real claim over B; he may have renounced his claim partly as a result of pressure from the wife's family (or her own lord). If so, this would suggest that the extent to which lords could appeal to written law to support their claims over people and property was limited by their ability to enforce their power in practice at the local level.[684] A may also have expected a counter-favour, and at any rate B and C's children were certainly expected to remain on his lands as free tenants and pay him dues. Naturally, it is impossible to tell how standard or how unusual the solution described here might have been, but the frequent occurrence of formulae of this type in different collections and manuscripts suggests that it was something scribes felt they needed to prepare for (compare Angers no. 59).[685]

Thus I, in God's name, A, to the woman B. It is not unknown that my slave named C married you through the crime of abduction against your parents' will and your own, and because of this he could have been in danger of [losing his] life. But through the intercession and mediation of friends[686] and good men,[687] it was agreed between us that, if any children are born to the two of you, they will retain full freedom. – And if she accepted the slave willingly, say: – It is known to all that you followed my slave named C willingly and accepted him as your husband. But although I could have forced you yourself and your progeny into my service, it pleased me, in the name of God and for the remission of my sins, to write for you the present document, so that, if there are any male or female children born to the two of you, neither ourselves nor our heirs nor anybody else may ever force them into our service at any point, but they should remain for all the time of their life under full freedom, as if they had been born of two free parents, and whatever possessions they may obtain will be granted [to them]. And they must remain under full freedom on the land of ourselves and our sons, without any prejudice to their free status, and let them pay the dues of the land every year, as is the custom for free persons, and always

---

the *Early Middle Ages*, pp. 405 and 560–61; Rio, 'Freedom and unfreedom', pp. 16–23. On the situation in the later Carolingian polyptychs, or estate-surveys, see Coleman, 'Medieval marriage characteristics'; Nelson, 'Family, Gender and Sexuality', p. 157.

684 See Rio, 'Charters, law-codes and formulae', pp. 25–26.

685 See also *Cartae Senonicae* no. 6; *Collectio Flaviniacensis* no. 102 (= Marculf, II, 29); *Formulae Salicae Merkelianae* no. 31; *Formulae Salicae Bignonianae* no. 11; *Formulae Salicae Lindenbrogianae* no. 20; *Formulae Morbacenses* nos. 18 and 19; *Formulae Augienses Coll. B* no. 41.

686 *Amici*: 'friends', or perhaps here 'relatives'.

687 See above, n. 515.

remain under full freedom, themselves as well as their descendants. And if someone, which we do not believe will happen, whether ourselves or one of our heirs or anybody else, tries to go against this document or wants to breach it, let him pay two pounds of gold, three pounds of silver to you or your heirs; and let him be unable to assert his claim, but let the present document of manumission remain firm for all time. With confirmation given below.[688] Made in D.

II, 30: Divorce document.

> This formula shows us a divorce by mutual consent, and is very similar to Angers no. 57, though with an added clause covering the possibility that one or both of these ex-spouses might choose to join a monastery.[689]

Since between A and his wife B there reigns not love according to God, but discord, and because of this they cannot live together at all, it pleased both to decide that they should separate from their marital association, which they did. Therefore they decided to have two documents of identical content[690] written and signed between them, so that each of them, if they want to enter into the service of God in a monastery or into [another] marriage union, should have the permission to do so, and should not have any claim [brought against them] by their counterpart because of this. But if one of them wants to change this or make a claim against the other, let him/her pay one pound of gold to the other, and, as they decided, let them remain separated from their union in the situation that they choose. Document made here, on day x, in year y of the reign of our most glorious lord King C.

II, 31: Mandate.

> A gave this mandate to B in order to allow him to represent him in court (either before the royal tribunal or in local courts) and negotiate a settlement on his behalf in a dispute over an inheritance. Compare Angers nos. 1b, 48 and 51–52; Marculf I, 21 and II, 38.

---

688 See above, n. 564.
689 See also *Formulae Turonenses* no. 19, *Cartae Senonicae* no. 47 (very similar to this formula) and *Formulae Salicae Merkelianae* no. 18. On divorce in this period, see d'Avray, *Medieval Marriage*, pp. 74–81; McNamara and Wemple, 'Marriage and divorce in the Frankish kingdom', pp. 96–124.
690 See above, Marculf I, 38.

To my lord brother[691] A, B. I pray and beg your authority, since I am seen to be involved in a dispute about an inheritance – or whatever – against the man named C in the palace – or wherever –, that you should take up this legal case before the court[692] and prosecute it on my behalf, and give an answer to the said C regarding this; and whatever you do or accomplish with him regarding this case, know that it will be approved and confirmed by me. Mandate made here, on day *x*.

II, 32: Here begin documents of manumission made in various manners. Manumission from the present day.

> As with the loan securities in II, 25–27, Marculf here gives three examples of manumissions, following different possibilities. This first of these was to be effective from the present day (rather than coming into effect after the master's death, as in the following formula). C was explicitly absolved from the service normally owed by a freedman ('libertinitatis obsequium'). The inclusion of a threat of excommunication in the penalty-clause was standard in manumissions, as in the case of gifts to the church: actions which entailed spiritual rewards also carried spiritual threats. Compare Angers nos. 20 and 23; Marculf I, 22 and II, 52.

He who unties a bond of service owed to him may be confident of earning salvation for himself before the Lord in the future. Thus I, in God's name A, and my wife B, for the redemption of our souls and an eternal reward, release you, [the man] C – or: [the woman] C –, belonging to our household, from all bond of servitude from the present day, so that you may live a free life thereafter, as if you had been born of free parents; and you will not owe service to any of our direct or indirect heirs or to anyone, nor the obedience of a freedman to any but God, to whom all things are subjected. The possessions that you have now or that you may acquire later [are] granted [to you]; and if it happens that you need to protect your freedom, you will have the right to the protection of the church or of anyone you care to choose, without any prejudice to your freedom, and you may lead your life forever well and completely free. And if someone, which we do not believe will happen, whether ourselves (and may this never happen) or one of our heirs or any other opposing person, tries to go against this your document of manumission or to breach it, or wants to force you into service, may divine vengeance strike him, and let him be excluded from the boundaries of churches and from communion, and furthermore let him pay one pound of gold to you,

---

691 See above, n. 626.
692 See above, n. 470.

the fisc compelling [him];[693] and let him be unable to assert his claim, but let the present document of manumission remain firm for all time. With confirmation given below.[694]

II, 33: Another manumission in another manner, after the death [of the owner].[695]

> This formula only shows what modifications to make in the preceding text if the manumission was only meant to become effective after the master's death.

To his dear [man] A – or: [woman] A –, B. Out of respect for the fidelity and obedience with which you serve me and for the remission of my sins, I release you from all bond of servitude, with this condition, however, that you should serve me while I live. But after my death, if you survive me, you should be free as if you had been born of free parents, and you will not owe service to any of my direct or indirect heirs, or to anybody. The possessions that you have now or that you may acquire are granted [to you], – etc.

II, 34: Another one for this, in another manner.

> This third example of manumission is similar to the previous two, but contains some added restrictions: B could only choose his legal 'protector' from among A's heirs (though the end of the formula also allows for the possibility of getting additional protection from a church), and also had to provide candles and hosts for his master's tomb, as in Marculf II, 17. Although the text emphasises that B would do all this 'as a free man', the arrangement therefore still involved a form of dependence. Ex-masters seem to have been conscious of the risk that legal 'protectors' might demand too much in return from the freedmen entrusted to them, and sometimes felt the need to protect the free status of their freedmen, and therefore the spiritual effectiveness of their gesture, by specifying that this duty of protection was 'not to oppress but to defend' ('non ad adfligendum sed ad defensandum' or 'ad defensandum non ad inclinandum').[696] Compare Angers no. 20.

If we release one of our servants[697] from the yoke of servitude, we are

---

693 See above, n. 394.
694 See above, n. 564.
695 This formula is copied almost word for word in *Cartae Senonicae App.* no. 4 (Zeumer, *Formulae*, p. 210).
696 *Formulae Salicae Bignonianae* no. 2 (Zeumer, *Formulae*, pp. 228–29); *Formulae Salicae Lindenbrogianae* no. 11 (p. 274).
697 The word is *servientes*, which Marculf uses to refer to unfree servants specifically. Compare Marculf I, 39, II, 3 and II, 27.

confident that we will earn salvation for ourselves because of this in the future. Thus I, A, in the name of God and for an eternal reward, release you, B, from all bond of servitude, so that from this day you may lead a free life, as if you had been born of free parents; and you will not owe service to any of my direct or indirect heirs or to anybody, except that you must have the protection, under full freedom, of whichever of my heirs you will choose, and must provide my hosts and lights every year in the place where my body lies. The possessions that you have now or that you may acquire; – or, if that is appropriate: the protection of the church of C – are granted [to you], and you may forever lead a free life. But if someone...

II, 35: Annulment.

> This formula shows us that the loss by the lender of a document recording a loan security could entail the complete annulment of the debt (for examples of such loan securities, see Marculf II, 25–27). In this case, as in Angers nos. 17 and 18, the loss of the document was apparently the only decisive factor, since the existence of the loan itself was not being contested.

To [my] lord brother A, B. It is known to all that *n.* years ago – or: last year – you received *n.* of our *solidi* for [your] benefit,[698] and for this you issued a loan security to us, as indeed you did,[699] according to which you were to return these *solidi* to us at such a time; but since we cannot find at present this loan security which you had issued to us, we therefore made this deed of annulment for you, so that you may remain freed and absolved for all time from [repaying] these *n. solidi*. And if this deed of security is found, or is presented at any time by ourselves or by our heirs, let it obtain no effect, but remain void and empty.

II, 36: If someone wants to give something to his slave or retainer.

> This is a gift of land to a dependant, in this case apparently a military retainer: the word used is *gasindus*, a Lombard word rarely found in Frankish documents. Marculf gives the word *servus*, 'slave', as its Latin equivalent, so that he seems to

---

[698] See above, n. 398.

[699] Although the phrase 'quod ita et fecisti' could be taken to refer to the repayment of the debt (in which case the loan would have been repaid as intended), this would be at odds with the rest of the document; the use of this same phrase in other formulae and comparison with other formulae of annulment also suggest it is more likely to refer to the issuing of the document itself.

have had in mind specifically a gift to an unfree retainer (or perhaps he meant it as an alternative: either way, this would show that he clearly considered giving land to an unfree dependant as a likely occurrence). This formula could thus constitute a rare and important piece of evidence for the ability of unfree persons to own land in this period.[700] B seems to have received the land in full ownership, since he was able to leave it to his heirs and 'do whatever he wanted with it' (a standard phrase linked with outright ownership), though Marculf also offered an alternative in which he would owe regular payments and ploughing service to his lord (the latter would be a little strange if B was indeed a military retainer: this clause may have been intended to apply in a different situation, or he may not have been intended to fulfil this duty personally, but to pass it on to his own dependants). Compare Angers no. 56 for a similar gift to a servant or dependant.

Those who serve us faithfully and with eager devotion are supported most justly by our gifts. I, in God's name A, to our faithful B. Out of respect for your fidelity and service, by which you did not cease to devote yourself to us, by a most ready decision we grant to you from the present day the small place called C – or: the *mansus* C – within the boundaries of our villa of D, with every appurtenance belonging to this small place – or: small *mansus* –, lands, houses, unfree servants,[701] vineyards, little meadows, little forests and the other benefits[702] belonging there, so that from this day you should take this into your power by right of ownership – if this is appropriate, or: [on condition of paying] the dues of the land –; and neither you nor your descendants should pay from it any charges or dues of the land, or any pasture, land or cartage dues, or anything else that can be named, to ourselves or to our heirs, or to whoever will own this villa after us, except – if this is what [the giver] wants – for ploughing service, but you must own this under immunity through all the days of your life and that of your heirs, and have the free power to do whatever you decide with it. And if someone, which we do not believe will happen, whether one of our heirs or anyone else, tries to act against this our grant or to take this property away from you, let him pay to you, the fisc compelling [him],[703] *n*. [amount of] gold, and let this document remain firm. With confirmation given below.[704]

---

700 See Rio, 'Freedom and unfreedom', pp. 25–27.
701 See above, n. 392.
702 See above, n. 518.
703 See above, n. 394.
704 See above, n. 564.

II, 37: How donations and testaments are entered in the [municipal] archive, in the manner of the Romans.

> Compare Angers no. 1a, which is virtually identical to this formula. It may seem surprising that a model concerning the *gesta municipalia* should be found in Marculf, since this would constitute very late evidence for them; on the other hand, the survival of this formal procedure did not necessarily imply that the civic context had remained the same, as church archives often seem to have taken the place of the *gesta* (see Appendix 2; for a negative view of the *gesta*, see Marculf II, 3).

In year x of the reign of King A, on day y, in the city of B, in the presence of the praiseworthy *defensor* C and all the municipal council of this city, the noble *prosecutor* D said: 'I ask, most excellent *defensor* and you, praiseworthy decurions and councillors, that you should order the public books to be opened for me, because I have something that I must enter in the archive'. The honourable *defensor* C and the decurions said: 'Let the public books be opened for you; enter what you want [there], and do not delay in making your declaration.' The noble *prosecutor* D said: 'The venerable man – or: illustrious man – E ordered me by his document of mandate to enter into the municipal archive on his behalf, as is the custom, this donation – testament or grant –, which he gave to the church – or: the holy place – of F – or: to the illustrious man F – from the present [day] – or: [taking effect] after his death.' The honourable *defensor* C said: 'You must now present or read out to us the mandate which you say was written for you.'

II, 38: Text of the mandate.

> This text is the continuation of the previous formula, and contains the mandate as well as the conclusion of the proceedings (though it does not contain the actual text of the donation). Compare Angers no. 1b–c, which are again very similar to this text.

'To my noble brother D, E. I ask and beg your kindness to bring forward in public in the city of B and to enter into the municipal archive on my behalf, according to custom, this document of donation – or: testament or grant –, which I gave out of my property of G to the church of F for the redemption of my soul – or: to the illustrious man F – [taking effect] after my death – or, if [that is the case]: from the present [day] –. Therefore we wrote this mandate for you, so that you should present and confirm [this] as described above. And know that whatever you do or achieve regarding this, it will be approved and confirmed by me. Mandate made at this time, in this place, in year x.'

After the reading out of the mandate, the honourable *defensor* C said: 'The mandate has been read out; let the said donation – testament or grant – which you say you have in your hands be read out in our presence, and, as you request, let it be confirmed in the public archive.' And the scribe[705] H read out this donation. After it was read out, the praiseworthy *defensor* C and the decurions said: 'Let the document that has been read out be inserted in the public archive, and let what the *prosecutor* D wants and asks for be given to him from the public archive.'[706] The *prosecutor* D said: 'It will be enough for me, good *defensor*, if you allow me to transfer the donation that has been read out into the archive.' The *defensor* C said: 'And because we know that the document of donation – or: grant, or: testament – and the mandate written for you were clearly made correctly and confirmed and signed by the hands of good men,[707] it is appropriate that you should be given a document from the archive, written and signed, regarding this, and that it should serve as a record in the public archive. Let it be issued.'

– [This is] how to write correctly both a mandate [to act] in someone's place and the whole text and the document for [its] execution; and afterwards the *defensor* and the decurions of the city and the others will sign and mark it.

II, 39: Document, if some persons have in their use the property of a church and are giving something from their property in return.

This is the first of three documents relating to grants of *precaria*: in this case, a bishop (whose own document is given in the following formula) agreed to grant to a couple a right of usufruct over an estate belonging to his church, but only in exchange for ownership of another estate, which was to be transferred to his church along with the property he had granted after the death of the couple. The mention that the *precaria* did not need to be renewed is here said to have followed 'the custom for everyone', which suggests that the need for renewal did not normally apply in the case of lifelong tenure (compare Marculf II, 5, 9 and 41). As in the rest of this formulary, no mention is made of any yearly payment (*census*), though the gift of another property clearly counted as a counter-gift.[708]

---

705 The word *professor* seems to refer in particular to scribes employed by the municipal council: compare *Formulae Bituricenses* nos. 7 and 15c (Zeumer, *Formulae*, pp. 171 and 176); *Cartae Senonicae* no. 39 and *App.* no. 1 (pp. 203 and 209).
706 This last part of the sentence seems to refer to a receipt or extract from the archive, given to D at the end of the text.
707 See above, n. 515.
708 See above, n. 585.

To the blessed and apostolic lord, lord and father in Christ, Bishop A, B and my wife C. Since your piety and kindness accepted our request that, while we both live, or while whichever one of us survives the other lives, you should allow us to cultivate for our benefit[709] a certain small place [belonging to] your church, called thus, situated here, which D gave for the redemption of his soul to your church of E, [built] in honour of Saint F, we were both seen, according to what was agreed, to give to you and your successors for the said church, both in exchange for this use and for the redemption of our soul, another small place called thus, situated here, after we are both dead, with this condition, however, that while we live we should possess the said places under usufruct, both the one you lent to us and that which we gave to this church for the redemption of our soul, without any prejudice to your church, without any diminution of any of this property. And after we are both dead, as we said, you and your successors or representatives will recover the said places to hold in perpetuity under your authority, without any other renewed *precaria*, as is the custom for everyone, through this document, without opposition or waiting for a transfer from any of our heirs or anybody else. And our possession [of these estates] must never entail any prejudice to you because of this. But if someone, which we do not believe will happen, whether ourselves or one of our heirs or any other person, wants to go against this document or diminish or take away anything from you out of these small places, let him be accountable to the said Lord F before the tribunal of Christ,[710] and furthermore let him pay *n.* to your church; and let him be unable to assert his claim, but let the present document remain firm. With confirmation given below.[711] Made here.

II, 40: *Prestaria* made by a bishop about the property of a church.

This formula complements the previous one, and gives the model for the bishop's side of the transaction: a *precaria* (from *precor*, 'to beg') documented the request for a grant of usufruct, while a *prestaria* (from *praesto*, 'to provide' or 'to lend') documented the grant itself. This document is very similar in its wording to II, 39, and both documents would no doubt have been expected to be produced by the same scribe.

To the children of the holy church in Christ – or, if that is what they are: illustrious persons – B–C, A, bishop by the grace of God. Since, in answer

---

709 See above, n. 586.
710 See above, n. 582.
711 See above, n. 564.

to your request, we promised that you could cultivate together for your benefit,[712] while you live, a certain small place called thus, situated here, and you gave in return to this church of Saint F, by your document, another small place, called thus, situated here, out of your property after you both die, both in exchange for this use and for the redemption of your souls, we therefore decided, with the agreement of our brothers, to write this document of *prestaria* for the two of you, so that, while you both live, or while whichever one of you survives the other lives, neither we nor our successors nor anybody representing our church should have the right to withdraw these small places from your authority, but, by our favour[713] and that of our successors, you should cultivate both small places in their entirety while you live, without any prejudice to our church or any diminution of any of this property; and after you both die, as stated in your document made by way of a *precaria*, without waiting for any transfer, we or our successors should recover them for our church. Document made...

II, 41: If someone wants to seize another person's property, which he is cultivating [under usufruct], but fails, and afterwards obtains it by *precaria*.

> This formula constitutes important evidence for lay people granting *precariae* in a similar way to churches, and also gives us an example of what could happen when such precarial arrangements went wrong: in this case, B held A's land under a right of usufruct, but apparently failed to keep his side of the bargain by trying to appropriate it fully (this probably meant that he had tried to alienate or divert some of it, which was the only thing precarists were not allowed to do with the property granted to them). Despite winning in this dispute, A nevertheless agreed, through the mediation of *boni homines*, to grant this right of usufruct over the same land back to B, but the new arrangement involved greater restrictions: B would lose the land unless he fulfilled some extra duties, 'as with [A's] other tenants' ('reliqui accolani'), suggesting the establishment of a stronger link of dependence and obligation (as perhaps emphasised by B addressing A as 'his own lord', 'mihi proprio domno'; compare Marculf II, 25). Such duties were not normally a feature of precarial arrangements, and were clearly imposed on B as a result of his failure in court. A could also recover the land whenever he pleased, as opposed to B being allowed to keep it until his death, as was normal in *precariae* (though this clause is also found in Marculf II, 9, which also dealt with a *precaria* arrangement made as a result of a dispute, and in which the precarist had found himself in a similarly weak bargaining position).

712 See above, n. 586.
713 See above, n. 398.

To my own lord, the illustrious lord A, B. Since, on the advice of evil men, which I should not have done, I tried to appropriate your land in the place called C, which I am seen to cultivate, and I wanted to seize this land as [my] property, but could not, as there was no justification [for this], and you and your representatives recovered it for yourselves and evicted us from there, but afterwards, at the request of good men,[714] you gave it back for us to cultivate, we therefore issue to your authority this *precaria*, so that, for as long as it pleases you [to allow] us to hold it without any prejudice to you, we swear to perform whatever [duties] your other tenants do. If we do not do [this], and are negligent, slow or shirking in this matter, [let us be] condemned publicly, as the law prescribes for the slow or negligent, through this *precaria*, as if it had always been renewed every five years, and you will have the right to evict us from this land. *Precaria* made here, on day x, in year y.

II, 42: Letter, when a bishop sends a gift[715] to another on [the day of] the resurrection of the Lord.

> The rest of Book II mostly contains letters of recommendation or conveying good wishes, rather than documenting particular legal actions (except for the last formula, II, 52, which mirrors Marculf I, 39). It is not difficult to see why such letters would have had their place in a formulary: like charters, they played an important part in starting or keeping up networks of patronage and clientelism. In this case, a bishop sent greetings and a gift to another for Easter. Despite its highly respectful tone, the letter seems to be addressed to a more junior bishop, as suggested in the answer given in the following formula. Uddholm remarked that the style of Marculf II, 42–51 strongly resembled that of the letters of Desiderius of Cahors, without, however, implying a textual link;[716] the highly conventional nature of these texts makes it difficult to be certain.

To the blessed lord, caring for the venerable apostolic see, lord and brother in Christ, Bishop A, B, bishop, though a sinner, by the grace of God. In what happy prosperity your industry – or: sanctity – stood to welcome and spend, with the protection of God himself, the mysteries of the feast of the resurrection of the Lord, by which the God Christ himself decided to untie

---

714 See above, n. 515.

715 The word *eulogias* could refer to different types of gift, but usually referred to consumables; it could, for instance, consist of a gift of host or blessed bread (this may have been the case here, as suggested by the reference to food and communion in Marculf II, 43).

716 *Epistulae S. Desiderii Cadurcensis*, ed. D. Norberg (Uppsala, 1961); Uddholm, *Marculfi formularum libri duo*, p. 305.

the bonds of hell, and, victorious over the beaten enemy, in triumph, 'led captivity captive, and gave gifts unto men',[717] and afterwards returned to heaven, the year's cycle beginning anew, we pray with particular veneration, [sending] an appropriate gift from your patron Saint C and duties of salutation, that you should deign to inform our lowliness more particularly by [your] worthy message.

II, 43: Answer to the bishop.

This is the answer to the preceding formula. The style is again far more elaborate than that of the other texts contained in this formulary: indeed, scribes seem to have had more trouble with this letter than with the rest of this formulary, so that the manuscripts offer a great variety of readings, making the meaning of the text very unclear. Zeumer and Uddholm suggested that the original may have contained a few lines of verse, in hexameters.[718]

To the blessed lord, apostolic through [his] merits, the much-loved lord and brother in Christ Bishop[719] A, Bishop B, a sinner. Know that, when our common venerable son C brought the sacred host[720] from your kindness, we received it as a suitable heavenly gift. Having consumed the wisdom of your letters[721] – he means the food –,[722] refreshed by your holy gift, much rejoicing in what the letter contained, as we learned that you and yours are in good health, and because your highness was so moved as to deign to notice a weak and inexperienced youth, we thank you, repaying in this a little more out of many [favours]. May the [divine] words – or: the songs of words – reveal what [actions] may merit a share in eternity. And we say this, that we must entreat you to remember us often in your prayers.

---

717 Ephesians 4:8.
718 Zeumer, *Formulae*, p. 101, n. 3; Uddholm, *Marculfi formularum libri duo*, p. 307, n. 1.
719 The word is *papa*; see above, n. 363.
720 *Communus* should probably be emended to *communio*, 'communion' or 'host' (or perhaps *commonitio*, a 'reminder' or 'exhortation', as in Zeumer's and Uddholm's editions).
721 Both Paris BnF lat. 10756 and Leiden BPL 114 have *apicum peritate*; Uddholm emends this second word to *veritate* ('truth'), but this is not really necessary.
722 Zeumer reconstructed the first two sentences differently, putting a full stop after 'the wisdom of your letters' (*apicum peritate*), and reading the *inquit* or *inquid* ('he says' or 'means') found after *aedulium* ('food') in the manuscripts as *in quid*, 'in that'. Uddholm's reconstruction, which takes *peritate* as depending from the same verb as *aedulium*, seems to make more sense here (though I have rejected his reading of *peritate* as *veritate*, since it seems unnecessary).

II, 44: How one should write greetings sent to a king, queen or bishop after the nativity of the Lord.

> This seems to be the early medieval equivalent of a Christmas card, here intended for particularly exalted recipients, no doubt in the hope of keeping up a relationship of patronage.

To the glorious and excellent son of the holy and universal catholic church King A, Bishop B. – To the glorious and excellent daughter of the holy and universal catholic church Queen A, B, bishop through God's mercy. – To the celebrated lord, worshipper of God and apostolic lord and brother in Christ Bishop A, Bishop B, a sinner. Since we rejoice generally at the coming of the nativity of the Lord, we hasten to deliver the tribute of [our] owed obedience, according to [our] vow, and thus sent – if addressed to the king: to your clemency – if addressed to a bishop: to your sanctity – gifts of salutation, with an appropriate gift[723] from your patron saint C. Showing every kind of humility to your utmost clemency, we request that you allow us to celebrate the fullness of your health, assiduously protected by [our] prayer, by a swift and worthy answer.

II, 45: Another one for the nativity of the Lord.

> This formula offers small variations to be added to the text of the previous formula to fit with possible slight differences in the circumstances: this time the letter seems to have been late, since it was sent after Christmas rather than before, and may have been meant to rectify this faux pas or oversight (though apparently the recipient had not sent anything either). The end of the letter was also modified in case the state of health of the recipient was already known to be poor.

Wishing to know the grace of mutual happiness universally brought by God, we sought to anticipate the letters sent by your clemency – or: your sanctity –, with an appropriate gift[724] from your patron [saint] A, requesting, with honourable and devoted care, that the conspicuous example of your sanctity should tell us with what joy you spent the feast of the nativity of the Lord. For the news of an improvement in your health will be a rich treasure of abundance to us.

---

723 See above, n. 715.
724 See above, n. 715.

II, 46: Letter of recommendation to a bishop one already knows.

> This is a letter of recommendation addressed to a bishop. The reference to the bearers of the letter coming to his diocese 'for the necessity of [our] brothers' suggests that the letter (like the one immediately following it) was written by an abbot, in a bid to enlist the bishop's help for monks sent out on business on behalf of their monastery.

To the most revered lord, elevated to the pontifical pinnacle, Bishop[725] A, B. Recalling the kind affection of your beatitude, with which, to obtain eternal rewards, you solicitously embraced our insignificant person in the intimacy of your heart, as if in a bond of unparalleled friendship, moved by this confidence, I confidently presumed to send to your dignity this letter from our lowliness through our brothers, your sons,[726] the present bearers, through whom I [also] presume to send to your kindness, if my presumption does not offend [you], gifts of salutation, as is fitting, not arrogantly but humbly. We ask that you should deign to receive suitably these [men], [who are] recommended in every way, for, going to your region so far away to provide for the necessity of [our] brothers, with Christ's protection, they are in need of support. For this help may you receive a most worthy hundredfold reward from God, who rewards all good men, [and may it be] added to the heap of His mercy forever. May our Lord God fill your pious crown with the memory of me, and with good things in the present, and reward [your] worthy [actions] in eternity, forever my lord.

II, 47: Another letter of recommendation, to an abbot one already knows.

> This letter has a purpose very similar to the preceding one, with the difference that it gives the appropriate model for one abbot writing to another. As in II, 46, the sender does not say on what business the monks had come; they may have been obtaining supplies for their monastery or dealing with its legal affairs in that region.

To the blessed lord, venerable through [his] merits, the holy father Abbot A, B sends his eternal salutations under God. Know that it gives us much joy when a suitable opportunity arises for us to send our little letters to your benevolence to obtain news of your health. Thus we ask your kindness, with the duties of salutations of [our] humble prayer, that you should not disdain to pray for us to the Lord of mercy, to whom you pour forth worthy and

---

725 The word is *papa*; see above, n. 363.
726 See above, n. 626.

diligent prayers, so that, strengthened by your prayers, we may deserve to go to our long desired home.[727] And we also presumed to recommend strongly to your beatitude the present bearers, your servants, our brothers in Christ, whom we sent there for the needs of our monastery, so that you should not disdain, out of divine consideration, to give them support in what they find necessary. Be well [and] pray for us, holy and blessed lord [our] father.

II, 48: Supplication for someone who wants to enter a monastery.

> According to the title given to this formula in the list of chapters at the beginning of Book II, this model applied not only to someone who wished to enter a monastery, but also to someone who had left it. This may be explained by the reference to an illness and the comparing of C to a sheep snatched 'from the jaws of the wolf', which suggest that C had been a monk before and had left his monastery, but that he was now being reintegrated, either into his own former monastery or into a new one. Since this letter was being sent by one abbot (presumably C's former abbot) to another, it seems more likely that he was moving to another monastery.

To the blessed lord and worshipper of God, my honourable brother in Christ Abbot A, B, wishing to send his salutation in Christ. First I request this, as if prostrated at present at your blessed feet, that when the little letter from my lowliness is put into your blessed hands, you may commend me as well as my brothers, my love for whom makes me request this before Christ, in your prayers to the Lord. Secondly: your servant, our brother in Christ C, inspired by the divine gift, wants to submit himself to your sanctity by [a vow of] obedience. He asked [that we should send] our little letter of recommendation to your kindness, in which we humbly ask that your diligence should lead back [this] sheep, freed from the jaws of the wolf by the hand of Christ, the good shepherd, into the fold of Christ's flock, and that, in place of both father and doctor, your pious vigilance should now apply itself to this patient. And if you present him along with the others to the shepherd of all, unharmed and returned to his former health, you know what [divine] mercy will follow from your labour, [since you are] highly learned in the divine words. Be well, in memory of me, venerable brother in Christ.

---

727 That is, heaven.

II, 49: General letter to all men.

> This is a letter for a pilgrim on his way to Rome, from an unknown sender (though presumably a bishop or abbot), asking all those to whom the letter was to be presented to provide help and supplies for him.[728] The mention that B was on a pilgrimage 'not, as is the habit for most people, in order to be idle' ('non, ut plerisque mos est, vacandi causa') reflects a suspicion, no doubt partly justified, that people went on pilgrimages to Rome for sightseeing as well as out of devotion.

To our orthodox lord Bishop[729] A, placed by God in the Roman apostolic see, and all the apostolic lords and fathers, or abbots and [women] dedicated to God living in monasteries, and illustrious men, *patricii*, dukes, counts and all those following the Christian religion in the divine cult, I, A, the lowliest sinner of all, presume to send my salutation under God. Since the present bearer B, inflamed by the divine rays, [and] desiring to go to the tombs of the holy apostles, the lords Peter and Paul, so as to flourish through [his] prayer, not, as is the habit for most people, in order to be idle, but for the name of God, [and] counting for little the difficult and painful journey, asked my littleness to recommend him by this little letter to your kindness and industriousness, by which I, the lowliest of all, presume to beg you, as if prostrated at the feet of each of you, to agree to pray for me, the smallest [of all], and to receive him, whom I recommend, on his way there and, if God allows it, on his way back, with [your] accustomed piety and for the name of God, and to give him as much as he needs, so that you may deserve to receive added mercy from Him who said that whatever one was seen to spend for His paupers was [also] paid to Him.[730]

II, 50: Letter of recommendation to illustrious laymen.

> This is an all-purpose letter of recommendation, presumably written by an abbot on behalf of some of his monks (his 'brothers'), to a powerful layman whom he did not know personally; compare the following formula, for a letter to laymen already known to the sender.

---

728 For other letters of introduction for pilgrims, see *Formulae Bituricenses App.* no. 9; *Formulae Salicae Bignonianae* no. 16; *Formulae Salicae Lindenbrogianae* no. 17. Compare *Formulae Bituricenses* no. 13, which gives a letter of introduction for a man sent in exile for having killed his brother.
729 The word is *papa*, here, for once, referring to the pope; see above, n. 363.
730 Namely, Christ; this refers to Matthew 25:40.

To the illustrious lord A, most magnificent in every way, and adorned and exalted by his noble lineage, B, a sinner, presumes to send his salutation under God. Although my littleness is not known at all to your excellence, I derived from the reports of many people your great devotion to the Lord and ready concern for the servants of God and his paupers, for [the sake of your] eternal salvation. Moved by this trust, we sent to your authority this letter of my lowliness for the present bearers, your servants, our brothers in Christ, through whom I presume [to send] many salutations to your industriousness, if my presumption does not offend you, and ask that you should agree to help them, for the name of God [and] with [your] accustomed piety, on their way there and back, in what they find necessary.

II, 51: Letter to powerful men of the palace whom one knows very well.

> This letter of recommendation differs from the previous ones in that it was addressed to a powerful layman with whom the sender was already very familiar (*maxime cognitus*, 'very well known', as opposed to merely *notus*, 'known', in the titles of II, 46 and 47): as a result, it referred to an established link of patronage, and took A's help more or less for granted.

To the illustrious Lord A, a man most magnificent in every way, B, a sinner, sends his eternal salutation before the Lord. We do not cease to inspire the plentiful charity of your industriousness towards us, by a preferential right, through ardent letters, by which, praising the benefit of your lively good nature,[731] we always receive plentiful fruit from you before the Lord; and since in this life the judge of [all] things gave you a position in which you have the support of both churches and friends, it should not cause [you] grief to undertake a task which will confer [upon you] the benefit of salvation in the future, and the support of many of your friends now. Grant, therefore, as a result of [your] pious obedience, [what] the bearers, my comrades, your servants, will request in your presence. Be well, man of strength and glory of your friends; may the piety of the omnipotent Lord deign, for the benefit of the churches, to preserve and guard you for a great length of time.

---

[731] The manuscripts consistently have the word *faciditatis* here, subsequently corrected in Paris BnF lat. 4627 and 2123 to *facilitatis*. Although this was only a later correction, it seems a more likely candidate than Uddholm's *facundetatis*, 'eloquence' (Uddholm, *Marculfi formularum libri duo*, p. 326).

II, 52: How the *domestici* of a royal villa must free [slaves] by their document at the king's order, on the occasion of the birth of his son.

> This last formula of Book II mirrors the penultimate formula of Book I (I, 39), containing the king's order relating to the same subject. It echoes many of the same themes, in particular with the concern to ensure God's protection for the king's son (*domnicillus*, 'little lord'). In other respects, however, this document of manumission follows a fairly standard form (compare Marculf I, 22 and II, 32–34; Angers nos. 20 and 23).

I, in God's name A, *domesticus*, though unworthy, of the glorious lord King B in his villas C–D, to E, from the king's household in the villa of C. Since all *domestici* have been sent a general order from the king to the effect that, for the birth of our little lord F, so that he may be better protected by God, three servants of either sex from each villa of the fisc should be released from service, and we received this order to do this, I therefore release you by this our letter, as I have been ordered, from all bond of servitude, so that you should thereafter lead a free life in no-[one's] service, as if you had been born of free parents; and you may never be forced into service, whether by us or by future *domestici*, or by anybody on behalf of the fisc, but you should remain well and fully free through all the days of your life by this document of manumission, [which] we were ordered to have made. And if someone wants to force you out of your free status, let him pay to you, the fisc compelling [him],[732] one pound of gold, and let him be unable to assert his claim, but let the present document remain firm. With confirmation given below.[733] Made here, on day *x*, in year *y* of the reign of the said lord, the most glorious King B.

---

732 See above, n. 394.
733 See above, n. 564.

SUPPLEMENT

[Although these six texts do not appear in the lists of chapter-headings, and therefore clearly did not form part of Marculf's original collection, they must have become associated with it at an early stage, since they are found in manuscripts belonging to every branch of the tradition.[734]]

No. 1: Immunity.

This royal immunity relates specifically to exemption from taxation on purchases made by a monastery. The impressive list of dues from which the monastery was to be exempt suggests that taxes on trade, at least, had remained alive and well in this period.[735] The content of this immunity is very similar to a late seventh-century toll exemption given to the abbey of St Denis by Theuderic III, though the formal resemblances between that document and this formula are only superficial, making the possibility of an actual textual link unlikely.[736] The cities mentioned are all situated on an itinerary following the river Rhône.

A, King of the Franks, to illustrious men, *patricii*, counts, toll-gatherers and all agents in the public service. If we do not cease to grant appropriate benefits[737] to the places of the saints, churches and priests, we are confident that we will without doubt be rewarded for it with eternal happiness. Therefore, let your greatness – or: your usefulness – know that we granted, at the request of the apostolic man B, bishop of the city of C, for the name of God and because his merits warranted it, this benefit:[738] know that his travelling agents[739] should not pay any toll or charges to our fisc out of the *n*. carts with which [they go] every year to buy lights[740] in Marseilles and in the other ports

---

734 See the list in Appendix 3, table 1, for the texts included in each manuscript; for lists of contents of the three main manuscripts of Marculf, see Appendix 3, table 2.

735 For a recent argument for the continuity of tolls levied on foreign trade during this period, see N. Middleton, 'Early medieval port customs, tolls and controls on foreign trade', *Early Medieval Europe* 13 (2005), pp. 313–58. On Merovingian taxation in general, see Goffart, 'Old and new in Merovingian taxation'.

736 Kölzer DM. 123, vol. 1, p. 313.

737 See above, n. 398.

738 See above, n. 398.

739 *Missi discurrentes* ('travelling *missi*') were later to become a staple of Carolingian government; see above, n. 462.

740 The word is *luminaria*, which probably referred to oil for lamps, since the monastery is unlikely to have sent envoys so far to obtain candles.

of our kingdom, or anywhere his agents[741] are seen to make purchases – or to go for a different need –. Therefore we decide by the present document, and we order [it] to stand in perpetuity, that neither yourself nor your subordinates and successors should require or demand from them any toll over these *n.* carts belonging to the pontiff B, in Marseilles, Toulon, Fos, Arles, Avignon, Soyons,[742] Valence, Vienne, Lyon, Chalon and the other cities and *pagi*, wherever tolls are levied in our kingdom, nor [demand] transport by sea or land, nor the toll levied on carts or bridges, nor labour or trade dues, nor compensation for [the damage they will make while] travelling,[743] nor any payment which our fisc could have expected out of these *n.* carts; but let this pontiff and his successors and the said church of the lord C have all this granted to them in every way for the name of God, and let it provide for the lights of this holy place.[744] And we decided to confirm this charter below by our own hand, [for it] to be valid in perpetuity.

No. 2: If someone wants to stand witness for a buyer in the presence of the king regarding what he sold to him, [this is] a royal document for this.

This is a royal confirmation for a sale, in order to provide additional assurance that there would be no dispute regarding the property sold.

King A to Count B. C – or his agent[745] on his behalf –, having come here in our palace, put it to the clemency of our rule that the man named D had been seen to sell to him his property – or: his villa – called E, in the *pagus* of F, whatever he had been seen to own there, by a title of sale, having received his money, and that [C] was seen to own it at present. And since this D was also present at that time, he was asked by ourselves and our great men to say presently whether he had made this sale of the said property in his name, as this C was now claiming, and whether he had sold the said property, and, if the necessity arose, whether he wanted to stand witness for him. And the said D declared this in our presence, that he had made this sale, and had

---

741 See above, n. 462.

742 Soyons is Zeumer and Uddholm's interpetation of the place-name 'Sugione'; E. de Rozière thought this referred to Sorgues (Zeumer, *Formulae*, p. 107, n. 1; Uddholm, *Marculfi formularum libri duo*, p. 335, n. 1).

743 *Cispitaticus*: this seems to have worked as a kind of tax, in compensation for the damage to fields created by the transport of goods (Niermayer, *Mediae Latinitatis Lexicon Minus*, 'caespitaticus').

744 See Fouracre, 'Eternal lights'.

745 See above, n. 462.

received the payment for the said property stipulated in the act of sale, and that he was standing witness for him now regarding this, and wanted to do so also in the future if the necessity arose. Therefore, since he declared this before us, we decide and order by the present document[746] that the said C should possess this villa – or: property – E, in the said place, in its entirety, [along with] anything that is read in this act of sale, in peace, without any opposition or claim from D or his heirs. And let C and his heirs have the free authority to do whatever they decide with it.

No. 3: Letter to the mayor of the palace.

> This letter of greetings is very similar to Marculf II, 44, on which it was no doubt based, and serves the function of adding the mayor of the palace to the list of possible recipients, which had originally included only a king, a queen and a bishop.

To the celebrated lord, ornament of the great men of the royal palace and son in Christ of the universal catholic church, the mayor of the palace A, B, bishop by God's mercy, though a sinner. When our lowliness inquires after the health of the charity of your highness in a suitable letter, this demonstrates the true loving affection of [our] eternal devotion. Therefore we presumed to send to your highness gifts of salutation, as is fitting, with an appropriate gift[747] from your patron [saint] Lord C, through your servant now [before you], [our] son in Christ D, through whom we humbly ask that they should be received by you with an affection equal to that with which they were sent by our devotion. And when he returns, let us deserve to learn of and delight in your prosperity through a written answer.

No. 4: Letter to relatives.

> This is a letter from a bishop to his mother, who seems to have become a nun as a widow (*deo sacrata*, 'consecrated to God'); the bishop specifies that A was his mother 'through the flesh' (*carnaliter*) at the same time as his daughter in Christ.[748]

To the lady consecrated to God, my mother through the flesh, and, since I received the pastoral office by the grace of the highest, daughter of the

---

746 See above, n. 388.
747 See above, n. 715.
748 Compare *Cartae Senonicae* no. 49 for another example of a man's letter to his mother (Zeumer, *Formulae*, p. 206).

holy church in Christ A, Bishop B, a sinner. Filial love and the solicitude of pastoral care inspire us to be concerned about you always. Therefore we sent this letter from my littleness to your kindness, with an appropriate gift[749] from your patron [saint], Lord C, in which we ask that you should deign to pray for us, and condescend to make known to us, in your answer through the present messenger, how things are with you, by God's mercy.

No. 5:[750] To a sister.

> This is an alternative address for the preceding text, if the letter was to the bishop's sister (apparently also a nun).

To the lady consecrated to God, my sister through the flesh, sister and daughter in Christ A, Bishop B, a sinner.

No. 6:[751] Charter regarding a bishopric.

> This formula was probably added to complement Marculf I, 5 and 6, both of which deal with the appointment of a bishop, and give notice of the king's decision, but without giving a model for the actual document of appointment. In this case, the chosen bishop seems to have been a former count, who requested this bishopric from the king; this was not an unusual occurrence, and shows how kings could use their control over bishops' appointments as part of wider strategies of patronage.

A, King of the Franks. Since, according to the words of the apostle, all power is given by God, and since the power by which all lands must be governed rests, after God, with the king, we must therefore deliberate with a sound counsel in order to establish as the guardians of the places of the saints those who are known to appear worthy of governing in this function. Therefore, since it was your request as well as that of the clergy and inhabitants of the city of B, that, having left the city of C, over which you were seen to rule and govern before, you should receive the pontifical see in the said city of B, and since your good way of life recommends you to our mind, and you are distinguished by [your] noble rank and adorned by the virtue of [your] habits – or: the compassion and honesty of [your] prudence –, following the advice and wish of our bishops and great men, according to the wish and agreement

---

749 See above, n. 715.
750 Uddholm numbers this text as *Supplementum* no. 4a (Uddholm, *Formula Marculfi*, p. 342).
751 Numbered in Uddholm as *Supplementum* no. 5 (Uddholm, *Formula Marculfi*, p. 344).

of the clergy and inhabitants of this city, in God's name we confer upon you the pontifical dignity in the said city of B. We therefore decide and order by the present document[752] that the said city and the property of its church and its clergy should be placed under your authority and government, and that you should always keep unwavering fidelity to our rule, and that, according to the canonical rule, you should strive to improve the people entrusted to you assiduously through sermons of predication and restrain them with no less piety than severity, and provide for the care of the poor and the necessity of the suffering with great care and love, and be able, having obtained and increased the salvation of your flock, to present it to the Lord's fold unsullied by any stain, so that, when you are seen actively to rule over and govern the church entrusted to you by divine dispensation, [its] prayers may increase the mercy of the eternal judge towards you. And you should pray to the boundless Lord assiduously for the burden of our sins.

---

752 See above, n. 388.

ADDITAMENTA: ADDITIONAL TEXTS FROM THE MANUSCRIPTS OF MARCULF

[This group gathers the flotsam of the Marculf tradition: new texts added or substituted to some Marculf formulae in individual manuscripts.]

No. 1

These texts are all prologues for a gift document to a church or monastery, appended to Marculf II, 2 in Paris BnF lat. 4627 in order to give a wider range of examples, offering variations on a single theme (exchanging earthly goods for heavenly ones). The givers seem to have been mostly laymen (only 1b gives an example for someone who had recently joined a monastery).

(a) Another prologue.

In the name of the Holy Trinity. It is known that it is a favourable and sound advice, and certainly a joyful one, that man should buy paradise with the property of this world, and exchange earthly possessions for celestial ones. Thus the Lord proclaimed with a splendid voice in the holy gospel, saying: 'Lay up for yourselves treasures in heaven, where the thief does not break through nor the moth pick holes'.[753]

(b) Prologue about a member of the clergy who is tonsured in a monastery, who gives his property to this place.

Each man must, with God's help, while he dwells in his body, prepare for the future and exchange fleeting objects for eternal ones, and whenever, by God's will, he comes to leave his body, he will obtain a dwelling in heaven for himself, bought out of the mammon of unrighteousness.[754] Therefore I, A, grant to the monastery of B, of which Abbot C is known to be the guardian and where I abandoned the hair of my head, and I want to live in this monastery according to the rule of the saints, and want this to be donated in perpetuity...

(c) Another prologue.

It is appropriate that each man, while he possesses earthly goods, should more often think of the good of his soul, so that I may deserve to have eternal

---

753 Abbreviated from Matthew 6:20.
754 This refers to Luke 16:9.

happiness. I, the illustrious man A, feel that I am weak in my body, and too much of a sinner in my soul. The divine power warns me – or: remorse came to me in my heart – that I should give something of my property to the places of the saints for the remission of my sins. Therefore I grant...

(d) Another prologue.

In the name of the Holy Trinity. We think it favourable, sound and certainly joyful that a man may lay aside the fleeting objects of this world to redeem his sins – or: what better advice is there, than that a man should buy paradise with the earthly property of this world, and exchange earthly sustenance for a celestial one? – Thus I, A, out of respect for God and in order to obtain salvation, so that the Lord may deign to grant me relief in the future – or: in order that my name may be written in the book of life[755] –, I give to the said monastery, [to provide for] the lights of the church[756] and the sustenance of the poor and the monks, and want it to be given by a legitimate right...

(e) Another prologue.

When [something] of this kind is known to have befallen someone, and we suffer desolation and every day suspect that the day of our death is at hand, it is necessary for each man, for the love of heaven's country, to embrace the benefits of devotion and to leave his property and give it for the needs of the saints and also the poor, so that the weight of sins which acts of penitence cannot dismiss should come to be alleviated more fully through their intercession.[757] Therefore I, A...

No. 2: Charter of protection given by a king and a prince.

> This text is offered as an alternative to Marculf I, 24 in Copenhagen Fabr. 84, where it follows immediately after it; in Paris BnF lat. 2123 it replaces I, 24 altogether, using the same title.[758] No doubt the scribe made the replacement because he thought the model would be more useful with an abbot as its only recipient, which suggests he was making his model for a monastery (I, 24 could apply to both a bishop and an abbot). The inclusion in the model of the part of the document containing the king's seal and witnesses' signatures is unusual in formulae, in which the end of documents tends to be cut short (this may be why this is the only reference to the king using a seal in this collection).

---

755 Revelation 21:27; Marculf II, 4. On *libri vitae* ('books of life'), see above, n. 581.
756 See Fouracre, 'Eternal lights'.
757 On the poor as privileged intercessors before God, compare Marculf II, 1 above.
758 See below, Appendix 3.

The illustrious man King A to the blessed lords and venerable fathers in Christ, all bishops and all abbots, and also illustrious men, dukes, counts, *vicarii*, *centenarii*, and all representatives and all our travelling agents,[759] and all our faithful followers and friends, both present and future, yours with good will. Let your greatness – or: your industriousness – learn this: the venerable man B, abbot of the monastery of Saint C, having come [to our palace], recommended himself to us more fully, both himself and his monastery with all its property, and we then received affectionately, with a glad spirit, the said venerable man, Abbot B, with this monastery and its men and all its affairs, under our protection and defence. Therefore, with greetings to your greatness – or: industriousness –, we ask and order you fully by this letter, that none of you are to trouble or pass a sentence against the said venerable abbot or his monastery or men, or its property which it is seen to possess at present or that may be added there by good men, with Christ's help, in the future; nor will you presume to diminish anything at all from its property, but you will allow both himself and his men to remain in peace by the grace of God and our protection and defence. And if any legal cases are brought against this Abbot B or his monastery or his men, which cannot be settled correctly in the *pagus* without [causing] him unjust expense, let them be in every way suspended and kept on hold until [they are heard] before us and later receive a definitive judgment before us according to the law and justice. And so that you may believe this more certainly, we signed by our own hand below and sealed it with our ring.

Seal + of the lord King A.

I, A witnessed this and signed it.

Given on day *x*, in year *y*, in the place of D.

No. 3: Privilege regarding all transactions.

This formula is inserted after Marculf I, 4 (appropriately following some documents of royal immunity) in Paris BnF lat. 2123 and Copenhagen Fabr. 84. It is based on no. 1 of the Supplement, and reproduces its text almost exactly, with the only difference that this version is slightly more general, as it does not include the list of different ports and does not specify the number of carts.

A, King of the Franks, to illustrious men, *patricii*, counts, toll-gatherers and all agents in the public service. If we do not cease to grant appropriate benefits[760] to the places of the saints, churches and priests, we are confident

---

759 See above, n. 739.
760 See above, n. 398.

that we will without doubt be rewarded for it with eternal happiness. Therefore, let your greatness – or: your usefulness – know that we granted, at the request of the apostolic man B, bishop of the city of C, for the name of God and because his merits warranted it, this benefit:[761] know that wherever in our kingdom his agents[762] are seen to make purchases – or to go for other needs –, neither himself nor his travelling agents[763] should pay any toll or charges to our fisc out of this. Therefore we decide by the present document,[764] and we want [it] to stand in perpetuity, that neither yourself nor your subordinates and successors should require or demand [from them] any toll in any cities or *pagi*, wherever tolls are levied in our kingdom, nor [demand] transport by sea or land, nor the toll levied on carts or bridges, nor labour or trade dues, nor compensation for [the damage they will make while] travelling,[765] nor dues relating to beasts of burden or to what men carry on their backs, nor any payment which our fisc could have expected out of this; but let this pontiff and his successors and the said church of Saint C have all this granted to them in every way for the name of God, and let it provide for the lights of this place.[766] And we decided to confirm this charter below by our own hand, [for it] to be valid in perpetuity.

---

761 See above, n. 398.
762 See above, n. 462.
763 *Missi discurrentes*; see above, n. 462.
764 See above, n. 388.
765 See above, n. 743.
766 See Fouracre, 'Eternal lights'.

A, B, C: THREE MORE TEXTS FROM THE MANUSCRIPTS OF MARCULF

[These three texts are found in all three main manuscripts of Marculf, and could therefore be said to form part of the Marculf corpus on an equal footing to the Supplement or Additional texts. They were not included in either Zeumer's or Uddholm's editions, which is why I include the edited Latin text here.[767] The manuscripts used are:

L: Leiden BPL 114, fols. 97–98
P1: Paris BnF lat. 10756, fols. 45–45v
P2: Paris BnF lat. 4627, fols. 125–126

P1 is used as the main witness.[768] This manuscript is badly damaged at this point, and there are some gaps in the text, marked in italics in the edited text. The Latin of these three texts is often obscure, and tends to defy literal translation; I have given the interpretation which seemed to me most likely.]

Incipit pro*logus ad omnes potentes* cupidus. *Opulens iamdudum auctor custas regolas in iambria* plusquam aurioso obto multi abuerunt, substancia rerum addepiunt sucessores, quod est vanitas, in quod infelix qui possessor transmigrat in sedibus altis, capiat multa pauca perenne.

a. prologus ad omnes potentes] prolocus ad homines potentes L || cupidus] cupidos L P2 || opullens] opolens L || regolas in iambria] regalis im gambris L || aurioso obto multi abuerunt] aurioso ob tumulti habuerint L areos obtomulti habuerunt P2 || substancia] substantia P2 || addepiunt] ademunt L P2 || quod est] quidem L P2 || in quod] inquid L P2 || infelix qui] infelix q: P1 felix *corr.* infelix quo *corr.* qui P2

---

767 Though Zeumer provided an edition of a and b in his article 'Über die älteren fränkischen Formelsammlungen', pp. 21–22 (using P2 as the main witness).
768 On this manuscript, see Appendix 3, pp. 265–70.

TRANSLATION

a) **Here begins a prologue addressed to all greedy powerful men.**

This first text is a prologue on the need for wealthy laymen to leave some of their property to religious foundations; it could very well have introduced a gift to a church or monastery. Apart from its threatening tone, it echoes similar concerns to the prologues (*arengas*) in Marculf II, 2 and *Additamenta* no. 1.

Many have more gold than the foundations of the keepers of the Rule, [and, their] father having already been rich for a long time, his descendants obtain his property, which is vanity, since he who travels to the higher regions a wealthy man is unhappy, for he will gain very little in eternity.

b) **Another text, addressed to young men who do not know how to write.**

This second text is much more unusual, and shows a teacher venting his disappointment at his pupil's failure to complete an exercise he had set for him, allowing us a rare glimpse of what could have happened in practice in an early medieval classroom. The teacher appears to have dictated a text to his pupils, who had to copy it on wax tablets which had been distributed to them (an ideal material on which to write school exercises repeatedly, since it was cheap and made almost infinitely reusable by melting and re-melting the wax). The text being dictated was described as an *epistula*, which could refer to a letter, but also to a legal document: 'b' could therefore constitute unique evidence for how future legal scribes were taught (perhaps even using Marculf itself a textbook).

Item alio dicto ad juvenis nescientes scripturas. Miro prosortam prolixa tempora aut nullum me sermone pagene consecutum, cuius eloquia vestri, velut ad verbo dictancium, polluti mutuati ceras afferunt, currunt articuli falsitatis; sed ubi venitur ad revolvendum, delisse magis quam scripsisse, pro solicissimum solicissimo referet; quando sperabam capitula epistolae finisse, nec inciperat in primo.[769]

b. item alio dicto] item alio dicatu L inter alio dictatu P2 ‖ juvenis] iovenis L iuvenes P2 ‖ miro] miror L P2 ‖ prosortam] prorsus tam P2 ‖ sermone] sermonem L ‖ pagene] pagine P2 ‖ eloquia] aeloquia L ‖ velut] velud L ‖ ad verbo dictancium] ad verba dictantium L P2 ‖ polluti] poluti *corr.* P2 ‖ ceras] caeras L ‖ articuli] articolis L articula P2 ‖ venitur] ventur *corr.* P2 ‖ scripsisse] scribisse P2 ‖ pro solicissimum solicissimo referet] pro solicissimum referit P1 pro solicismum solicismo refert P2 ‖ capitula] capitola L P2

Item alio prologo. Oportunum aduenisse tempus congratulor refugium ad Christus sarcinassem iecta secularis mundi curis expetitur sanctuarium ingrediar vestrum in sanctorum cenubia claustra sedens fratrum. Ibi dulciora mellis alimentis profruar laetus diliciarum affluens scripturarum iugiter ferre deus; ibi mens secura quasi iuge convivii et celestis agetur vita documenciis floribus inlustrium pro vestigia doctorum trita; ibi mens floribus pro candencia lilia campi; ibi certatem militis Christi supernam appetunt palmam; ibi triumfhum expediunt victores coronam; ibi summi acincis in aciem membra solent adsistere bina; ibi *dupli*cem hostem adversus speciem propugnare dira; ibi mundana fugit a me omnis amoris affectus, in monaste*rio* illo sedens mansurum. Ad consilio letate regis *cunctis mu*ndi curis inter potentes consistere iugiter non vale*unt pa*rvi sic ergo non merente esse ultimum largiente do*num primorum* qui regnas in secula saeculorum. Amen. [*P1 continues:* Pater noster qui [regnas in cae]lis cred[o…]

c. prologo] prolocu L ‖ oportunum] oportunam L ‖ congratulor] congratulatur P2 ‖] a te Christi sarcinare L a te Christe sarcinare P2 ‖ iecta] iacta P2 ‖ secularis] saecularis L ‖ expetitur] expeditur P2 ‖ sanctuarium] sanctoarium L ‖ cenubia claustra] caenobia cluaustra L ‖ sedens] resedens P2 ‖ ibi] ubi L ‖ profruar] perfruar L P2 ‖ affluens] affluenter L ‖ scripturarum] scribturarum L ‖ convivii] convivi L ‖ celestis agetur] caelestis agitur L ‖ documenciis] documentis L ‖ pro vestigia] per uestigia L per uestigium P2 ‖ doctorum] datorum P1 ‖ pro candencia lilia campi] per

---

[769] On this text, see D. Ganz, 'Bureaucratic shorthand and Merovingian learning', in P. Wormald, ed., *Ideal and Reality in Frankish and Anglo-Saxon Society: Studies Presented to J.M. Wallace-Hadrill* (Oxford, 1983), pp. 58–75, p. 61.

I wonder that, after such a long time, my speech has in no way been followed on the page, and the borrowed writing tablets which are brought back soiled with your text, as if from dictation, are filled with the wrong words; and when it comes to handing them over, he has erased more than he has written down, replacing one solecism with another. When I was expecting him to have finished the sections of the document, he had not even begun.

c) Another prologue.

> This third text is described as a prologue; it is rather unusual, and proclaims, in a highly flowery style, a layman's joy at being admitted into a monastery. It may have been intended to introduce a grant of that person's property to this monastery (compare *Additamenta* no. 1b). The reference to advising the king in the company of great men suggests he had been quite a grand person.

I rejoice that the appropriate time has come for me to take refuge in Christ, leaving aside the cares of the secular world, desiring to enter your sanctuary in the monastery of the saints, residing [there] as a brother. There I shall enjoy food sweeter than honey, as well as rejoice in the flow of delightful scriptures that God brings; there life is spent with a secure mind, as if at a heavenly feast, through the flowers of the testimony of the illustrious apostles; there the mind glows with flowers like the lily in the field;[770] there the soldiers of Christ long for the heavenly palm; there the victors attain a crown[771] in triumph; there great efforts continually bring assistance in the battle [fought] between two sides; there the treacherous enemy[772] is fought against with horror; there all the passion of love from this world will fly from me, residing in this monastery. Living with all the cares of this world among great men for the joy of advising the king is worth little, and is not worth the smallest of the great gifts bestowed by Him who reigns for the eternity of time. Amen

---

770 This refers to Matthew 6:28.
771 This is a play on words: *corona* could refer either to a crown or to a tonsure.
772 That is, the devil.

candencia lilia campi L per candentia libeat campi P2 ǁ certatem] certatis L certatim P2 ǁ militis] milites P2 ǁ triumfhum] triumphum L ǁ victores] victoris L ǁ acincis] capitis L P2 ǁ duplicem] duplice L ǁ mundana] mundane P2 ǁ omnis amoris] omnes amores L ǁ in monasterio] im monasterio L ǁ mansurum] mansurus L P2 ǁ consilio letate] consoliditate L consiliditate P2 ǁ cunctis] cunt L ǁ inter potentes] in te potentis L ǁ valeunt] valiunt L ǁ primorum] praemiorum L ǁ regnas] regnis P2 ǁ secula] saecula L P2 ǁ amen] *om.* P1

APPENDICES

APPENDIX I
THE ORIGINAL DATE OF THE ANGERS COLLECTION: THE STATE OF THE QUESTION

The question of exactly when the formulary of Angers was originally compiled has been the object of much debate, and of arguments of increasing complexity. Karl Zeumer, in his printed edition of this collection for the *Monumenta* series, followed the order of texts found in the single surviving manuscript of this collection (Fulda D1), but distinguished between three different groups of formulae within it, which he thought had been composed at different dates, the earliest at the beginning of the sixth century, the latest at the end of the seventh.[773]

Copied in between nos. 57 and 58 in the manuscript (fols. 181v–182) is a series of instructions on calculating computus, followed by a short chronological text which Zeumer did not include in his edition, though Mabillon, who produced the earliest printed version of this text, had included it in his.[774] Zeumer established his main distinction in terms of dating between the formulae copied before this text and the ones copied after it in the manuscript: since he thought that this text had no rightful place in a formulary, he concluded that the formulae copied after it must only have been added later, as an afterthought, and that its presence therefore signalled a different phase of composition. The scribes of our surviving manuscript would then have found this text in the middle of the formulae in their exemplar, and copied it along with them without realising that it was not in fact a formula itself. This view has been accepted ever since in studies of this collection.

This chronological text is introduced with the title *Incipit compotum annorum ab inicio mundi u[s]quae annum III Theudorigo regis* ('Here begins the reckoning of the years from the beginning of the world to the

---

773 Zeumer, *Formulae*, pp. 1–25; for a fuller discussion, see Zeumer, 'Über die älteren fränkischen Formelsammlungen', pp. 91–95. For earlier editions, see also Mabillon, *Libri de re diplomatica supplementum*, and E. de Rozière, *Formulae Andegavenses, d'après le manuscrit de Weingarten actuellement à Fulde*, Extrait des pièces justificatives de l'histoire du droit français au Moyen-Age par M. Ch. Giraud (Paris, 1844).

774 Mabillon, *Libri de re diplomatica supplementum*.

third year of the reign of King Theuderic').[775] There were, however, several Merovingian kings named Theuderic, and it is difficult to tell which one was being referred to here. The text calculates that 5,229 years had elapsed from the creation of the world to Christ's death, and 5,880 years from creation to the third year of Theuderic's reign. This therefore places Theuderic's third year of rule 651 years after Christ's death, and therefore well into the 680s. Unfortunately for us, this does not correspond to the third year of the rule of any king named Theuderic; Zeumer chose the nearest chronological candidate for this name, that is, Theuderic III (who ruled in the Frankish kingdom of Neustria, to which Angers then belonged, from 673 to 690/91).[776] Zeumer therefore designated the year in which this chronology was made as 676, and dated the formulae found with it accordingly, assigning a date at some point before 676 to all the texts preceding it in the manuscript (nos. 1–57), while he considered nos. 58, 59 and 60, which follow after it, to have been added shortly after this date in the same lost exemplar.

Zeumer further subdivided nos. 1–57 into two groups: nos. 1–36 on the one hand, and nos. 37–57 on the other. Nos. 1 and 34 are the only two formulae in this collection to preserve the dates of the documents on which they were based, which in both cases happened to be the fourth year of the reign of a King Childebert. Zeumer considered it safe to suppose that all the texts copied in-between these two formulae would also have been copied in that same year, and also added nos. 35 and 36 to that group, because of their general air of similarity to these previous texts. As in the case of Theuderic, however, there are several possible Merovingian candidates for this king's name. Mabillon changed his mind several times as to which one the formulae were referring to, hesitating between Childebert I (511–558), Childebert II (575–596) and Childebert III (695–711).[777] Zeumer argued that Childebert III, since his reign was later than that of the Theuderic III to whom he thought the chronological text referred, could not have been at the origin of this supposedly earlier group. He also argued that, since Childebert

---

775 The full text is transcribed in Zeumer, *Formulae*, p. 2.

776 Theuderic III admittedly did not become king of Austrasia until 687, closer to the date suggested in the chronology, but there would have been no reason for his regnal years to have been counted only from that time in Angers.

777 Mabillon, *Vetera analecta*, vol. 4 (Paris, 1685), pp. 232–70; *Annales ordinis S. Benedicti*, p. 419; *Libri de re diplomatica supplementum*, p. 68. To complicate matters, there is also another Childebert known as 'Adoptivus', who had been adopted by the Merovingian king Sigibert III, and reigned from 656 to 662 as a result of a coup instigated by his biological father, the mayor of the palace Grimoald, a member of the Pippinid family from which the Carolingian kings later descended.

II ruled in Austrasia, and not in the Loire valley, where Angers is situated, the only possible candidate left was Childebert I. As a result, he placed the year of composition of nos. 1–36 in 514/5.

Zeumer's second chronological group came into being more or less by default, through being wedged in-between the first and the last group. Zeumer thought this new group would have started with no. 37, a transfer of property from parents to their son, which mentions a war with the Bretons and Gascons (*Wascones*), no doubt fought between them and the Franks. Zeumer took this to refer to Chilperic's campaign against the Breton ruler Waroch in c. 574–578, which included a contingent from Anjou,[778] and concluded that nos. 37–57 must date from this period.

Bruno Krusch immediately expressed doubt as to the accuracy of Zeumer's dating in his review of the first instalment of the *Monumenta* volume: he thought Childebert II was a more likely candidate than Childebert I, and thus moved the first group of formulae forward to 595/6, since Childebert II ruled in Angers from the death of his uncle Guntram in 592.[779] This new date has the virtue of restoring unity to the collection: nos. 1–57 thus need only be one group instead of two, since by this reconstruction the fourth year of Childebert's reign no longer predates the war in Brittany. This avoids a rather artificial division, since all the texts in this collection tend to look very similar to each other. Nos. 58–60 were still, however, firmly kept in 676.

Werner Bergmann, in a more recent study, offered yet another different set of dates.[780] He dated nos. 1–57 to 578/9, that is, the fourth year of Childebert's reign counting from the death of his father Sigibert in 575, and not from the death of Guntram. This fits the war mentioned in no. 37 closely, though we are still left to wonder why the compiler would have dated his documents by Childebert's regnal years rather than Chilperic's, another uncle of his, who would have been in control of the region at that time. Bergmann explained this through the history of power struggles between kings in the region. The diocese of Angers fell under the jurisdiction of the metropolitan see of Tours, which, according to the division agreed between Guntram, Chilperic and Sigibert after the death of their brother Charibert I in 567, was taken over by Sigibert, Childebert II's father, after a brief conflict with Chilperic, who had moved to take control of both Tours and Poitiers.[781] After Sigibert's

---

778 See Gregory of Tours, *Histories* V, 26.
779 B. Krusch, 'MGH Legum sectio V. Formulae Merowingici et Karolini aevi', *Historische Zeitschrift* 51 (1883), pp. 512–19. Felgenträger agreed with Krusch in a later article (Felgenträger, 'Zu den Formulae Andecavenses').
780 Bergmann, 'Verlorene Urkunden nach den *Formulae Andecavenses*', at pp. 8–15.
781 Gregory of Tours, *Histories* IV, 45.

assassination in 575, Chilperic took control of the region.[782] After Chilperic's own death in 584, Guntram ordered all cities which had belonged to Sigibert to swear an oath to Childebert II (585).[783] Bergmann inferred from this that the cities of the Loire valley had never fully accepted Chilperic's rule, and used this argument to explain the dating of Angers documents according to the regnal years of Childebert instead, whom they would have perceived as their rightful lord. Bergmann also points out that Gregory of Tours, who was bishop of Tours at that time, himself dated his *Histories* by Childebert's regnal years from the very beginning of his reign in 575: Gregory's dates follow the reigns of Clovis, Theudebert I, Sigibert I and Childebert II, without taking any notice of Chilperic, with whom Gregory had rather strained relations. Of course, this way of dating may have been brought into the *Histories* only in retrospect, which weakens Bergmann's point somewhat. Angers did ultimately fall under the jurisdiction of the bishopric of Tours, but this does not imply it would have been associated with it in the territorial division of the kingdoms. Similarly weak is Bergmann's use of a passage from Gregory's *Histories*, VIII, 18, in which Theodulf, count of Angers, was driven out of the city and required military help to assert himself there: Theodulf was expelled not by an outraged pro-Childebert population, but by Domigisel, one of Chilperic's old supporters, which makes it difficult to use this story as evidence for Childebert's support in the region, as Bergmann takes it to be. Theodulf's appointment as count of Angers was moreover explicitly ascribed by Gregory to Guntram's desire to take under his personal government the kingdom of Chilperic's son Chlothar II, which would imply that Angers did not in fact fall under Childebert's jurisdiction.[784] Either way, however, it does not really make much difference, given the long-term development of formulary texts,[785] whether nos. 1–57 are dated to 578/9, as in Bergmann's hypothesis, or to 595/6, as Krusch suggested.

Let us now consider the last group of formulae in this collection, nos. 58–60, dated by Zeumer to 676 or shortly afterwards. Bergmann also offered a new date for these. He based his argument on connections between the chronology found in our manuscript and Gregory of Tours's own calculations in his *Histories* (IV, 51 and X, 31).[786] A comparison between Gregory's chronology and that of the Fulda manuscript gives the result shown in the following table.

---

782 Gregory of Tours, *Histories* V, 13.
783 Gregory of Tours, *Histories* VII, 26.
784 Bergmann, 'Verlorene Urkunden nach den *Formulae Andecavenses*', p. 10.
785 See above, pp. 28–33.
786 Bergmann, 'Verlorene Urkunden nach den *Formulae Andecavenses*', pp. 13–15.

252 THE FORMULARIES OF ANGERS AND MARCULF

Events	Gregory IV, 51	Gregory X, 31	Fulda D1 computation
Creation to Flood	2242 years	2242 years	2242 years
to birth of Abraham	+ 942		+ 940
to departure from Egypt	+ 462	+ 1404	3689 from Creation
to building of Temple	+ 480		
to exile in Babylon	+ 390		
to death of Christ	+ 668	+ 1808	5229 from Creation
to death of Saint Martin	+ 412	+ 412	
to death of Clovis	+ 112		
to death of Theudebert	+ 37		
to death of Sigibert	+ 29		
	(= 5774 from Creation)		
to Childebert II's 19th regnal year		+ 197 (= 5792 from Creation) *(real total 6063)*	
to Theuderic's 3rd regnal year			5880 from Creation

The number of years from creation to Christ's death amounts to 5,229 in Fulda D1, but only to 5,184 according to Gregory in IV, 51, amounting to a difference of 45 years. This led Bergmann to postulate that the chronology found with the Angers formulary could be brought into line with Gregory's, and their two accounts synchronised, by the simple expedient of substracting 45 years from the dates contained in our manuscript. Bergmann separately noted that Gregory dates Sigibert's death, which we know to have occurred in 575, to 590 years after Christ's death. Judging from this gap, Bergmann inferred that substracting fifteen years from Gregory's calculations would allow one to obtain a date consistent with our own reconstruction of the history of this period, counting from Christ's *birth* rather than his death. One could already argue at this point that these purely arithmetic relationships are too automatic, and rely on the assumption that both chronologies remained strictly consistent internally. In a methodological *salto mortale*, Bergmann conflated these two results in order to establish a rule whereby one might infer the correct date on the basis of the numbers of years given in our manuscript: this he did by first substracting 45 years from the number given in our manuscript, in order to arrive at a date consistent with Gregory's calculations, and then substracting another fifteen years to translate Gregory's own calculations into the 'correct' date counting from Christ's birth. Bergmann concluded that substracting 60 years was all that was required to translate our manuscript's chronology into our modern system of dating. The third year of Theuderic's reign mentioned in our chronology would therefore have come not 651 years after Christ's death, as calculated in the text, but 591 years after his birth, since $651 - 60 = AD\ 591$. This brings us closer to the reign of Theuderic II (596–613), whose third regnal year was 597/8, than to that of Theuderic III, thus placing nos. 58–60 closer in date to the bulk of the text, in the late sixth century.

Taking a step back from this rather bewildering array of calculations, it has to be said that Bergmann's reasoning here is in many respects highly problematic. It is too much to hope for these texts to match so systematically. Gregory's own two accounts themselves differ in some significant ways: he thus counted 1,808 years for the period between the crossing of the Red Sea and Christ's death in Book X of his *Histories*, but only 1,538 years in Book IV. The total number of years from creation is therefore different in Gregory's two accounts, adding up to 5,774 years by the time of Sigibert's death in 575 according to IV, 51, but to 6,063 years by the nineteenth year of Childebert's reign (in 594) according to X, 31. Gregory, however, only offered a total of 5,792 years in X, 31, which does not match the actual numbers given, but does match very nearly the calculation in IV, 51 ($5,774 + 19 = 5,793$), which suggests that Gregory did not recalculate his grand total from scratch, but instead used his earlier result. There is therefore already a difference of 270 years between Gregory's own two accounts, which puts the extra 45 years detected by Bergmann in our manuscript into perspective.

Bergmann also exaggerates the link between Gregory's chronology and that found in our manuscript, which makes his combining of results derived from them in order to obtain a single method of dating difficult to justify. The calculations in our manuscript are substantially different from those in Gregory's first chronology (IV, 51). They too allow for a period of 2,242 years from creation to the flood, but the similarity stops there. There is already a small discrepancy in the number of years allowed for the intervening period between the flood and the birth of Abraham: this is

940 years in our manuscript, 942 according to Gregory IV, 51. The departure from Egypt and the 'initiation of the children of Israel to the divine mystery' took place 3,689 years after creation according to our manuscript, while both of Gregory's versions allowed for only 3,646 years. The number of years from creation to Christ's death given in our manuscript is 5,229; according to Gregory, it totalled either 5,184 years (according to IV, 51) or 5,454 (according to X, 31). The similarities in the selection of chronological points of reference are far from an exact match, and only work for Old Testament events, which are rather predictably chosen for both texts in any case. Gregory's more idiosyncratic use of the death of Saint Martin as a reference point is not echoed in our manuscript. There is therefore nothing to justify the application of the '− 15 years' rule derived from Gregory's chronology in the case of our own manuscript text. Even after all this, 591 is still not an exact match for the third regnal year of any Theuderic. Clearly these chronologies were not yet standardised in any meaningful sense. It is therefore impossibly optimistic to expect the chronology in the Angers collection to fit our own reconstructed dates for this period merely through the application of a simple and constant mathematical formula.

Furthermore, it should be noted that all this only helps to date the chronology, but not necessarily the formulae themselves. How much should we infer from the presence of this chronological text in our collection in any case? It has been assumed as a matter of course that its presence was a key feature in terms of dating, but making so much of it may be a mistake. Since the collection only survives in a single late eighth-century witness, its manuscript tradition escapes us completely: much could have happened in the intervening time between the compilation of the collection and the copying of this manuscript. We cannot know for sure whether nos. 58–60 were really appended to the text only after the chronology was included, or whether the chronology was simply inserted at some later point in the middle of a pre-existing collection: the fact that formulae followed after it in the manuscript therefore does not mean that they could only have been added at a later point. This relies on the idea that a scribe would never deliberately have included a text so foreign in character as this chronology in a formulary, but then one finds many strange things in the middle of formularies,[787] and it is dangerous to base an argument for the dating of a collection on the organisation of its manuscript.

---

787 See above, p. 13.

APPENDIX II
THE *GESTA MUNICIPALIA*

The question of the survival into the early middle ages of Roman-style municipal archives (*gesta municipalia*) has been the object of a long-standing debate.[788] Their disappearance is associated with a transition from a form of documentary practice in which legal documents were issued, authenticated and preserved by a public authority to one in which they were issued by private persons or institutions, and preserved by particular beneficiaries. Knowing precisely when the *gesta* ceased to exist is made difficult by the fact that no actual example of such an archive survives for either Roman Gaul or early medieval Francia. Their absence from our surviving record may have been due to deliberate destruction,[789] or simply to the possibility that such documents had mainly been written on papyrus (a material known to have been used down to the late seventh century, at least by the Merovingian chancery), which has a very limited shelf-life in a European climate: records made on papyrus had little chance of surviving unless particular ecclesiastical institutions had a vested interest in preserving them, as in the case of some Italian papyri, dating from the fifth and sixth centuries, which had originally formed part of the *gesta municipalia* of Ravenna, but were preserved through an episcopal archive.

Although the *gesta* were clearly a Roman civic institution, their existence is very rarely mentioned in Roman sources, and it may seem paradoxical that

---

[788] See in particular the discussion in Classen, 'Fortleben und Wandel'. See also H. Bresslau, 'Urkundenbeweis und Urkundenschreiber im älteren deutschen Recht', *Forschungen zur deutschen Geschichte* 26 (1886), pp. 1–66, and, more recently, E. Ewig, 'Das Fortleben Römischer Institutionen in Gallien und Germanien', in E. Ewig, *Spätantikes und frühmittelalterliches Gallien: Gesammelte Schriften (1952-1973)*, ed. H. Atsma (Zurich/Munich, 1976), vol. 1, pp. 409–34; W. Bergmann, 'Fortleben des antiken Notariats im Frühmittelalter', in Peter Schuler, ed., *Tradition und Gegenwart. Festschrift zum 175-jährigen Bestehen eines badischen Notarstandes* (Karlsruhe, 1981), pp. 23–35; Wood, 'Disputes in late fifth- and sixth-century Gaul: some problems', pp. 12–14; Davies and Fouracre, *The Settlement of Disputes*, p. 208; McKitterick, *The Carolingians and the Written Word*, p. 24, n. 5, and p. 89; Wickham, *Framing the Early Middle Ages*, pp. 110–11 and p. 601.

[789] As suggested in Davies and Fouracre, *The Settlement of Disputes*, p. 208.

far more references to them should be found in sources dating from the early medieval period, by which time it is generally assumed they had become extinct: these occur in Angers no. 1 and Marculf II, 37–38, as well as in other formulae and documents ranging from the sixth to as late as the ninth century.[790] The main point of the question is therefore to decide whether these early medieval references to the *gesta* should be read as constituting exciting evidence that these municipal archives had survived long after the breakdown of Roman government in the West, or whether they were merely archaic hangovers, copied out of respect for the Roman tradition rather than out of a practical need, in order to confer a symbolic sense of dignity on the proceedings.

Since there is no material evidence for municipal archives in Gaul for any period, the consensus that they had definitively stopped functioning by the beginning of the eighth century can of course only remain a conjecture: one cannot, therefore, discount out of hand the possibility that the *gesta* were still extant in the late eighth century. Since no other source refers to them, the whole argument boils down to the question of knowing what to do with the evidence for the *gesta* provided by formulae and by still extant documents. Although one might expect the evidence from formulae and the evidence from surviving charters to prop each other up, making their combined evidence more secure as a result, this is not in fact the case, since references to the *gesta* in actual documents are likely to have been due precisely to the use of such formulae as models, and cannot therefore really be counted as independent evidence (which certainly shows, at least, that the

---

790 References to the *gesta municipalia* in formulae include Angers nos. 1, 32, 41 and 48; Marculf II, 3, 17, 37 and 38; *Formulae Arvernenses* nos. 1 and 2; *Formulae Turonenses* nos. 2, 3, 20 and 23; *Formulae Bituricenses* nos. 3, 6 and 15; *Cartae Senonicae* nos. 38, 39, 40 and 46, and Appendix no. 1; and, for a non-Frankish example, in *Formulae Visigothicae* nos. 21 and 25; two further collections reproduce *gesta* formulae copied from Marculf: *Formulae Augienses* A no. 13 (= Marculf II, 3) and *Collectio Flaviniacensis* no. 8 (= Marculf II, 17) (all of these are included in Zeumer, *Formulae*). Surviving charters mentioning the *gesta* are from Poitiers in 677–678 (J. Tardif, 'Les chartes mérovingiennes de Noirmoutier', *Nouvelle revue de droit français et étranger* 22 [1898], pp. 763–90, at pp. 783–85; see also L. Lemaître, 'Cunauld, son prieuré et ses archives', *Bibliothèque de l'Ecole des Chartes* 59 [1898], pp. 231–61, at pp. 239–45); Le Mans in 616 and 643 (*Actus pontificum cenomannis in urbe degentium*, ed. G. Busson and A. Ledru [Le Mans, 1901], pp. 141 and 162); Orléans in 667 and Murbach in 728 (Pardessus, *Diplomata* nos. 358 and 544); Flavigny in 717–719 (Wideradus's testaments, in *Cartulaire de Flavigny*, nos. 1 and 57), and Angers in 804 (H. Beyer, ed., *Urkundenbuch zur Geschichte der jetzt die Preussischen Regierungsbezirke Coblenz und Trier bildenden mittelrheinischen Territorien*, vol. 1, *Von den ältesten Zeiten bis zum Jahre 1169* (Coblenz, 1860), pp. 47–49, no. 42).

presence of archaic features is a problem affecting *all* documentary evidence from this period, not just formulae).

Several features of these formulae and documents warn against taking this evidence at face value. The most important objection relates to their referring not only to the *gesta municipalia*, but also, simultaneously, to a whole range of Roman civic institutions that are even less likely to have survived by the time these formulae and documents were written. Angers no. 1 thus consistently refers to a Roman setting involving not only the municipal archives, but also a municipal council (*curia*), a city magistrate (*defensor*), a master of soldiers (*magister militum*), and the forum as the major public space of the city. Although some or all of these things may still have been in place in the Loire valley at the end of the sixth century, when this collection was probably first put together, it is more difficult to explain the inclusion of these texts in the late eighth-century manuscript in which this collection survives, since by that time all of these other Roman institutions, given here as the background for the *gesta*, had certainly become defunct. This shows that at least part of Angers no. 1 did refer to archaic features which did not correspond to this eighth-century context. This in turn implies that even if documents were still being written on the basis of such formulae (as they clearly were[791]), the reality of the proceedings could not possibly have corresponded exactly to those described in this ritual dialogue, in which case there would be little justification in singling out the *gesta* as the sole 'live' institution among this range of anachronistic references. It would be even more difficult to explain references to all of these Roman features in Marculf, in the late seventh century, or in a Prüm document dating from 804 (the latest reference to the *gesta* in a document) through the hypothesis of actual survival.

Such texts therefore constitute evidence for the survival of a particular documentary form rather than of a real institution. It does not follow, however, that scribes were necessarily conjuring up a fantasy world which no longer related to anything concrete. They may well have had *something* in mind when they referred to the *gesta*, much as they clearly had particular people in mind when they referred to Roman-style officials or *curiales* (by which they may have meant the sort of local bigwigs referred to as *boni homines* in other types of document), or particular 'public' places when they referred to a *curia publica*.[792] Even if none of these things survived in their original form,

---

791 See above, n. 790.
792 See above, p. 44.

as clearly most if not all of them did not, the same words could still have been used to express, in this particularly formal type of document, similar relationships in a different context. The ecclesiastical context of the transmission of our formulae suggests that the function of the *gesta* could have been transferred to new centres of power and publicity, and that they could have survived as a notional entity, though admittedly in a very different form to their original one, through ecclesiastical institutions.[793] In an adaptation of Marculf II, 17, found in no. 8 of the Flavigny collection, the phrase 'so that... [our testament] may be validated at the municipal archive at their request' ('ut... gestis rei publici municipalibus titulis eius prosecutionibus muniatur') was thus copied with the significant clarification: '... and I have decided that it should be preserved in the archive of the church of Saint X' ('et in archivis basilice sancti illius conservandum decrevi'). This would fit in quite well with the increasing role of religious houses in the production and preservation of documents for lay people (suggested by their need to keep formulae relating to lay transactions). The *gesta* documentary form may have been one possible option among many for document-holders, providing them with a more formal style of public recognition and symbolic authentication for the documents issued to them, even though no longer in the original context envisaged in these texts. The content of the transactions described in documents written in this manner (a *dos* in Angers no. 1, a gift of property in Marculf II, 37–38) was not different from that of documents written without reference to the *gesta*: using this form when writing a new document was therefore not the result of an automatic lapse of scribes into archaic practices in the case of one particular type of document, but a deliberate choice, which could apply to virtually any transaction. Postulating a complete opposition between practical and symbolic needs may therefore not be the most helpful approach: even if references to the *gesta* in eighth- and ninth-century documents were only 'ritual',[794] the use of such a ritual is still meaningful.

---

793 Davies and Fouracre, *The Settlement of Disputes*, p. 209.
794 Wickham, *Framing the Early Middle Ages*, p. 601.

APPENDIX III
THE MARCULF COLLECTION: MANUSCRIPTS AND EDITIONS

THE MANUSCRIPT TRADITION

Zeumer's original discussion was based on the four manuscripts used by Eugène de Rozière in his earlier edition (1859–71): Paris BnF lat. 4627, Paris BnF lat. 2123, Paris BnF lat. 10756 and Leiden BPL 114, all dated to the ninth century.[795] A further two, Munich lat. 4650 and Leiden Voss. lat. O. 86, constitute branch 'C' of the tradition, and Zeumer did not rely on them to reconstitute the *Urtext*. After the publication of Zeumer's edition for the *Monumenta*, a new manuscript was found (now in Copenhagen, Kongelige Bibliothek, coll. Fabric. 84), which had been used by Lindenbruch in his edition of 1613 but had since disappeared; this manuscript was discussed by Zeumer in a later article in which he tackled the relationship between it and the very closely related Paris BnF lat. 2123.[796]

Paris BnF lat. 4627 and Paris BnF lat. 10756 are the most complete manuscripts, and present Marculf more or less in the order reproduced by Zeumer in his edition.[797] Leiden BPL 114, Paris BnF lat. 2123 and the Copenhagen manuscript, on the other hand, present the Marculf formulae in a very different order and context. Leiden BPL 114 contains a large number of formulae (including the so-called 'Bourges Formulae'), by no means all drawn from Marculf; what does belong to Marculf has its order rearranged and parts missing.[798] Zeumer ascribed these changes to faults in the exemplar, such as wrong arrangement of the quires, or missing pages, and to faults in the scribe, whom he often accused of carelessness. There are problems with this interpretation, as the changes could just as easily, and

---

795 Zeumer, 'Über die älteren fränkischen Formelsammlungen', pp. 13–41. E. de Rozière, *Recueil général des formules*.

796 K. Zeumer, 'Die Lindenbruch'sche Handschrift der Formelsammlung von Flavigny', *Neues Archiv* 14 (1889), pp. 589–603. This manuscript was rediscovered by the Danish scholar H.O. Lange, 'En Codex redivivus af de marculfinske Formler', in *Opuscula philologica: Mindre Afhandlinger udgivne af det philologisk-historiske Samfund* (Copenhagen, 1887), pp. 39–52.

797 For a detailed list of which formulae are contained in which manuscripts, see Table 1.

798 See above, pp. 119–20; for a list of contents of this manuscript, see below, Table 2.

more plausibly, represent deliberate scribal choices. Paris BnF lat. 2123 and the Copenhagen manuscript, which Zeumer counted as his 'B' tradition for Marculf, certainly represent a set of scribal choices of such a kind. They also mix the Marculf texts with a number of formulae taken from different sources, including the Tours formulary, thereby effectively constituting a new and distinct collection. This collection was edited separately as the Flavigny collection (*Collectio Flaviniacensis*), but was also used for the edition of Marculf itself. It is obvious even from a very cursory study of the various manuscripts that formularies were not copied like literary texts, but that scribes could change the contents of a formulary by omitting old material and including new texts, no doubt so as better to suit their own or their patron's purposes. This confers a certain fluidity on any formulary text, even in the case of Marculf, despite its alleged archetypal status.[799]

Three formulae, which Zeumer referred to as 'a', 'b' and 'c', are found together with Marculf in Paris BnF lat. 4627 and 10756 and the Leiden manuscript.[800] Their presence establishes a clear link between these three manuscripts: all three must have derived from an exemplar which had included these texts, which implies that 'a', 'b' and 'c' were added at an early stage in the tradition.

Zeumer also established a link between Paris BnF lat. 4627, the Leiden manuscript and the B tradition (Paris BnF lat. 2123 and the Copenhagen manuscript), because they have in common a series of other formulae which Zeumer called the Supplement, which he considered to have been a deliberate addition meant to fill some gaps in Marculf's original coverage. These formulae are not present in Paris BnF lat. 4627. Zeumer thought that this meant that the branch from which Paris BnF lat. 4627 derived had become separated from the main tradition before the Supplement had been added, as he found it improbable that a scribe who had bothered to copy 'a', 'b' and 'c', despite what he saw as their inherent uselessness, should fail to copy a supplement consisting of respectable, genuine formulae, particularly as he considered Paris BnF lat. 4627 to be the most complete manuscript of Marculf.[801] Zeumer later changed his mind, and decided in the introduction to his edition of Marculf that the omission of the Supplement must have been due to an error: 'I am now in doubt as to whether I was correct in supposing that the exemplar for A2 [Paris BnF lat. 4627] had become separated from the common source before the Supplement was added, and I

---

[799] See above, pp. 117–23.
[800] See above, pp. 121–22, and pp. 240–44 for an edition and translation of these texts.
[801] Zeumer, 'Über die älteren fränkischen Formelsammlungen', p. 24.

prefer to think that the Supplement was missed out as a result of an omission or a mistake'.[802] He gave, however, no further explanation for this change of heart. Despite the link between Paris BnF lat. 10756 and Leiden BPL 114 established through the presence of the Supplement, Zeumer thought that their traditions had gone their separate ways already in Merovingian times, which is supported by the fact that Paris BnF lat. 10756 includes a variant referring to the mayor of the palace in Marculf I, 39, instead of the count found in Leiden BPL 114 (the replacement of a count by a mayor of the palace only makes sense in the Merovingian period).[803]

On the other hand, Zeumer found a close link between Paris BnF 10756 and 2123: both lack *hominibus* after *Deum timentibus* in I, 1; both have *dignanter annuere* instead of *anuere* in I, 7 (although this may indeed be the correct reading, as Uddholm thought in his later edition); both have *agnuscite* instead of *cognoscite* in I, 16; both regularly have *exoratione* instead of the more likely candidate *exortatione* found in Leiden BPL 114 and Paris BnF lat. 4627. The significance to be ascribed to these common variants was doubted by later scholars, in particular by Krusch.[804] Uddholm suggested that the readings from Leiden BPL 114 and Paris BnF lat. 4627 could well have been the erroneous ones, while Paris BnF lat. 10756 and 2123 had the correct readings. On the whole, Uddholm admitted that the evidence for a link between Paris BnF lat. 10756 and 2123 was strong;[805] yet his reconstruction of the manuscript tradition differed rather sharply from that of Zeumer.[806]

Uddholm made a convincing case for a link between Paris BnF lat. 4627 and Paris BnF lat. 10756 (see Table 3): they share readings in II, 3 (*fiunt* instead of *sunt*); in II, 4 (*perfruantur* instead of *potiantur*); in II, 8 (*ubicumque* instead of *undecumque*); in II, 10 (*supradicta* instead of *suprascribta*); in II, 17 (*memorauimus* instead of *nominauimus*).[807] Uddholm also found that

---

802 Zeumer, *Formulae*, pp. 35–36: 'Iam uero dubius, an recte ibi suspicatus sim, codicis A2 exemplar iam ante Supplementum additum e communi fonte fluxisse, credere maluerim, Supplementum errore seu quolibet uitio in illo esset omissum.'

803 The variant found in Paris BnF lat. 10756 cannot be the original reading in this case, because the Copenhagen manuscript, which is likely to have derived from the same branch of the tradition as Paris BnF lat. 10756, also has *illo comite* (see Krusch, 'Der Staatsstreich des fränkischen Hausmaiers Grimoald I', p. 414 n. 6; Krusch, 'Ursprung und Text', p. 268).

804 Krusch, 'Ursprung und Text', pp. 267–71.

805 Uddholm, 'Le texte des *Formulae Marculfi*', p. 42.

806 For a comparison of their respective stemmata, see below, Tables 6, 7 and 8.

807 Uddholm also counted in his list of errors shared between these two manuscripts a phrase in II, 20, for which Paris BnF lat. 4627 has 'liberum perfruatis arbitrium' and Paris BnF

Paris BnF lat. 4627 shared readings with the B tradition (Paris BnF lat. 2123 and the Copenhagen manuscript) which are not present in Paris BnF lat. 10756: for instance, Paris BnF lat. 4627 has *ligum–* and the other two *ligumina* in I, 11, while the following *ligna* is omitted in both Paris BnF lat. 4627 and the Copenhagen manuscript; there are also common omissions, such as the *ac ponteficale culmine sublimato* in II, 46 or *subnexa* in II, 1. This would suggest that Paris BnF lat. 4627 was actually closer to the B tradition than to Paris BnF lat. 10756.

The table of common readings (Table 3) shows significant concordances between Paris BnF lat. 4627 and 10756 and the B tradition; it also shows concordances between Paris BnF lat. 4627 and Leiden BPL 114, which is itself unrelated to Paris BnF lat. 10756 and 2123. The Leiden manuscript and Paris BnF lat. 4627 thus share in I, 2 *sanctorum* instead of *seruorum*, which is certainly the most striking error, in itself sufficient to establish a link; otherwise they share mainly omissions, such as the *ut* in I, 5, or the *dignanter* in I, 7. Uddholm's case for links between Paris BnF lat. 4627 and Leiden BPL 114 is somewhat less convincing here. In support of Uddholm's claim, one could also mention that Leiden BPL 114 and Paris BnF lat. 4627 often have common readings, against Paris BnF lat. 10756, in 'a', 'b' and 'c'. In short, according to Uddholm's reconstruction, Paris BnF lat. 4627 was linked to both the Leiden manuscript and the group of related manuscripts Paris BnF lat. 10756, Paris BnF lat. 2123 and Copenhagen coll. Fabr. 84, but these two branches were not themselves related. Uddholm stressed that many corrections could be observed in Paris BnF lat. 4627, in which the readings from Leiden BPL 114 seem to have been altered into readings from Paris BnF lat. 10756 or the B tradition (and vice-versa). Uddholm therefore concluded that Paris BnF lat. 4627 was the result of a contact between the two traditions, and that its scribe was working with a manuscript from each.

Now for Zeumer's reconstruction of the B tradition, also known as the Flavigny collection, found in Paris BnF lat. 2123 (B1) and Copenhagen Fabr. 84 (B2). The Flavigny collection contains some texts from the Tours formulary, most of the formulae from Marculf, some model letters,[808]

---

lat. 10756 'liberum perfruatur arbitrium', instead of 'liberam habeas potestatem' in the other manuscripts. I take the reading from Paris BnF lat. 10756 to be the correct one, which only slightly weakens Uddholm's point. 'Liberam habeas potestatem' is a more usual turn of phrase in formulae, and it is more likely that a scribe decided to normalise the phrase rather than the contrary (see above, n. 658).

808 See above, p. 115.

and some completely unrelated formulae which may have originated in Burgundy (where the monastery mentioned in nos. 43 and 44 is said to have been situated).[809] Some parts of this collection are present in the Paris manuscript but not in the Copenhagen one, and some other parts are present in the Copenhagen manuscript but appear in the Paris one only in the list of chapter headings. Neither of these manuscripts can therefore have relied on the other for its exemplar. The Copenhagen manuscript in general has a tendency to try to shorten the formulae, and reorders them quite extensively, whereas the Paris manuscript remains reasonably close to its sources as far as order is concerned (the first book of Marculf thus appears more or less in its original order, as do the 33 formulae from Tours). The Paris manuscript therefore reflects the order used in the common model, while the Copenhagen manuscript was drawn from an exemplar in which the order of the material in the original formularies had been substantially changed. The Copenhagen manuscript cannot have been copied straight from the common exemplar, as, despite the reordering and renumbering of the formulae, nos. 48 and 49 are missing from the text, and the numbering in the manuscript goes straight from no. 47 to no. 50. The two formulae therefore went missing in a copy made after the collection had already been reordered and numbered.

Uddholm suspected that the B tradition had undergone the 'influence occulte d'un bon ms.' (a rather needlessly sinister way of putting it).[810] He went on to list a series of cases in which both of these manuscripts actually matched Leiden BPL 114 rather than Paris BnF lat. 4627 and 10756, and other cases in which he judged that the two B manuscripts actually had the correct reading against every other manuscript. It is here that Uddholm's discussion is at its weakest: the few readings common to the Leiden manuscript and the B tradition cannot really be considered to be significant, since all could easily have been the result of coincidence or independent correction: *causa suspensa* instead of *causas suspensas* in the title of I, 23, for instance, is hardly of an earth-shattering nature. The other connections established by Uddholm are in a similar category. In most cases they are

---

809 There is also a very strong case for a textual link between *Collectio Flaviniacensis* nos. 8 and 43, present in both manuscripts, and the two testaments of Widerad which constituted the foundation charters of the monastery of Flavigny in Burgundy (*Cartulary of Flavigny* nos. 1 and 2, probably dating from 717 and 719 respectively; see above, n. 65). Zeumer did not refer to the link between *Collectio Flaviniacensis* no. 43 and no. 58 of the Flavigny cartulary in 'Über die älteren fränkischen Formelsammlungen', although he was certainly aware of it by the time he prepared his edition.

810 Uddholm, 'Le texte des *Formulae Marculfi*', p. 47.

not even a definite match: in I, 11, for instance, the fact that B2's *dactalos* and B1's *dactiles* are closer to Leiden's *dactalus* than Paris BnF lat. 4627's *dactolas*, Paris BnF lat. 10756's *dactol–*, or Munich lat. 4650 and Leiden Voss. lat. O. 86's *dactilas* seems rather insignificant in view of the bewildering number of different readings in all of the manuscripts (see Table 4 for a list of all of Uddholm's examples). As to the text appearing more like a Merovingian original in the B manuscripts 'à en juger par le contenu et par la langue', this is not a very compelling argument, as in every case Uddholm seems to have preferred the reading in the B manuscripts because it was more grammatically satisfying, and that is not in itself sufficient to hold it to be Marculf's own. Indeed, the writer of the common source for Paris BnF lat. 2123 and the Copenhagen manuscript seems to have been a highly intelligent scribe, who did not like copying things which he thought made no sense: he therefore often altered the text, or even in one case left a blank space instead of copying a phrase he did not understand (he thus omitted the confusing 'et decimo illo sunt ellitis' in I, 20). The fact that he was using Marculf as only one among several sources for his own brand new and independent collection points to a certain licence in the use of his texts. One could also accuse Uddholm of having double standards here, as it was precisely the lack of 'correctness' of the Leiden manuscript that made him think it was 'better' and more authentic. Here are some examples of cases in which Uddholm thought the B tradition preserved the original reading, and my reasons for dismissing them: in I, 2, the *sancti* in *monasterium in honore* [B: *sancti*] *illius* was easy to supply; the same goes for the *sancti* in II, 45. In I, 4, Uddholm rejected the *iam dicta ecclesia* found in the 'A' manuscripts, and favoured the reading *superius memorata / memoratam* found in the B manuscripts: it seems to me the *iam dicta* reading is more convincing, especially as it is preceded by *iam dictis principibus*.[811] Most surprising is Uddholm's choice in I, 33 to accept the reading *tam quod* found in B when Paris BnF lat. 4627 has *quam pro quod*, and Leiden BPL 114 and Paris BnF lat. 10756 both have *quam per quod*. This goes against his own view that the Leiden manuscript and Paris BnF lat. 10756 were not linked, and that readings were shared by them only when they corresponded to the common original. Uddholm did not list this in his list of common errors for Leiden and Paris BnF lat. 10756, even though it would be very significant if it were a common error rather than the correct reading. The correct reading here has

---

[811] Uddholm in fact changed his mind in his edition; Uddholm, *Marculfi Formularum libri duo*, p. 42.

to be *quam per quod*, and not the reading found in the B tradition. This is only one of several examples in which the Leiden manuscript and Paris BnF lat. 10756, without being directly related, both give what seems to be the original reading against all the other manuscripts, which suggests that Paris BnF lat. 10756 actually gives a more authentic text than Paris BnF lat. 4627 (see below). On the whole, Uddholm's idea that the B tradition was influenced by a better manuscript therefore seems unconvincing, and one should perhaps not trust the B manuscripts as much as Uddholm recommended.

Zeumer's C tradition (Munich 4650 and Leiden Voss. lat. O. 86) gives an adaptation of Marculf made in the Carolingian period, and is therefore relatively unimportant for editing purposes, although it is very interesting as evidence for the continued use of Marculf.[812] Its order is broadly related to that of the B tradition (the formula which Zeumer calls Supplement no. 6 is in both traditions inserted between I, 6 and I, 7), and there are no great differences in specific readings, although, since the C tradition does not share several of the common readings found between the B manuscripts and Paris BnF lat. 4627, Uddholm concluded that the C tradition had broken off from the main tradition before B did.

On the whole the reconstructions of Zeumer and Uddholm are not difficult to reconcile: the only really significant change brought about by Uddholm's version (apart from the uncontroversial place of the C tradition, in which Zeumer was not in the least interested) is the demonstration that Paris BnF lat. 4627 was influenced by two unrelated traditions, that of Leiden BPL 114 on the one hand, and that of Paris BnF lat. 10756 and the B tradition on the other. This of course shows that Zeumer's later view was correct, and that the absence of the Supplement in Paris BnF lat. 4627 does not indicate that the branch broke off from the main tradition before the Supplement came to be included in the collection (for a comparison of the different possible stemmata, see Tables 6, 7 and 8).

EDITIONS OF MARCULF AND THE HIERARCHY OF MANUSCRIPTS

For a long time, arguments over the manuscript hierarchy mainly had to do with whether the 'best' manuscript was Leiden BPL 114 or Paris BnF lat. 4627 – and by 'best', Marculf's editors always meant the most Merovingian-looking, and as a result tended to look for the least classical

---

812 See above, p. 31.

grammar and spelling. Eugène de Rozière and Adolphe Tardif were both convinced of the greater authenticity of Paris BnF lat. 4627; Zeumer and Uddholm were equally convinced of that of the Leiden manuscript. Judging from the rather aggressive exchanges between Zeumer and Tardif, this seems to have become an issue of national pride, French scholars generally preferring the Paris manuscript and German scholars the Leiden one.[813] Tardif discussed this point mainly in relation to problems of dating and to the tired question of whether Landeric was bishop of Paris, Metz or Meaux,[814] and he conflated all the dispute onto the precise point of deciding whether Marculf I, 25 had or had not originally included a reference to the presence of the mayor of the palace at the royal tribunal: the Leiden manuscript and Paris BnF lat. 10756 do have a *maior domus* present, whereas Paris BnF lat. 4627 does not. Tardif was doubtless right in pointing out that 'the dogma of universal suffrage and of the sovereignty of the highest number has not yet been extended to textual criticism' (writing in 1885, let us not forget),[815] but in this particular case his argument is further weakened by Uddholm's subsequent discovery that Paris BnF lat. 4627 was actually the result of a contact between the traditions of the Leiden manuscript and of Paris BnF lat. 10756. The reference to the *maior domus* would therefore have been dismissed as anachronistic in the Paris BnF lat. 4627 tradition at some point after the disappearance of that office in 751, pointing to a later tradition in relation to the other manuscripts rather than to an earlier one. The *maior domus* reading is therefore clearly the original one, and constitutes another instance of the Leiden manuscript and Paris BnF lat. 10756 both giving the correct reading against Paris BnF lat. 4627.

Uddholm's reconstruction therefore affects the hierarchy of manuscripts, so that, in contrast to the idea generally accepted before Zeumer according to which Paris BnF lat. 4627 was the 'best' manuscript, before being demoted by Zeumer to the status of runner-up to Leiden BPL 114, it actually falls to third place. The most authentic manuscript turns out to be either Paris BnF lat. 10756 or the Leiden manuscript: Paris BnF lat. 4627, as a compromise between these two traditions, cannot be used as a separate witness.[816]

813 See above, n. 313.
814 See above, pp. 107–10.
815 'Le dogme du suffrage universel et de la souveraineté du nombre n'a pas encore été étendu à la critique des textes... on peut soutenir, dans le domaine de la science, qu'un bon avis vaut mieux que trois mauvais; un bon ms. que trois médiocres: *numerentur sed ponderentur*', Tardif, 'Nouvelles observations sur la date du formulaire de Marculf', p. 371.
816 Uddholm, *Formulae Marculfi: Etudes sur la langue et le style*, p. 22.

Zeumer did not really explain why he rated Paris BnF lat. 10756 as less trustworthy than either Leiden BPL 114 or Paris BnF lat. 4627. He simply asserted that although it was interesting in many ways, it 'could not compare' with the Leiden manuscript,[817] and went on to say that Paris BnF lat. 4627 was *unerreicht* ('unrivalled') in completeness and authenticity and that he would follow it for his edition. As he later went on to say that Leiden was the most 'Merovingian' and therefore the 'best' manuscript, his message becomes rather confusing. Uddholm also thought that Leiden was the best manuscript but similarly failed to give any reasons.[818] This lack of interest in Paris BnF lat. 10756 is all the more surprising as both editors agreed that there were cases in which it was the only manuscript to preserve the original reading against all the others: it is thus the only manuscript to contain the full text of II, 37. Only Krusch was doubtful as to the advisability of making systematic editing choices on the basis of the manuscript hierarchy, and criticised Zeumer for failing to take the other manuscripts more into account, pointing out several cases in which he thought one should follow Paris BnF lat. 10756 against all the others.[819]

It is now generally thought that Leiden BPL 114 is the manuscript of Marculf closest to the original, despite the fact that it does not stick to the general order found in the other manuscripts, and does not even really purport to be Marculf. Zeumer and Uddholm agreed on this. The general idea, therefore, was that one should follow the order given in Paris BnF lat. 10756 and Paris BnF lat. 4627, but that the individual readings in Leiden BPL 114 tended to be better.

Zeumer believed that Leiden BPL 114 was the best manuscript for several reasons. One was that he thought the spelling and grammar in this manuscript were appalling, and therefore would probably have been closer to Marculf's Merovingian Latin than the 'better' Latin of the other manuscripts, which he suggested were the result of corrections made by conscientious Carolingian scribes (one should point out that in terms of bad grammar Paris BnF lat. 10756 comes next, not Paris BnF lat. 4627). In particular, the scribe of Leiden BPL 114 consistently hypercorrected 'e' to 'ae', but since this extends beyond Marculf to other parts of the manuscript,

---

817 '...obwohl in vielen Einzelheiten recht gut, muss gegen L zurücktreten, wie am besten ein vergleichender Blick auf die nur in diesen beiden Handschriften enthaltenen Stücke des Supplements zeigt' (Zeumer, 'Über die älteren fränkischen Formelsammlungen', p. 28).

818 Uddholm, *Formulae Marculfi: Etudes sur la langue et le style*, p. 50.

819 Krusch, 'Der Staatsstreich des fränkischen Hausmaiers Grimoald I', p. 414, n. 6; Krusch, 'Ursprung und Text', pp. 268–73.

this is likely to have been a regional or scribal idiosyncrasy rather than constituting proof that the spelling was somehow more authentic. Uddholm also used the argument of spelling to explain his preference for the Leiden manuscript. This is a rather unconvincing part of his argument, in particular when he decided to follow the Leiden readings purely on the basis that their spelling was closer to what he thought would have been the spelling used in St Denis at the time (by comparison with original documents from St Denis). He is even more unsound when he considers the reading in Leiden to be correct but, the spelling not being 'bad' enough, recommends a compromise by accepting the reading but using another spelling for it, exchanging it for one closer to what he thought would have been used in St Denis.[820] Not only, as I suggested earlier, is it not at all clear that Marculf did write in St Denis,[821] but, whether he did or not, one should not forget that the formulae in Marculf were modelled on a variety of different existing charters, which must themselves have had their differences in terms of spelling and grammar (as Uddholm himself points out).[822] Merovingian scribes were known to change their spellings, and their attitude to this problem was apparently not as systematic or as fussy as that of modern scholars. To sum up, not only is it impossible to know what spelling Marculf would originally have used, but it is also unclear why we should care: in itself it can tell us very little, at least as far as reconstructing the original text is concerned. It certainly does not constitute a decisive argument in terms of the relative authenticity of manuscripts. There is no absolute, immediate and specific link to be made between non-classical Latin and the Merovingian period, especially in the case of documents such as these, which were kept for their practical rather than their literary value. Furthermore, the Latin used in the other manuscripts of Marculf is also far from classical, and it seems rather odd to dismiss Paris BnF lat. 10756 simply because its Latin is a little less bizarre.

In terms of individual readings, it does seem that Leiden BPL 114 is sometimes correct where none of the others are. Of course one cannot suppose that Marculf necessarily had the most satisfying reading himself in the first place; but there are cases in which the reading in the Leiden manuscript makes sense while none of the others do, and in which it would be difficult to explain how the scribe could have reconstituted a meaningful sentence on his own without the assistance of a better manuscript: one such

---

820 Uddholm, *Formulae Marculfi: Etudes sur la langue et le style*, p. 31, on the reading for *aquarum* in Marculf I, 13.

821 See above, pp. 113–17.

822 Uddholm, *Formulae Marculfi: Etudes sur la langue et le style*, p. 26.

instance is II, 3, with the reference to the *gesta municipalia*: Leiden BPL 114 has 'nequaquam a curialium uilitate', which makes sense, whereas Paris BnF lat. 4627 has 'nequiquam aurialium' and Paris BnF lat. 10756 'nequiquam auguriale uel uilitate', neither of which can be right. To give another example: in I, 40 Leiden BPL 114 has *leudesamio* in both text and chapter-heading, whereas Paris BnF lat. 10756 has the bizarre *leudesamicicia* and *leodes amicicia* and Paris BnF lat. 4627 *leode et samio* and *leo desamio* (though this is a less compelling case, as it would not have been very difficult for a scribe who knew the word to reconstitute it from some of these other versions). In particular, some gaps in the main manuscript tradition appear to be filled in the Leiden manuscript. Zeumer concluded that it was corrected with the help of a better exemplar. This does not mean, of course, that Leiden BPL 114 is systematically right: apart from these two instances in which Leiden BPL 114 clearly preserves the original reading, some of Zeumer's other choices in favour of this manuscript against the others seem more arbitrary (see Table 5). Zeumer's method in determining whether a particular expression was authentic was to compare it with existing Merovingian diplomas.[823] There are a number of problems with this, not least in that he often used for this comparison forgeries[824] and documents that were only preserved through cartularies, so that they may well preserve an altered reading themselves. Even in the case of originals, the survival rate of documents in general seems too low, as a rule, to allow us to form definite conclusions about whether any particular expression was current or not.

Furthermore, there has to be a fundamental problem with using as the most authentic text for Marculf a manuscript which does not even attempt to reproduce the text in any accurate way. It would seem fair to consider Leiden BPL 114 not as a manuscript of Marculf at all, but as a manuscript of a different collection altogether, which relies heavily on Marculf, and matters for the Marculf tradition itself only insofar as it preserves some convincing readings. Leiden BPL 114 does not preserve Marculf as a distinct collection: its preface and structure are ignored, and it is mixed up with other formulae. The same goes for Paris BnF lat. 2123 and the Copenhagen manuscript. More worryingly, the scribes of these new collections, which only use Marculf as one source among others, actually strike one as being the most competent, in the sense that they did not copy the text uncritically. As such, they are more likely to have produced a text that made sense. Leiden BPL

---

823 Zeumer, 'Über die älteren fränkischen Formelsammlungen', p. 33.
824 Such as Kölzer DM. †49 (pp. 126–28); see above, p. 112.

114 does seem to preserve some convincing readings; but in view of the extensive reworking of the Marculf material in this manuscript, its level of authenticity is necessarily inconsistent. On the other hand, it now seems safe to rehabilitate Paris BnF lat. 10756 as the most reliable manuscript of Marculf, though it should be noted that it is generally inadvisable to rely very systematically on any single manuscript for texts that were by their very nature highly flexible and adaptable.

APPENDICES

Table 1 The Marculf corpus in the manuscripts

	Paris 4627	Paris 10756	Leiden 114	Paris 2123	Fabricius 84	Leiden Voss. lat. 86	Munich 4650
Preface	x			x			
I, 1	x	x	x	x	x		
I, 2–4	x	x	x	x	x		x
I, 5	x	x	x	x	x		
I, 6–7	x	x	x	x	x		x
I, 8	x	x	x	x	x	x	
I, 9	x	x	x	x		x	
I, 10	x	x	x	x		x	x
I, 11	x	x	x	x	x	x	x
I, 12–13	x	x	x	x	x		
I, 14–16	x	x	x	x	x		x
I, 17	x	x	x		x		x
I, 18	x	x	x		x		
I, 19–20	x	x	x	x	x		
I, 21	x	x	x		x		
I, 22	x	x	x	x	x		x
I, 23	x	x	x	x	x		
I, 24	x	x	x	= Add. 2	x		
I, 25–28	x	x	x	x	x		
I, 29	x	x	x	x	x	x	x
I, 30–32	x	x	x	x	x		
I, 33	x	x	x	x	x		x
I, 34	x	x	x	x	x	x	x
I, 35	x	x	x	x	x		
I, 36–40	x	x	x		x		
II, 1	x	x	x	x	x		
II, 2	x	x	x				
II, 3	x	x	x	x			
II, 4	x	x	x				
II, 5	x	x	x	x			
II, 6–8	x	x	x				
II, 9	x	x	x	x			

THE FORMULARIES OF ANGERS AND MARCULF

	Paris 4627	Paris 10756	Leiden 114	Paris 2123	Fabricius 84	Leiden Voss. lat. 86	Munich 4650
II, 10	x	x	x				
II, 11	x	x	x	x			
II, 12	x	x	x	x	x		
II, 13	x	x	x				
II, 14	x	x	x	x	x		
II, 15	x	x	x		x		
II, 16–17	x	x	x				
II, 18	x	x	x	x	x		
II, 19	x	x	x		prologue		
II, 20	x	x	x				
II, 21	x	x					
II, 22–24	x	x	x				
II, 25–29	x	x		x	x		
II, 30	x	x					
II, 31–34	x	x		x	x		
II, 35	x	x			x		
II, 36	x	x	end	x			
II, 37–38	x	x		part			
II, 39–40	x	x	x	x	x		
II, 41	x	x	x				
II, 42–43	x	x	x		x		
II, 44–45	x	x			x		
II, 46	x	x	x	x			
II, 47	x	x	x	x		x	x
II, 48–51	x	x	x	x			
II, 52	x	x	x		x		
Suppl. 1		x	x				
Suppl. 2		x	x		x		x
Suppl. 3		x	x		x	x	x
Suppl. 4		x	x		x		x
Suupl. 5		x	title				
Suppl. 6		x	x	x	x	x	x
Add 1	x						
Add 2–3				x	x		
a, b, c	x	x	x				

APPENDICES

Table 2 List of contents of the three main manuscripts

	fol. nos.	list of contents
Leiden BPL 114	1-8	Isidore, *Etymologiae* IX, 5 and 6
	8-88	Aegidius's epitome of the *Lex Romana Visigothorum*
	89-91v	*Formulae Bituricenses* Appendix 1-12
	91v-97	Marculf II, 42, 43, 46-52
		Marculf *Supplementum* 3, 4, 6
	97-98	a, b, c
	98-101v	*Formulae Bituricenses* 8-13
	101v-103	*Formulae Bituricenses* * 1-3
	103-104v	*Formulae Bituricenses* 14
	104-158	Marculf *Supplementum* 1-2
		Marculf I, 1-40
		Marculf II, 1-2
		Marculf *Additamenta* 1 a-e
		Marculf II, 3-20, 22-24 (end 36), 39-41
	158v-160v	letter Chrodobert-Boba in formula style (discarded by Z.)
	161-166v	*Formulae Bituricenses* 15-19
Paris 4627	2-27v	*Formulae Senonenses (Senonicae)* 1-51
	27v-29	*Formulae Senonenses (Senonicae)* Additam. 1-5
	29-31v	*Formulae Senonenses (Senonicae)* Appendix 1-6
	32-59v	*Lex Salica*
	59v	catalogue of Frankish kings (Theoderic to Childeric)
	59v-60	Marculf preface
	60v-61	Chapters list for Marculf I
	61v-85	Marculf I, 1-40
	85v	Chapters list for Marculf II
	86-125	Marculf II, 1-52
	125	a, b, c
	127-145	*Formulae Senonenses recentiores* 1-18
Paris 10756	1-1v	chapter list for Marculf I
	2-2v	chapter list for Marculf II
	3-4v	Marculf *Supplementum* 1-6
	4v-21	Marculf I, 1-40
	22-45	Marculf II, 1-52
	45-45v	a, b, c (ms. damaged)
later bound with:	46-61	*Formulae Turonenses*
later bound with:	62-64	*Formulae Bituricenses* nos. 1-6 (Merovingian copy)
	64v-69v	computus; lists and annotations in Tironian notes*

Table 3 Shared readings in the manuscripts of Marculf

		BPL 114	Paris 4627	Paris 10756	B tradition
sua *om.*	I, 2	X	X		
seruorum	I, 2	X	X		
ut *om.*	I, 5	X	X		
dignanter *om.*	I, 7	X	X		
proprietate(m)	I, 9	X	X		
inprimitus *om.*	II, 6	X	X		
ei dedi	II, 9	X	X		
uolui *om.*	II, 41	X	X		
propria manu subscripsimus	I, 24		X	X	
fiunt	II, 3		X	X	
perfruantur	II, 4		X	X	
ubicumque	II, 8		X	X	
memorauimus	II, 17		X	X	
supradicta	II, 10		X	X	
uestitum	II, 13		X	X	
prefatae *om.*	II, 15		X	X	
quia	II, 1		X	X	
successoribus	II, 3		X	X	
fragilitatis	II, 4		X	X	
quod *om.*	I, 1		X	X	X
hominibus *om.*	I, 1			X	X
agnuscite	I, 16			X	X
exoratione *pro* exortatione				X	X
ligum(ina)	I, 11		X		X
ac ponteficale culmine sublimato *om.*	II, 46		X		X
subnexa *om.*	II, 1		X		X

APPENDICES   275

Table 4 Uddholm's readings for the B tradition

	Paris 2123	Copenhagen	Leiden BPL 114	Paris 4627	Paris 10756
I, 1	ab ill	ab ill	ab⁻ [= abba] ill	*om.*	abb il
I, 2	sancti	sancti	*om.*	*om.*	*om.*
I, 4	superius memorata	superius memoratam	iam dicta	iam dicta	iam dicta
I, 11	dactiles	dactalos	dactalus	dactolas	dactol⁻
I, 14d	termino	termino	termino	termine	termine
I, 23	causa suspensa	causa suspensa	causa suspensa	causas suspensas	causas suspensas
I, 32	ipsius	ipsius	*om.*	*om.*	*om.*
I, 33	tam quod per	tam quod per	quam per quod	quam pro quod	quam per quod
I, 40	*formula missing*	leudissamio	leodesamio	leude samio	leodes amicicia
II, 18	fistuco	fistuco	fistuco	fistuca	fistuca
II, 42	*formula missing*	cum	*om.*	*om.*	*om.*
II, 42	*formula missing*	propere	prepropere	propterea	quapropter
II, 42	*formula missing*	qua	qua	que,	que
II, 43	*formula missing*	dictu. Adicimus	dictua Dicimus	dictua Dicimus	dictua Dicimus
II, 43	*formula missing*	reminiscatis orationibus	reminiscat oratio	reminiscat oratio	reminiscat oratio
II, 45	*formula missing*	sancti	*formula missing*	*om.*	*om.*
II, 46	commendatos	*om.*	cum indoctis	commendetur	commendetur
II, 52	*formula missing*	regi	rege	regis	regis
II, 52	*formula missing*	uita ei concedatur	melius conseruetur	melius conseruetur	melius conseruetur
Supl. 6	ad	ad	ad	a	a

Table 5 The case for the authenticity of Leiden BPL 114

	Leiden BPL 114	Paris 10756	Paris 4627	B
I, 1	cui hinc furmola habere placuerit	cui hic	cui haec	*heading missing*
I, 24	subter decreuimus	subscripsimus	subscripsimus	subscripsimus (B2)
I, 25	ill. maiorem domus	ill. maiorem domus	*om.*	ill. maiorem domus
I, 29	rauba	rauba	raupa	rauba
I, 35	gloriosi regni nostri	gloriae regni nostri	gloriae regni nostri	glorie regni nostri
I, 36	saciendi	saciendi	sancciendi	saciendi (B2)
I, 37	abiectisset	*om.*	abiectus sit	*om.*
I, 40	leudesamio	leodes amicicia	leode et samio	leodisamio (B2)
I, 40	leudesamio	leudesamicicia	leo desamio	leudisamio (B2)
II, 3	nequaquam a curialium uilitate	nequiquam auguriale vel vilitate	necquiquam aurialium	*om.*
II, 15	tanodono	tañ (tanto) dono	tanto dono	t- no (B2)
II, 16	tanodo	tano dono	tanto domo	t- no (B2)
II, 41	ad proprietate sacire	ad proprietate sacire	ad proprietate scire	*om.*
II, 41	ad proprietate sacire	ad proprietate sacire	ad proprietate satire	*om.*

APPENDICES

Table 6 Zeumer's stemma

Based on K. Zeumer, 'Über die älteren fränkischen Formelsammlungen', *Neues Archiv* 6 (1881), pp. 9–115; K. Zeumer, 'Die Lindenbruch'sche Handschrift der Formelsammlung von Flavigny', *Neues Archiv* 14 (1889), pp. 589–603; K. Zeumer, *Formulae Merowingici et Karolini Aevi*, MGH *Legum* V Hanover, 1886), pp. 32–127

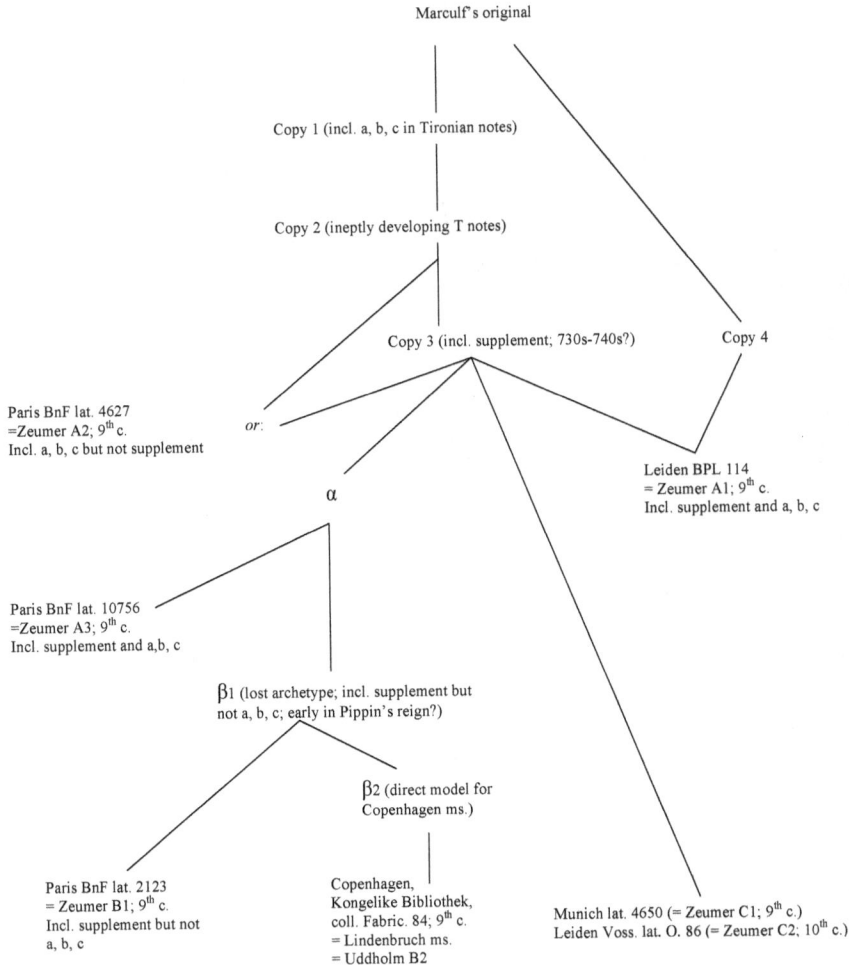

Table 7 Uddholm's stemma

A. Uddholm, 'Le texte des *Formulae Marculfi*', *Eranos* 55 (1957), pp. 38–59, p. 51

Marculf's original

α

β

γ

Leiden BPL 114

δ

Paris BnF lat. 10756

ε

ζ

η   Munich lat. 4650   Leiden Voss. lat. O. 86

Paris BnF lat. 2123   Copenhagen, Kongelike
                       Bibliothek, coll. Fabric. 84

x   y

Paris BnF lat. 4627

APPENDICES

Table 8 Another possible reconstruction
This integrates Zeumer's reconstruction of the B tradition with Uddholm's view that Paris BnF lat. 4627 was the result of a contact between the traditions of Paris BnF lat. 10756 and Leiden BPL 114 (but rejecting his hypothesis of the influence of another, 'better' manuscript on the B tradition).

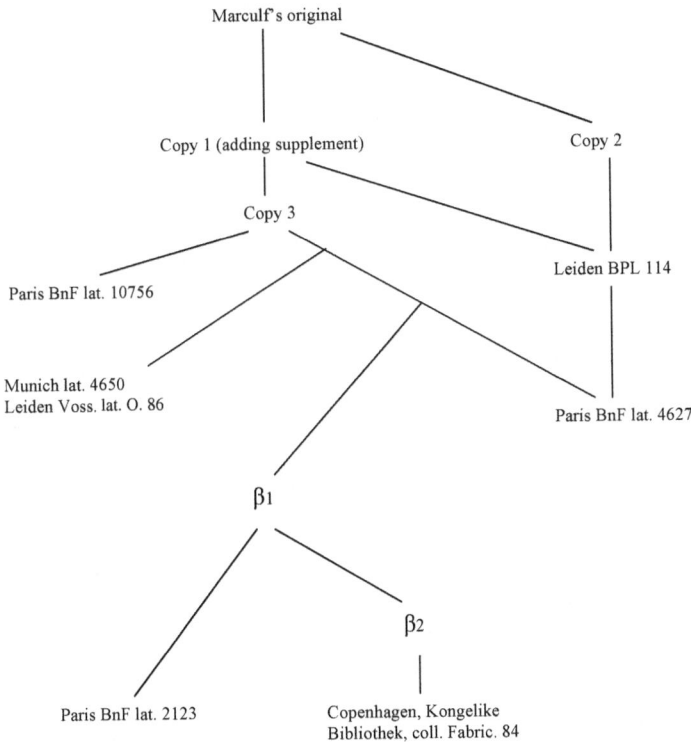

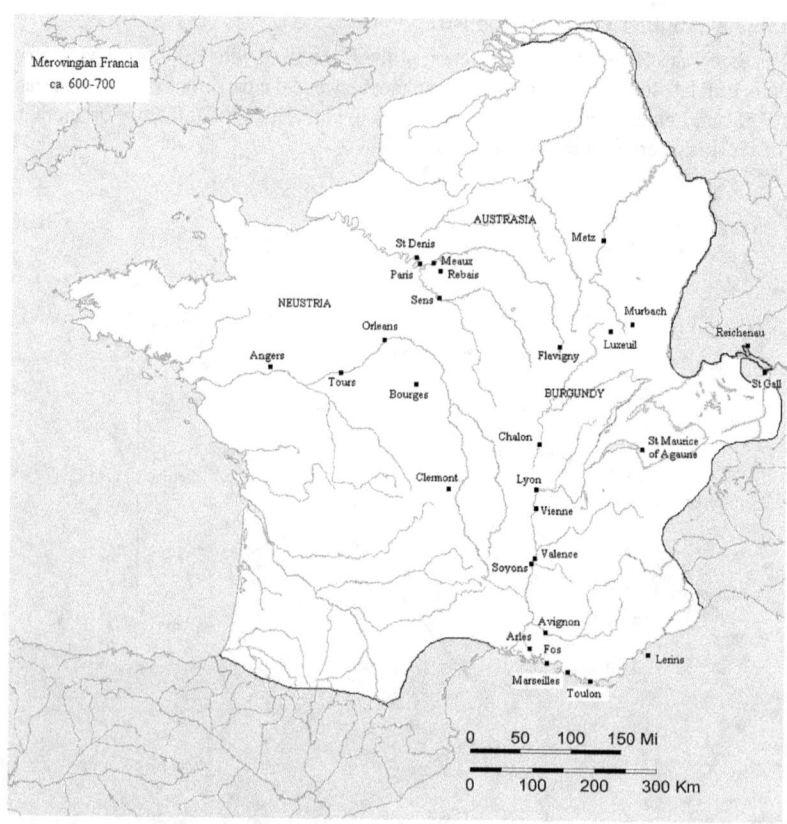

Merovingian France, c. 600–700

GLOSSARY

appennis: a procedure allowing the replacement of lost documents (for instance when the owner's house had burned down). The claimant had to present accounts from witnesses to prove he had lost his documents, and could then petition to have the rights that had been recorded in them generally reasserted, by having a document of *appennis* displayed in a public place.

beneficium: the main meaning of this word is 'favour' or 'benefit', particularly in relation to a grant or a loan (and also, in descriptions of property, to refer to revenues linked to the land), but it later acquired, probably only after the end of the Merovingian period, the more technical meaning of 'land benefice', that is, land held under a right of usufruct, usually obtained through a *precaria*. Allocating the revenues of lands (particularly lands belonging to the church) according to this form of tenure seems to have become a common way of rewarding dependants and followers from the Carolingian period onwards.

boni homines: the phrase 'good men', in a legal context, referred to men who could be called upon to act as witnesses or to arbitrate in a dispute. Such men would have been responsible for dealing with legal cases at the lowest and most local level, which explains their greater prominence in Angers than in Marculf.

cartulary: collections compiling copies of charters concerning the land transactions of particular churches or monasteries. The earliest surviving examples of such collections for West Francia date from the tenth century, though they often contained much older documents, the wording of which was often modified in the process of copying.

centenarius: leader in charge of a *centena*, a type of administrative district ('hundred', and so a 'hundred man', though what exactly this number referred to is unclear). It has been argued that *centena* was the East Frankish/Burgundian equivalent of *condita*, but this is unlikely, since the word is also found in West Frankish documents (in Normandy, Maine,

Quercy and the Toulousain, for example).[825]

charter (*carta* or *charta*, pl. *cartae*): a legal document in the form of a contract, recording particular rights and transactions, and typically containing, in order: a protocol consisting of an invocation (for instance 'In the name of the Holy Trinity'), an *intitulatio*, announcing the title of the party issuing the document, and an address naming and saluting the recipient; an *arenga* or formal introduction containing general statements of purpose and motivation, which could vary in length considerably; a *narratio* outlining the circumstances leading up to the agreement made in the document; a dispositive section stating the action taken through the document, and often containing a penalty-clause; a corroboration reinforcing the act, usually with reference to the signatures of witnesses; and an eschatocol containing the place and date. Formulae did not always contain all of these, and sometimes shortened or omitted some parts. See also *notitia*.

condita: a type of administrative district, and a subdivision of the *pagus*.

count (*comes*, pl. *comites*): counts were royal representatives appointed to govern local districts (in formulae usually described as *pagi*), and in charge of administration and justice for secular matters (while bishops were in principle in charge of the equivalent for matters involving the clergy; in practice, however, bishops and counts could often come into conflict over borderline cases). This office clearly remained in principle dependent on the king's favour until the tenth century (though there is debate as to whether, and when, it might have become hereditary in practice). In the Angers formulary, the count appears to have been involved in practice only in the most serious cases (such as murder or *appennis* procedures), while most other disputes were settled less formally by *boni homines* or before an abbot.

count of the palace (*comes palatii*): palace official, in charge of formally witnessing decisions taken at the royal tribunal.

---

[825] R. Schröder, 'Über die fränkischen Formelsammlungen', *Zeitschrift der Savigny-Stiftung für Rechtsgeschichte, Germanistische Abteilung* 4 (1883), pp. 75–112, at pp. 86–94; E. Zadora-Rio, ed., *Des paroisses de Touraine aux communes d'Indre-et-Loire : la formation des territoires*, Supplément à la Revue Archéologique du Centre (Tours, forthcoming), part 2, chapters 1 and 3; J.P. Brunterc'h, 'Le duché du Maine et la marche de Bretagne', in H. Atsma, ed., *La Neustrie: les pays au nord de la Loire de 650 à 850* (Sigmaringen 1989), pp. 29–127; F. Hautefeuille, 'Structures de l'habitat rural et territoires paroissiaux en bas-Quercy et haut-Toulousain du VIIe au XIVe siècle', PhD thesis, Université de Toulouse II-Le Mirail (1998), vol. 1, p. 135. See A.C. Murray, 'From Roman to Frankish Gaul: *centenarii* and *centenae* in the administration of the Merovingian kingdom', *Traditio* 44 (1988), pp. 59–100.

GLOSSARY

cubicularius (pl. *cubicularii*): a dignitary of the royal household. The word suggests they were attached to the king's 'chamber', though the office seems to have involved wider functions, such as witnessing judgments made at the royal tribunal (as in Marculf I, 25), or acting as a royal agent (a *cubicularius* by the name of Berthar thus took part in the capture of Theudebert II in 612; Fredegar IV, 38).

curator: a city official under the late Roman empire.

decurions (*curiales*): members of the municipal council (*curia*) of a city under the Roman empire.

defensor: under the Roman empire, a city magistrate (first documented in 365) in charge of protecting those without legal standing. It is unclear what the term came to mean after the end of the Roman empire in the West (though bishops could sometimes be described as *defensores*).

denarius (pl. *denarii*): a silver coin.[826] Throwing a *denarius* was a symbolic gesture associated with one particular form of manumission (Marculf I, 22).

domesticus (pl. *domestici*): this word seems to have referred to representatives of the Frankish kings, either at court or for the purpose of managing estates of the fisc, in a fairly general and non-specialised sense: a count is thus described as one the king's *domestici* in Marculf I, 39.

dos: a marriage-gift made by the husband to his wife on the day of their wedding, often consisting of both lands and moveable goods such as jewellery. This would in principle have counted as her own property, but some *dos* arrangements forbade the woman to alienate any of it, and reserved it for the husband's own heirs.

duke (*dux*, pl. *duces*): a royal agent with military as well as judicial authority, governing over larger regions than counts.

festuca: this 'rod' was used in court proceedings as a symbol to sanction various legal procedures.[827] Although this tends to be seen as a specifically Frankish phenomenon, it can also be found in a description of Roman judicial proceedings, with a description of accompanying gestures, in the second-century *Institutes* of Gaius (IV, 16). Even in his day Gaius described it as an archaic practice: on its origins, he speculated that 'rods stood for spears, as a symbol of legitimate ownership, because it was thought that the most legitimate form of ownership was over the

---

826 On Merovingian coinage, see P. Grierson and M. Blackburn, *Medieval European Coinage* (Cambridge, 1986), vol. 1, at pp. 80–154.

827 On this word, see Fouracre, 'The nature of Frankish political institutions', p. 287; Barnwell, 'Emperors, jurists and kings', p. 24.

spoils taken from the enemy' ('festuca autem utebantur quasi hastae loco, signo quodam iusti dominii, quamdo iusto dominio ea maxime sua esse credebant quae ex hostibus cepissent').

fidelis (pl. *fideles*): this term seems to have designated members of the Frankish aristocracy. It has also been argued that it referred to the fidelity owed to the king by his subjects in general,[828] but some of the people described in royal documents were pointedly not described as *fideles* (as in Marculf I, 19), which would imply that the word had a more technical meaning. It is unclear in any case how far the notion of 'subject' would have applied in relation to early medieval models of kingship.[829]

fisc *(fiscus)*: this could refer to the royal treasury (particularly in the context of the collection of dues or fines), or to estates belonging to the king.

gesta municipalia: under the Roman empire, municipal archives (see Appendix 2). The word *gesta* could also describe a document produced for such an archive.

juchus (pl. *juchi*): literally 'a team of oxen', used in formulae as a measure of land (as in the amount of land that could be ploughed in a day with a team of oxen).

mallus: place of public assembly, also functioning as a local court.

mansus (pl. *mansi*): a landed estate, including land and houses, but designating a smaller unit of land than a *villa* (since *mansi* could be situated on the lands of a *villa*, as in Marculf II, 36). *Mansus* later became the favoured unit of reference in Carolingian polyptychs (descriptions of estates).

master of soldiers *(magister militum)*: the highest military office under the Roman empire.

mayor of the palace *(major domus)*: initially merely at the head of the palace administration, the nature of the office changed drastically during the seventh century, when it became occupied by increasingly powerful figures, in particular the Pippinids, later to become the Carolingian ruling dynasty. The office was discontinued after Pippin III deposed the last Merovingian king in 751.

missus (pl. *missi*): an agent or envoy (*missi discurrentes* were 'travelling' agents). Although the use of *missi* has been mostly associated with the Carolingian style of government, Merovingian kings had also used them, as had bishops (as in Marculf I, 26, Supplement no. 1 and *Additamenta*

---

[828] Reynolds, *Fiefs and Vassals*, pp. 88–89.
[829] Nelson, 'Kingship and empire', p. 223.

no. 3), though perhaps less systematically than the early Carolingians.

modius (pl. *modii*): a measure of volume of grain or liquid (equivalent to about 40 to 55 litres in the Carolingian period).[830]

notitia (pl. *notitiae*): a legal record (in the Angers formulary referring in particular to a 'record of judgment'). This type of document was much more narrative in style than a charter, and tended to give more detail regarding the circumstances leading up to the agreement or the court's decision (they were therefore also usually far longer). This form of document apparently came to supersede the charter form, before replacing it altogether, during the course of the eleventh century.[831]

pagensis (pl. *pagenses*): the inhabitant of a *pagus*.

pagus: a local administrative district (in formulae usually designating the territory under the jurisdiction of a count).

patricius (pl. *patricii*): a royal representative in charge of a province (similar in this sense to dukes and counts, though apparently of a higher rank).

penalty-clause: this is a clause appended at the end of charters specifying the fines and punishments to be imposed on anyone attempting to breach the contract. Also referred to as comminatory or sanction clause.

placitum (pl. *placita*): this could refer either to a judicial hearing (in local courts as well as at the royal tribunal), or to the date scheduled for a hearing (for instance for the repayment of loans), or (by modern historians) to the type of document produced as a result of a hearing.[832] People who had to go to a *placitum* were apparently allowed three days within which to turn up; if they did not come within that time without offering a reasonable excuse (*sunia*), they were considered as having defaulted on their obligation (see *solsadia*).

praepositus: this could refer to any person 'in charge', and usually refers in formulae to someone presiding over a judicial hearing.

precaria: literally 'a begging letter', by which people requested the right of usufruct over land belonging to someone else. This practice mostly related to people who had given their land to a church, and then asked to retain the revenues of this property until their death, but it also seems to have been used in other cases (see, for instance, Marculf II, 41). A

---

830 J.-P. Devroey, *Économie rurale et société dans l'Europe franque (VIe–IXe siècles): Fondements matériels, échanges et lien social* (Paris, 2003), at p. 71.

831 D. Barthélemy, *La société dans le comté de Vendôme de l'an mil au XIVe siècle* (Paris, 1993), pp. 19–127.

832 On this type of document, see Fouracre, '*Placita* and the settlement of disputes in later Merovingian Francia'.

precaria technically needed to be renewed at particular intervals of time, though this need was usually negated in documents.

prestaria: this refers to the type of document issued in response to a *precaria*, and granting usufruct over some land.

prosecutor: in general, a claimant; in formulae, this word refers only to persons asking for the insertion of a document in the *gesta municipalia*.

rachinburgii: apparently members of the local elite, usually described in sources as assisting a count during judicial hearings. This term may have referred to the same sort of person as *boni homines*.

referendary: a notary in the royal chancery (also in charge of the king's seal).

Salic law: a Frankish law code, probably first compiled in the late fifth century (though it was subsequently modified: there are six extant recensions, including a Carolingian version).

scriptorium, pl. *scriptoria*: a community of scribes, usually belonging to an ecclesiastical institution (as well as the place where they worked).

senescalcis: officials of the royal household; the word (from which the word 'seneschal' is derived) seems to have originally referred to the 'eldest' among palace stewards. Their exact functions are not really known; they tend to appear only in *placita* as witnesses in the royal tribunal, as in Marculf I, 25.

solidus (pl. *solidi*): a gold coin, the highest extant denomination.[833]

solsadia: a document establishing someone's failure to appear at their appointed *placitum* within three days.[834]

Theodosian code (*codex Theodosianus*): a compilation of late Roman imperial law issued in 438 by the Eastern Roman emperor Theodosius II. It remained current in the West after the end of Roman rule through an abbreviated Visigothic version, the Breviary of Alaric.

Tironian notes: a form of specialised shorthand used by early medieval scribes.

usufruct: this refers to the right of 'use' over the land, that is, the right to exploit it and retain its revenues, as opposed to full ownership. Usufruct agreements (see *precaria*) usually included clauses forbidding the beneficiary from alienating (selling or giving) any of the property or from diminishing its value in any way.

---

833 On Merovingian coinage, see Grierson and Blackburn, *Medieval European Coinage*, vol. 1, at pp. 80–154.

834 See Fouracre, 'The nature of Frankish political institutions', pp. 287–88.

vicarius (pl. *vicarii*): the deputy of a count.
villa (pl. *villae*): in formulae, a landed estate, including lands and buildings; in some contexts, the word could also be used to refer to a village (for an overview of this term, see Wickham, *Framing the Early Middle Ages*, pp. 510–13).
wergeld: this was the price to be paid in compensation for murder to the victim's family. Determining the amount of the *wergeld* depending on the social status, gender or age of the victim was an important part of early medieval law-codes (the higher the status, the higher the *wergeld*). The particular circumstances of the crime could also affect the amount to be paid (the sum was thus tripled if the body had been concealed, as 'hidden' murder was thought a far more serious crime).

BIBLIOGRAPHY

Editions of Angers and Marculf

Bignon., J., ed., *Marculfi monachi formularum libri duo* (Paris, 1613)
Lindenbruch, F., ed., *Codex legum antiquarum* (Frankfurt, 1613)
Mabillon, J., ed., *Libri de re diplomatica supplementum* (*Formulae Andecavenses*) (Paris, 1704)
Migne, J.-P., ed., *Marculf et alii*, in *Patrologia Latina* (1844–64), vol. 87
Rozière, E. de, ed., *Formulae Andegavenses, d'après le manuscrit de Weingarten actuellement à Fulde*, Extrait des pièces justificatives de l'histoire du droit français au Moyen-Age par M. Ch. Giraud (Paris, 1844)
——, *Recueil général des formules* (Paris, 1859–71)
Uddholm, A., ed., *Marculfi formularum libri duo* (Uppsala, 1962)
Zeumer, K., ed., *Formulae Merowingici et Karolini Aevi*, MGH *Leges* V (Hanover, 1886)

Primary sources

Actus pontificum cenomannis in urbe degentium, ed. G. Busson and A. Ledru (Le Mans, 1901)
Anthemius, *Epistula de observatione ciborum*, ed. E. Liechtenhan, *Corpus Medicorum Latinorum* vol. 8:1 (Leipzig, 1963)
Capitularia regum Francorum, ed. A. Boretius, MGH *Leges* II (Hanover, 1883)
Cartulary of Flavigny, ed. C. Bouchard (Cambridge, MA, 1991)
Cassiodorus, *Variae*, ed. T. Mommsen, MGH *Scriptores Auctores Antiquissimi* XII (Berlin, 1898) [English translation: S.J.B. Barnish, *Cassiodorus: Selected Variae* (Liverpool, 1992)]
Chartae latinae antiquiores XIII, ed. H. Atsma and J. Vezin (Dietikon-Zurich, 1981)
Codex Theodosianus, ed. T. Mommsen and P.M. Meyer (Berlin, 1905) [English translation: C. Pharr, *The Theodosian Code and Novels and the Sirmondian Constitutions* (Princeton, 1952)]

Concilia aevi Karolini (742-842), ed. A. Werminghoff, MGH *Concilia* II.1 (Hanover, 1906)

Epistulae S. Desiderii Cadurcensis, ed. D. Norberg (Uppsala, 1961)

Fredegar, *Fredegarii et aliorum Chronica. Vitae Sanctorum*, ed. B. Krusch, MGH SS rer. Merov. II (Hanover, 1888) [English translation: J.M. Wallace-Hadrill, *The Fourth Book of the Chronicle of Fredegar* (London, 1960)]

Gaius, *Institutes*, ed. J. Reinach, 4th edn revised by M. Ducos (Paris, 1991)

Gesta episcoporum Cameracensium, in *Chronica et gesta aevi Salici*, ed. G.H. Pertz, MGH *Scriptores* VII (Stuttgart, 1846)

Gregory of Tours, *Opera* Teil 1: *Libri historiarum X*, ed. B. Krusch, MGH SS rer. Merov. I, 1 (Hanover, 1937) [English translation: L. Thorpe, *The History of the Franks* (Penguin, 1974)]

Isidore of Seville, *Etymologiae sive origines*, ed. W.M. Lindsay (Oxford, 1911) [English translation: S.A. Barney, W.J. Lewis, J.A. Beach and O. Berghof, *The Etymologies of Isidore of Seville* (Cambridge, 2006)]

Leges Alamannorum, ed. K.A. Eckhardt and K. Lehmann, MGH *Leges* I, 5, 1 (Hanover, 1966)

Leges Burgundionum, ed. L.-R. von Salis, MGH *Leges* I, 2, 1 (Hanover, 1892)

Lex Ribuaria, ed. F. Beyerle, MGH *Leges* I, 3, 2 (Hanover, 1954)

Lex Romana Visigothorum, ed. Gustav Hänel (Berlin, 1849)

Il Liber epistolarum *della cancelleria austrasica (sec. V-VI)*, ed. E. Malaspina (Rome, 2001)

Liber Iudiciorum: sive, Lex Visigothorum, in *Leges Visigothorum*, ed. K. Zeumer, MGH *Leges* I, 1 (Hanover, 1902)

Orosius, *Historiae adversum paganos*, ed. M.-P. Arnaud-Lindet (Paris, 1990)

Pactus Legis Salicae, ed. K.A. Eckhardt, MGH *Leges* I.4.1 (Hanover, 1962)

Pardessus, J.-M., ed., *Diplomata, chartae, epistolae, leges: aliaque instrumenta ad res Gallo-Francicas spectantia* (Paris, 1843-1849)

Die Urkunden der Merovinger, ed. T. Kölzer, MGH *Diplomata regum Francorum e stirpe merovingica* (Hanover, 2001)

Die Urkunden Pippins, Karlmanns und Karls des Grossen, ed. E. Mühlbacher, MGH *Diplomata* (Hanover, 1906)

Urkundenbuch zur Geschichte der jetzt die Preussischen Regierungsbezirke Coblenz und Trier bildenden mittelrheinischen Territorien, vol. 1, *Von den ältesten Zeiten bis zum Jahre 1169*, ed. H. Beyer (Coblenz, 1860)

Vita Austrigisili episcopi Biturigi, in Passiones vitaeque sanctorum aevi Merovingici et antiquorum aliquot (II), ed. B. Krusch, MGH Scriptores IV (Hanover, 1902)

Secondary sources

Althoff, G., *Family, Friends And Followers: Political and Social Bonds in Early Medieval Europe*, tr. C. Carroll (Cambridge, 2004)

Amory, P., 'The meaning and purpose of ethnic terminology in the Burgundian laws', *Early Medieval Europe* 2 (1993), pp. 1–28

Anderson, T., 'Roman military colonies in Gaul, Salian ethnogenesis and the forgotten meaning of Pactus Legis Salicae 59.5', *Early Medieval Europe* 4 (1995), pp. 129–44

Auerbach, E., *Literatursprache und Publikum in der lateinischen Spätantike und im Mittelalter* (Bern, 1958)

Banniard, M., *Viva voce: communication écrite et communication orale du IVe au IXe siècle en Occident latin* (Paris, 1992)

Barnwell, P.S., 'Emperors, jurists and kings: law and custom in the late Roman and early medieval West', *Past and Present* 168 (2000), pp. 6–29

Barthélemy, D., 'Qu'est-ce que le servage, en France, au XIe siècle ?', *Revue historique* 287(2) (1992), pp. 233–84

——, *La société dans le comté de Vendôme de l'an mil au XIVe siècle* (Paris, 1993)

Bartlett, R., *Trial by Fire and Water: the Medieval Judicial Ordeal* (Oxford, 1986)

Bautier, R.-H., 'La chancellerie et les actes royaux dans les royaumes carolingiens', *Bibliothèque de l'Ecole des Chartes* 142 (1984), pp. 5–80

Becher, M., *Eid und Herrschaft. Untersuchungen zum Herrscherethos Karls des Grossen* (Sigmaringen, 1993)

Beneyto Pérez, J., *Fuentes de Derecho histórico español* (Barcelona, 1931)

Bergmann, W., 'Die Formulae Andecavenses, eine Formelsammlung auf der Grenze zwischen Antike und Mittelalter', *Archiv für Diplomatik* 24 (1978), pp. 1–53

——, 'Fortleben des antiken Notariats im Frühmittelalter', in Peter Schuler, ed., *Tradition und Gegenwart. Festschrift zum 175-jährigen Bestehen eines badischen Notarstandes* (Karlsruhe, 1981), pp. 23–35

——, 'Verlorene Urkunden nach den *Formulae Andecavenses*', *Francia* 9 (1981), pp. 3–56

Berkhofer, R.F., *Day of Reckoning: Power and Accountability in Medieval France* (Philadelphia, 2004)

Beszard, L., *La langue des formules de Sens* (Paris, 1910)

Beumann, H., 'Gregor von Tours und der Sermo Rusticus', in K. Repgen and S. Skalweit, eds, *Spiegel der Geschichte. Festschrift für Max Braubach zum 10. April 1964* (Münster, 1964), pp. 69–98

Beyerle, F., 'Das Formelbuch des westfränkischen Mönchs Marculf und Dagoberts Urkunde für Rebais a. 635', *Deutsches Archiv für Erforschung des Mittelalters* 9 (1951), pp. 43–59

——, 'Das Formel-Schulbuch Markulfs', in H. Büttner, O. Feger and B. Meyer, eds, *Aus Verfassungs- und Landesgeschichte. Festschrift zum 70. Geburtstag von Theodor Mayer dargebracht von seinen Freunden und Schülern*, vol. 2: *Geschichtliche Landesforschung. Wirtschaftsgeschichte. Hilfswissenschaften* (Constanz 1955), pp. 365–89

Biedenweg, J.G.O., *Commentatio ad formulas Visigothicas novissime repertas* (Berlin, 1856)

B. Bischoff, 'Die Hofbibliothek unter Ludwig dem Frommen', in J.J.C. Alexander and M.T. Gibson, eds, *Medieval Learning and Literature: Essays presented to Richard William Hunt* (Oxford, 1976), pp. 3–22; reprinted in B. Bischoff, *Mittelalterliche Studien* vol. 3 (Stuttgart, 1981), pp. 171–86

Bonnassie, P., 'Survie et extinction du régime esclavagiste dans l'Occident du haut moyen âge (IVe-XIe s.)', *Cahiers de civilisation médiévale* 28 (1985), pp. 307–43

Bougard, F., Feller, L. and Le Jan, R., eds, *Dots et douaires dans le Haut Moyen Age*, Collection de l'Ecole Française de Rome 295 (Rome, 2002)

Bougard, F., La Rocca, C. and Le Jan, R., eds, *Sauver son âme et se perpétuer: Transmission du patrimoine et mémoire au haut moyen-âge*, Collection de l'Ecole Française de Rome 351 (Rome, 2005)

Boswell, J., *The Kindness of Strangers: The Abandonment of Children in Western Europe from Late Antiquity to the Renaissance* (New York, 1988)

Bresslau, H., 'Urkundenbeweis und Urkundenschreiber im älteren deutschen Recht', *Forschungen zur deutschen Geschichte* 26 (1886), pp. 1–66

——, *Handbuch der Urkundenlehre für Deutschland und Italien*, 2nd edn by H.-W. Klewitz (Berlin/Leipzig, 1931)

Brown, W., 'When documents are destroyed or lost: lay people and archives in the early Middle Ages', *Early Medieval Europe* 11 (2002), pp. 337–66

——, 'Conflicts, letters, and personal relationships in the Carolingian formula collections', *Law and History Review* 25 (2007), pp. 323–44

Brunner, H., 'Die Erbpacht der Formelsammlungen von Angers und Tours und die spätrömische Verpachtung der Gemeindegüter', *Zeitschrift der Savigny-Stiftung für Rechtsgeschichte, Germanistische Abteilung* 5 (1884), pp. 69–83

——, *Deutsche Rechtsgeschichte*, 2nd edn (Leipzig, 1906)

Brunterc'h, J.P., 'Le duché du Maine et la marche de Bretagne', in H. Atsma, ed., *La Neustrie: les pays au nord de la Loire de 650 à 850* (Sigmaringen, 1989), pp. 29–127

Buchner, R., *Deutschlands Geschichtsquellen im Mittelalter: Vorzeit und Karolinger. Beiheft: Die Rechtsquellen* (Weimar, 1953)

Bührer-Thierry, G., 'Femmes donatrices, femmes bénéficiaires: les échanges entre époux en Bavière du VIIIe au Xe siècle', in Bougard, Feller and Le Jan, *Dots et douaires*, pp. 329–51

Bullimore, K., 'Folcwin of Rankweil: the world of a Carolingian local official', *Early Medieval Europe* 13 (2005), pp. 43–77

Calboli, G., 'Il latino merovingico, fra latino volgare e latino medioevale', in E. Vineis, ed., *Latino volgare, latino medioevale, lingua romanze, Atti del Convegno della S.I.G., Perugia 28–29 marzo 1982* (Pisa, 1984), pp. 63–81

——, 'Aspects du Latin mérovingien', in J. Herman, ed., *Latin vulgaire – Latin tardif, Actes du premier colloque international sur le latin vulgaire et tardif* (Pécs, 2–5 septembre 1985) (Tübingen, 1987), pp. 19–35

——, 'Bemerkungen zu einigen Besonderheiten des merowingisch-karolingischen Latein', in M. Iliescu and W. Marxgut, eds., *Latin vulgaire – Latin tardif III, Actes du Troisième Colloque International sur le latin vulgaire et tardif (Innsbruck, 2–5 septembre 1991)* (Tübingen, 1992), pp. 41–61

Catalogus codicum manuscriptorum Bibliothecae Regiae 3, 3 (Paris, 1744)

Clanchy, M., *From Memory to Written Record: England 1066-1307*, 2nd edn (Oxford, 1993)

Classen, P., 'Fortleben und Wandel spätrömischen Urkundenwesens im frühen Mittelalter', in P. Classen, ed., *Recht und Schrift im Mittelalter*, Vorträge und Forschungen 23 (Sigmaringen, 1977), pp. 13–54

Coleman, E.R., 'Medieval marriage characteristics: a neglected factor in the history of serfdom', *Journal of Interdisciplinary History* 2 (1971), pp. 205–19

Collins, R., 'Law and ethnic identity in the Western kingdoms in the fifth and sixth centuries', in A.P. Smyth, ed., *Medieval Europeans: Studies in ethnic identity and national perspectives in medieval Europe* (London/New York, 1998), pp. 1–23

Curtis, R.I., 'A. Umbricius Scaurus of Pompeii', in R.I. Curtis, ed., *Studia Pompeiana & Classica in Honour of Wilhelmina F. Jashemski* (New York, 1988), vol. 1, pp. 19–50

d'Avray, D., *Medieval Marriage: Symbolism and Society* (Oxford, 2005)

Davies, W., *Small Worlds: The Village Community in Early Medieval Brittany* (London, 1988)

Davies, W. and Fouracre, P., eds, *The Settlement of Disputes in Early Medieval Europe* (Cambridge, 1986)

——, *Property and Power in the Early Middle Ages* (Cambridge, 1995)

Depreux, P., *Les Sociétés occidentales du milieu du VIe à la fin du IXe siècle* (Rennes, 2002)

——, 'La tradition manuscrite des "Formules de Tours" et la diffusion des modèles d'actes aux VIIIe et IXe siècles', in Depreux and Judic, *Alcuin de York à Tours*, pp. 55–71

Depreux, P. and Judic, B., eds, *Alcuin de York à Tours: Écriture, pouvoir et réseaux dans l'Europe du Haut Moyen Age* (Rennes/Tours, 2004)

Deroux, C., 'Anthime, un médecin gourmet du début des temps mérovingiens', *Revue belge de philologie et d'histoire* 80:4 (2002), pp. 1107–24

Devroey, J.-P., *Économie rurale et société dans l'Europe franque (VIe-IXe siècles): Fondements matériels, échanges et lien social* (Paris, 2003)

——, *Puissants et misérables: Système social et monde paysan dans l'Europe des Francs (VIe–IXe siècles)*, Classe des Lettres series 3, vol. 40 (Brussels, 2006)

De Waha, M., 'À propos d'un article récent: quelques réflexions sur la matricule des pauvres', *Byzantion* 46 (1976), pp. 354–67

Dominicy, M.A., *De treuga et pace in bellis privates* (Paris, 1669)

Du Pin, L.E., *Nouvelle bibliothèque des auteurs ecclésiastiques*, vol. 6 (Paris, 1692)

Durliat, J., *De l'Antiquité au Moyen-Age: l'Occident de 313 à 800* (Paris, 2002)

Dutton, P. E., tr., *Charlemagne's Courtier: The Complete Einhard* (Broadview, 1998)

Ewig, E., *Spätantikes und Fränkisches Gallien: Gesammelte Schriften (1952-1973)*, vols. 1 and 2, ed. H. Atsma (Zurich/Munich, 1976–1979)
——, 'Das Fortleben Römischer Institutionen in Gallien und Germanien', in Ewig, *Spätantikes und frühmittelalterliches Gallien*, vol. 1, pp. 409–34
——, 'Beobachtungen zu den Klosterprivilegien des 7. und frühen 8. Jahrhunderts Adel und Kirche', in Ewig, *Spätantikes und fränkischen Gallien*, vol. 2, pp. 411–26
——, 'Das Formular von Rebais', in Ewig, *Spätantikes und fränkischen Gallien* vol. 2, pp. 456–84
——, 'Das Privileg des Bischofs Berthefrid von Amiens für Corbie von 664 und die Klosterpolitik der Königin Balthild', in Ewig, *Spätantikes und Fränkisches Gallien* vol. 2, pp. 538–83
——, 'Marculfs Formular "De privilegio" und die merowingischen Bischofs-privilegien', in H. Mordek, ed., *Aus Archiven und Bibliotheken. Festschrift für Raymund Kottje zum 65. Geburtstag* (Frankfurt, 1992), pp. 51–69
Fabricius, J.A., *Bibliotheca latina mediae et infimae aetatis* (Hamburg, 1735–46)
Falkowski, R. 'Studien zur Sprache der Merowingerdiplome', *Archiv für Diplomatik* 17 (1971), pp. 1–125
Felgenträger, W., 'Zu den Formulae Andecavenses', in M. Kaser, H. Kreller and W. Künkel, eds, *Festschrift P. Koschaker zum 60. Geburtstag überreicht von seinen Fachgenossen*, vol. 3 (Weimar, 1939), pp. 366–75
Fichtenau, H., *Arenga: Spätantike und Mittelalter im Spiegel von Urkundenformeln* (Graz/Cologne, 1957)
Fouracre, P. '"*Placita*" and the settlement of disputes in later Merovingian Francia', in Davies and Fouracre, *The Settlement of Disputes in Early Medieval Europe*, pp. 23–43
——, 'Eternal lights and earthly needs: practical aspects of the development of Frankish immunities', in Davies and Fouracre, *Property and Power in the Early Middle Ages*, pp. 53–81
——, 'Attitudes towards violence in seventh- and eighth-century Francia', in G. Halsall, ed., *Violence and Society in the Early Medieval West* (Woodbridge, 1998), pp. 60–75
——, 'The nature of Frankish political institutions in the seventh century', in I.N. Wood, ed., *Franks and Alamanni in the Merovingian Period: An Ethnographic Perspective*, Studies in Historical Archaeoethnology 3 (Woodbridge, 1998), pp. 285–316
——, *The Age of Charles Martel* (London, 2000)

Fouracre, P. and Gerberding, R.A., *Late Merovingian France: History and Hagiography, 640–720* (Manchester, 1996)

Fustel de Coulanges, N.D., 'Etude sur l'immunité mérovingienne', *Revue Historique* 22 (1883), 249–90; 23 (1883), pp. 1–27

——, *La monarchie franque*, Histoire des institutions politiques de l'ancienne France, vol. 3 (Paris, 1888)

Ganshof, F.L., 'Charlemagne's use of the oath', in F.L. Ganshof, *The Carolingians and the Frankish Monarchy: Studies in Carolingian History*, tr. J. Sondheimer (London, 1971), pp. 111–24

Ganz, D., 'Bureaucratic shorthand and Merovingian learning', in P. Wormald, ed., *Ideal and Reality in Frankish and Anglo-Saxon Society: Studies Presented to J.M. Wallace-Hadrill* (Oxford, 1983), pp. 58–75

——, 'Paris BN Latin 2718: theological texts in the chapel and the chancery of Louis the Pious', in *Scientia veritatis: Festschrift für Hubert Mordek zum 65. Geburtstag*, ed. O. Münsch and T. Zotz (Ostfildern, 2004), pp. 137–52

Garrison, M., '"Send more socks": on mentality and the preservation context of medieval letters', in M. Mostert, ed., *New Approaches to Medieval Communication* (Turnhout, 1999), pp. 69–99

Geary, P.J., 'Ethnic identity as a situational construct in the Early Middle Ages', *Mitteilungen der anthropologischen Gesellschaft in Wien* 113 (1983), pp. 15–26

——, *Furta Sacra: Thefts of Relics in the Central Middle Ages*, 2nd edn (Princeton, 1990)

——, *Phantoms of Remembrance: Memory and Oblivion at the End of the First Millenium* (Princeton, 1994)

——, 'Land, language and memory in Europe, 700–1100', *Transactions of the Royal Historical Society*, 6th series, vol. 9 (1999), pp. 169–84

——, *The Myth of Nations: The Medieval Origins of Europe* (Princeton, 2002)

Gil, J., '*Formulae Wisigothicae*', in *Miscellanea Wisigothica* (Seville, 1972), pp. 70–112

Gobin, L., 'Notes et documents concernant l'histoire d'Auvergne. Sur un point particulier de la procédure mérovingienne applicable à l'Auvergne: "l'institution d'*apennis*"', *Bulletin historique et scientifique de l'Auvergne* (1894), pp. 145–53

Goetz, H.-W., 'Serfdom and the beginnings of a "seigneurial system" in the Carolingian period: a survey of the evidence', *Early Medieval Europe* 2 (1993), pp. 29–51

―――, *Frauen im frühen Mittelalter: Frauenbild und Frauenleben im Frankenreich* (Weimar, 1995)

Goetz, H.-W., Jarnut, J., and Pohl, W., eds, *Regna and gentes: the relationship between late antique and early medieval peoples and kingdoms in the transformation of the Roman world* (Leiden, 2003)

Goffart, W., 'Old and new in Merovingian taxation', *Past & Present* 96 (1982), pp. 3–21

Grierson, P. and Blackburn, M., *Medieval European Coinage* (Cambridge, 1986)

Guillot, O. (1995) 'La justice dans le royaume franc à l'époque mérovingienne', in *La giustizia nell' alto medioevo (secoli V–VIII)*, Settimane di studio del centro italiano di studi sull' alto medioevo XLII (Spoleto), vol. 2, pp. 653–731

Hägermann, D., 'Einige Aspekte der Grundherrschaft in den fränkischen formulae und in den leges des Frühmittelalters', in A. Verhulst, ed., *Le grand domaine aux époques mérovingienne et carolingienne / Die Grundherrschaft im frühen Mittelalter* (Ghent, 1985), pp. 51–77

Halsall, G., *Warfare and Society in the Barbarian West, 450–900* (London, 2003)

Hautefeuille, F., 'Structures de l'habitat rural et territoires paroissiaux en bas-Quercy et haut-Toulousain du VIIe au XIVe siècle', PhD thesis, Université de Toulouse II-Le Mirail (1998)

Heather, P., 'Literacy and power in the migration period', in A. Bowman and G. Woolf, eds, *Literacy and Power in the Ancient World* (Cambridge, 1994), pp. 177–97

Heidrich, I., 'Titulatur und Urkunden der arnulfingischen Hausmeier', *Archiv für Diplomatik* 11/12 (1965/66), pp. 71–279

Herlihy, D., 'Land, Family and Women in Continental Europe (701-1200)', *Traditio* 18 (1962), pp. 89–120

Herman, J., 'Sur quelques aspects du latin mérovingien: langue écrite et langue parlée', in M. Iliescu and W. Marxgut, eds, *Latin vulgaire – Latin tardif III, Actes du Troisième Colloque International sur le latin vulgaire et tardif (Innsbruck, 2–5 septembre 1991)* (Tübingen, 1992), pp. 173–86

Histoire littéraire de la France, vol. 3 (Paris, 1735)

Hummer, H., *Politics and Power in Early Medieval Europe: Alsace and the Frankish Realm, 600–1000* (Cambridge, 2005)

Immink, P.W.A., 'Propriété ou seigneurie? A propos des « baux perpétuels » des formules d'Angers et de Tours', *Tijdschrift voor rechtsgeschiedenis* 29 (1961), pp. 416–31

Innes, M., 'Memory, orality and literacy in an early medieval society', *Past & Present* 158 (1998), pp. 3–36
———, *State and Society in the Early Middle Ages: The Middle Rhine Valley, 400–1000* (Cambridge, 2000)
Innes Miller, J., *The Spice Trade of the Roman Empire: 29 BC to AD 641* (Oxford, 1969)
Johanek, P., 'Herrscherdiplom und Empfängerkreis. Die Kanzlei Ludwigs des Frommen in der Schriftlichkeit der Karolingerzeit', in R. Schieffer, ed., *Schriftkultur und Reichsverwaltung under den Karolingern*, Abhandlungen der Nordrhein-Westfälichen Akademie der Wissenschaften 97 (1996), pp. 167–88
John, W., 'Formale Beziehungen der privaten Schenkungsurkunden Italiens und des Frankenreiches und die Wirksamkeit der Formulare', *Archiv für Urkundenforschung* 14 (1936), pp. 1–104
Karras, R. M., 'The history of marriage and the myth of *Friedelehe*', *Early Medieval Europe* 14 (2006), pp. 119–51
Kienast, W., *Die fränkische Vassalität* (Frankfurt, 1990)
Krusch, B., 'MGH Legum sectio V. Formulae Merowingici et Karolini aevi', *Historische Zeitschrift* 51 (1883), pp. 512–19
———, 'Der Staatsstreich des fränkischen Hausmaiers Grimoald I', in M. Krammer, ed., *Historische Aufsätze. Karl Zeumer zum sechzigen Geburstag als Festgabe dargebracht von Freunden und Schülern* (Weimar, 1910), pp. 411–38
———, 'Ursprung und Text von Marculfs Formelsammlung', in *Nachrichten von der Königlichen Gesellschaft der Wissenschaften zu Göttingen, Phil. hist. Klasse* (Berlin, 1916), pp. 234–74
Lange, H.O., 'En Codex redivivus af de marculfinske Formler', in *Opuscula philologica: Mindre Afhandlinger udgivne af det philologisk-historiske Samfund* (Copenhagen, 1887), pp. 39–52
Launoy, J., *Inquisitio in chartam immunitatis quam beatus Germanus parisiorum episcopus suburbano monasterio dedisse fertur* (Paris, 1689)
Lauranson-Rosaz, C. and Jeannin, A., 'La résolution des litiges en justice durant le haut Moyen-Age: l'exemple de l'*apennis* à travers les formules, notamment celles d'Auvergne et d'Angers', in *Le règlement des conflits au Moyen-Age, XXXIe Congrès de la SHMES (Angers, juin 2000)* (Paris, 2001)), pp. 21–33
Lehmann, K., 'Monumenta Germaniae Historica. Legum Sectio V: Formulae Merowingici et Karolini aevi, edidit Karolus Zeumer', *Kritische*

Vierteljahrschrift für Gesetzburg und Rechtswissenschaft 29 (1887), pp. 331–46

Le Jan-Hennebicque, R., 'Aux origines du douaire médiéval (VIe–Xe siècles)', in M. Parisse, ed., *Veuves et veuvage dans le haut moyen âge* (Paris, 1993), pp. 107–21

Le Jan, R., Bougard, F. and La Rocca, C., eds, *Les transferts patrimoniaux en Europe occidentale, VIIIe–Xe siècle*, Mélanges de l'École française de Rome, Moyen Âge, 111–12 (Rome, 1999)

Lemaître, L., 'Cunauld, son prieuré et ses archives', *Bibliothèque de l'Ecole des Chartes* 59 (1898), pp. 231–61

Levillain, L., 'Le formulaire de Marculf et la critique moderne', *Bibliothèque de l'Ecole des Chartes* 84 (1923), pp. 21–91

——, 'Note sur l'immunité mérovingienne', *Revue historique du droit français et étranger* 6 (4th series) (1927), pp. 38–67

Levison, W., 'Zu Marculfs Formularbuch', *Neues Archiv* 50 (1935), pp. 616–19

——, 'Kleine Beiträge zu Quellen der fränkischen Geschichte', *Neues Archiv* 27 (1902), pp. 331–408

Liebs, D., 'Sklaverei aus Not im germanisch-römischen Recht', *Zeitschrift der Savigny-Stiftung für Rechtsgeschichte. Romanistische Abteilung* 118 (2001), pp. 286–311

Mabillon, J., *Vetera analecta*, vol. 4 (Paris, 1685)

——, *Annales ordinis S. Benedicti, occidentalium monachorum patriarchae, in quibus non modo res monasticae, sed etiam ecclesiasticae historiae non minima pars continetur*, vol. 1 (Paris, 1703)

Magnou-Nortier, E., 'Etude sur le privilège d'immunité du IVe au IXe siècle', *Revue Mabillon* 60 (1981–84), pp. 465–512

Marilier, J., 'Notes sur la tradition textuelle des testaments de Flavigny', *Mémoires de la Société pour l'histoire du droit et des institutions des anciens pays bourguignons, comtois et romands* 23 (1962), pp. 185–99

McCormick, M., *Origins of the European Economy* (Cambridge, 2001)

McKitterick, R., *The Carolingians and the Written Word* (Cambridge, 1989)

—— ed., *The Uses of Literacy in Early Medieval Europe* (Cambridge, 1990)

McNamara, J.-A. and Wemple, S.F., 'Marriage and divorce in the Frankish kingdom', in S.M. Stuard, ed., *Women in Medieval Society* (Philadelphia, 1976), pp. 96–124

Mersiowsky, M., 'Saint-Martin de Tours et les chancelleries carolingiennes', in Depreux and Judic, *Alcuin de York à Tours*, pp. 73–90

Middleton, N., 'Early medieval port customs, tolls and controls on foreign trade', *Early Medieval Europe* 13 (2005), pp. 313–58

Moorhead, J., 'Papa as "bishop of Rome"', *Journal of Ecclesiastical History* 36 (1985), pp. 337–50

Mordek, H., *Bibliotheca capitularium regum francorum manuscripta: Überlieferung und Traditionszusammenhang der fränkischen Herrschererlasse*, MGH Hilfsmittel 15 (Munich, 1995)

Muller, H. F., 'When did Latin cease to be a spoken language in France?', *The Romanic Review* 12 (1921), pp. 318–34

——, *L'Epoque mérovingienne: Essai de synthèse de philologie et d'histoire* (New York, 1945)

Murray, A.C., 'From Roman to Frankish Gaul: *centenarii* and *centenae* in the administration of the Merovingian kingdom', *Traditio* 44 (1988), pp. 59–100

——, 'Immunity, Nobility, and the Edict of Paris', *Speculum* 69 (1994), pp. 18–39

——, *From Roman to Merovingian Gaul: A Reader* (Broadview, 2000)

Nelson, J.L., 'Queens as Jezebels: Brunhild and Balthild in Merovingian history', in D. Baker, ed., *Medieval Women: Essays dedicated and presented to Professor Rosalind M.T. Hill* (Oxford, 1978), pp. 31–77; reprinted in J.L. Nelson, *Politics and Ritual in Early Medieval Europe* (London, 1986), pp. 1–49

——, 'Dispute settlement in Carolingian West Francia', in Davies and Fouracre, *The Settlement of Disputes in Early Medieval Europe*, pp. 45–64

——, 'Kingship and empire', in J.H. Burns, ed., *The Cambridge History of Medieval Political Thought c.350–c.1450* (Cambridge, 1988), pp. 211–51

——, 'Literacy in Carolingian government', in McKitterick, *The Uses of Literacy in Early Medieval Europe*, pp. 258–96

——, 'The wary widow', in Davies and Fouracre, *Property and Power in Early Medieval Europe*, pp. 82–113

——, 'Family, Gender and Sexuality', in M. Bentley, ed., *Companion to Historiography* (London, 1997), pp. 153–76

——, 'Peers in the early middle ages', in P. Stafford, J.L. Nelson and J. Martindale, eds, *Law, Laity and Solidarities: Essays in honour of Susan Reynolds* (Manchester, 2001), pp. 27–46

——, 'England and the Continent in the Ninth Century: III, Rights and Rituals', *Transactions of the Royal Historical Society* 14 (6th ser.) (2004), pp. 1–24

Niermayer, J.F., *Mediae Latinitatis Lexicon Minus*, 2nd edn (Leiden, 2004)

Nonn, U., 'Merowingische Testamente: Studien zum Fortleben einer römischen Urkundenform im Frankreich', *Archiv für Diplomatik* 18 (1972), pp. 1–129

Norberg, D., *Syntaktische Forschungen auf dem Gebiete des Spätlateins und des frühen Mittellateins* (Uppsala, 1943)

——, *Manuel pratique de latin médiéval* (Paris, 1968)

Pei, M.A., *The Language of the Eighth-century Texts in Northern France: A Study of the Original Documents in the Collection of Tardif and other Sources* (New York, 1932)

Pfister, C., 'Note sur le formulaire de Marculf', *Revue Historique* 50 (1892), pp. 43–63

Pirenne, H., 'De l'état de l'instruction des laïques à l'époque mérovingienne', *Revue Bénédictine* 46 (1934), pp. 165–77

——, *Mahomet et Charlemagne* (Paris, 1937)

Pirson, J., 'Le latin des formules mérovingiennes et carolingiennes', *Romanische Forschungen* 26 (1909), pp. 837–944

Pohl, W., and Reimitz, H., eds, *Strategies of Distinction: The Construction of Ethnic Communities, 300-800* (Leiden, 1998)

Reuter, T., 'The insecurity of travel in the early and high middle ages: criminals, victims and their medieval and modern observers', in T. Reuter, *Medieval Polities and Modern Mentalities*, ed. J.L. Nelson (Cambridge, 2006), pp. 38–71

Reynolds, S., *Fiefs and Vassals: The Medieval Evidence Reinterpreted* (Oxford, 1994)

——, 'Our forefathers? Tribes, peoples, and nations in the historiography of the age of migrations', in A.C. Murray, ed., *After Rome's Fall: Narrators and Sources of Early Medieval History* (Toronto, 1998), pp. 17–36

Riché, P., 'L'instruction des laïcs en Gaule mérovingienne au VIIe siècle', in *Settimane di studio del Centro italiano di studi sull' alto medioevo* 5 (Spoleto, 1958), pp. 873–88

——, *Education et culture dans l'Occident barbare, VIe-VIIe siècles* (Paris, 1962)

——, *Enseignement du droit en Gaule du VI au XIe siècle* (Milan, 1965)

——, 'La formation des scribes dans le monde mérovingien et carolingien', in W. Paravicini and K.-F. Werner, eds, *Histoire comparée de l'administration (IVe-XVIIIe siècles): Actes du XIVe colloque historique franco-allemand (Tours, 27 mars-1er avril 1977)*, Beihefte der Francia 9 (Munich, 1980), pp. 75–80

Richter, M., '"*Quisquis scit scribere, nullum potat abere labore*". Zur Laienschriftlichkeit im 8. Jahrhundert', in J. Jarnut, U. Nonn and M. Richter, eds, *Karl Martell in seiner Zeit* (Sigmaringen, 1994), pp. 393–404

Rio, A., 'Freedom and unfreedom in early medieval Francia: the evidence of the legal formulae', *Past & Present* 193 (2006), pp. 7–40

——, 'Formulae, written law and the settlement of disputes in the Frankish kingdoms', in P. Andersen, ed., *Law Before Gratian: III. Carlsberg Academy Conference on Medieval Legal History* (Copenhagen, 2007), pp. 21–34

——, 'Charters, law-codes and formulae: the Franks between theory and practice', in Paul Fouracre and David Ganz, eds, *Frankland: The Franks and the World of Early Medieval Europe: Essays in honour of Dame Jinty Nelson* (Manchester, 2008), pp. 7–27

——, 'Les formulaires mérovingiens et carolingiens: tradition manuscrite et réception', *Francia*, 35 (2009), pp. 327–48

——, *Legal Practice and the Written Word in the Early Middle Ages: Frankish Formulae, c.500–1000* (Cambridge, forthcoming)

Rosenwein, B., *Negotiating Space: Power, Restraint, and Privileges of Immunity in Early Medieval Europe* (Ithaca, NY, 1999)

——, 'Property transfers and the Church, eighth to eleventh centuries: an overview', *Mélanges de l'Ecole Française de Rome: Moyen âge* 3:2 (1999), pp. 563–75

Rouche, M., 'La matricule des pauvres: évolution d'une institution de charité du Bas-Empire jusqu'à la fin du Haut Moyen Âge', in M. Mollat, ed., *Études sur l'histoire de la pauvreté* (Paris, 1974), vol. 1, pp. 83–110

Sas, L.F., *The Noun Declension System in the Merovingian Period* (Paris, 1937)

Schröder, R., 'Über die fränkischen Formelsammlungen', *Zeitschrift der Savigny-Stiftung für Rechtsgeschichte, Germanistische Abteilung* 4 (1883), pp. 75–112

——, *Lehrbuch der deutschen Rechtsgeschichte*, 6th edn. revised by E.V. Künssberg (Berlin, 1922)

Schwerin, C. von, 'Sobre las relaciones entre las Fórmulas visigóticas y las andecavenses', *Annuario de Historia del derecho Español* 9 (1932), pp. 177–89

Sickel, T., *Acta regum et imperatorum Karolinorum digesta et enarrata. Die*

Urkunden der Karolinger, vol. 1: *Urkundenlehre* (Vienna, 1867)

Sprömberg, H., 'Marculf und die fränkische Reichskanzlei', *Neues Archiv* 47 (1928), pp. 77–142

Tardif, A., 'Etude sur la date du formulaire de Marculf', *Nouvelle revue historique de droit français et étranger* 8 (1884), pp. 557–65

——, 'Nouvelles observations sur la date du formulaire de Marculf', *Nouvelle revue historique de droit français et étranger* 9 (1885), pp. 368–75

Tardif, J., 'Les chartes mérovingiennes de Noirmoutier', *Nouvelle revue de droit français et étranger* 22 (1898), pp. 763–90

Uddholm, A., *Formulae Marculfi: Etudes sur la langue et le style* (Uppsala, 1953)

——, 'Le texte des *Formulae Marculfi*', *Eranos* 55 (1957), pp. 38–59

Valois, A. de, *Disceptationis de basilicis defensio* (Paris, 1660)

Vielliard, J., *Le latin des diplômes royaux et des chartes privées de l'époque mérovingienne* (Paris, 1927)

Wickham, C., *Framing the Early Middle Ages: Europe and the Mediterranean, 400–800* (Oxford, 2005)

Woll, I., *Untersuchungen zu Überlieferung und Eigenart der merowingischen Kapitularien*, Freiburger Beiträge zur mittelalterlichen Geschichte 6 (Frankfurt, 1995)

Wood, I.N., 'Disputes in late fifth- and sixth-century Gaul: some problems', in Davies and Fouracre, *The Settlement of Disputes in Early Medieval Europe*, pp. 7–22

——, 'Administration, law and culture in Merovingian Gaul', in McKitterick, *The Uses of Literacy in Early Medieval Europe*, pp. 63–81

——, *The Merovingian Kingdoms, 450–751* (London, 1994)

——, 'Teutsind, Witlaic and the history of Merovingian *precaria*', in Davies and Fouracre, *Property and Power in the Early Middle Ages*, pp. 31–52

Wood, S., *The Proprietary Church in the Early Middle Ages* (Oxford, 2006)

Wormald, P., '*Lex scripta* and *verbum regis*: legislation and Germanic kingship from Euric to Cnut', in P.H. Sawyer and I.N. Wood, eds., *Early Medieval Kingship* (Leeds, 1977), pp. 105–08; reprinted in P. Wormald, *Legal Culture in the Early Medieval West: Law as Text, Image and Experience* (London, 1999), pp. 1–43

——, *The Making of English Law* (Oxford, 1999)

Wright, R., *Late Latin and Early Romance in Spain and Carolingian France*

(Liverpool, 1982)

———, *A Sociophilological Study of Late Latin* (Turnhout, 2002)

Zatschek, H., 'Die Benutzung der *Formulae Marculfi* und anderer Formularsammlungen in den Privaturkunden des 8. bis 10. Jahrhunderts', *Mitteilungen des Instituts für Österreichische Geschichtsforschung* 42 (1927), pp. 165–267

Zeumer, K., 'Über den Ersatz verlorener Urkunden im fränkischen Reiche', *Zeitschrift der Savigny-Stiftung für Rechtsgeschichte, Germanistische Abteilung* 1 (1880), pp. 89–123

———, 'Über die älteren fränkischen Formelsammlungen', *Neues Archiv* 6 (1881), pp. 9–115

———, 'Über die alamannischen Formelsammlungen', *Neues Archiv* 8 (1883), pp. 473–553

———, 'Der Maior domus in Marculf I, 25', *Neues Archiv* 10 (1885), pp. 383–88

———, 'Neue Erörterungen über ältere fränkische Formelsammlungen', *Neues Archiv* 11 (1886), pp. 313–58

———, 'Die Lindenbruch'sche Handschrift der Formelsammlung von Flavigny', *Neues Archiv* 14 (1889), pp. 589–603

———, 'Zur Herkunft der Markulfischen Formeln. Eine Antwort an G. Caro', *Neues Archiv* 30 (1905), pp. 716–19

Zadora-Rio, E., 'De la haie au bocage: quelques remarques sur l'Anjou', in L. Feller, P. Mane and F. Piponnier, eds, *Le Village médiéval et son environnement: Études offertes à Jean-Marie Pesez* (Paris, 1998), pp. 671–82

———, 'The making of churchyards and parish territories in the early medieval landscape of France and England in the 7th-12th centuries: a reconsideration', *Medieval Archaeology* 47 (2003), pp. 1–19

——— ed., *Des paroisses de Touraine aux communes d'Indre-et-Loire: la formation des territoires*, Supplément à la Revue Archéologique du Centre (Tours, forthcoming)

Zimmermann, M., 'Un formulaire du Xème siècle conservé à Ripoll', *Faventia* 4 (1982), pp. 25–86

INDEX

abbess 87–88, 170–71
abbot 54, 70, 87–88, 130–31, 132, 138,
    149, 169, 170–71, 181, 183–86,
    189–90, 207–08
  accused of appropriating land
    160–61
  letters to and from 225–28
  president of a court 56–57, 71–72,
    89
  receiving *mundeburdium* from the
    king or mayor of the palace
    157–58, 236–37
adoption 196–97
Angers, formulary of, *see Formulae
    Andecavenses*
annulment, *see vacuaturia*
antrustion 151–52
appennis, apennis (replacement of lost
    documents) 40n, 73–76, 166–68,
    281
Augustine of Hippo 13
arenga 20–21, 26, 148–49, 178, 183,
    199, 204, 211–12, 235–36,
    240–43

Baluze, Étienne 118
Bergmann, Werner 42, 250–53
biblical quotes 26, 132, 145, 148, 153,
    179–80, 183, 184, 187, 223, 227,
    242–43
Bignon, Jérôme 3n, 107, 108, 113, 118
bishop 106, 128–33, 149–50, 156,
    157–58, 169–71, 179, 181–82,
    186–88, 205–06, 207, 219–21

appointment of 137–40, 232–34
asked to discipline a follower
    160–61
at the royal tribunal 159
letters to and from 222–25, 227,
    232–33
president of a court 74–75
receiving a royal immunity 134–37,
    230–31, 237–38
receiving *mundeburdium* from the
    king or mayor of the palace
    157–58
sent on an embassy 142–44, 156–57
summoned to the royal tribunal
    159–60
boni homines 45, 53, 60, 64, 74, 80,
    85, 86, 89, 94–95, 97–98, 106,
    166–67, 192, 199–200, 212, 219,
    221–22, 257, 281
boundary clauses 54–55, 66, 67, 81, 95,
    205, 206, 207, 208
Breviary of Alaric 13, 140
Brown, Warren 31
Burgundians 140–41

cartae paricolae (document in two
    identical copies) 55, 87, 172–74,
    191, 198, 208, 209, 213
  in the case of *appennis* 75
cartularies 5, 16, 112, 281
Cassiodorus, *see Variae*
Charibert I 250
Charlemagne 14, 56, 87n, 134n, 144,
    156, 175

charters
  and the written word 5, 17
  sections of 282
  preservation of 4–5, 27–28
  see also cartae paricolae, formulae, notitiae
Childebert, Merovingian king 41, 42, 48, 249–51
Chilperic I 41, 250–51
Chlothar II 251
Chrodegang, bishop of Metz 129
churches and monasteries
  as providers of documents 12, 44–45
  growth under the Carolingians 12–13
  network of, in Northern Francia 15–16
  see also abbot, bishop, gifts, kings, monks, mundeburdium
Collectio Flaviniacensis 33n., 99n, 115, 120, 212n, 256n, 258, 260, 262–63
Cordoba 14
count (comes) 132, 171–72, 174, 176, 227, 230, 237, 282
  appointed bishop 233–34
  appointment of 140–41
  asked by the king to discipline a pagensis 161
  of the palace 159, 172, 173, 282
  president of a court 45, 59, 74–75, 91–92
curia, curia publica 48–50, 74, 90, 218, 257
curiales (decurions) 74, 183–85, 218–19, 257, 283

Dagobert I 132, 175
Desiderius of Cahors 222
disputes, in Angers and Marculf 45, 106–07
  over an assault 53, 161–62, 171–72
  over boundaries 70–71
  over labour 56–57, 62–63
  over land 159–60, 161
  over inheritance 192–93, 214
  over murder 59–60, 91–92, 203–04
  over property or valuables 52–53, 61–62, 71–72, 85
  over *raptus* 69–70, 85–86, 199–200, 211–12
  over a slave 160–61, 172–74
  over theft 50–52, 58, 60–61, 80–81, 85
  over the scattering and killing of animals 68
  over vineyards 72, 89–90, 94–95
  settled before the king 158–62, 171–74
  see also judgment; security, deed of; *solsadia*
divorce 97–98, 213
domesticus 174, 229, 283
Domigisel, supporter of Chilperic I 251
dos 47–50, 73, 75, 76–77, 81–82, 95–96, 192–93, 194, 198–200, 283
duke (*dux*) 140–41, 159, 227, 237, 283
Du Pin, Louis Ellies 107–08

embassies 141–44, 156–57
enslavement, see self-sale
Ewig, Eugen 111, 128–29
exchange, document of 54–55, 73, 75, 76, 131–33, 164, 167, 168, 207–09
exemption, episcopal 128–31, 179

Fabricius, Johann Albert 107, 108
fideijussor (legal guarantor) 135–37, 160–61, 172
fidelis, fideles 147, 148, 151, 152, 155, 159, 160–62, 165–66, 167, 170, 174, 284
fisc 141, 146, 153, 154, 284

and the confiscation of property 165–66
collecting a share of fines 51, 52, 53, 55, 64, 70, 79, 84, 85, 86, 88–89, 96, 133, 134, 135, 137, 179, 182, 186, 187, 189, 191, 203, 204, 207, 209, 215, 217, 229
collecting tolls 230–31, 238
estates of 132, 148–49, 151, 162–63, 229
servants or tenants of 148–49, 229
Flavigny, *see Collectio Flaviniacensis*, Widerad
formulae, formularies
and charters 4–5, 25–28, 32, 35, 112–13
and forgeries 26, 27, 108, 112, 114
and law-codes 35, 79n.
and literacy 22–25
in Germanic-speaking areas 22, 24n.
and teaching 12–13, 16, 124–26, 240–43
and the royal centre 8–9, 13–16
contextualisation, problems of 6–8, 34–35
dating 25–26, 28–33, 41–42
disappearance 16–17
exchanged between institutions 15, 34
geographical distribution 14–15, 33–34
language 17–22
manuscripts 8–17, 28, 30–34, 42
see also individual entries under manuscripts
process of selection 5, 27–28, 31
Formulae Andecavenses (Angers) 14, 33, 38–101
and late Roman institutions 39–40, 44–45, 47
date 41–43, 248–254

language 19–21
manuscript, *see* manuscripts: Fulda D1
organisation 45–46
Formulae Argentinenses (Strasbourg) 65n
Formulae Arvernenses (Clermont) 14, 33, 73n, 166n, 256n
Formulae Augienses (Reichenau) 33, 65n, 99n, 105n, 183n, 190n, 191n, 212n, 256n
Formulae Bituricenses (Bourges) 14, 33, 79n, 120, 157n, 219n, 227n, 256n, 259
Formulae Imperiales 8–9, 105, 142n, 157n
Formulae Codicis Laudunensis (Laon) 33
Formulae Collectionis S. Dionysii (St Denis) 33n
Formulae Marculfi 104–244
and surviving charters 26n., 27, 28
and St Denis 107, 113–17, 268
and the royal court 9, 105–06, 113–17
date 107–13
language 21–22, 267–68
manuscript tradition 15, 31, 34, 105, 117–23, 259–79
privileged status in early modern and modern scholarship 3, 104, 117–18
Formulae Morbacenses (Murbach) 33, 99n, 212n
Formulae Salicae Bignonianae 33n, 65n, 99n, 118, 197n, 212n, 215n, 227n
Formulae Salicae Lindenbrogianae 33n, 65n, 99n, 194n, 199n, 212n, 215n, 227n
Formulae Salicae Merkelianae 33n, 65n, 97n, 99n, 105n, 112n, 120–21, 194n, 195nn, 197n, 199n, 212n, 213n

Formulae Sangallenses (St Gall) 12n, 15, 114–15
Formulae Senonenses (Sens) 33, 59n, 63n, 73n, 97n, 99n, 118, 166n, 168n, 195n, 197n, 206n, 210n, 211n, 212n, 213n, 215n, 219n, 232n, 256n
Formulae Turonenses (Tours) 14, 15, 33, 34, 73n, 79n, 91, 97n, 105n, 112n, 121, 166n, 184n, 194n, 195–97nn, 199nn, 205n, 213n, 256n, 260
Formulae Salzburgenses (Salzburg) 14, 33
Formulae Visigothicae (Visigothic) 12, 14, 39n, 79n, 82n, 256n
Formularum Codicis S. Emmerami Fragmenta 105n
Fredegar 175
freedmen, freedwomen 202, 214
Fustel de Coulanges, Numa Denis 7n, 132n

gasindus 156–58, 165–66, 216–17
gesta municipalia 40, 44, 45, 47–50, 84, 94, 183–85, 201, 218–19, 255–58, 284
gifts 75, 76, 164, 167, 168, 202, 218–19
 between childless spouses 82–84, 145–46, 190–92
 between *fideles* of the king 146–47
 for Easter 222–23
 from the king 148–51
 to a church or monastery 87–89, 148–50, 178–87, 189–90, 235–36
 to a *fidelis* 148–51
 to a grandson 194–95
 to a nephew 77–78
 to a servant 96–97, 216–17
 to a son 78–79, 98–99
 see also dos
Gregory of Tours 39, 126., 251–54

Guntram, Frankish king 250–51

Heidrich, Ingrid 112

immunity, royal 132–37, 150
 from tolls 230–31, 237–38
 granted to a layman 148–49, 151, 179, 181
inheritance
 of daughters 195–96, 201–02
 of grandsons 193–94
 sharing of 96, 153–54, 197–98
 see also gifts: between spouses / to a son, testament
Isidore of Seville 13

John, Wilhelm 116
judex, judices 133, 135–37, 149–51, 181, 185, 188, 189
 cruelty of 136, 185
judgment (*judicius*) 57–58, 61–62, 68, 70–72, 73, 75, 76, 92, 171–72
 see also disputes, *placitum, solsadia*

kings
 appointing bishops and lay officials 137–41, 233–34
 confirming lay agreements and transactions 145–47, 154–56, 164–65, 170–71, 231–32
 confiscating the property of a rebel 165–66
 demanding oaths of fidelity 175–76
 exchanging land 162–64
 giving permission for someone to enter the priesthood 152–53
 intervening in the partition of an inheritance 153–54
 letters to 141–42, 224
 making grants of land 148–51
 manumitting servants on the birth of a son 174, 229
 putting legal cases on hold 156–57

settling disputes 158–62, 171–74
  see also antrustion; embassies;
  formulae, and the royal centre;
  immunity royal; *mundeburdium*
Krusch, Bruno 109n, 110, 116, 142–43,
  250, 251, 261, 267

Landeric, bishop 107–10, 115–16,
  124–25, 266
Launoy, Jean de 107–08
Lérins, island-monastery 130
lesewerpus 146–47
letters
  between kings 141–42
  of recommendation 225–28
  on church feasts 222–24
  to relatives 232–33
  to the mayor of the palace 232
Liber epistolarum 115
Lindenbruch, Friedrich 259
loan document (*cautio*) 75, 76, 100–01,
  209–10, 216
  in exchange for labour 63–64,
    79–80, 210
  in exchange for usufruct of a
    vineyard 66–67
Louis the Pious 8, 14
  see also *Formulae Imperiales*
Luxeuil, monastery 130

Mabillon, Jean 3n, 107n, 118, 248, 249
mandate 47–49, 90, 93–94, 155,
  213–14, 218–19
manumission 65–66, 67–68, 183, 185,
  202, 211–13, 214–16
  by *denarius* 155–56
  on the birth of the king's son 174,
    229
manuscripts
  Copenhagen, Kongelige Bibliothek,
    coll. Fabr. 84 118n, 119, 163n,
    171n, 174n, 198n, 236–237,
    259–265, 269

Fulda D1 16, 34, 40, 43–44
Leiden BPL 114 34, 118n, 119–22,
  139n, 158n, 198n, 259–70
Leiden Voss. lat. O. 86 13n, 31n,
  118n, 119, 259, 265
Munich Clm. lat. 4650 31n, 118n,
  119, 259, 265
Paris BnF lat. 2123 13n, 109n,
  118n, 119, 120, 122, 146n,
  163n, 171n, 186n, 198n, 236–37,
  259–65, 269
Paris BnF lat. 2400 13n.
Paris BnF lat. 2718 8–9
Paris BnF lat. 4410 13n
Paris BnF lat. 4627 13n, 118n, 121,
  139n, 158n, 163n, 163n, 186n,
  198n, 235, 259–67, 269
Paris BnF lat. 4629 13n, 34, 120
Paris BnF lat. 4841 13n
Paris BnF lat. 10756 11, 34, 118n,
  120, 121, 130n, 139n, 158n,
  163n, 171n, 174n, 198n, 259–70
Paris BnF lat. 11379 13n
Paris BnF lat. 13686 118n
Vatican Reg. lat. 612 13n
Marculf, formulary of, see *Formulae
  Marculfi*
marriage, see divorce; *dos*; servants,
  marriage of; women
Martin, Saint 173, 254
matricularii 90–91
mayor of the palace 110–11, 157–59,
  168, 232, 236–37, 266, 284
McKitterick, Rosamond 24
Merkel, Jean 121
missus, of a bishop 160, 230, 238
  of a layman 231
  of the king 153–54, 175–76, 237,
    284–85
monks 128–34, 185–86
  as *pauperes* 179–82, 228
  giving property to a monastery 235,
    242–43

joining a different monastery 226
mundeburdium 157–58, 236–37
municipal council, *see curia*
murder, *see* disputes

Nelson, Janet L. 24
Norberg, Dag 19–20
notary (*amanuensis, notarius, professor*) 48–49, 201, 219
independent lay 10, 11–12
notitiae, overtaking charters as the preferred documentary form 16, 285
see also disputes

oaths, oath-swearing, oath-helping 24, 56–57, 58, 60–62, 68, 71–72, 91–92, 173–74
of fidelity 175–76

patricius 140–41, 159, 169, 227, 230, 237, 285
pilgrimage 227
Pippin II, mayor of the palace 110
Pirenne, Henri 23n, 125n, 143–44
placitum 59–62, 80, 94, 106, 110, 114, 158–59, 171–72, 173–74, 209, 285
pope, letter of recommendation to 227
poverty, claims of 49n, 64, 81n, 196–97
precaria, prestaria 53–54, 187–88, 193, 219–22, 285–86
see also usufruct
privilege, episcopal, *see* exemption

queen, letter to 224

rachinburgii 92, 286
raptus, see disputes, over *raptus*
Rebais, monastery 108, 129
Rechtsschule 7
see also Krusch, Bruno; Zeumer, Karl

Riché, Pierre 116–17
Rosenwein, Barbara 129
Rozière, Eugène de 2n, 259, 266

sale, document of (*vinditio*) 73, 75, 76, 164, 167, 168, 202
single field 66, 206
land 70
newborn child 90–91
slave 55, 206–07
urban property 205–06
villa 204–05
vineyard 52
see also self-sale
Salic law 13, 51, 140, 152, 156, 193, 195–96, 199–200, 211, 286
scribes 4, 13, 8–17, 30–33, 122, 125n, 146n, 163n, 175n, 200n, 212, 220, 223, 257, 264, 269
see also notaries
security, deed of (*securitas*) 52–53, 69–70, 73, 75, 76, 85–86, 203–04
self-sale 50–52, 62–63, 64, 68–69, 211
see also loan document, in exchange for labour
servants, slaves, unfree tenants 50, 55, 64, 85–86, 134, 135, 153, 211
escaped 93, 172–74
gifts to 96–97, 216–17
marriage of 86–87
between free woman and unfree man 99–100, 211–13
in lists of property 54, 78, 81, 83, 84, 88, 96, 98, 133, 147, 149, 154, 163–64, 165, 167, 169, 170, 181, 185, 186, 189, 190, 194, 195, 196, 198, 199, 200, 205, 208, 217
stolen 160–61, 172–74
see also disputes, freedmen, manumission, sale, self-sale
Sigibert I 250–51, 252

Sigibert III 175
Sigrada, freedwoman of Charlemagne 156
Sirmond, Jacques 121
slaves, *see* servants
solsadia (notice of default) 59–62, 94–95, 171–72, 286
spices 143–44
St Denis, monastery 230
  see also Formulae Marculfi, and St Denis
St Gall, monastic archive 12n, 24
St Martin of Tours, monastery 8
St Maurice of Agaune, monastery 130

Tardif, Adolphe 109n, 110, 266
testament 200–03, 218–19
theft, *see* disputes over theft
Theodulf, count of Angers 251
Theuderic, Merovingian king 41, 42, 248–49, 253–54
Theuderic III 111, 230
tractoria 142–44

Uddholm, Alf 111, 114n, 121, 153n, 154n, 223, 261–68
unfree, *see* servants
usufruct 53–54, 66–67, 81–82, 95, 145–47, 183–86, 187–90, 192–93, 201–02, 219–22, 286–87

vacuaturia (annulment) 62–64, 73, 75, 76, 216
Valois, Adrien de 107–08
Variae of Cassiodorus 12, 23
vinditio, see sale, document of

Waroch, Breton ruler 41, 250
wergeld 152, 203, 287
Widerad, testament of 26n, 256n, 263n
witchcraft 59
witnesses 74–76, 89–90
  see also oaths
women
  acting jointly with their husbands 50, 55, 63, 69, 70, 73, 78, 82–84, 88, 100, 184–88, 200–03, 214–15, 219–20
  in court 47–49, 59–60, 61–62, 69–70, 71–72
  letters to 224, 232–33
  unfree 85–87
  see also dos, inheritance, servants

Zeumer, Karl 29–30, 32, 34, 41–42, 108, 109n, 110, 118–23, 223, 248–51, 259–62, 265–67, 269

www.ingramcontent.com/pod-product-compliance
Lightning Source LLC
Chambersburg PA
CBHW052149300426
44115CB00011B/1586